SPORT ENTREPRENEURSHIP AND INNOVATION

This book features international authors discussing the role of entrepreneurship and innovation in the sports context. It focuses on topics such as the role of entrepreneurial marketing in sport, how technological innovation has changed the way sport is played and viewed, the globalization of sport as a product and service, the new types of sports that have emerged, athlete entrepreneurs and their related business endeavors and how sport influences innovation in other industries.

The main themes of the book include: 1) the development of sport entrepreneurship and innovation, 2) entrepreneurship and sport, 3) innovation in sport, 4) internationalization and entrepreneurial behavior in sport, 5) entrepreneurial sport marketing, 6) sport in entrepreneurial universities and 7) the future for sport entrepreneurship and innovation. This interdisciplinary book will appeal to entrepreneurship, innovation and sport management scholars, students and practitioners.

Vanessa Ratten is Associate Professor of Entrepreneurship and Innovation at the Department of Management and Marketing, La Trobe Business School, Australia.

João J. Ferreira is Associate Professor in Management at the University of Beira Interior and NECE Research Unit in Business Sciences, Portugal.

SPORT ENTREPRENEURSHIP AND INNOVATION

Edited by Vanessa Ratten and João J. Ferreira

LONDON AND NEW YORK

First published 2017
by Routledge
2 Park Square, Milton Park, Abingdon, Oxon OX14 4RN

and by Routledge
711 Third Avenue, New York, NY 10017

Routledge is an imprint of the Taylor & Francis Group, an informa business

© 2017 selection and editorial matter, Vanessa Ratten and João J. Ferreira;
individual chapters, the contributors

The right of Vanessa Ratten and João J. Ferreira to be identified
as the authors of the editorial material, and of the authors for their
individual chapters, has been asserted in accordance with sections 77
and 78 of the Copyright, Designs and Patents Act 1988.

All rights reserved. No part of this book may be reprinted or reproduced
or utilised in any form or by any electronic, mechanical, or other means,
now known or hereafter invented, including photocopying and recording,
or in any information storage or retrieval system, without permission in
writing from the publishers.

Trademark notice: Product or corporate names may be trademarks or registered
trademarks, and are used only for identification and explanation without
intent to infringe.

British Library Cataloguing in Publication Data
A catalogue record for this book is available from the British Library

Library of Congress Cataloging in Publication Data
A catalog record for this book has been requested

ISBN: 978-1-138-94173-1 (hbk)
ISBN: 978-1-138-94174-8 (pbk)
ISBN: 978-1-315-39338-4 (ebk)

Typeset in Bembo
by RefineCatch Limited, Bungay, Suffolk

CONTENTS

List of figures	*vii*
List of tables	*ix*
Notes on contributors	*xi*
Foreword by Matt Winkler	*xv*
Preface	*xvii*
Acknowledgements	*xx*

1	Sport entrepreneurship and innovation: concepts and theory *Vanessa Ratten and João J. Ferreira*	1
2	Innovation capability of non-profit sport organisations *Mathieu Winand and Larena Hoeber*	13
3	Influence of sports events in local tourism *Héctor Valentín Jiménez Naranjo, Mari Cruz Sánchez Escobedo and José Luis Coca Pérez*	31
4	Innovation for social inclusion in sport *Anne Tjønndal*	42
5	The influence of Total Quality Management in the innovative capacity of municipal sport firms *Gastão Sousa and Maria José Madeira*	59

vi Contents

6 Sport leadership, psychology and innovation 75
Vanessa Ratten

7 A blue ocean strategy in a sport context: a systematisation of literature 88
Elsa Regina M. Vieira and João J. Ferreira

8 The relevance of the social impact of sports events in the context of public financing of sport 117
David Parra Camacho, Ferran Calabuig Moreno, Juan Núñez Pomar and Josep Crespo Hervás

9 Sport entrepreneurship and community development in Japan 141
Isao Okayasu and Duarte B. Morais

10 Coherence, the beginning and end of everything 153
Marco Arraya

11 Sport, innovation and public policy 179
Vanessa Ratten

12 "Not Out"? A sociomaterial perspective on decision review systems in professional cricket 192
Ian McLoughlin and Patrick Dawson

13 Consumer behavior analysis: an innovation approach in non-profit sports organizations 209
Dina Miragaia and João J. Ferreira

14 Exploring motivation of marathon runners 221
Konstantinos Koronios, Marina Psiloutsikou and Athanasios Kriemadis

15 Sport entrepreneurship and the emergence of opportunities: towards a future research agenda 242
Vanessa Ratten and João J. Ferreira

Index 257

FIGURES

2.1	Innovation capability of non-profit sport organisations	19
3.1	Research analysis approach	34
3.2	Users of sporting events	36
3.3	Proposed model	37
5.1	Basic constructs and study design	64
5.2	Number of coded references to TQM practices in municipal firm EM1	68
5.3	Number of coded references to TQM practices in municipal firm EM2	69
5.4	Number of coded references to TQM practices in municipal firm EM3	70
5.5	Comparing the number of coded references to TQM practices	71
5.6	Number of coded references to innovation	71
7.1	Blue ocean strategy conceptual strategy applied to fitness/health clubs	112
9.1	The total number of comprehensive community sport clubs	143
9.2	The number of inbound/outbound tourists and the rate of Japanese yen to US dollars	144
9.3	The image of the sport club in Hatsukaichi City	145
9.4	The number of tourists in summer and winter season at Niseko Town	148
9.5	The number of guests at the Outdoor Sport Programs Company from 2008 to 2014	150
9.6	The number of foreign guests at the Outdoor Sport Programs Company in 2014	150
10.1	DNA, environmental factors, performance and adaptation	158
10.2	Customer target identification variables	161

viii Figures

10.3	The life cycle stages	172
10.4	The four competitive advantage and coherence building blocks	174
14.1	The proposed model about factors influencing participation in marathon events	230

TABLES

3.1	Testing hypotheses	38
4.1	Drivers and barriers for innovation in sport	46
4.2	Innovation drivers and barriers for inclusion of girls and women in skateboarding	53
5.1	Dimensions used in the interview guide	66
6.1	Sport and business leadership differences	80
6.2	Sport coaching attitudes	82
7.1	Systematising the conceptual studies on the blue ocean strategy	90
7.2	Systematising the empirical studies on the blue ocean strategy	94
8.1	Theoretical frameworks for assessing the social impact of sport events	125
8.2	Examples of the impacts of sports events	127
9.1	An analysis of skills/experience in the Sport Club of Hatsukaichi	145
9.2	An analysis of skills/experience in the Outdoor Club of Niseko	147
9.3	An analysis of skills/experience in the Outdoor Club of Minakami	149
10.1	The VRIO framework elements	166
10.2	The coherency diagnostic	170
11.1	Sport entrepreneurial ecosystem participants	188
12.1	Critical incidents identified concerning DRS in an Ashes Test Match	198
12.2	DRS reviews initiated by teams	199
13.1	Factor loadings of the reasons motivating swimmers	213
13.2	Ranking of swimmers' motivation and coaches' perception and significant differences	214

x Tables

14.1 Independent samples t-test for the motivation of runners in different events   235

14.2 Correlation coefficients between intention to participate in future running events and motivation factors   236

14.3 Regression analysis for the proposed research model   237

CONTRIBUTORS

Marco Arraya is a manager and consultant in the health sector and sports organizations. He holds a PhD in Strategic Management from Universidade Aberta, Portugal, a Master of Administration from University of South Africa, a Master in Sports Management from Universidade Técnica de Lisboa / FMH, Portugal, and a degree in Marketing Administration from IPAM, Portugal. His research interests are in business management practices, dynamic capabilities, resource-based view, learning organization and KPI. He is Handball Master Coach (Rink convention).

David Parra Camacho is a research assistant in the Department of Physical Education and Sport at Universitat de València, Spain, research specialist in Sports Management, and PhD candidate in Sciences of Physical Activity and Sport (sport management specialization). He has participated in several research projects in sports management and has published several articles about the social impact of sporting events.

Patrick Dawson is Emeritus Professor at the University of Aberdeen. He holds a PhD in Industrial Sociology from the University of Southampton and he has held positions in universities in Australia, England, Sweden, Denmark and Scotland. As an international expert on change and temporality, Patrick has worked on a number of Australian Research Council (ARC) and Economic and Social Research Council (ESRC) funded projects in collaboration with scholars at other universities. He has published over 60 refereed academic journal articles, 50 book chapters and 12 books, and he is regularly invited to present keynote addresses at major international conferences.

João J. Ferreira is Associate Professor in Management at the University of Beira Interior and NECE Research Unit in Business Sciences, Portugal.

xii Contributors

Josep Crespo Hervás received his PhD in Sport Sciences (Sport Management) from the Universitat de València, Spain, where he is currently Assistant Professor at the Faculty of Physical Activity and Sport Sciences. He has published several articles in prestigious international journals regarding sport event management. He is also the main manager of the Hockey Federation of Valencia and he has been the director of several international sporting events held in Valencia.

Larena Hoeber is Associate Professor in the Faculty of Kinesiology & Health Studies at the University of Regina. Her research interests include gender and sport, use of contemporary research methods in sport management, sport volunteerism, organizational culture and values in sport, and innovation in amateur sport organizations. She has published her research in the *Journal of Sport Management*, *Sport Management Review*, *European Sport Management Quarterly*, *Gender, Work & Organization*, *Qualitative Research in Sport, Exercise & Health*, *International Journal of Sport Management and Marketing* and *Sex Roles*.

Konstantinos Koronios is a PhD candidate in Marketing and a research staff member of the Department of Sports Organization and Management at the University of Peloponnese, Greece. He received his first Master's degree in Business Administration from the University of Piraeus, Greece, and his second Master's degree in Marketing and Communication with new technologies from Athens University of Economics and Business. His recent publications include "Sport Sponsorship: The Impact of Sponsor Image on Purchase Intention of Fans", for the *Journal of Promotion Management*, Vol. 22, 2016. His research interests include marketing, business strategy, coopetition, sports marketing and management. He is currently completing his PhD thesis in sport sponsorship effectiveness.

Athanasios Kriemadis is Professor teaching Strategic Management and Total Quality Management at the University of Peloponnese and the University of Athens.

Maria José Madeira is Assistant Professor at the University of Beira Interior (UBI), Covilhã, Portugal. Her academic background includes a PhD in Management, specialising in innovation, UBI and habilitation (Agregação) in management. She is Coordinator of the postgraduate course in Technological Entrepreneurship, Director of 2nd Cycle degree in Entrepreneurship and Business Creation and Scientific Coordinator of Project International INESPO II. She is a research fellow at CIEO – Centre for Spatial and Organizational Dynamics. Her areas of expertise are innovation and technology entrepreneurship.

Ian McLoughlin is Professor of Management at Monash University, Australia.

Dina Miragaia is Auxiliary Professor at the University of Beira Interior, Portugal, and the course director of the Undergraduate Program in Sport Sciences. She is also a member of the Research Unit of Business Sciences – NECE. Her research interests include sport management, consumer profile, organizational behavior and strategy.

Duarte B. Morais is Associate Professor at North Carolina State University, USA, a Visiting Associate Professor at the University of Johannesburg, South Africa, and the lead in(ve)stigator of the People-First Tourism Lab – a transdisciplinary network of researchers devoted to studying and enabling dignified and sustainable livelihoods glocally through frugal IT innovation and micro-entrepreneurship. He explores how tourism and IT innovations can be used by subaltern people to earn human agency and break away from hegemonic control of local elites, industry and the state.

Ferran Calabuig Moreno is Vice Dean of the Faculty of Physical Activity and Sport Sciences at Universitat de València, Spain. He has published several articles about the perceived quality of sports consumers and about the social impact of sporting events. He lectures in different Masters of Sport Management in Spain and is author of around 10 books and chapters on sport management and its research. He has published several articles in international prestigious journals about service quality and social impact of sporting events.

Héctor Valentín Jiménez Naranjo attends the University of Extremadura, and has a Master in Sports Law from the University of Lleida, Spain.

Isao Okayasu is Associate Professor at Hiroshima University of Economics. He completed the PhD Program of Juntendo University, Japan. He investigates how sport and recreation effect community enhancement-related social capital, and recreational sport events such as marathons through participants behaviors and attitudes. He designs the possibility of micro-entrepreneurship in nature-based tourism in rural area as well.

José Luis Coca Pérez is Associate Professor at the School of Finance, Business and Tourism, University of Extremadura, Spain.

Juan Núñez Pomar is Professor at the Faculty of Physical Activity and Sports Sciences at Universitat de València, Spain. He teaches strategic planning and organization of sporting events. He is Professor of various Master's programs in Spain and a public sports management expert, as well as the author of several articles and book chapters on sport management.

Marina Psiloutsikou is Professor at the Department of Sport Management at the University of Peloponnese, Greece.

Vanessa Ratten is Associate Professor of Entrepreneurship and Innovation at the Department of Management and Marketing, La Trobe University, Australia.

xiv Contributors

Mari Cruz Sánchez Escobedo is Associate Professor at the School of Finance, Business and Tourism, University of Extremadura, Spain.

Gastão Sousa is Assistant Professor at the University Institute of Maia – ISMAI, Portugal, and researcher at CIDESD-ISMAI. He has a PhD in Management with specialization in sport innovation. He is Director of Master and Bachelor Programs in Sport Management at ISMAI and former President of the Portuguese Sport Management Association.

Anne Tjønndal is a sport scientist (MSc Sport Science, Norwegian University of Science and Technology), and is currently employed as a PhD Research Fellow at the Faculty of Social Sciences, Nord University, Bodø, Norway. Her research interests include innovation and social inclusion in sport, gender studies and boxing. She is a regular contributor and blogger on the Nordic Sport Science Forum (www.idrottsforum.org).

Elsa Regina M. Vieira is Professor of Sport Management at the Sport Sciences School of Rio Maior Sports, Polytechnic Institute of Santarém, Portugal. She is a doctoral student in Management at the University of Beira Interior and has investigated in the field of blue ocean strategy applied to the sports sector. She is also a member of the Research Unit of the Polytechnic Institute of Santarém (UIIPS).

Mathieu Winand is Lecturer in Sport Management in the Faculty of Health Sciences and Sport at the University of Stirling, UK. He is also an associate researcher at the Belgian Olympic Chair, Université catholique de Louvain (Belgium). He is Deputy Editor of *Sport, Business and Management*. His research expertise is in the area of sport governance, performance management and innovation in sport.

Matt Winkler is a faculty member at American University, Washington DC, USA.

FOREWORD

In the sports world, the only constant is change . . .

Sport is a $213 billion dollar industry and growing steadily, according to the *SportsBusiness Journal*. In fact, 90 of the 400 wealthiest Americans – nearly one in every four as measured by *Forbes* magazine in 2016 – are financially invested in sports. And why not? Sport has its own special ecosystem and its environment is interactively linked with a constantly changing global community for a wide variety of players.

Through *Sport Entrepreneurship and Innovation*, Vanessa Ratten and João Ferreira demonstrate how the business of sports has been transformed by economic and social dynamics and how entrepreneurship and innovation have changed the way we design, launch and run sports-related businesses in the twenty-first century.

While the measurement of success and failure in the sporting arena comes via victory and defeat – wins and losses (and draws) – its success is not easily defined in the entrepreneurial space. It still involves processes, services, products, technologies and business models and the application of solutions to address new challenges, requirements and, more prevalent today, cultural needs.

Nowadays, we must envision how a newer variety of sports, such as surfing and futsal, can influence the future of high-performance sports, athletes, brands, fans, media and sponsors to create new properties. This book explores what the next generation of sport might look like with the foresight that envisions its social impact, sustainability and legacy.

The growth opportunities in today's sports space appear in many technical areas including interactive spectatorship, performance analytics, e-sports and virtual reality, to name a few. But now, soft skills are desired, and often acquired organically through social impact and public policy.

To be successful in the modern sports marketplace, professionals must be skilled in business planning, developing pragmatic outcomes, changing management and improving return on investment and engagement. This book, therefore, connects with readers who are willing to apply such entrepreneurial concepts and theories to the sports industry, whether as part of a start-up, a private venture, an investor, employee or student.

Over the last few years here in the United States, the brand Under Armor has provided us with an illustration of exactly what Ratten and Ferreira so masterfully set out as a blueprint for success in sports entrepreneurship and innovation. Kevin Plank, Under Armor's founder, launched this American sports clothing and accessories company from his grandmother's basement here in Washington, DC.

Plank started by identifying a need: athletic clothing that didn't soak through with sweat. He provided a solution in the form of a moisture-wicking synthetic fabric that was practical, comfortable, and "cool." Then, using grass-roots marketing techniques and strategic brand-building partnerships, Under Armor captured the imagination of athletes and teams, helping to create brand awareness and mystique with millennials in particular.

In a marketplace that includes two of the world's biggest brands, Nike and Adidas, Under Armour gained market share by expanding into footwear and women's clothing, both domestically and, eventually, internationally. Recently, Plank and Under Armour have mapped out their future in the digital fitness space by investing in and acquiring mobile or wearable devices and applications that measure and improve health and fitness, thereby tapping into an even broader audience.

As the sports industry continues to evolve through new technologies and innovation, savvy business leaders should follow the money. Venture capital funding and investments target the intersection of sports as a cultural passion with the promise of digital and other technologies that enhance the consumer engagement experience. This revenue generation will impact a bottom line that is critical to investment and investors.

Moving forward, the future of sports, however, may take place in the virtual world. eSports, the competitive video gaming space, has seen massive investment bring it a boundless audience. In addition, integrating women and children into the market space can generate additional licensing opportunities in that space.

Overall, *Sport Entrepreneurship and Innovation* emphasizes the need to adjust to technological innovation and new social enterprises. Still in their nascent stages, there is much work to be done to fully understand and leverage them. But executives, athletes, managers, investors, academics, students and fans will find valuable insights and resources throughout this book, rendering it a virtual blueprint to the future of the business of sports.

Matt Winkler
American University, Washington, DC
Founder, Georgetown University, Sports Industry Management
Founder, The Sports Events Marketing Experience (The SEME)

PREFACE

Sport is inherently entrepreneurial because of its capability to change based on societal and technology trends. This ability to change comes from our global society including a number of different sports, which are adapting based on innovative developments. Lifestyle and adventure sports are commonly referred to as being innovative due to their ability to connect with cultural needs. Examples of lifestyle and adventure sports include surfing, which has seen a global increase in fan engagement. Despite the emphasis on new sports for bringing innovation into the marketplace, traditional sports such as tennis have also seen an increase in the usage of new equipment and changing playing conditions.

This book begins with a chapter on sport entrepreneurship and innovation by Vanessa Ratten and João Ferreira. This chapter serves as a good introduction to the book as it explains the concepts and theories behind the emergence of sport entrepreneurship and innovation theory. The authors explain how sport management and innovation management need to be integrated more. The second chapter is about innovation capability of non-profit sport organizations by Mathieu Winard and Larena Hoeber. As there is an abundance of non-profit entities in sport, the chapter explains how innovation can be harnessed using a more social perspective. The third chapter focuses on the influence of sports events in local tourism by Héctor Valentín Jiménez Naranjo, Mari Cruz Sánchez Escobedo and José Luis Coca Pérez. The authors highlight the big role sport tourism has had on society with innovative developments in marketing being stated.

The fourth chapter is about innovation for social inclusion in sport by Anne Tjønndal. In the chapter, the author discusses the role that sport has in society by bringing together people from diverse socio-cultural backgrounds. This helps to understand how innovation can develop in sport by focusing more on the societal rather than financial benefits of sport. The fifth chapter highlights the influence of total quality management in the innovative capacity of municipal sport firms by Gastão Sousa and Maria José Madeira. In the chapter the role of production and supply chains is addressed in terms of how they help sport firms innovate. This is important given the role municipal sport firms play both in local government policy and in the international sporting arena. The sixth chapter discusses sport leadership, psychology and innovation by Vanessa Ratten. In her chapter, the importance of sport leaders in encouraging innovation is examined. This helps understand the role sport psychology plays in encouraging entrepreneurial ecosystems to develop in sport.

The seventh chapter focuses on a blue ocean strategy in a sport context by conducting a systematization of literature by Elsa Regina M. Vieira and João J. Ferreira. This chapter links sport innovation to strategic management, which is an important step in increasing the interdisciplinary nature of sport studies. The eighth chapter discusses the relevance of the social impact of sport events in the context of public financing of sport by David Parra Camacho, Ferran Calabuig Moreno, Juan Núñez Pomar and Josep Crespo Hervás. This chapter highlights the role of innovation in informing sport policy, which has important implications for public financing. This emphasis of sports events is important in understanding how innovation can be used to increase social impact of sports. The ninth chapter is about sport entrepreneurship from a community development perspective in Japan by Isao Okayasu and Duarte B. Morais. This chapter highlights how sport is increasingly seen as a way to develop communities as it links people together for a common purpose.

The tenth chapter is about coherence, the beginning and the end of everything, by Marco Arraya. This chapter provides an important conceptual application of sport to innovation and entrepreneurship. The eleventh chapter discusses sport, innovation and public policy by Vanessa Ratten and states how these concepts are linked together as they have mutually similar aims. The chapter focuses on the key role sport plays in innovative public policy in the global sport context. The twelfth chapter by Ian McLoughlin and Patrick Dawson shows how digital technologies play an increasing role in the production and consumption of sport. Drawing upon the insights offered by a sociomaterial perspective, they challenge the assumption that technologies have inherent properties of accuracy and human agents properties of fallibility in the international cricket context.

The thirteenth chapter by Dina Miragaia and João J. Ferreira aims to identify the consumer behavior of swimming according to the motivational approach through the perceptions of athletes and coaches. The authors conclude that coaches highlight the competitive aspects and social status as the main motives for attracting young people to participate in swimming competitions.

The fourteenth chapter by Konstatinos Koronios, Marina Psiloutsikou and Athanasios Kriemadis focuses on the key variables in the sport participation context, and more specifically examines how motivational factors influence individuals' participation in running events

The fifteenth chapter concludes the book and addresses the role of sport entrepreneurship and the emergence of opportunities in fostering a future research agenda by Vanessa Ratten and João Ferreira. This chapter provides a good conclusion to how the discipline of sport entrepreneurship and innovation is growing based on the popularity of sport in the global business environment.

ACKNOWLEDGEMENTS

We are very excited about this book on sport entrepreneurship and innovation. There have been many technological and societal advances that have changed the nature of sport and how we view sport. Sport as a business has increased largely as a result of the entrepreneurship and innovation occurring within the industry. This has been in conjunction with the internationalization and professionalization of sport.

The process of editing and writing this book was a long process but we are delighted with the final book. We thank our Editor Yongling Lam for her enthusiasm, professionalism and support. She has been a tremendous asset and we are very much appreciative of her help. We also thank our production assistant Samantha Phua for her attention to detail and assistance with our book. In addition, we are grateful for the editorial and marketing team at Routledge Publishing for their guidance with the book.

Lastly, but also very importantly, we thank our family, friends and colleagues around the world for their encouragement with this book. The book is a collection of international authors who have been very good to work with and we look forward to working with them again in the future. On a personal note, Vanessa would like to thank her mum, Kaye, for her encouragement, wisdom and fun; her dad David, and of course her two brothers, Hamish and Stuart, for all their support and "advice," and Hamish's wife Tomomi. João would also like to thank his family for their support. We hope you will enjoy reading this seminal book about sport entrepreneurship and innovation.

1

SPORT ENTREPRENEURSHIP AND INNOVATION

Concepts and theory

Vanessa Ratten and João J. Ferreira

Introduction

The sport industry is a competitive market in which innovation is important for its sustained success (Ratten, 2010). Sport innovation is important to organizations, individuals and governments due to the important role sport has in the global marketplace. Despite the growing popularity of sport-related innovations there has been minimal progress in theory development unifying the field. This lack of unifying framework for sport innovation makes it difficult to progress research and establish its legitimacy in the management research field. There is research about sport and innovation but there is a disconnect in providing sport innovation as a theoretical framework. This chapter discusses the way sport innovation can provide a school of thought for understanding the way innovation in the sport context is different to other contexts. This will enable researchers, practitioners and public policy planners to use sport innovation theory to identify problems and suggest solutions in the interconnected global business world.

The main focus of innovation in the sport context concerns sports organizations innovating to increase membership numbers and to add more services (Thibault *et al.*, 1993). This is the result of consumers playing a crucial role in sport organizations by generating new ideas as they have more emotional attachment (Franke and Sha, 2003). Innovation in sport is sometimes developed by consumers or participants because of the high level of involvement they have with sport (Newell and Swan, 1995). This means that sport innovation is different to other types of innovation, which is usually developed internally within an organization through research and development activities (Franke and Shah, 2003).

Most organizations develop innovations by spending time and money on internal processes that they control and which lead to commercialization. Sport innovation differs as often the users innovate the equipment themselves instead of waiting for an organization to do this. This leads to the innovation in sport being dynamic as it is refined by members of the sport community. The resulting innovation is then diffused within the sport context and can be used in a variety of different contexts depending on demand. Sport innovation by users instead of manufacturers is popular due to the reward in performance coming from the change. This user-driven innovation can occur in organizations who want to keep the innovation secret whilst benefitting from it for revenue-sharing reasons (von Hippel, 2007).

Some organizations must reveal their innovation because of government regulations that lessen their ability to keep innovations secret. Innovations can take an explorative or exploitative function depending on the level of risk and control involved (Tushman and Smith, 2002). Explorative sport innovations involve looking at ways to use existing knowledge and services to improve design efficiency. Exploitative sport innovations involve the use of resources in ways that have not been done before. Some innovations in sport are not considered innovative at the time they are introduced. This is due to the innovations such as electronic sport games having been invested into other contexts including the manufacturing industry. Sport innovation tends to focus on the idea of improvement in how sport is played, viewed or watched. Some sport innovations are transferred from other industries such as online sport betting.

The purpose of this chapter is to bring the sport and innovation literature together in order to address the following questions: How is sport innovation defined? Why does sport innovation constitute a separate area of innovation management study? And, how can sport innovation be used as a theoretical framework for future research? The consequences of answering these research questions are to encourage future research on sport innovation and to establish sport innovation as a coherent field of research. By doing so, this chapter will pave the way for the systematic development of sport innovation as an important area of business management research.

This chapter is organized over the following sections. The first section discusses the importance of having an innovative perspective within sport. This leads to an exploration of the literature on innovation management. The next section presents a theoretical framework for sport innovation that focuses on the distinctiveness of the field with the innovation management literature. The final section concludes the chapter by highlighting how sport innovation is defined and developed. Implications for sport managers and suggestions for future study and research about sport innovation are stated.

Literature review

Innovation involves the successful exploitation of new ideas that can generate value (Damanpour, 1996). This is important for improving the attractiveness and delivery of a product, process, service or technology (Oke *et al.*, 2007). Some organizations develop streams of innovation over time as changes occur and trends influence behavior (Smith and Tushman, 2005). This has led to organizations having a history of innovation due to their ability to develop better effectiveness with implementation of successful innovations (Damanpour *et al.*, 2009). The implementation of innovation is important to the growth of resources devoted to creative activity (Damanpour and Schneider, 2006).

Some organizations explore innovation by creating new markets that can be used in the international environment. These innovations often bring about radical change as they involve the use of new resources. The range of innovations available in an organization is constrained by internal and external control mechanisms (Hull and Lio, 2006). This means that organizations have less market freedom in some circumstances to incorporate innovative strategies (Damanpour, 1996). Resource constraints both in terms of time and money may further limit the innovative capability of some organizations due to their strategic goals.

Innovation strategy describes the way an organization positions itself in its competitive environment for new product and market development. Part of an organization's innovation strategy involves management making specific decisions about innovation goals. Organizational innovation is defined as the "implementation of an idea – whether pertaining to a device, systems, process, policy, program, or service – that is new to the organization at the time of adoption" (Damanpour and Evan, 1984, p. 393). Sometimes the strategic direction an organization will take involves focusing on the resource allocation decisions that lead to innovation (Li and Atuahene-Gima, 2001).

Innovation strategy operates within the context of an organization so it can commit to developing new products and markets. The interaction between innovation and strategy will be embedded in an organization's actions, behavior and culture. The key attributes of innovation strategy are proactiveness, risk taking and commitment to innovation (Saleh and Wang, 1993). These attributes combine with the top management leadership in an organization to link innovation strategy with overall business goals (Pinto and Prescott, 1988). Organizational leadership that has a long-term commitment to innovation is part of their strategic vision.

In an organization, resources need to be allocated to innovation goals in order for new products and services to be developed. This resource allocation is part of an organization's strategic objectives that shape innovation (Tipping and Zeffren, 1995). The strategic leadership of managers is important in making innovation happen. Managers can champion innovation by having a clear strategic direction based on communication. Furthermore, managers who tolerate change are able to support and champion innovation in an organization (Damanpour, 1991). Providing the climate for implementing innovation is important in order to facilitate change. This is impacted by the managerial attitude towards innovation that includes having practical support for change in an organization. Some managers expect innovation in an organization as they offer ways of doing new and improved practices.

Innovation management literature distinguishes between the adoption and appropriation process (Clark, Staunton and Rogers, 1989). Newell and Swan (1995) discuss how this is important in the sport context with adoption involving decisions to use a new idea for a specific purpose. The adoption process of the idea can promote and help an activity be introduced but might not always mean it will be implemented (Rogers, 2010). Appropriation involves translating the idea into reality within an organization (Newell and Swan, 1995). The appropriation process means making it appropriate for the context in which an organization operates (Clark, Staunton and Rogers, 1989). Some organizations will design the innovation differently so it is appropriate within their environmental setting. Rogers (2010) in his discussion about adoption and appropriation also refers to the reinvention process as being linked between both phases of innovation. Reinvention means some innovations come from doing things differently with an innovation that in the past has not been successful (Newell and Swan, 1995). Innovation adoption and appropriation can be considered from a function and psychological perspective (Antioco and Kleijnen, 2010).

Service innovation

Service innovation is relevant to sport as the delivery of services is at the core of many organizations in terms of how they adopt and appropriate innovation (Newell and Swan, 1995). Service innovation involves introducing new services to a group of customers in order to increase quality rates (Walker, 2008). The effectiveness of an organization is impacted by service innovations as they link to customer satisfaction. Some service innovations already exist in other industries but when introduced in a new context they become innovative. This comes from new knowledge, acts or processes resulting in service innovation (Hipp and Grupp, 2005). When new services are developed they are intangible in form as they cannot be physically defined (Damanpour, 1991). Lovelock and Gummesson (2004) state that services are purchased for a time period with a certain location and this is the main way they are distinguished from other types of innovation.

Services occur when consumption and production take place at the same time for a consumer (Hipp and Grupp, 2005). Innovation in the service sector can include the service itself in terms of the way it is done or the conditions surrounding the service (Edvardsson and Olsson, 1996). Hoeber and Hoeber (2012) in a study on community soccer organizations discussed how new electronic devices are developed. They found that service innovation needs a connection between staff and managers that includes good communication.

The creation of new knowledge by exploring opportunities is important for organizations that rely on innovation to stay competitive. The willingness of an organization to explore new ideas is an important determinant of whether an innovation will be successful (Damanpour, 1991). The creation of new knowledge is impacted by the commitment an organization has towards innovation. Innovation is facilitated in an organization when there is a favorable attitude towards knowledge development (Rogers, 2010). This attitude can be incorporated into staff behavior that encourages knowledge development (Bierly *et al.*, 2009). Innovation can be implemented into an organization more easily when staff are engaged with the knowledge process (Walsh and Ungson, 1991). The ability of an organization to innovate is related to how they assimilate knowledge by valuing good ideas (Hull and Lio, 2006).

Process innovation

Innovation is different to invention as it involves something perceived as new and often incorporates processes (Rogers, 2010). Invention refers to the creation of a product, service or process that has not been done before. The invention of new materials such as quick-drying material in sports clothing and aluminium baseball bats are innovations that were originally developed in other industries. Adoption perspectives of innovation focus on understanding how innovation develops from changes in the environment (Kimberly and Evanisko, 1981). These changes make some organizations more receptive to innovation than others.

The diffusion perspective of innovation focuses on why and how innovation spreads in society (Kimberly and Evanisko, 1981). In order to diffuse innovation more quickly it is important to coordinate both the design and marketing approaches. This enables innovation to incorporate both the adoption and diffusion process when they are integrated in an organization. The decision to adopt an innovation involves making use of the innovation because it is the best course of action (Rogers, 2010). The diffusion of innovation includes the adoption process as a social system communicates the reasons why an innovation should be adopted (Rogers, 2010). Diffusion can occur over a time period to increase the probability that other people in the social system will adopt an innovation. Communication of innovations can take a variety of different forms including through social networks that are common in sport communities in which individuals have a common interest in performance outcomes.

Theoretical framework for sport innovation

Sport innovation takes place in a variety of different forms depending on the context. This chapter proposes that a useful theoretical framework for analyzing sport innovation is to focus on usage, value, risk, psychology and image (Antioco and Kleijnen, 2010). This helps to understand the reasons for the innovation taking place in a sport context and to evaluate how it adapts to the sport context. By focusing on each area this provides a structure for future evaluation of sport innovations. Each of these sport innovation areas will now be discussed.

Usage reasons

There are usage barriers to adopting innovations when there is a conflict with existing patterns (Ram and Sheth, 1989). Some innovations face conflict as the status quo is difficult to change due to the investment spent on the existing innovation (Holak and Lehman, 1990). This is a concern for innovations that improve user experience but may take some time to implement due to the learning and cost involved (Antioco and Kleijnen, 2010). Some innovations require a long time before they are accepted in the market as they require changes in behavior (Herbig and Day, 1992).

Sometimes consumers are suspicious of innovations as they are unclear about the need for them (Lee and Clark, 1996). The ability to recognize the benefits from an innovation may take some time. Some innovations need to be integrated into existing patterns and this takes time for people to understand (Antioco and Kleijnen, 2010). Consumers will resist innovations when there is uncertainty about the benefits of the innovation for the long term (Kleijnen *et al.*, 2009).

In the sport context, innovations are developed for different usages, from improving on-field performance to increasing team outcomes. Innovations have also occurred in the salary cap by placing limits on some sport teams in terms of how much they can pay players. These innovations have made sport more equitable but also in line with societal trends. The National Football League draft has been televised, which was an innovation in the way players were chosen based on performance statistics. In addition, innovations in clothing and footwear such as quick-dry technology and performance gear have made it better for athletes.

Value incentives

Value is considered different depending on the context and type (Antioco and Kleijnen, 2010). Innovations exhibit a great variety that can make them unstable and uncertain when in the initial stage of development. Past research by Parasuraman and Grewal (2000) discusses how perceived value affects the adoption of innovations and the importance on performance for behavioral intentions. The lack of perceived value is an impediment for innovation adoption due to the lack of incentive (Kleijnen *et al.*, 2009). The success of an innovation is determined by its extrinsic value in terms of future usages (Lee and O'Connor, 2003). Sometimes it is difficult to ascertain the value of an innovation when there is a lack of alternatives. This means that some innovations will have no substitutes and that makes it hard to assess the future success of the innovation (Wood and Moreau, 2006).

Value innovations in sport include increased money and time spent on sport sponsorship and television broadcasts. This has meant there has been more value for sport teams and athletes from televising events to global audiences. In addition, the marketing of specific sport players in a team has meant that value has been derived from clothing and merchandise sales. This value proposition from sport innovation is also apparent in increased education in schools about the benefits and potential harms from sport.

Risk reasons

Risk is commonly discussed in relation to the adoption and usage of innovations (Antioco and Kleijnen, 2010). Most innovations have some risk involved when they are introduced into the marketplace (Herzenstein *et al.*, 2007). These risks mean that consumers will wait until the innovation has been proven successful before adopting it (Ram and Sheth, 1989). Some consumers will develop functional barriers that lessen the potential side effects that may occur from using the innovation (Klerck and Sweeney, 2007). Antioco and Kleijnen (2010) propose that financial and performance issues comprise the two main types of risk. Financial risk involves monetary and resource issues with adopting the innovation. Many consumers are money conscious when spending resources on an innovation (Stone and Grønhuag, 1993). This means that consumers may act conservatively and be hesitant about sport innovations that affect their performance when there is an opportunity cost involved. Some consumers will invest in innovations when they have more information about the usages and benefits (Antioco and Kleijnen, 2010). Consumers will evaluate financial risk by examining the price versus reward for using the innovation (Song and Chintagunta, 2003). Performance risk is an issue for innovations that are difficult to assess because of their features (Antioco and Kleijnen, 2010). This means that many technology innovations have higher performance risk factors because of the uncertainty with the product or service (Agarwal and Teas, 2001). In order to lessen performance risk, knowledge transfer may take place amongst consumers (Moreau *et al.*, 2001). The overall functionality of an innovation is a major influence of adoption and diffusion decisions (Woodside and Biemans, 2005). Sometimes the lack of information about the innovation may hinder the usage of an innovation (Farrell and Saloner, 1986). Functionality can include having features on the innovation that are currently not available elsewhere.

Depending on the sport innovation, some consumers will disregard the risk because of prior experience and knowledge about the sport. Adventure and adrenaline sports have increased because of increased risks athletes are prepared to take and the audience who will pay to watch these sports. The risk of some sports has decreased with better safety equipment being invented. This has been made possible by international sporting bodies governing the way sport is played and viewed by society. Although with the increased usage of the internet there have been risks from sports betting and usage of illegal substances to increase sports performance.

Psychological factors

There are psychological barriers to adopting an innovation that differ depending on a person's culture, personality and age (Antioco and Kleijnen, 2010). Some of the psychological factors affecting innovation stem from the conditions existing in society based on societal expectations. Consumers may prefer to do things a certain way and this can lead to unwillingness to use an innovation (Kleijnen *et al.*, 2009). This is referred to as behavioral intent to continue to associate with certain traits that take time to change. Social networks can lessen psychological barriers to innovation when innovations are used by people in their community (Chang and Cheung, 2001). Sometimes social changes will force a consumer to use an innovation as people within their group require this usage. When consumers can assess all the consequences of an innovation then their behavior may change in a positive or negative manner (Antioco and Kleijnen, 2010).

Positive associations with an innovation will result when there is less change in tradition and the current way of thinking. Negative associations will come from fear in changing current behaviors. Both types of behavior influence psychological barriers but may be different in the sport context depending on the willingness of a person in an organization to perform well. Some athletes and teams will adopt innovations faster when they perceive the performance outcomes outweigh the psychological barriers. Examples of psychological innovations in sport are the increased focus on women in sport and their participation rates. There have also been technological innovations that have changed the rules of the game from goal scoring technology.

Image incentives

The image of an innovation in terms of how it looks and feels is an important consideration for consumers. As more money is spent on innovations consumers will examine the functionality of an innovation but also its brand image and reputation in the marketplace. Kleijnen *et al.* (2005) discuss how image is an influential force behind innovation adoption decisions. This is due to images being related to certain ideas or expectations about how a person will behave in society. Some consumers focus on the social risk in adopting an innovation (Stone and Grønhaug, 1993). The social risk can affect the image a consumer projects to their peers. This is because if a consumer chooses a wrong innovation that does not fit their reputation it will affect their image (Berger and Heath, 2007). Some consumers see images as impacting their social status amongst their peer group. Some images are purchased more quickly by consumers when they impact their social status (Plouffe *et al.*, 2001). Some images are stereotypes that are embedded in societal thinking (Ram, 1989). These stereotypes are also affected by a lack of information and knowledge about the innovation (Antioco and Kleijnen, 2010). Images that are unfavorable are less likely to be adopted by consumers. Some consumers postpone buying innovations when there is uncertainty about performance. Consumers need to be reassured about making the right decision when investing in an innovation.

The image of some sports has changed based on innovations. A good example of this is the World Fighting Championship, which changed its rules to enable usage of the Octagon instead of the ring in which fights take place. This image change is also seen in athletes developing better physical strength and endurance as evidenced by the increased viewership of ultra sports events such as marathons. Due to the competitive nature of the sport industry, the different images of sport perceived by consumers, businesses and governments have changed. Luxury sport brands such as Moncler use images to associate their brand with social status. Other sport brands, including lifestyle ones such as Rip Curl, use images like maintaining a healthy lifestyle to encourage people to adopt their innovations.

Managerial implications

The theoretical arguments discussed in this chapter have important managerial implications and point to significant avenues for future sport managers. The focus of the chapter has been on developing a theory of sport innovation, which is a key focus for many sport associations that rely on innovation for their continued success. The theory of sport innovation provides guidance to managers about identifying innovation with sport. Some managers and firms will differ in their ability to innovate in sport due to resource, time and aptitude constraints. A future direction for managers to take is to study how some forms of sport innovation may be more accessible in some organizations and easier to commercialize. This is due to some organizations being more adept at formulating and solving problems based on their ability to process knowledge (Vanhaverbeke and Cloodt, 2014). Other organizations may discover innovative ways to interact with sport fans as part of their linkage to clubs. An opportunity for future work is to study the managerial factors that shape sport innovation.

The contribution of this chapter for sport managers is to provide an in-depth explanation of sport innovation and to offer a conceptual understanding of this area. This will enable the development of sport innovation as a distinct area of innovation management that can provide a basis for managers to further develop in the sport and innovation field. This chapter also contributes to the literature on innovation management by contextualizing sport and its relationship with dynamic growth activity in the business world.

Future research suggestions

More research needs to utilize the theoretical framework developed in this chapter to understand and consider the nature of sport innovation. Future research should use the definition of sport innovation discussed in this chapter to build sport innovation as a coherent field of research. By understanding the idea of sport innovation this will lead to more research focusing on the distinctiveness of the field. The community of sport management and innovation management scholars should establish sport innovation as a field of research combining both sport and innovation. Sport innovation is practically relevant for many businesses and not-for-profit organizations due to the integral nature of sport in society.

Approaches to sport innovation research need to target different stakeholders in terms of their diversity in innovation adoptions. For example, research should attend to the specific economic and social innovations that contribute to sport. Social, behavioral and organizational science research is required to understand sport innovation and to inform research. Efforts are needed to join the sport and innovation disciplines to provide a more holistic view of sport innovation. The growing recognition of the importance of innovation to society, and especially sport, highlights the need for different discipline engagements with sport innovation. There is a need for a whole-of-science agenda for sport innovation related research. This chapter places importance for scholars across the sport and innovation sciences to stress the need to engage with sport innovation research.

Conclusion

This chapter has introduced the concept of sport innovation as a theoretical framework and it is hoped future research will more fully develop this concept. The innovation view of sport focused on value generation, which can have both a financial and non-financial basis. Further research is called for that widens the conceptualization of sport and business to incorporate a view of innovation to help reframe the dynamic nature of the sport industry.

There are some limitations of developing sport innovation as a field of research due to the complex nature of the concepts. The concepts of sport and innovation are contested because of the broad meanings and applications they have in the literature. Sport and innovation are complex concepts due to the way they change depending on the type of sport or innovation studied. This may complicate the application of sport innovation depending on whether the innovation is radical or incremental, social or technological, or a combination of both. In addition, professional sport versus amateur sport provides a different way of looking at sport innovation. Nevertheless, this chapter provides a good basis for understanding sport innovation and is a useful conceptual tool for furthering future research.

References

Agarwal, S. & Teas, R. K. (2001). 'Perceived value: mediating role of perceived risk', *Journal of Marketing Theory and Practice*, *9*(4), 1–14.

Antioco, M. & Kleijnen, M. (2010). 'Consumer adoption of technological innovations: effects of psychological and functional barriers in a lack of content versus a presence of content situation', *European Journal of Marketing*, *44*(11/12), 1700–1774.

Berger, J. & Heath, C. (2007). 'Where consumers diverge from others: identity signaling and product domains', *Journal of Consumer Research*, *34*(2), 121–134.

Bierly, P. E., Damanpour, F. & Santoro, M. D. (2009). 'The application of external knowledge: organizational conditions for exploration and exploitation'. *Journal of Management Studies*, *46*(3), 481–509.

Chang, M. K. & Cheung, W. (2001). 'Determinants of the intention to use Internet/WWW at work: a confirmatory study'. *Information & Management*, *39*(1), 1–14.

Clark, P. A., Staunton, N. & Rogers, E. M. (1989). *Innovation in technology and organization.* London: Routledge.

Damanpour, F. (1991). 'Organizational innovation: a meta-analysis of effects of determinants and moderators'. *Academy of Management Journal*, *34*(3), 555–590.

Damanpour, F. (1996). 'Organizational complexity and innovation: developing and testing multiple contingency models'. *Management Science*, *42*(5), 693–716.

Damanpour, F. & Evan, W. M. (1984). 'Organizational innovation and performance: the problem of "organizational lag"'. *Administrative Science Quarterly, 29*, 392–409.

Damanpour, F., Walker, R. M. & Avellaneda, C. N. (2009). 'Combinative effects of innovation types and organizational performance: a longitudinal study of service organizations'. *Journal of Management Studies, 46*(4), 650–675.

Damanpour, F. & Schneider, M. (2006). 'Phases of the adoption of innovation in organizations: effects of environment, organization and top managers'. *British Journal of Management, 17*(3), 215–2.

Edvardsson, B. & Olsson, J. (1996). 'Key concepts for new service development'. *Service Industries Journal, 16*(2), 140–164.

Farrell, J. & Saloner, G. (1986). 'Installed base and compatibility: innovation, product preannouncements, and predation'. *The American Economic Review, 76*(5), 940–955.

Franke, N. & Shah, S. (2003). 'How communities support innovative activities: an exploration of assistance and sharing among end-users'. *Research Policy, 32*(1), 157–178.

Herbig, P. A. & Day, R. L. (1992). 'Customer acceptance: the key to successful introductions of innovations', *Marketing Intelligence & Planning, 10*(1), 4–15.

Herzenstein, M., Posavac, S. S. & Brakus, J. J. (2007). 'Adoption of new and really new products: the effects of self-regulation systems and risk salience'. *Journal of Marketing Research, 44*(2), 251–260.

Hipp, C. & Grupp, H. (2005). 'Innovation in the service sector: the demand for service-specific innovation measurement concepts and typologies'. *Research Policy, 34*(4), 517–535.

Hoeber, L. & Hoeber, O. (2012). 'Determinants of an innovation process: a case study of technological innovation in a community sport organization'. *Journal of Sport Management, 26*(3), 213–223.

Holak, S. L. & Lehmann, D. R. (1990). 'Purchase intentions and the dimensions of innovation: an exploratory model'. *Journal of Product Innovation Management, 7*(1), 59–73.

Hull, C. E. & Lio, B. H. (2006). 'Innovation in non-profit and for-profit organizations: visionary, strategic, and financial considerations'. *Journal of Change Management, 6*(1), 53–65.

Kimberly, J. R. & Evanisko, M. J. (1981). 'Organizational innovation: the influence of individual, organizational and contextual factors on hospital adoption of technological and administrative innovations'. *Academy of Management Journal, 24*(4), 689–713.

Kleijnen, M., De Ruyter, K. & Andreassen, T. W. (2005). 'Image congruence and the adoption of service innovations'. *Journal of Service Research, 7*(4), 343–359.

Kleijnen, M., Lee, N. & Wetzels, M. (2009). 'An exploration of consumer resistance to innovation and its antecedents'. *Journal of Economic Psychology, 30*(3), 344–357.

Klerck, D. & Sweeney, J. C. (2007). 'The effect of knowledge types on consumer-perceived risk and adoption of genetically modified foods'. *Psychology & Marketing, 24*(2), 171–193.

Lee, H. G. & Clark, T. H. (1996). 'Market process reengineering through electronic market systems: opportunities and challenges'. *Journal of Management Information Systems, 13*(3), 113–136.

Lee, Y. & O'Connor, G. C. (2003). 'New product launch strategy for network effects products'. *Journal of the Academy of Marketing Science, 31*(3), 241–255.

Li, H. & Atuahene-Gima, K. (2001). 'Product innovation strategy and the performance of new technology ventures in China'. *Academy of Management Journal, 44*(6), 1123–1134.

Lovelock, C. & Gummesson, E. (2004). 'Whither services marketing? In search of a new paradigm and fresh perspectives'. *Journal of Service Research, 7*(1), 20–41.

Moreau, C. P., Lehmann, D. R. & Markman, A. B. (2001). 'Entrenched knowledge structures and consumer response to new products'. *Journal of Marketing Research*, *38*(1), 14–29.

Newell, S. & Swan, J. (1995). 'Professional associations as important mediators of the innovation process'. *Science Communication*, *16*(4), 371–387.

Oke, A., Burke, G. & Myers, A. (2007). 'Innovation types and performance in growing UK SMEs'. *International Journal of Operations & Production Management*, *27*(7), 735–753.

Parasuraman, A. & Grewal, D. (2000). 'The impact of technology on the quality-value-loyalty chain: a research agenda'. *Journal of the Academy of Marketing Science*, *28*(1), 168–174.

Pinto, J. K. & Prescott, J. E. (1988). 'Variations in critical success factors over the stages in the project life cycle'. *Journal of Management*, *14*(1), 5–18.

Plouffe, C. R., Vandenbosch, M. & Hulland, J. (2001). 'Intermediating technologies and multi-group adoption: a comparison of consumer and merchant adoption intentions toward a new electronic payment system'. *Journal of Product Innovation Management*, *18*(2), 65–81.

Ram, S. (1989). 'Successful innovation using strategies to reduce consumer resistance: An empirical test'. *Journal of Product Innovation Management*, *6*(1), 20–34.

Ram, S. & Sheth, J. N. (1989). 'Consumer resistance to innovations: the marketing problem and its solutions'. *Journal of Consumer Marketing*, *6*(2), 5–14.

Ratten, V. (2010). 'Developing a theory of sport-based entrepreneurship'. *Journal of Management & Organization*, *16*(4), 557–565.

Rogers, E. M. (2010). *Diffusion of innovations*. Simon and Schuster.

Saleh, S. D. & Wang, C. K. (1993). 'The management of innovation: strategy, structure, and organizational climate'. *IEEE Transactions on Engineering Management*, *40*(1), 14–21.

Smith, W. K. & Tushman, M. L. (2005). 'Managing strategic contradictions: a top management model for managing innovation streams'. *Organization Science*, *16*(5), 522–536.

Song, I. & Chintagunta, P. K. (2003). 'A micromodel of new product adoption with heterogeneous and forward-looking consumers: application to the digital camera category'. *Quantitative Marketing and Economics*, *1*(4), 371–407.

Stone, R. N. & Grønhaug, K. (1993). 'Perceived risk: further considerations for the marketing discipline'. *European Journal of Marketing*, *27*(3), 39–50.

Thibault, L., Slack, T. B. & Hinings, B. (1993). 'A framework for the analysis of strategy in nonprofit sport organizations'. *Journal of Sport Management*, 7, 25–43

Tipping, J. W., Zeffren, E. & Fusfeld, A. R. (1995). 'Assessing the value of your technology'. *Research Technology Management*, *38*(5), 22.

Tushman, M. L. & Smith, W. (2002). 'Organizational technology' in *Blackwell Companion to Organizations*, J. A. C. Baum (ed.) Blackwell, 386–414.

Vanhaverbeke, W., & Cloodt, M. (2014). 'Theories of the firm and open innovation' in *New Frontiers in Open Innovation*, H. Chesbrough, W. Vanhaverbeke & J. West (eds.) Oxford University Press Oxford, 256–278.

Von Hippel, E. (2007). *The sources of innovation*, Springer.

Walker, R. M. (2008). 'An empirical evaluation of innovation types and organizational and environmental characteristics: towards a configuration framework'. *Journal of Public Administration Research and Theory*, *18*(4), 591–615.

Walsh, J. P. & Ungson, G. R. (1991). 'Organizational memory'. *Academy of Management Review*, *16*(1), 57–91.

Wood, S. L. & Moreau, C. P. (2006). 'From fear to loathing? How emotion influences the evaluation and early use of innovations'. *Journal of Marketing*, *70*(3), 44–57.

Woodside, A. G. & Biemans, W. G. (2005). 'Modeling innovation, manufacturing, diffusion and adoption/rejection processes'. *Journal of Business & Industrial Marketing*, *20*(7), 380–393.

2

INNOVATION CAPABILITY OF NON-PROFIT SPORT ORGANISATIONS

Mathieu Winand and Larena Hoeber

Introduction

Researchers and practitioners realise the importance of studying innovation. Thousands of academic articles have dealt with this central topic in an organisational context (for an overview see Crossan and Apaydin, 2010). Scholars have pointed out that innovation is a source of competitive advantage, in the public, private and non-profit sectors, through improved effectiveness and efficiency (Damanpour and Aravind, 2012; Dess and Picken, 2000; Han *et al.*, 1998; Lee *et al.*, 2009; McDonald and Srinivasan, 2004; Tushman and O'Reilly, 1996). Indeed, organisations have to adapt to the competitive environment they face. They need to change in order to meet the expectations of their consumers or to create added value for users through innovation. The for-profit sector is often seen as the most dynamic sector of the sport market as competition leads to innovation (e.g., Gratton and Taylor, 2000; Robinson, Hewitt and Harris, 2000; Vos and Scheerder, 2014). However, little is known about innovation outside the for-profit sector, and the focus on patents and R&D departments. As Crossan and Apaydin (2010, p. 21) stated, "innovation research is fragmented, poorly grounded theoretically, and not fully tested in all areas".

Non-profit sport organisations (NPSOs), such as voluntary sport clubs or sport federations, are encouraged to change to satisfy and meet new expectations of their members. Indeed, their ability to innovate is just as important as for other organisations (Newell and Swan, 1995), in part because of the growing commercialisation and professionalisation of the sport industry. NPSOs are increasingly challenged by for-profit sport providers, but also face competition from other NPSOs. For example, non-profit sport clubs may be competing with each other for members and scarce resources such as finances, facilities and volunteers (Newell and Swan, 1995; Vos *et al.*, 2012). That competition, as perceived by the management board, leads NPSOs to innovate (Winand *et al.*, 2013).

14 Mathieu Winand and Larena Hoeber

According to Newell and Swan (1995), issues faced by NPSOs are unique and require a context-specific framework with which to address innovation. Yet, research on innovation in this context is rare. Very few studies have paid attention to the notion of innovation in NPSOs (exceptions include Caza, 2000; Hoeber and Hoeber, 2012; Newell and Swan, 1995; Winand *et al.*, 2013), and none of them have developed a conceptualisation of innovation in NPSOs, which could form the basis for further research. This chapter aims to feature innovation types in the context of NPSOs and to identify the opportunities and constraints that lie within the context of NPSOs with regard to innovation, with the goal of establishing a model of innovative capability in NPSOs.

First, innovation in non-profit organisations is outlined according to the specific characteristics of these organisations that lead them to approach innovation differently from for-profit organisations. Then, innovation types in the sport context are described and findings from the literature on innovation in the non-profit sport sector are outlined. Finally, a model of constraints and opportunities for innovation in non-profit sport organisations is presented and discussed. The chapter concludes with suggestions for further research directions.

Innovation in non-profit organisations

Scholars in many disciplines have paid attention to innovation at different levels of analysis: sector, industry, organisation, firm, group and at the individual level (Camisón-Zornoza *et al.*, 2004; Crossan and Apaydin, 2010; Damanpour, 1996). At the organisational level, which is the focus of this chapter, innovation has been broadly and often defined as the adoption of an idea or behaviour that is new for the organisation (Crossan and Apaydin, 2010; Daft, 1978; Damanpour, 1996; Damanpour and Evan, 1984; Damanpour and Schneider, 2006; Hage, 1999; Hansen and Wakonen, 1997; Van de Ven, 1986). That is, even though it may have been developed by other organisations, it is new for the adopter (Mohr, 1969; Rogers, 1995; Zaltman *et al.*, 1973). The new idea should not only be adopted by the organisation, but successfully brought into use.

The range of non-profit organisations (NPOs) is broad and given the difficulty to identify specific types and core activities for non-profits, it is challenging to classify types of innovation. NPOs develop new administrative processes, services, organisational designs or cultures and products/devices. The main shared feature is their non-profit mission that influences their ability to innovate. Indeed, the range of organisational values is restricted for non-profits. They have low flexibility (or none) in their market choice orientation due to the fact that their market is usually a fundamental part of their societal or social mission (Hull and Lio, 2006). It is therefore crucial for non-profits that innovations be consistent with their mission, values, experience and needs (Wolfe, 1994). NPOs are accountable to and scrutinised by external political and regulatory institutions (Damanpour, 1996; Perry and Rainy, 1988) and internal stakeholders like members. These external and internal control mechanisms restrict their decision-making flexibility (Dean *et al.*, 1991).

For example Slack and Hinings (1994), Skille (2009) and Vos *et al.* (2011) found evidence for coercive pressures of governments on NPSOs. These pressures are related to regulations, ethical and/or cultural considerations, dependency on financial resources, etc. (Vos *et al.*, 2011). The high levels of centralisation, formalisation and procedures standardisation of some NPOs (Perry and Rainey, 1988), as well as the high degree of control, would limit the extent of innovation or inhibit it all together (Damanpour, 1996; Pierce and Delbecq, 1977). However, not all NPOs are centralised, formalised and standardised. On the contrary, some have just become formalised and standardised and some are still quite informal (e.g. local club sports) (Kikulis *et al.*, 1995; Taylor, 2004; Theodoraki and Henry, 1994).

Hull and Lio (2006) suggested that resistance to innovation, and broadly to change, is greater in NPOs than in for-profits. Staff of NPOs may not see the benefit or necessity for their organisation to innovate. The authors highlighted risk taking as one factor that is crucial to explain why NPOs tend to be less innovative than for-profits. Risk taking has been linked with innovation (Covin and Slevin, 1998; Miller, 1983), with some suggesting that innovation requires it (Damanpour, 1996). Because NPOs are more risk-averse, take fewer risks in their strategic decisions, due to their fragile structure, complex distribution of responsibilities and non-profit goals, they are more reluctant to innovate (Hull and Lio, 2006). Furthermore, it is common for service organisations, like some non-profit organisations, when they seek to develop new services not to use the word innovation but to highlight the outcomes of innovations, such as clients' satisfaction or quality improvement (Gallouj, 2002; Preissl, 2000; Sundbo and Gallouj, 2000; Toivonen and Tuominen, 2006). Consequently, it may even be more difficult to detect how innovative they are as they do not value or even incorporate the innovation terminology. Additionally, there is no patent protection for a new service that would facilitate its identification. This lack of protection could also reduce the incentive for this kind of innovation (Hipp and Grupp, 2005).

In response to the restrictions and challenges NPOs face in considering innovation, Hull and Lio (2006, p. 61) suggested that the label of "process innovation" is a "better fit with the interests of non-profits than are product innovations". According to the authors, process innovation is less risky, less expensive in the short term and may provide immediate benefits to support the organisation's mission and what their members can value. McDonald (2007, p. 258) stated that "successful non-profit organisations will strive for innovation to serve their missions". NPOs develop innovations, which are compatible with their mission and values, to attract and satisfy their users and members. Innovations within the non-profit sport sector would likely be sport related (e.g. sport services) or in support of the sport organisations' activities.

Innovation in sport

The type of innovation refers to the aspect of the organisation to which the innovation is most relevant. Types of innovations are usually conceptualised as a dichotomy of technical or administrative innovations (Crossan and Apaydin, 2010; Daft, 1982; Damanpour, 1996; Gopalakrishnan and Damanpour, 2000). Technical innovations are directly linked to the core activity of the organisation and could include products, services, processes and technologies. Administrative innovations are the structural, administrative and managerial aspects needed to achieve the organisation's core activity. In the sport industry, two main types of technical innovations are developed: new sport products (e.g. sport equipment, sport devices, sport technologies) and new sport services (e.g. training programmes for athletes, coaches, referees). Administrative innovations are related to the organisations' non-sport services such as a new affiliation system, an online inter-active tool and updated schedules of sport competitions.

Sport is an entrepreneurial process where being innovative, favouring risk, being proactive and creating value are crucial (Ratten, 2010, 2011a, 2011b). Market opportunities are exploited by organisations through product or service innovation to create value to users. However, Desbordes (2002) noted that some product innovations did not appear in the sport industry due to resistance from consumers and international sport federations. Nevertheless, he argued sport product innovation firms attach great importance to the sport consumers they want to satisfy and integrate during the product development (e.g. pre-tests of sport equipment). According to Franke and Shah (2003) and Lüthje (2004), sport consumers play an important role in generating new ideas. The authors noted innovative sport consumers are not driven by profit but aim to fulfil an individual need, usually to improve their sport practice.

A similar conclusion could be applied to service innovations. They are new acts or processes (Hipp and Grupp, 2005), and hence cannot be physically manip-ulated or possessed. Service innovations are all new services that are introduced by the organisation for the first time to increase users' satisfaction, its effectiveness or its quality to the users (Damanpour and Aravind, 2012). Users can either be customers purchasing new services or members paying a membership fee to access a range of services, including new ones. When customers purchase a service, they do not receive ownership, but access to the service for a defined period of time, price (fee), within a limited area, using specific materials (Lovelock and Gummesson, 2004). For example, sport participants receive access to sport facilities and sport programmes or gain the right to use a sport trainer's expertise. Sport providers may act on the different possibilities of access to make it more attractive. Services are characterised by customers' integration where production and consumption are simultaneous (Gallouj and Weinstein, 1997; Hipp and Grupp, 2005). A new training programme for sport coaches is only visible when coaches are following it. The interaction of the training provider represented by an expert and the future sport coaches following the new programme represent the sport service innovation. The intangible characteristic of services makes it more difficult to detect a modification or an improvement in comparison with new products. Although services are intangible before their use, they could have mental and physical tangible effects (Lovelock and Gummesson, 2004). To illustrate, sport activities, considered as physical acts to users' bodies, result in an experience that is highly tangible.

Additionally, new sport disciplines or activities have emerged that have been recognised as service innovations. Zumba (i.e. a dance fitness programme) is an example of new recreational physical activities emerging in the 90s. We argue that new sports or recreational physical activities are a specific kind of service innovation. Indeed, as underlined by Edvardsson and Olsson (1996), in service innovation, it is not the service itself that is produced but new conditions for the service to take place. Similarly, for Zumba, these conditions include fitness instructors who have followed Zumba training, participants with Zumba skills, a room adapted for that type of activity, etc. Service innovation theory applies to all new sport or recreational physical activities as far as consumers partake in the activity, i.e. they do not passively watch (sport spectators to a football match). Another example of a new sport service innovation (i.e. technical innovation type) is a new training programme called "Run For You" developed by athletic sport federations and sport clubs in Belgium to assist people from all ages to get active and run five kilometres. Other examples of sport service innovations include "360ball" – a new way of playing squash-tennis created in 2011 – and "Zorbing" – the recreation of rolling downhill inside a transparent orb. These new sports are sport activities that are offered during a defined period of time, for a particular price (or fee) in order to use the limited area and specific equipment. These elements form the conditions for these new sports to be experienced. Note that when sport consumers decide to buy new materials for these new sports and practise whenever and wherever they want (e.g. a Zorb), it should not be conceived as a service they pay for in a defined period of time, but a product they bought and own.

Walker (2008) called for more knowledge about the nature of service innovation. He suggested understanding service innovation through the relationship with the user in meeting his or her need or a market need. He identified three types of service innovations (Osborne, 1998; Walker *et al.*, 2002) following the combinations of new or existing services provided to new or existing users. *Total innovation* refers to new services provided to new users; *expansionary innovation* involves the provision of existing services to new users; and *evolutionary innovation* refers to new services provided to existing users (Walker, 2008). The objective of total innovation would be to attract new consumers, whereas the objective of evolutionary innovation would be to satisfy or retain current consumers. Expansionary innovation depends on how newness is defined and by whom it is perceived. Given that all services integrate users' experience and are performed for a particular user's satisfaction, each service is unique. If the unit of analysis is the user, the same service provided to different users consists of multiple innovations. If the unit of analysis is the organisation or the service sector, then a service is innovative when it is first introduced or used in an organisation or in the sector (Drejer, 2004).

NPSOs develop sport and non-sport innovations as a means to induce change in their organisational process, services and management. Since the core activity of NPSOs is oriented to the delivery of sport services (e.g. organising sport competitions, running sport programmes, offering training opportunities), they will mainly develop service innovations as opposed to product innovations. Furthermore, the context in which NPSOs operate leads them to comprehend innovation differently from commercial sport organisations or other non-profits. The following section addresses innovation in the context of NPSOs.

Innovation in non-profit sport organisations

NPSOs differ from other sport organisations on four main criteria (Bayle, 2005; Bayle and Robinson, 2007). Their mission is social and/or sport oriented rather than financially profit oriented. They are run by volunteers and/or paid staff. They have a mixed economy balancing between grants, subsidies, revenues from sponsorship and membership fees. They operate via a sport network and thus are regulated by national and international sport systems. In comparison to other non-profit organisations, NPSOs are highly dependent on volunteers, tend to be smaller but more financially self-sufficient, and often have varying levels of resource capacity (Gumulka *et al.*, 2005). One of the key features for the viability of non-profit sports clubs is the strong commitment of volunteers that make their workforce available (Vos, Breesch and Scheerder, 2012).

Innovation represents a worthwhile opportunity for NPSOs as demonstrated by Winand *et al.* (2011) in a study on determinants of high organisational performance within the context of sport federations where innovative activities were a key determinant to success. Nevertheless, studies on innovation in this context are rare. So far, only a few relevant studies have been published on this concept for sport users (Franke and Shah, 2003), both amateur and professional sport organisations (Gilmore and Gilson, 2007; Hoeber and Hoeber, 2012; Wolfe *et al.*, 2006) as well as sport federations (Caza, 2000; Newell and Swan, 1995; Winand, Qualizza *et al.*, 2013; Winand *et al.*, 2013).

In contrast with firms where innovation is usually developed internally, and is controlled and commercialised, NPSOs frequently exploit both internal and external sources to innovate. Innovation in NPSOs is sometimes developed by users (e.g. sport participants) (Franke and Shah, 2003). Innovation can thus be achieved through close interaction with members of sport organisations. Furthermore, not only NPSOs, but also sport participants can benefit from cooperation between (sport) providers. These benefits include innovation, service and quality (Vos and Scheerder, 2014). It shows a valuable illustration of inter-active and open innovation (Chesbrough, 2003) in which external sources (e.g. users, but also other NPSOs, sport networks and regulatory agencies) influence the innovation process of NPSOs.

Examples of case studies of innovation in the sport organisation literature range from new staff philosophy in a soccer club (Gilmore and Gilson, 2007), new sport equipment (Franke and Shah, 2003), new programmes, online services and partnerships with external stakeholders (Hoeber *et al.*, 2009), new computer scoring systems and athlete ranking systems (Caza, 2000), to new technological innovation (i.e. Electronic Game Sheet; Hoeber and Hoeber, 2012). The next section looks at the opportunities and constraints NPSOs face which influence their innovation capability.

Innovation capability of non-profit sport organisations

Innovation capability has been defined as the ability for organisations to mobilise individuals' skills and resources to create new knowledge leading to new services, products or processes (Cohen and Levinthal, 1990; Damanpour, 1991; Kogut and Zander, 1992). According to Newell and Swan (1995), the innovative capability of governing bodies of sport is critical to acquiring (new) resources to survive and to promote their sport, as well as to develop the sport in general in diffusing innovations, new practices or new rules for instance. NPSOs have specific opportunities and constraints that impact on their innovation capability. Based on the work of Bayle and Robinson (2007), Gumulka et al. (2005) and Hull and Lio (2006), four main dimensions are highlighted which influence the ability of NPSOs to innovate (see Figure 2.1): (i) a strategic dimension, (ii) a user dimension, (iii) a financial dimension and (iv) a human resources dimension.

The strategic dimension includes the NPSO environment of competitors in the sport service market, apex bodies within the sport system and stakeholders'

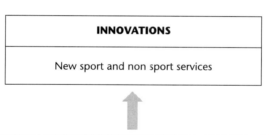

FIGURE 2.1   Innovation capability of non-profit sport organisations

expectations. Thibault *et al.* (1993) identified NPSOs as innovators when they show strong competitive position (i.e. low investment needed to participate) and low programme attractiveness, but want to get people involved in their sports and retain them. The ability of NPSOs to innovate is reduced to the range of freedom in their market. Their market is restricted to the sport and social values they promote and constrained by the rules and regulations imposed by umbrella organisations (e.g. international sport organisations and public authorities). Indeed, the environment in which NPSOs operate has a strong influence on their ability to innovate. Key agencies (e.g. government, national councils, international and national sport governing bodies and the International Olympic Committee) play a central role in affecting innovations in the organisation of sport (Newell and Swan, 1995). It could be argued that stakeholders will be influenced by the extent to which the consequence of an innovation is visible or observable (Wolfe, 1994). They would be more receptive to highly visible and easily understandable new services or processes in line with the organisation's non-profit and sport purposes. Note that partnerships developed by NPSOs with commercial organisations in their network are also of importance as the latter can assist the development and implementation of new ideas as mentioned by Hoeber and Hoeber (2012). Moreover, organisations might copy other organisations in order to gain legitimacy and to tackle uncertainty. According to DiMaggio and Powell (1983) this process of mimetic isomorphism might explain why sports organisations have a tendency to take on attributes of other organisations they interact with and/or depend on.

Another opportunity is the influence of sport members, consumers and users in innovation within NPSOs. The user dimension refers both to their expectations of new sport and non-sport services to increase their satisfaction, as well as their involvement in the innovation process, including the conceptualisation of new ideas (Franke and Shah, 2003). This has an impact on the degree of resistance users will have against the new idea, and indirectly how the idea will be perceived by staff and stakeholders (e.g. sponsors and funding agencies).

Financial dimension concerns the monetary resources NPSOs attract from members, sponsors, funding agencies and public authorities, which influence their level of autonomy and the cost of new investments. NPSOs receive scarce resources and as such, strive for financial balance. As part of their mandate, any profits must be reinvested in their activities (Winand *et al.*, 2012). Their funding streams impact their dependence on stakeholders/funders and their autonomy in developing new ideas. Sport sponsorship is a funding stream of NPSOs with particular requirements in terms of media coverage and participation base (Berrett and Slack, 2001). Indeed, as stated by Newell and Swan (1995), sponsorship revenues are associated with increasing demands on NPSOs for change to better serve the interests of the sponsors. Therefore, core sponsors might expect or even require NPSOs to develop new activities they would support which increase their visibility in return.

Financial investment required by innovations (Wolfe, 1994) might be seen as a barrier to innovate especially for some non-profits with scarce resources.

However, a study by Winand *et al.* (2013) showed that perceptions of low economic health within sport federations might foster innovation. The rationale suggested by the authors is that these sport federations innovate in order to differentiate from competitors and create opportunities to increase resources to grow and survive. A study by Wicker *et al.* (2013) on resource dependence theory within non-profit sport clubs, which are known as traditional and rather non-innovative organisations, showed that in case of serious resource problems there is a need to gain more external resources and to have interorganisational relationships. Partner organisations (e.g. sponsors, schools or other NPSOs) could encourage innovations by providing NPSOs with defined financial support or other physical (e.g. sport facilities) or human resources (e.g. volunteers) to develop innovative activities in order to raise interest from participants, which in return benefit the funder/partner. Agencies in the sport movement have made a business of connecting voluntary sport organisations (or athletes) with commercial partners, hence providing marketing partnerships to NPSOs, which do not have the capability to develop such practice.

A large part of the success of innovation is due to careful management alongside its implementation (Caza, 2000). The human resources dimension includes the individuals within the NPSOs who make the decisions to adopt and implement new ideas. Paid staff and/or volunteers are involved in decision-making at different levels of the organisation. They might have different motives which impact on the process of innovation within their NPSOs and the implementation of new ideas over time. However, the value of tradition in sport and resistance from decision-makers could serve as a barrier to innovation (Newell and Swan, 1995; Wolfe *et al.*, 2006). Volunteers are crucial in influencing innovation in NPSOs because most rely (partially or entirely) on them. It is common that decision-makers, particularly in voluntary sports clubs, want to maintain the status quo, which could be done through self-monitoring and internal recruitment processes (Thiel and Mayer, 2009). The attitude of staff towards change and newness is also critical in the non-profit sport context (Winand, Qualizza *et al.*, 2013), as some operate with mixed staff (i.e. commission volunteers, volunteer board members, technical and administrative professionals). Successful implementation of innovation requires managerial support and a committed staff, a simple structure and a small staff size, resulting in good communication and flexibility (Hoeber and Hoeber, 2012). Additionally, the process of innovation needs leadership commitment (Hoeber and Hoeber, 2012). Winand *et al.* (2013) highlighted that the support and attitude of employees and volunteers within NPSOs is critical during the innovation process. It helps to create an entrepreneurial atmosphere. It is important in the sport context, no matter whether professional (Wolfe *et al.*, 2006) or amateur (Hoeber and Hoeber, 2012), to rely on someone advocating for the need to innovate all along the process. This individual, mentioned as the "innovation champion" in the literature (Damanpour and Schneider, 2006; Wolfe, 1994), can be found in the role of technical or sport professional in NPSOs as discussed by Winand *et al.* (2013).

The ability to develop innovations is delimited by the four dimensions highlighted in the model. NPSOs innovate in order to satisfy new users' expectations and answer challenges they face from their environment. They aim to provide added value to membership as perceived by current and potential members (Walker, 2008).

Discussion of the model of innovation capability in non-profit sport organisations

Innovations in NPSOs could be initiated (or inhibited) by professionals and board members, sport members and users or sport networks, competitors and agencies. The NPSO characteristics – size, membership, financial resources, staff and tradition – have a strong influence all along the process of innovation (Newell and Swan, 1995), as well as the specificities of the sport promoted by the NPSO, its ways and place of practice, its media coverage, its potential attractiveness and its competitive position, as mentioned by Thibault et al. (1993). NPSOs exist in a sport system of national and international umbrella organisations and/or the Olympic movement that has a substantial impact on their activities. The organisations of some sport competitions are exclusive (and regulated) services. The monopolistic control of a sport, like regulation in football, has an impact on the ability of NPSOs to innovate. While some sports are developing very fast with the emergence of associated sports (e.g. beach volleyball, snowboard cross) and evolution of rules (e.g. moving the three-point line back in basketball), others stay unchanged and attached to their tradition (e.g. football). International sport federations have considerable impact on innovation at lower levels. No matter how new the idea, it cannot be implemented if it is contrariwise to the essence of the game being promoted. At the same time, the idea should comply with the rules of other regulatory organisations in the sport sector (e.g. World Anti-Doping Agency and Court of Arbitration for Sport). A study by Winand et al. (2013) suggested that sports federations preferably innovate with regard to non-sport services to provide added value to membership, instead of developing new sport services, sporting activities or sports due to regulatory and legal constraints from apex bodies (e.g. international sport federations and public authorities).

The model presented has some limitations to consider. NPSOs range from large, professional organisations attracting a lot of resources from membership, sponsors and media (e.g. Fédération Internationale de Football Association; International Olympic Committee) to small, amateur organisations run by volunteers that have few resources from grants and membership (e.g. regional sport federations, local sport clubs). As Newell and Swan (1995, p. 312) underlined: "achieving innovation in SOs [governing bodies of sport] is likely to be dependent on their starting point (i.e., in terms of size, membership, media coverage, level of funding)." Taylor (2004) identified two types of voluntary sport organisations (or NPSOs) that lie at opposite sides of a continuum. On the one hand, some NPSOs are traditional/informal and appear to resist current management concepts. On the other hand, some NPSOs are contemporary/formal and are concerned about organisational performance. Response to change and innovation in these two opposite NPSOs would be different. The latter might be more proactive for members' need or responsive to members' expectations. The constraints and opportunities with regards to innovation highlighted in the model could be adapted to the category (e.g. amateur sport clubs, national sport federations, national Olympic committees), size (e.g. large versus small), sport (traditional versus contemporary sport) or policy context (e.g. international or national sport policy level). Nevertheless, they are all – to a certain extent – constrained by similar factors (e.g. mixed financial resources, sport network and market, combination of volunteers and professionals, and non-profit sport mission), which make them non-profit and sport organisations and influence their innovative capability.

Conclusion and further research

The present chapter analysed the concept of innovation in NPSOs. NPSOs innovate with regard to new sport services (technical innovation type) or new non-sport services (administrative innovation type) in order to create added value to users and stakeholders, satisfy users, gain effectiveness and/or increase quality to users. Sport service innovations are linked to the core activity of NPSOs. Non-sport service innovations are related to the structure, administrative processes and managerial aspects needed to achieve sport services. NPSOs could also develop new sport products (technical innovation type) that can be owned by sport consumers, but it seems less common and requires partnership with expertise organisations in the development of those products. NPSOs will thus mainly innovate in services directly related to sport (i.e. sport services) or in support of sporting activities (i.e. non-sport services). For that purpose they create the conditions for these new services to take place.

The context in which NPSOs exist and the specific constraints they face lead them to approach innovation differently. NPSOs, which belongs to a sport network that regulate their activities, are driven by professionals and volunteers aiming at attracting mixed financial resources in order to fulfil their social and sport missions. Taking into account their context, the model developed throughout this chapter establishes a conceptual framework to generate and test hypotheses related to innovation in non-profit sport organisation research. Constraints and opportunities within four main dimensions (i.e. strategy, human resources, finance and users) have been highlighted as a starting point for further research on innovation in NPSOs.

NPSOs such as national sport federations and sport clubs operate via a sport network regulated by international and national sport systems. As a result, the development of innovations, answering new sport expectations and challenges, should comply with their social, societal and/or sport missions, as well as regulations that prevail in their sport and country. Sport culture might be different from one sport to another, as well as the policy context in which NPSOs operate.

These non-profit sport organisations need to comply with national regulations and laws from their country/region while at the same time are required to follow international sport regulations or rules, such as from the international sport federation or the World Anti-Doping Agency (WADA). Beach volleyball was diffused as an innovative sport in the 90s (but invented in the 1920s to 40s) with its integration into the programme of the Olympic Games. Following the popularity of beach volleyball, volleyball federations and clubs have adopted this new way of playing volleyball at the national level. The development of this new sport in turn led to new services such as training programmes for athletes, referees and coaches, and new championships to organise with new rules, facilities and equipment. The process of diffusion of new sports and its consequence at the national level needs further explanation. According to Brunsson *et al.* (2012) it is not clear whether organisations adapt to policies or whether policies are adapted to better fit local contexts, organisations' characteristics and what organisations can accept. Further research could examine the implementation of new sport policies (e.g. anti-doping policies) at national level and how NPSOs manage to satisfy both international sport and national legal regulations.

Decision-making processes regarding innovation within non-profit sport organisations should be investigated further given the human resources constraints. Indeed, NPSOs are managed by volunteers and professionals who might have different motives and might not see the incentive to innovate or be more risk-averse. Therefore, once a new idea has been highlighted questions remain as to how it is being adopted by the board and implemented. Key individuals would influence the process of innovation in NPSOs. Research has highlighted that support from innovation champions is a key element in that process, but no clear explanation as to how this individual proceeds as well as his/her profile has been examined or discussed (Hoeber and Hoeber, 2012; Winand *et al.* 2013). Thus, profiles of innovation champions in NPSOs could be investigated further. Furthermore, most NPSOs mainly rely on volunteers who might not have the skills, resources or time to develop innovations in a timely fashion. The influence of other organisations and partners that help them to develop, adopt and implement new ideas needs further understanding. Moreover, the impact of innovation success (or failure) on decision-making processes should be investigated further within NPSOs given the different stakeholder groups involved in their development, including volunteers, professionals, sport members, partners and sponsors. Their attitude towards innovations, the constraints (e.g. cost, time and adaption) associated with implementing them, would considerably influence the decision to adopt new ideas.

NPSOs have a mixed economy based on grants, sponsorship, membership fees and other sources of revenue, and strive to reach financial balance. The financial return of innovation for NPSOs could be investigated. While NPSOs innovate to compete for resources, no study has yet identified how organisations support innovation cost, how successful innovation was in non-profits, and if it were whether potential profits were re-invested into new ideas. Examples suggest that private organisations and sponsors fund new ideas but the investment and return to the organisation and funders in financial term or to members' satisfaction have not yet been addressed in the non-profit sector.

Sport members or users are critical considering innovations' aim to satisfy them. In the sport sector, it has been shown that these individuals could be involved in innovation not for profit, but for their own enjoyment. Further research should analyse the relationship between NPSOs and their members with regards to innovation. How do members perceive or value newness and the need for innovation in the non-profit sport sector? For how long would sport members perceive an idea as new? How pervasive is a new idea, that is, how long does it last before users come to other interests? How much are they involved in the development of new ideas and their refinement?

It is assumed throughout this chapter that NPSOs need to innovate. However, NPSOs might not always benefit from innovation. The traditional sport culture of NPSOs does not require innovation, at least not in all of its activities. Additionally, some members of NPSOs could be against new programmes or activities having a negative impact on current ones. Innovation could also push members away. The impact of innovation on users' satisfaction and organisational performance needs further research especially in service-based organisations. However, it must be noted that satisfaction of innovative services can only be evaluated once the service has been purchased or consumed.

Four dimensions have been highlighted in the model that influence, inhibit or facilitate the development, adoption and implementation of innovation within NPSOs. Further study could investigate how these dimensions act and interact within NPSOs and lead to innovation success or high performance. We call for more research on causal complexity theory on innovation where a combination of variables leads NPSOs to innovate. For instance, it could be argued that a positive attitude of volunteers towards newness or change is necessary in NPSOs or that strong competitive position is sufficient to facilitate innovations.

The implication of some potential studies highlighted in this chapter implies that researchers need to address the challenges of measuring innovation in NPSOs, particularly service innovation. Due to intangibility and users' integration it is challenging to identify the innovativeness of an organisation. The number of innovations implemented during a defined period of time has been used by researchers (Gopalakrishnan and Damanpour, 2000; Jaskyte and Dressler, 2005; Winand et al., 2013). However, this does not make any distinction between the significance of the different innovations. The level of change they have induced to NPSOs' processes or users' behaviour could be used as it would distinguish strong (radical) and weak (incremental) service innovations.

This chapter has managerial implications to consider. Due to features such as their policy imperative, the significant growth of the number of for-profit sport providers in recent decades, and the commercialisation and professionalisation of the sport sector, there is a clear need for NPSOs to be innovative (Vos et al., 2011). We encourage managers of NPSOs to develop new ideas and to be open to them coming from sport members and their networks. Being a non-profit organisation should not be an excuse to not respond to or anticipate members' expectations of new services. Through the model highlighted in this chapter, NPSOs' managers could identify the constraints and opportunities for developing innovations. Success of innovation depends on multiple factors at managerial level (e.g. decision-makers' attitudes towards newness and innovation champions), organisational level (e.g. users' involvement and organisation's features such as financial capacity) and environmental level (e.g. competitors, stakeholders, sponsors, apex bodies and agencies). It is also important for NPSOs to communicate with staff, users/members and stakeholders in general about their innovation given it could impact on its success and the development of future new ideas. Success of previous innovations might lead to more innovations and a positive atmosphere favouring newness and change. Furthermore, repetition of different types of innovation, not a single innovation, has been related to higher performance (Damanpour *et al.*, 2009). Managers might implement both sport and non-sport service innovations to create added value for sport members, increase the organisation's effectiveness and quality to members while answering their new needs and expectations.

References

Bayle, E. (2005). *Management des organisations sportives. Contributions à l'analyse du management des organisations hybrides*. Mémoire d'habilitation à diriger des recherches, Université Claude Bernard Lyon 1: Lyon, France.

Bayle, E. and Robinson, L. (2007). 'A framework for understanding the performance of national governing bodies of sport'. *European Sport Management Quarterly, 7*(3), 249–268.

Berrett, T. and Slack, T. (2001). 'A framework for the analysis of strategic approaches employed by non-profit sport organisations in seeking corporate sponsorship'. *Sport Management Review, 4*(1), 21–45.

Brunsson, N., Rasche, A. and Seidl, D. (2012). 'The dynamics of standardization: Three perspectives on standards in organization studies'. *Organization Studies, 33*(5–6), 613–632.

Camisón-Zornoza, C., Lapiedra-Alcamí, R., Segarra-Ciprés, M. and Boronat-Navarro, M. (2004). 'A meta-analysis of innovation and organizational size'. *Organization Studies, 25*, 331–361.

Caza, A. (2000). 'Context receptivity: Innovation in an amateur sport organization'. *Journal of Sport Management, 14*(3), 227–242.

Chesbrough, H. W. (2003). *Open innovation: The new imperative for creating and profiting from technology*. Boston: Harvard Business School Press.

Cohen, W. M. and Levinthal, D. A. (1990). 'Absorptive capacity: A new perspective on learning and innovation'. *Administrative Science Quarterly, 35*(1), 128–152.

Covin, J. G. and Slevin, D. P. (1998). 'Adherence to plans, risk taking, and environment as predictors of firm growth'. *The Journal of High Technology Management Research, 9*(2), 207–237.

Crossan, M. M. and Apaydin, M. (2010). 'A multi-dimensional framework of organizational innovation: A systematic review of the literature'. *Journal of Management Studies, 47*(6), 1154–1191.

Daft, R. L. (1978). 'A dual-core model of organizational innovation'. *Academy of Management Journal, 21*(2), 193–210.

Daft, R. L. (1982). 'Bureaucratic versus non-bureaucratic structure and the process of innovation and change'. In S. B. Bacharach (ed.), *Research in the sociology of organizations.* Greenwich, CT: JAI Press, 129–166.

Damanpour, F. (1991). 'Organizational innovation: A meta-analysis of effects of determinants and moderators'. *Academy of Management Journal, 34*(3), 555–590.

Damanpour, F. (1996). 'Bureaucracy and innovation revisited: Effects of contingency factors, industrial sectors, and innovation characteristics'. *Journal of High Technology Innovation Management, 7,* 149–173.

Damanpour, F. and Aravind, D. (2012). 'Organizational structure and innovation revisited: From organic to ambidextrous structure'. In M. Mumford (ed.), *Handbook of organizational creativity.* London: Elsevier, 479–509.

Damanpour, F. and Evan, W. M. (1984). 'Organizational innovation and performance: The problem of organizational lag'. *Administrative Science Quarterly, 29*(3), 392–409.

Damanpour, F. and Schneider, M. (2006). 'Phases of the adoption of innovation in organizations: Effects of environment, organization, and top managers'. *British Journal of Management, 17*(3), 215–36.

Damanpour, F., Walker, R. M. and Avellaneda, C. N. (2009). 'Combinative effects of innovation types on organizational performance: A longitudinal study of public services'. *Journal of Management Studies, 46*(4), 650–675.

Dean, J. W., Sharfman, M. P. and Ford, C. M. (1991). 'Strategic decision-making: A multiple-context framework'. In J. R. Meindl, R. L. Cardy and S. M. Puffer (eds.), *Advances in information processing in organizations.* Greenwich, CT: JAI Press, 77–110.

Desbordes, M. (2002). 'Empirical analysis of the innovation phenomena in the sports equipment industry'. *Technology Analysis & Strategic Management, 14*(4), 481–498

Dess, G. G., and Picken, J. C. (2000). 'Changing roles: Leadership in the 21st century'. *Organizational Dynamics, 28*(3), 18–34.

DiMaggio, P. J. and Powell, W. W. (1983). 'The iron cage revisited: Institutional isomorphism and collective rationality in organizational fields'. *American Sociological Review, 48*(2), 147–160.

Drejer, I., 2004. 'Identifying innovation in surveys of services: A Schumpeterian perspective'. *Research Policy, 33*(3), 551–562.

Edvardsson, B. and Olsson, J. (1996). 'Key concepts for new service development'. *Service Industries Journal, 16*(2), 140–164.

Franke, N. and Shah, S. (2003). 'How communities support innovative activities: An exploration of assistance and sharing among end-users'. *Research Policy, 32*(1), 157–178.

Gallouj, F. (2002). *Innovation in the service economy.* Cheltenham, UK: Edward Elgar.

Gallouj, F. and Weinstein, O. (1997). 'Innovation in services'. *Research Policy, 26(4–5),* 537–556.

Gilmore, S. and Gilson, C. (2007). 'Finding form: Elite sports and the business of change'. *Journal of Organizational Change Management, 20*(3), 409–428.

Gopalakrishnan, S., and Damanpour, F. (2000). 'The impact of organizational context on innovation adoption in commercial banks'. *IEEE Transactions on Engineering Management, 47*(1), 1–13.

Gratton, C. and Taylor, P. (2000). *Economics of sport and recreation.* London: Spon Press.

Gumulka, G., Barr, C., Lasby D. and Brownlee, B. (2005). *Understanding the capacity of sports & recreation organizations: A synthesis of findings from the National Survey of Nonprofit and Voluntary Organizations and the National Survey of Giving, Volunteering, and Participating.* Toronto, ON: Imagine Canada.

Hage, J. T. (1999). 'Organizational innovation and organizational change'. *Annual Review of Sociology, 25*(1), 597–622.

Han, J. K., Namwoon, K. and Srivastava, R. (1998). 'Market orientation and organizational performance: Is innovation a missing link?' *The Journal of Marketing, 62*(4), 30–45.

Hansen, S. O., and Wakonen, J. (1997). 'Innovation, a winning solution?' *International Journal of Technology Management, 13*(4), 345–358.

Hipp, C. and Grupp, H. (2005). 'Innovation in the service sector: The demand for service-specific innovation measurement concepts and typologies'. *Research Policy, 34*(4), 517–535.

Hoeber, L., Doherty, A., Hoeber, O., Wolfe, R., Misener, K. and Cummings-Vickaryous, B. (2009). *An exploration of the nature of innovations in community sport organizations*. Oral presentation at the North American Society for Sport Management Conference, Columbia, South Carolina.

Hoeber, L. and Hoeber, O. (2012). 'Determinants of an innovation process: A case study of technological innovation in a community sport organization'. *Journal of Sport Management, 26*(3), 213–223.

Hull, C. E. and Lio, B. H. (2006). 'Innovation in non-profit and for-profit organizations: Visionary, strategic, and financial considerations'. *Journal of Change Management, 6*(1), 53–65.

Jaskyte, K. and Dressler, W. W. (2005). 'Organizational culture and innovation in nonprofit human service organizations'. *Administration in Social Work, 29*(2), 23–41.

Kikulis, L. M., Slack, T. and Hinings, B. (1995). 'Sector-specific patterns of organizational design change'. *Journal of Management Studies, 32*(1), 67–100.

Kogut, B. and Zander, U. (1992). 'Knowledge of the firm, combinative capability and the replication of technology'. *Organization Science, 3*(3), 383–397.

Lee, R. P., Ginn, G. O. and Naylor, G. (2009). 'The impact of network and environmental factors on service innovativeness'. *Journal of Services Marketing, 23*(6), 397–406.

Lovelock, C. and Gummesson, E. (2004). 'Whither services marketing?: In search of a new paradigm and fresh perspectives'. *Journal of Service Research, 7*(20), 20–41.

Lüthje, C. (2004). 'Characteristics of innovating users in a consumer goods field: An empirical study of sport-related product consumers'. *Technovation, 24*(9), 683–695.

McDonald, R. E. (2007). 'An investigation of innovation in nonprofit organizations: The role of organizational mission'. *Nonprofit and Voluntary Sector Quarterly, 36*(2), 256–281.

McDonald, R. E. and Srinivasan, N. (2004). 'Technological innovations in hospitals: What kind of competitive advantage does adoption lead to?' *International Journal of Technology Management, 28*(1), 103–117.

Miller, D. (1983). 'The correlates of entrepreneurship in three types of firms'. *Management Science, 29*(7), 770–791.

Mohr, L. B. (1969). 'Determinants of innovation in organizations'. *The American Political Science Review, 63*(1), 111–126.

Newell, S. and Swan, J. (1995). 'The diffusion of innovations in sport organizations: An evaluative framework'. *Journal of Sport Management, 9*(3), 317–333.

Osborne, S. P. (1998). 'Naming the beast: Defining and classifying service innovations in social policy'. *Human Relations, 51*(9), 1133–1155.

Perry, J. L. and Rainey, H. G. (1988). 'The public-private distinction in organization theory: A critique and research strategy'. *Academy of Management Review, 13*(2), 182–201.

Pierce, J. L., and Delbecq, A. L. (1977). 'Organizational structure, individual attitudes, and innovations'. *Academy of Management Review, 2*(1), 26–37.

Preissl, B. (2000). 'Service innovation: What makes it different? Empirical evidence from Germany'. In J. S. Metcalfe, and I. Miles (eds.), *Innovation systems in the service economy. Measurement and case study analysis* 124–148. Boston: Kluwer Academic Publishers, 124–148.

Ratten, V. (2010). 'Developing a theory of sport-based entrepreneurship'. *Journal of Management & Organization, 16*(4), 573–582.

Ratten, V. (2011a). 'Social entrepreneurship and innovation in sports'. *International Journal of Social Entrepreneurship and Innovation, 1*(1), 42–54.

Ratten, V. (2011b). 'Sport-based entrepreneurship: Towards a new theory of entrepreneurship and sport management, *International Entrepreneurship and Management Journal, 7*(1), 57–69.

Robinson, D., Hewitt, T. and Harris, J. (2000). 'Why inter-organisational relationships matter'. In D. Robinson, T. Hewitt and J. Harris (eds.), *Managing development – understanding inter-organizational relationships*. London: Sage, 1–16.

Rogers, E. M. (1995). *Diffusion of innovations* (4th ed.). New York: The Free Press.

Skille, E. A. (2009). 'State sport policy and voluntary sport clubs: The case of the Norwegian sports city program as social policy'. *European Sport Management Quarterly, 9*(1), 63–79.

Slack, T. and Hinings, B. (1994). 'Institutional pressures and isomorphic change: An empirical test'. *Organization Studies, 15*(6), 803–827.

Sundbo J. and Gallouj, F. (2000). 'Innovation as a loosely coupled system in services'. In J. S. Metcalfe, and I. Miles (eds.), *Innovation systems in the service economy. Measurement and case study analysis*. Boston: Kluwer Academic Publishers, 43–68.

Taylor, P. (2004). 'Driving up sport participation: Sport and volunteering'. In Sport England (ed.), *Driving up participation: The challenge for sport*. London: Sport England, 103–110.

Theodoraki, E. I. and Henry, I. P. (1994). 'Organisational structures and contexts in British national governing bodies of sport'. *International Review for the Sociology of Sport, 29*(3), 243–263.

Thibault, L., Slack, T. and Hinings, B. (1993). 'A framework for the analysis of strategy in nonprofit sport organizations'. *Journal of Sport Management, 7*(1), 25–43.

Thiel, A. and Mayer, J. (2009). 'Characteristics of voluntary sports clubs management: A sociological perspective'. *European Sport Management Quarterly, 9*(1), 81–98.

Toivonen, M. and Tuominen, T. (2006). *Emergence of innovations in services: Theoretical discussion and two case studies*. Paper presented at the International ProACT Conference, Tampere, Finland.

Tushman, M. L. and O'Reilly, C. A. (1996). 'Ambidextrous organizations: Managing evolutionary and revolutionary change'. *California Management Review, 38*(4), 8–30.

Van de Ven, A. H. (1986). 'Central problems in the management of innovation'. *Management Science, 32*(5), 590–607.

Vos, S. and Scheerder, J. (2014). 'Fact or fiction? An empirical analysis of cooperation between mass sport providers at the local level'. *European Journal for Sport and Society, 11*(1), 7–34.

Vos, S., Breesch, D. and Scheerder, J. (2012). 'Undeclared work in non-profit sports clubs: A mixed method approach for assessing the size and motives'. *VOLUNTAS: International Journal of Voluntary and Nonprofit Organizations, 23*(4), 846–869.

Vos, S., Breesch, D., Késenne, S., Van Hoecke, J., Vanreusel, B. and Scheerder, J. (2011). 'Governmental subsidies and coercive pressures. Evidence from sport clubs and their resource dependencies'. *European Journal for Sport & Society, 8*(4), 257–280.

Walker, R. M. (2008). 'An empirical evaluation of innovation types and organizational and environmental characteristics: Towards a configuration approach'. *Journal of Public Administration Research and Theory, 18*(4), 591–615.

Walker, R. M., Jeanes, E. and Rowlands, R. O. (2002). 'Measuring innovation: Applying the literature-based innovation output indicator to public services'. *Public Administration, 80*(1), 201–214.

Wicker, P., Vos, S., Scheerder, J. and Breuer, C. (2013). 'The link between resource problems and interorganisational relationships. A quantitative study of Western European sport clubs'. *Managing Leisure, 18*(1), 31–45.

Winand, M., Qualizza, D., Vos, S., Zintz, T. and Scheerder, J. (2013), 'Fédérations sportives innovantes: Attitude, perceptions et champions de l'innovation [Innovative sport federations: Attitude, perceptions and innovation champions]'. *Revue Interdisciplinaire sur le Management et l'Humanisme, 6*, 6–21.

Winand M., Rihoux, B., Qualizza, D. and Zintz, T. (2011). 'Combinations of key determinants of performance in sport governing bodies'. *Sport, Business and Management: An International Journal, 1*(3), 234–251.

Winand, M., Vos, S., Zintz, T. and Scheerder, J. (2013). 'Determinants of service innovation: A typology of sports federations'. *International Journal of Sport Management and Marketing, 13*(1/2), 55–73.

Winand M., Zintz, T. and Scheerder, S. (2012). 'A financial management tool for sport federations'. *Sport, Business and Management: An International Journal, 2*(3), 225–240.

Wolfe, R. A. (1994). 'Organizational innovation: Review, critique and suggested research directions'. *Journal of Management Studies, 31*(3), 405–431.

Wolfe, R., Wright, P. M., and Smart, D. L. (2006). 'Radical HRM innovation and competitive advantage: The Moneyball story'. *Human Resource Management, 45*(1), 111–126.

Zaltman, G., Duncan, R. and Holbek, J. (1973). *Innovations and organizations*. New York: Wiley.

3

INFLUENCE OF SPORTS EVENTS IN LOCAL TOURISM

Héctor Valentín Jiménez Naranjo,
Mari Cruz Sánchez Escobedo and José Luis Coca Pérez

Introduction

In this chapter sporting events will be studied as manifestations of a concept that includes sports tourism.

Through our research we have found that "sport" and "tourism" are two complementary activities. Sporting events generate tourism, and tourists do different activities, including sporting activities, while enjoying their leisure. The relationship between the two terms is revealed for the first time in the work of Anthony (1966), although there have been many scholars who have made statements on the issue of sports tourism, for example: Delpy (1998), Keller (2001), Gibson (2003) and Weed (2006, 2009). The relevance between both terms in our society is collected by Latiesa and Paniza (2006, p. 133), where it is stated that "the interconnection between tourism and sport is evident in advanced societies." In 2001 Barcelona hosted the first World Conference on Sport and Tourism, focusing on the relationship between the two sectors, and demonstrating the importance of sports tourism, as the link between the sectors was analyzed. In some respects this forum is still in force more than a decade later, and its conclusions are key to understanding the current topic of sports tourism. Among other findings, the conference highlighted the chronic lack of statistics and information relating to the sector, establishing this as one of the great challenges for the future of this activity. For this reason in 2008, international recommendations for tourism statistics suggest the Tourism Satellite Accounts (TSA) keep a watch on sports and leisure as one of the emerging tourism industries.

Spain is one of the world's leading countries in tourism. Looking at the data collected in sports statistics yearbooks for the years 2013 and 2014, travel of residents in Spain primarily made for reasons related to sport grew by more than 60 per cent in the period between 2007 and 2012, from 1534.4 (million trips), to 2573.2 (million trips) in that period; which generated an increase in total expense arising from this type of tourism of 39.7 per cent, corresponding to 384.1 million euros spent in 2007, and 536.6 million euros in 2012. This data indicates the importance of this sector in the Spanish economy, showing that sport is one of the market segments growing quickly in the tourism sector. Sporting events, as one of several examples of sports tourism, have been of special interest to researchers in recent years, coming to be regarded as one of its major components, and perhaps the most significant in relation to the number of tourists and economic impact (Getz, 2003; Deery, Jago and Fredline, 2004).

Our interest is in analyzing the socio-economic impact on specific sporting events. For that reason sporting events will be classified by their size or dimensions (Gratton, Dobson and Shibli, 2000; Barajas, Salgado and Sánchez, 2012) for the purpose of this thesis. Major sporting events, or sporting mega-events have been thoroughly analyzed in relation to their economic impact on their host cities (Henderson *et al.*, 2010; Ziakas and Boukas, 2012; Li *et al.*, 2013); however, we must emphasize the importance of sports for smaller events, which represent wealth creation in the environment where they are held, mainly due to the influx of attendees and competitors (Hurtado *et al.*, 2007; Barajas and Sánchez, 2011). Based on the foregoing, we formulate our hypothesis about events that are not identified as large events, but which are characterized as being held on a regular basis in regards to their periodicity, and the difficulty in predicting interested viewers, resulting in minor evidence regarding the economic impact which they could generate (Gratton *et al.*, 2000; Barajas *et al.*, 2012).

In this sense, some authors like Lee (2001) and Hurtado *et al.* (2007) state that the organization of sports competitions is a source of benefits to the places where they are held. Basically these benefits are realized in terms of enhancement of the image of the city and/or the environment, direct income and also in economic terms of revitalization and development of the overall socio-economic fabric of the territory.

The involvement of government in sporting events is not just limited to building activity. Their actions also generate consequences for hosting cities. These consequences or outcomes are difficult to quantify, mainly because of the lack of data for analysis, as we indicated above; so through the socio-economic impact of a sporting event we can identify those factors that are crucial to maximize the benefit to the environment where it takes place. Once these factors are clear, we will be interested in their behavior to obtain information to facilitate decision-making for both government and organizers.

In order to judge the socio-economic impact, we have analyzed the different methodologies used to develop the economic magnitudes of sport (Pedrosa and Salvador, 2003; Hurtado *et al.*, 2007; Barajas and Sánchez, 2011; Barajas *et al.*, 2012) highlighting, through cost-benefit analysis, the importance of consumption of the participants on the impact study. In relation to consumption, we are referring to the costs incurred by participants in the venue of the event and other payments made during the session (OMT, 1998; Sancho, 2001). Therefore, we must focus on finding out why the "cost" varies and which factors we can attribute the changes to. The variable to be explained can be seen as dependent on other variables observed or not, and these are interrelated (García-Ferrando, 2008). This focuses us to perform the analysis of sporting events from the perspective of consumer behavior that involves the study of sociological factors, so that the theoretical foundation is established on the basis of doctrines which contain such variables (Becker, 1964; García-Ferrando, Puig and Lagardera, 2002; Turco, Swart, Bob and Moodley, 2003; Kim, Gursoy and Lee, 2006).

There arises a social problem due to the importance of this sector in the economy, and for the few studies that address the behavior of individuals in the sporting events. This problem affects the development of the events and decisions of the organizers in different ways, mainly by the failure to identify the factors that create impact in the places where they are held. So, as to optimize its consequences, we identify the variables that can influence the socio-economic impact of sports events, and design a model to analyze their relationships which allows us to predict their behavior. In this way we can provide information to facilitate decision-making by the organizers through a model that is functional as a tool for planning and management of sporting events, and which may be relevant for the design of public policies in societies where these events are celebrated.

The analysis from the perspective of consumer behavior focuses on understanding individual decisions, and how behavior is influenced by a wide range of factors. For this study the characteristics of the people who consume goods and services during a sporting event and the motivation for these expenditures are examined to try to understand, explain and predict human actions related to expenditure on events. Specifically we will question the influence of certain individuals' internal variables, and behavior related to the consumption engaged during sporting events. That is, we know the relationship that may exist between their personal characteristics and their consumption during the event. We will analyze variables such as gender, age and education.

Furthermore, there also arise questions related to the influence of other variables held during consumption, such as the assessment or the perception of the event. These are issues of concern to both the organizers and the institutions that support the promotion of such activities, as well as the society of the place where the event is to be held.

As for the individuals who participate in sporting events, we will conduct our research on one of the two distinct groups, who classify according to their participation in the event and can be passive or active in relation to sport. We refer to the attendees (Hall, 1992; Gammon and Robinson, 1997; Standeven and De Knop, 1999), and will analyze the impact that the selected research variables have on their behavior, thus obtaining information to help make decisions in a differentiated manner. Therefore, and taking into account the aforementioned, we will try to answer the questions related to the variables that influence the

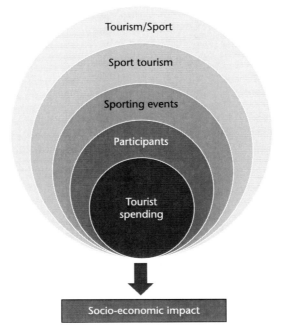

FIGURE 3.1 Research analysis approach

Source: Jiménez-Naranjo, H.V. (2015).

spending of attendees at sporting events, in order to predict behavior to optimize their impact. We summarize the focus of our research in Figure 3.1, which shows that based on the general theoretical concepts, we can identify the people who generate economic impact through tourism spending.

Through our research we will try to identify variables that influence sporting events to generate information that facilitates decision-making.

Finally, and following Cazorla (2006), it can be considered that sport is one of the most important and widespread forms of entertainment, with great ability to mobilize masses of people. The author indicates that many people that attend events are passive participants, who are often the first ones that generate the most revenue for the city that organizes the event. By highlighting the economic importance that tourist spending has for the cities, it will become clear that cities hosting sports events will benefit from the arrival of tourists, or as a result of domestic tourism which causes significant economic benefits such as the redistribution of wealth.

Participants in sporting events

Our research will highlight the importance of analyzing the socio-economic impact of sporting events because it will enable the identification of variables that may influence spending by those involved in such events. In this way, we can meet those characteristics and incorporate tourism resources in the localities where sporting events are held, so as to complement the seasonality of the tourism sector.

When analyzing sports events participants must be emphasized according to Deery *et al.* (2004), because it is important for the future of tourism segmentation that markets are defined exactly. The research profiles of the segments will benefit the sector and provide a higher level of accuracy with policy and planning purposes.

Tourist sporting events can attract different types based on the classifications made by different authors (Gratton *et al.*, 2000; Barajas *et al.*, 2012), who note that all have a similar component (Johnson, 2010). Żauhar and Kurtzman (1997) postulate that religious pilgrimages of the past have been replaced by modern pilgrimages to events like the Olympics, world championship tournaments and smaller events like national and regional championships. They point to events as one of the types of sports tourism where the goal of tourists is to be spectators at the event. Accordingly, Weed (2009) has developed expertise in relation to such marketing in tourism due to the economic impact that sporting events generate.

This section identifies participants in sporting events as, according to Fernández (2014), tourists who come to the city where the sporting event is taking place and spend money. To diversify tourism and the ability of each city to attract visitors, it stands in the interest of public officials to attract and promote this potential source of revenue and profits for the city. In this regard, participants in sporting events can be divided into assistants, competitors, and officers and employees (Deery *et al.*, 2004). As explained below, in our research we will address attendees and competitors.

Moreover, we note that the WTO (World Tourism Organization) identifies visitors as travelers, unrelated to tourism itself. The differentiation between those who stay and those who do not leads to the definition of "tourists" and "visitors" respectively (OMT, 1995). Thus it is observed that sporting events involve people who can be categorized within the concepts that have been defined: tourists and visitors. There are other travellers who cannot be considered in these terms, but they attend the event, so participate in the event, and they are discussed below.

In analyzing the economic impact of sports events, we believe that we must consider all those involved in the events, including travelers (tourists or visitors) and residents in the city that hosts the event. So we identify the participants and users of sports events regardless of their origin, although the source is a variable that must be considered if we want to know more about the participants. Therefore both attendees who reside in the city that hosts an event and those who do not form part of our analysis, along with competitors (see Figure 3.2).

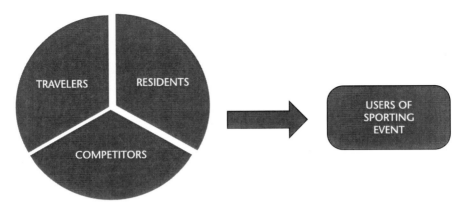

FIGURE 3.2 Users of sporting events
Source: Jiménez-Naranjo, H.V. (2015).

Analysis model

Below we propose our model identifying the expenditure incurred by participants during these events as an indicator of the consumption made by participants, and one of the factors affecting the socio-economic impact of sports events. In our research only the costs incurred in the destination of travel and other payments made during the session (Sancho, 2001) will be included.

By raising our model we must emphasize the importance of analyzing the socio-economic characteristics to understand consumption patterns associated with sports tourism (Turco et al., 2003) and the importance of this for understanding the impacts of these events on the host community (Johnson, 2010). It is therefore necessary to analyze the main explanatory variables in relation to the models of buying behavior in tourism, to understand the conditions that affect the expenditure incurred by those attending a sporting event the most. We can therefore distinguish between internal and external in regards to the individual variables, following groupings made by Swarbrooke and Horner (1999), Decrop (2005) and Sirakaya and Woodside (2005). In our study we will focus on the influence on spending in relation to certain internal variables of the individual, so that following the work of Aragonés (2013), the personal characteristics of the purchaser, the perception of sports events, and the valuation quality of sports events are internal variables of the individual who will submit to analysis to position them in relation to the spending of participants in sporting events.

Figure 3.3 displays the first approximation of our model, which reflected that the output will be the primary dependent variable model.

The relationships between constructs define the hypotheses proposed in this research.

H_1: The Valuation's variable influence on spending.
H_2: The Socio-economic Characteristics' influence on spending.
H_3: The Perception's variable influence on spending.

Influence of sports events in local tourism 37

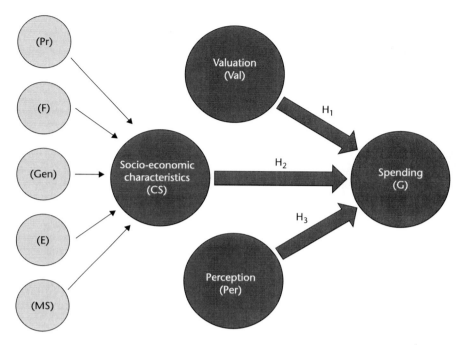

FIGURE 3.3 Proposed model
Source: Jiménez-Naranjo, H.V. (2015).

The proposed model contains a multidimensional construct (Edwards, 2001) called Socio-economic characteristics (CS), which is a formative variable (Barroso, Cepeda and Roldán, 2006), and the dimensions that will make the origin (Pr), training (F), gender (G), age (E) and social motivation (MS).

Methodology applied

To test these hypotheses we used a dual approach: Descriptive Statistics and Multivariate Analysis. In this case the tools used are SPSS (v. 21) and Excel (2010). Meanwhile, the Multivariate Analysis (Uriel & Aldás, 2005) has been based on the use of structural equation models deploying the technique of Partial Least Square-based variance (PLS). In this case the tool used was the SmartPLS v. 2.0.M3 (Ringle, Wende and Will, 2005).

Sources of information and sample used

The sporting event analyzed is "Cáceres International Open", celebrated in Cáceres in May 2013. It is a paddle tournament organized by World Paddle Tour, and is considered the first professional circuit paddle.

TABLE 3.1 Testing hypotheses

Hypotheses	Path Coef.	Error St.	t-test	Sig.
H_1: CS -> G	0.5746	0.032	4.465	★★★
H_2: Val -> G	0.0136	0.0347	0.678	ns
H_3: Per -> G	0.0645	0.036	−1.166	ns

Following the concepts discussed, we conducted research on some of the participants in sporting events, in particular on the attendees. There were a total of 670 random surveys (670 attendees).

Results

The existence of a multidimensional construct or construct second-order approach requires two steps (two-stage approach) for treatment (Edwards, 2001). We will then analyze the measuring instrument for variables.

The values of variance (R2) for spending (G) is 0.34, moderate following the criteria of Chin (1998).

Finally, the analysis of the structural model is done through boostrapping (Hair et al., 2014). The data for these variables is reflected in Table 3.1.

Discussion

For events held it can be seen that, in the case of those attending, the influence of socio-economic characteristics of the participants on the expenditure made at sporting events is accepted. It has also been possible to establish a hierarchy of second-order variables – dimensions – based on their weights. So that the dimension has more weight in the variable "CS" is the origin "Pr" followed by motivation "MS". It indicates that higher spending is generated in those who come from outside and go to the event, motivated primarily by their attendance in the city. Behind these indicators appears the "E", age, and finally the formation, "F".

Therefore it is necessary to rely on the descriptive analysis to identify those age groups and the training that contributes most to spending. However, in the proposed model, gender, "Gen", is not a valid indicator of the socio-economic characteristics in relation to expenditure, so it is not possible to assess influence on spending in regards to this variable.

Conclusion

The model is valid to analyze the influence regarding expenditure of some specific variables of sports events participants: socio-economic characteristics, perception and valuation. We can consider that the socio-economic characteristics of the participants at the event explain the behavior of spending.

The multidimensional variable socio-economic characteristics show that neither gender nor origin provide a significant weight so are excluded from the model. A model that serves as the basis for the analysis of the behavior of sports tourists arises.

Managers of sports events must plan events that attract participants from out of town, and the duration of these events should encourage them to stay. This recommendation is demonstrated through the influence of socio-economic characteristics in spending. We believe that research could be replicated in other sporting events to observe variations in the analyzed scenarios.

References

Anthony, D. (1966). *Sport and tourism.* Central Council for Physical Recreation. London, UK.

Aragonés, C. (2013). *La transferencia entre un gran evento deportivo y la marca patrocinadora: La visión del visitante deportivo.* Tesis doctoral. Departamento de Comercialización e Investigación de Mercados, Universitat de Valencia, Valencia. España.

Barajas, A. & Sánchez, P. (2011). 'Aplicación del análisis coste-beneficio (ACB) al Campeonato de España de Natación Master 2011'. *Comunicación presentada al I Gijón Workshop de Economía del Deporte: El Impacto Económico en el Deporte,* Gijón, Universidad de Oviedo, Oviedo, España.

Barajas, A., Salgado, J. & Sánchez, P. (2012). 'Problemática de los estudios de impacto económico de eventos deportivos'. *Estudios de Economía Aplicada,* 30(2), 441–462.

Barroso, C., Cepeda, G. & Roldán, J. L. (2006). 'Constructos latentes y agregados en la Economía de la Empresa'. *Comunicación presentada en AEDEM,* Palma de Mallorca, España.

Becker, G. S. (1964). *Human capital: a theoretical analysis with special reference to education.* National Bureau for Economic Research, Columbia University Press, New York and London.

Cazorla, L. M. (2006). 'Deporte: ocio y negocio'. *Temas para el debate,* 141, 65–67.

Chin, W. W. (1998). 'The partial least squares approach to structural equation modeling'. In Marcoulides, G.A. (Ed.), *Modern Methods for Business Research.* Erlbaum, Mahwah.

Decrop, A. (2005). 'Group processes in vacation decision making'. *Journal of Travel and Tourism Marketing,* 18(3), 23–36.

Deery, M., Jago, L. & Fredline, L. (2004). 'Sport tourism or event tourism: are they one and the same?'. *Journal of Sport Tourism,* 9(3), 235–245.

Delpy, L. (1998). 'An overview of sport tourism: building towards a dimensional framework'. *Journal of Vacation Marketing,* 4(1), 23–38.

Edwards, J. R. (2001). 'Multidimensional constructs in organizational behavior research: An integrative analytical framework'. *Organizational Research Methods,* 4(2), 144–192.

Fernández, M. T. (2014). 'El impacto turístico de los eventos deportivos: un estudio de caso'. *Cuadernos de turismo,* 33, 59–76.

Gammon, S. & Robinson, T. (1997). 'Sport and tourism: a conceptual framework'. *Journal of Sport Tourism,* 4(3), 11–18.

García-Ferrando, M. (2008). *Socioestadística. Introducción a la estadística en sociología.* Alianza Editorial, Madrid, España.

García-Ferrando, M., Puig, N. & Lagardera, F. (2002). *Sociología del Deporte.* Alianza Editorial, Madrid, España.

Getz, D. (2003). 'Sport Event Tourism: Planning, Development, and Marketing'. In Hudson, S. (Ed.), *Sport and Adventure Tourism*, Haworth Hospitality Press, New York, USA, 49–85.

Gibson, H. J. (2003). 'Sport tourism: an introduction to the special issue'. *Journal of Sport Management*, 17(3), 205–213.

Gratton, C., Dobson, N. & Shibli, S. (2000). 'The economic importance of major sports events: a case-study of six events'. *Managing Leisure*, 5(1), 17–28.

Hair, J. F., Sarstedt, M., Hopkins, L. & Kuppelwieser, V. G. (2014). 'Partial least squares structural equation modeling (PLS-SEM): an emerging tool in business research'. *European Business Review*, 26(2), 106–121.

Hall, C. M. (1992). 'Adventure, sport and health'. In Hall, C. M. & Weiler, B. (Eds.), *Special Interest Tourism*. Pluto Press, London, UK.

Henderson, J. C., Foò, K., Lim, H. & Yip, S. (2010). 'Sports events and tourism: the Singapure Formula One Grand Prix'. *International Journal of Event and Festival Management*, 1(3), 60–73.

Hurtado, J. M., Ordaz, J. A. & Rueda, J. M. (2007). 'Evaluación del impacto económico y social de la celebración de grandes eventos deportivos a nivel local: el caso del Campeonato de Tenis femenino de la ITF en Sevilla en 2006'. *Revista de métodos cuantitativos para la economía y la empresa*, 3, 20–39.

Jiménez-Naranjo, H. V., Coca-Pérez, J. L., Gutiérrez-Fernández, M. & Sánchez-Escobedo, M. C. (2015). 'Cost-benefit analysis of sport events: the case of world paddle tour'. *Aceptado en Mayo de 2015 en la Revista Investigaciones Europeas de Dirección y Economía de la Empresa*. DOI:10.1016/j.iedee.2015.04.001.

Jiménez-Naranjo, H. V. (2015). *Análisis del impacto socioeconómico de los eventos deportivos*. Tesis Doctoral, Departamento Economía Financiera y Contabilidad, Universidad de Extremadura.

Johnson, D. (2010). *A comparative study of the management and socioeconomic impacts of sport tourism events in Durban and Cape Town*. Doctoral Thesis. Cape Peninsula University of Technology, Cape Town, South Africa.

Keller, P. (2001). *Sports & Tourism: Introductory report*. World Tourism Organization, Madrid, España.

Kim, H., Gursoy, D. & Lee, S. (2006). 'The impact of the 2002 World Cup on South Korea: comparisons of pre- and post-games'. *Tourism Management*, 27(1), 86–96.

Latiesa, M. & Paniza, J. L. (2006). 'Turistas deportivos. Una perspectiva de análisis'. *Revista Internacional de Sociología*, 64(44), 133–149.

Lee, S. (2001). 'A review of economic impact study on sport events'. *The Sport Journal*, 4(2), 32–39.

Li, S., Blake, A. & Thomas, R. (2013). 'Modelling the economic impact of sports events: the case of the Beijing Olympics'. *Economic Modelling*, 30, 235–244.

OMT (1995). *Conceptos, definiciones y clasificaciones estadísticas de turismo: Manual técnico*. Organización Mundial del Turismo. Madrid, España.

OMT (1998). *Recomendaciones sobre estadísticas en turismo*. Organización Mundial del Turismo. Madrid, España.

Pedrosa, R., & Salvador, J. A. (2003). 'El impacto del deporte en la economía: Problemas de medición'. *Revista Asturiana de Economía*, 26, 61–84.

Ringle, C. M., Wende, S. & Will, A. (2005). *SmartPLS 2.0 (beta)*, SmartPLS, Hamburg, Germany.

Sancho, A. (2001). *Apuntes de metodología de la investigación en turismo*. Organización Mundial del Turismo, Madrid, España.

Sirakaya, E. & Woodside, A. (2005). 'Building and testing theories of decision making by travellers'. *Tourism Management*, 26(6), 815–832.

Standeven, J. & De Knop, P. (1999). *Sport tourism*. Human Kinetics Publishers, Champaign, IL, USA.

Swarbrooke, J. & Horner, S. (1999). *Consumer behaviour in tourism*. Butterworth-Heinemann. Oxford, UK.

Turco, D. M., Swart, K., Bob, U. & Moodley, V. (2003). 'Socio-economic impacts of sport tourism in the Durban UniCity, South Africa.' *The Journal of Sport Tourism*, 8(4), 223–239.

Uriel, E. & Aldás, J. (2005). *Análisis multivariante aplicado*. Thomson Editores Spain, Paraninfo SA, Madrid, España.

Weed, M. E. (2006). 'Sports tourism research 2000–2004: a systematic review of knowledge and a meta-evaluation of method'. *Journal of Sports & Tourism*, 11(1), 5–30.

Weed, M. E. (2009). 'Progress in sports tourism research? A meta-review and exploration of futures'. *Tourism Management*, 30(5), 615–628.

Zauhar, J. & Kurtzman, J. (1997). 'Sport tourism. A window of opportunity'. *Journal of Sports Tourism*, 3, 11–16.

Ziakas, V. & Boukas, N. (2012). 'A neglected legacy'. *International Journal of Event and Festival Management*, 3(3), 292–316.

4

INNOVATION FOR SOCIAL INCLUSION IN SPORT

Anne Tjønndal

Introduction

Social exclusion and social inequality are as evident in sport as in any other area of society. The physical and psychological health benefits of sport participation and physical activity are well documented (e.g. Pyle *et al.*, 2003; Malina, *et al.* 2004; Malina, 2006; Seigel *et al.*, 2009). Hence, from a social science and public health perspective, it would be highly beneficial to minimize social exclusion and inequality in sport and physical activity. In other words, to increase social inclusion and equality of access in sport. Therefore, it is a serious problem that there is an apparent social divide when it comes to physical activity and sport participation globally. In the case of Norway, studies have shown that Norwegians with advanced degrees[1] are more physically active and have higher participation rates in sport, compared to Norwegians with high school education (Breivik and Rafoss, 2012; Ommundsen and Aadland, 2009). Similarly, studies have also demonstrated that Norwegians with a high level of income are more active and physically fit than Norwegians earning minimum wages (Anderssen *et al.*, 2009; Ulseth, 2008). Some studies have also investigated the correlation between personal income and educational level, as well as parents' educational level and household economy. Again, these studies show a clear correlation between social class and participation in sport and physical activity (Breivik and Rafoss, 2012; Rafoss and Breivik, 2009). Similar tendencies have also been documented in studies of health and social exclusion in other countries, such as England (Collins, 2014).

It has been estimated that approximately 32 per cent of adults in Norway fulfill the Norwegian government's recommendation for a minimum of 30 minutes of daily physical activity (Helsedirektoratet, 2015). In other words, it is likely that a large part of the Norwegian population can be described as inactive. Living an inactive lifestyle is associated with a variety of health issues and lifestyle diseases such as certain types of cancer and diabetes. A common reason for inactivity is social exclusion from participation in sport and physical activity (Spaaij, Magee & Jeanes, 2014). How, then, can social exclusion in sport and physical activity be eliminated, or greatly reduced? My aim in writing this chapter is to discuss how and in what ways innovation contributes to social inclusion in sport. I will do this by firstly discussing the innovation term and innovation research, before I go into potential drivers of and barriers to innovation for social inclusion in sport. Subsequently, I will link innovation literature to studies of sport and sport science. Additionally, I will discuss social exclusion and inclusion in sport, as well as some of the central factors related to exclusion. Following this, I will discuss how innovation promotes social inclusion, focusing on the risks and possibilities associated with innovation for social inclusion in sport. Finally, I end this chapter with a short empirical example of innovation and social inclusion from my research on innovation and gender-based inclusion in skateboarding. In this paper, I define sport innovation as any new idea, change, process or innovation taking place in a sports context.

Innovation

Innovation as a theoretical concept and as a field of study might be relatively new, but as a phenomenon is not new at all (Fagerberg, 2004). In their article, Baregheh Rowley and Sambrook (2009) proposed that there are more than 60 academic definitions of innovation, spanning different scholarly fields such as business and management, organizational studies, technology, marketing, knowledge management and economics. In other words, innovation is a term used in a wide variety of empirical settings. Because of its popularity and many uses in different contexts, it can be problematic to define what innovation actually is. Innovation is even utilized as its own type of political strategy by municipalities and governments, and as a term, it is almost always associated with improvement and efficiency.

Innovation scholars have described innovation in a number of different ways. Economist and innovation pioneer Schumpeter (1942, 1983) classified innovations according to their type, distinguishing between five types of innovation: new products, new methods of production, new sources of supply, the exploitation of new markets, and new ways to organize business. Sørensen and Torfing (2011) argue that innovation, independent of type, always involves four phases: 1) the generation of ideas, 2) the selection of ideas, 3) the implementation of new ideas and 4) the dissemination of new practices.

Innovation researcher Fagerberg (2004) points out an important distinction between innovation and invention. An invention can be characterized as the first occurrence of a new idea, but innovation is the first attempt to carry it out into practice, to bring it to life in the real world (Fagerberg, 2004; Behn, 2008). Innovation often involves lengthy and unlinear processes. Kline & Rosenberg (1986, p.283) argued that it is a serious mistake to treat innovation as if it was a well-defined, homogenous thing that could be easily identified.

Definitions of innovation range from short catchy phrases, to detailed and context-dependent descriptions. Some simple definitions of innovation include: "new stuff that is made useful" (McKeown, 2008), "new ideas that work" (Mulgan and Albury, 2003) and "novelty in action" (Altschuler and Zegans, 1997). Although these definitions are fairly short, and to some extent vague, they grasp the essence of the innovation term; *new ideas put into practice*. An important difference between how innovation is viewed by innovation researchers is related to whether or not innovation should be seen as a normative term. In other words, does innovation only imply new ideas, change and practices that are good? Or can innovations be equally destructive? Is innovation simply discontinuity, incorporating any form of new practice? Or is it change aimed at some sort of improvement?

Building on Willumsen and Ødegård's (2015) argument that how one views innovation is always context-specific, when studying practices of social exclusion and inclusion in an innovation perspective – innovation must always be normative. That is, when I investigate how sports organizations implement new ideas and change to enhance social inclusion, these innovations must always be with the intention of changing daily practices for the better in terms of increasing social inclusion in sport. As Sørensen & Torfing (2011, p. 849) describe the innovation term: "An intentional and proactive process that involves the generation and practical adoption and spread of new and creative ideas, which aim to produce a qualitative change in a specific context." However, there are (almost) always some practical implications of innovations. They do not always turn out positive, benefitting "everyone" or "the greater good". Many historical innovations have had great impact on the social world, and there are many examples of innovations that have had disastrous implications for humanity, such as the development of the atom bomb, the guillotine, or the gas chambers used by Nazis during the war. One could argue that these innovations benefitted some, for instance, the guillotine undoubtedly came as an improvement to executioners, but it would be a far stretch to call innovations of these kinds a positive contribution to the world, or a "social innovation".

There are many similarities between the term "social innovation" and my perspective of innovation in this chapter. Social innovation is about novelty and change where the human dimension is central, and where collaboration between different individuals and organizations is crucial (Willumsen, Sirnes and Ødegård, 2015). Murray *et al.* (2010) provide a definition of social innovation, which I find particularly useful:

> Social innovation is about new ideas that work to address pressing unmet needs. We simply describe it as innovations that are both social in their ends and in their means. Social innovations are new ideas (products, services and models) that simultaneously meet social needs (more effectively than alternatives) and create new social relationships or collaborations.
>
> *(p.3)*

When I study how and in what ways innovation can promote social inclusion in sport, the "unmet need" is a solution to practices of social exclusion in sports organizations. In other words, these kinds of innovations are both social in their ends (increasing inclusion, combatting inequalities) and their means (development of new ideas, activities, ways of organizing sport). These kinds of innovation processes also hold the potential to create new social relationships and collaborations between different individuals and organizations within the sport sector.

Innovation drivers and barriers

Who (and what) constitutes the sources, or drivers of the innovation process impacts the result of the innovation. Researchers have identified different kinds of innovation drivers. Some of the more commonly used innovation drivers are described as top-down innovations, bottom-up innovations, democratic innovation, collaboration, employee-driven innovation and management-driven innovation (Høiland and Willumsen, 2015; Fagerberg, 2004; Gjelsvik, 2007; Hartley, 2005, 2013; Sørensen and Torfing, 2010). "Top-down" innovation is initiated by the organization's management or leader (Halvorsen *et al.*, 2005; Fuglsang, 2010; Høiland & Willumsen, 2015). In sports, "top-down" innovations could come from the leader (or board) of a sports club, from a national sport federation, or even from an international governing body of sport, such as international sport federations, or the International Olympic Committee. "Bottom-up" innovation on the other hand, sometimes referred to as "bricolage" (Fuglsang, 2010), includes processes where innovations take place on a day-to-day basis. Employees or other professionals with the knowledge to create better solutions and new ideas (Høiland and Willumsen, 2015) often initiate these types of innovations. "Bottom-up" innovations can occur spontaneously, without any apparent leadership strategy to initiate them. Within the context of sport, these could be innovations initiated by coaches or even athletes, seeking to improve a particular aspect of sport. A third common innovation driver is often referred to as "democratic innovation" (von Hippel, 2005; Høyrup, 2010). Here, the users (of the product or service) constitute the driving force of the innovation process. Examples of democratic innovations in sport could be consumers of sporting goods actively participating in the process of developing new products such as athletic wear and shoes.

Just as there can be many different drivers for any innovation process, there can be a number of innovation barriers. Financial (or economic) barriers are perhaps the types of innovation barriers given the most empirical attention by innovation researchers regardless of empirical context (Arundel, 1997; Tourigny and Le, 2004; Savignac, 2006, 2008; Tiwari *et al.*, 2007; Mancusi and Vezzulli, 2010). Lack of economic resources, or financial obstacles otherwise, can have a significant impact on an organization's ability to innovate (D'Este *et al.*, 2012). Sport organizations require material and economic resources to initiate and maintain activities. In order to develop a new project, a new activity or new

46 Anne Tjønndal

competition, sport organizations need sufficient economic resources. If a sport organization barely has enough material resources to maintain its core activities, it will be difficult to innovate and implement new ideas into practice. In other words, it is likely that (lack of) economic resources makes up some of the innovation barriers that sport organizations face when seeking to develop new ideas and practices.

Second, many firms, organizations and even individual entrepreneurs experience knowledge barriers during their innovation process. By knowledge barriers, I mean that many innovators at some point realize that they lack the necessary knowledge to develop or implement their new idea, product or service. For example, a football player seeking to develop new and improved shoes to maximize their performance on the field probably does not have the necessary technological knowledge to design and implement the idea into creating actual new football shoes. A sport organization could have ideas about how to promote inclusion and equality of access within their activities, but lack the necessary knowledge needed to implement their ideas as an innovation put into practice in the real world.

The last types of innovation barrier I consider particularly relevant for innovation and social inclusion in sport are structural and regulation barriers (Iammarino *et al.*, 2009). These types of barriers are often discussed by management scholars in relation to barriers firms face with markets and regulations from governments (Baldwin and Lin, 2002; Baldwin and Hanel, 2003; Dougherty, 1992; Ferriani *et al.*, 2008). However, all sport organizations face structural constraints and regulations they must conform to if they want to be a part of a larger institutionalized system of their particular sport. Sport organizations are obliged to follow the rules and regulations of national governments, national sport federations and international governing bodies of sport. As a result, small sport organizations can often find themselves stuck in a conflict between innovation and membership in larger, both national and global, sport organizations. Table 4.1 provides an overview of potential barriers and drivers for innovation in sport.

Sport innovation

Even though the term "innovation" is relatively new in sport and studies of sport, innovation as a phenomenon is not new to sport. Sport has always changed and

TABLE 4.1 Drivers and barriers for innovation in sport

	Innovation Drivers	*Innovation Barriers*
1	"Top-down" innovation	Financial barriers
2	"Bottom-up" innovation	Knowledge barriers
3	"Democratic" innovation	Structural barriers
4	Collaboration	

adapted alongside society (Goksøyr, 2008). In other words, without innovation, sport as we know it today would look very different. Imagine high jumping without the development of the 'Fosbury flop' technique. All elite high jumpers now use this technique, but previously it was the straddle[2] which dominated as the 'best technique' in this sport. Or think of how boxing would be practised today without the introduction of the Queensberry rules in 1867. The Queensberry rules determined a set amount of rounds, rules of conduct within the ring, weight divisions and guidelines for boxing equipment – completely changing boxing competitions. On the other hand, imagine ice hockey, baseball and American football without the use of video refereeing, or instant replay. The introduction of these particular new forms of technology has revolutionized refereeing of these sports. These are just two small examples of how innovation has changed how sport is practised and organized.

In spite of its undeniable importance, sport innovation has not received the scholarly attention it deserves. To some extent, this is now changing. Some researchers have investigated certain aspects of innovation in sport and discussed the importance of innovation for sport (e.g. Mullin *et al.*, 2007; Schwarz and Hunter, 2008; Ratten, 2011). Ringuet-Riot *et al.* (2013) argue that technology-based innovation plays a vital role in sport today, while Trabal (2008) studied resistance to technological innovation in elite sport. Pill *et al.* (2012) investigated the significance of innovation for physical education (P.E.)[3] teacher education, and claimed that innovation is essential to the improvement of P.E. teacher education. Winand *et al.* (2013) examined service innovation in the sports sector and found that innovation is critical for sports organizations because innovation provides a way to grow within a competitive environment. In their study, Khromin *et al.* (2014) demonstrate how a strategic approach to system innovation can be efficient for increasing physical activity and sports participation in local municipalities. Fuller *et al.* (2007) studied innovation in online basketball communities and concluded that members of online sports communities are a great source of sport-based innovation.

Speed and Roberts (2011) as well as Johnson (2010) have examined innovation in the context of sports medicine. In another study, Ringuet-Riot *et al.* (2014) found that innovation is crucial to the sports sector as it provides solutions to pre-defined problems when developing sport and maximizing the experiences and performances of individuals and organizations. Building on Ringuet-Riot *et al.* (2014), social exclusion can be understood as a pre-defined problem in sport, to which innovation could be a potential solution.

These studies illustrate how innovation occurs in a number of ways in sport, both at an organizational and at an individual level. Boutroy *et al.* (2015) suggest that sport provides a unique setting for studying and observing intense innovative situations, and that further research should explore sport from an innovation perspective. As all of the studies mentioned here demonstrate, innovation, or sport innovation, comes in many different forms and is applied in a wide spectrum of settings. In this chapter I define sport innovation as any new idea, change,

48 Anne Tjønndal

process or innovation taking place in a sports context. Viewing sport innovation in such a broad perspective means taking a multifaceted and interdisciplinary approach to studies of how innovation takes place (and is made useful) in sport.

Social exclusion and inclusion in sport

There are many misconceptions about the term "social exclusion", a common one being that social exclusion is synonymous with poverty. Poverty is a much more static concept, and social exclusion does not only mean insufficient income (Rigaux, 1994; Collins, 2004, 2014; Price and Parker, 2003).

A definition derived from Madanipour *et al.* is:

> Social exclusion is defined as a multi-dimensional process, in which various forms of exclusion are combined: participation in decision making and political processes, access to employment and material resources, and integration into common cultural processes.
>
> *(2002, p. 22)*

Building on these definitions social exclusion in sport is here defined as exclusion from sport participation based on one or several personal (or environmental) factors or linked problems. These factors include, but are not limited to, socio-economic status, gender, ethnicity, age and disability (Collins, 2014). In contrast to social exclusion in sport, social inclusion in sport is about equal access to participation, regardless of these factors and linked problems. Sport England provides a clear definition of social inclusion in sport:

> social inclusion and "sports equity" is about fairness in sport, equality of access, recognizing inequalities and taking steps to address them. It is about changing the structure of sport to ensure that it becomes equally accessible to all members of society, whatever their age, gender, race, ethnicity, sexuality, or socio-economic status.
>
> *(Sport England, 2001)*

Social exclusion is one of many tough problems in modern sport, and combatting exclusion has proven to be a seemingly intractable challenge for sport organizations. How can sport organizations minimize social exclusion? What possible solutions to this resilient problem are there? Howaldt *et al.* (2015) as well as Ringuet-Riot *et al.* (2014) argue that innovation could provide sustainable solutions to pre-defined problems in sport, such as social exclusion. If sport as we know it today is plagued by social exclusion, then clearly new ideas, change and innovation is needed in order to ensure that sport participation becomes inclusive for all, regardless of social class, gender, religion, sexual orientation and ethnicity. Social exclusion takes many shapes and can appear in diverse ways in different sports contexts (Spaaij, Magee and Jeanes, 2014). Innovations, at least innovations involving social change, are equally dependent of context (Evers and Ewert, 2015).

Innovation for social inclusion in sport: Possibilities and risks

Modern sport as it is organized and practised today is plagued by social exclusion. This means that in many contexts, the way sport is organized now promotes exclusion from participation in one way or another. It could be exclusion based on age, skill, gender, ethnicity, race, social class, rurality, or a number of other factors. Often, several factors like the ones mentioned here interact and cause social exclusion from participation in sport (Collins, 2014). The groups that dominate sport participation also generally control the organization and management of sport (Numerato and Baglioni, 2011). In general, middle-class men with majority-ethnic backgrounds control organized sport in most countries (Spaaji *et al.*, 2014).

There is no easy answer to how one should go about combatting social exclusion in sport participation and physical activity. However, one thing is certain; the way we organize sport today does not promote social inclusion adequately. In the introduction of this chapter, I used some activity numbers illustrating the situation of social exclusion in Norwegian sport. But Norway is not the only country where sport is troubled by social exclusion and social inequality. Globally, large groups of the population do not have the opportunity to participate in sport and physical activity. Therefore, in order to promote social inclusion in sport, something must change in regards to the way we organize and practise modern sport today. If the organization of sport continues the same way it does today, year after year, generation after generation, social exclusion will never diminish or be eliminated. To put it simply, change is needed to promote social inclusion in sport globally. This is how innovation promotes social inclusion in sport – by introducing new ideas, new ways of organizing sport and even entirely new sports activities to the world.

Innovation does undoubtedly hold the potential to promote social inclusion in sport. Innovation provides opportunities to think "outside of the box", try out new ideas, create projects and promote change for a more inclusive sports movement globally. When linked to social inclusion, sports innovations must always have the aim of changing sport organizations for the better at some point or in some way. However, innovation does not magically change sport for the better. Sports innovations aimed at promoting social inclusion do, just like any other innovation process, involve risks. As previously discussed, innovations are not always successful (Sørensen & Torfing, 2011). Sometimes they fail, and in the worst-case scenario, they could promote change for the worse. In this case, causing practices which promote exclusion rather than inclusion. Therefore, it is essential that innovation drivers in sport are aware of the potential risks of their own innovation process. If things do not work out the way we want them

50 Anne Tjønndal

to, what could happen? Who would suffer most if the innovation should fail? These are important questions to consider before embarking on any innovation journey. It is crucial that sport organizations are willing to take risks, but are also able to assess the risks that come with implementing innovations aimed at promoting social inclusion. Here, the worst-case scenario would be creating and implementing an innovation that ends up promoting social exclusion rather than inclusion.

Just as innovation researchers have identified different innovation drivers in large organizations and firms, if one looks closely at sport, one will be able to identify both "top-down", "bottom-up" and democratic innovations within sports organizations locally, nationally and globally. I would like to end this chapter with an empirical example of innovation for social inclusion in sport. This example deals with gender-based exclusion in skateboarding. Skateboarding, as well as most lifestyle sports, is considered to be a highly masculine sport environment (Wheaton, 2000, 2004; Sisjord, 2005; Turner, 2013). The archetypical skateboarder, or lifestyle-sport enthusiast, can be described as a young, white, middle-class male (Booth, 2004; Anderson, 1999). In other words, many potential societal groups could be experiencing social exclusion from skateboarding as well as other lifestyle sports. This chapter follows a local skateboarding club struggling to attract girls and women as active members, and the club's innovation process, work and strategies for including women in their sporting activities.

Innovation for inclusion of girls and women in skateboarding

My empirical example of how innovation can promote social inclusion in sport comes from a local skateboarding club in Norway. Before getting into how and what type of innovation promoted inclusion in this particular sport organization, I feel it is necessary to clarify the unique position skateboarding has in Norway. Norwegian sports are all organized under the Norwegian Olympic and Paralympic Committee and Confederation of Sports (NIF). Skateboarding, however, is not part of NIF[4] and is therefore not clearly classified as a sport in Norway. Norway is also one of the few countries where skateboarding has been illegal by law (from 1978 to 1989). This means that skateboarding is organized somewhat differently compared to other sports in Norway. Perhaps this also provides skateboarding clubs with a unique ability to be innovative? When skateboarding and Norwegian skateboarding clubs stand outside of the NIF this means that they are not obligated to follow the same organizational, ideological and political guidelines as other sports and sports organizations in Norway. This could result in greater possibilities for innovation because their structural and regulational barriers are different (and perhaps smaller) than those of sports organizations within NIF.

Norwegian skateboarding clubs have founded their own organization outside of NIF called the Norwegian Skateboarding Organization, or NORB.[5] This organizational model has both practical and ideological implications for Norwegian skateboarding. While all sport clubs and organizations associated with NIF are obligated to abide by their rules, regulations, political goals and ideology, skateboarding clubs do not need to adhere to these regulations and structural barriers. One of the top priorities of the NIF is promoting inclusion, or "sport participation for all" (Norges Idrettsforbund, 2014). Hence, all sports organizations within the NIF should work actively towards promoting inclusion of marginalized groups in sport. Taking this into consideration one would think that sport organizations within NIF would all take action to increase social inclusion, while skateboarding clubs organized by NORB have the same pressure to promote inclusion. However, in spite of these regulations and political goals, not all sports organizations within NIF are taking measures to combat social exclusion in sport. Some of the reason why not all sport organizations within NIF are equally interested in social inclusion could be that there are few actual repercussions or consequences for sport organizations that do not follow the overall ideology and political aims of the confederation.

While doing research for my PhD thesis, I came across a local skateboarding club in the process of implementing their own innovation. Their overall aim for the innovation process was to increase gender-based inclusion in the club. Meaning that they wanted to attract more girls and women to participate in skateboarding. As a sport scientist, I found this innovation process particularly interesting, as Norwegian skateboarding clubs are not obligated to promote inclusion in the same way as other sports organizations connected to NIF are. The club, located in a medium-sized Norwegian city, was founded in 2005 and has no full-time employees. The skateboarding club is managed mainly through the volunteer work of a few enthusiastic skateboarders. In 2008, the club received municipal funding to build an indoor skating park to utilize for their activities. The club's daily activities are organized into four different types: 1) "Girl Skate" for girls and women only, 2) "Kidskate" for children (both boys and girls), 3) "adult sessions" for members over 18 years (women/men) and 4) "open sessions" for everyone. There are coaches available to provide instruction for members during all of the different types of sessions except the "open session".

During my fieldwork within the skateboarding club, I interviewed the leaders, trainers and several members. I followed the efforts of the trainers as the club worked to recruit and include more girls and women. During my fieldwork, I realized that this particular sport innovation process appeared to have several drivers, incorporating elements of both "bottom-up" innovation, "democratic" innovation, and to some extent also "top-down" innovation (Fuglsang, 2010; Hartley, 2005, 2013; von Hippel, 2005). During my interviews and conversations trainers and members of the club explained how they had struggled with high dropout rates among girls and women for many years. While many girls came to skate with them, not many stayed active within the club for longer periods.

White, young middle-class men constitute the dominant group in skateboarding (Turner, 2013), as is the case with most other lifestyle sports, such as surfing and wind surfing (Wheaton, 2000). This is also the case for Norwegian skateboard clubs in general, and it was the case for the skateboarding club I followed in my study. Previously, the club had organized skateboarding sessions for all club members, regardless of skill, age and gender. Here, women and girls had stood out as a clear minority among the participants in the club's activities. The training environment was mixed-sex, but dominated by men and male ways of interacting, which might have been part of the reason why girls and women dropped out more frequently than boys and men. Reflecting on how the organization of their activities might contribute to increased dropout among women and young girls, some of the leaders and older members of the club decided to try to change the way the club organized its activities in order to provide skating activities that might appeal more to women and girls.

Together with club members, the trainers and leaders of the club came up with three new ideas aimed specifically at recruiting and keeping girls and women as active members. Firstly, the club decided that being a "leading club for women's skateboarding" in Norway should be one of their top priorities, and they incorporated this goal into the club's bylaws. Secondly, they created and implemented a concept called "Girl Skate" in which they set specific times in their skating hall where only girls and women were allowed to practise together. These sessions were introduced as a supplement for the regular skating sessions (open for all members of the club), meaning that girls could now choose between skating in all-girl sessions or in sessions with both girls and boys. Thirdly, the club introduced a special training camp called "Girl Skate Camp": several days with multiple sessions with trained skateboarders as coaches, where girls from all over the country could come and skate with other girls.

Innovation drivers and barriers within the skateboarding club

Following my definition of sport innovation, as well as the innovation literature this chapter is based on, the new ways of organizing and the new activities in the skateboarding club are, in many ways, a good example of a successful innovation for social inclusion in sport. Through the innovation process of introducing new organizational goals and new ways of organizing their activities, the skateboarding club increased its number of female members and decreased its dropout rates. Here, it appears to be the members of the club itself that stand out as the drivers of the innovation process, a characteristic associated with "democratic" innovation (von Hippel, 2005) and "bottom-up" innovation (Høiland & Willumsen, 2015). This is particularly visible in the daily practices of the new (innovative) activities "Girl Skate" and "Girl Skate Camp", which both members and coaches organized and carried out.

During my fieldwork in the club I identified some innovation drivers often associated with "top-down" innovation. In regards to "top-down" innovation, an apparent characteristic of this type of innovation driver is the club's incorporation of the innovation (and the aim of the innovation process) directly into the club's bylaws and policies (Halvorsen *et al.*, 2005). Seeing how several different kinds of innovation drivers could be identified in the case of the skateboarding club reflected Fagerberg's (2004) description of how innovation often involves complicated, lengthy and ulinear processes.

Collaboration also appeared to be an innovation driver in this case (Sørensen & Torfing, 2011). The process of developing and implementing the ideas for "Girl Skate Camp" and "Girl Skate" involved a high degree of collaboration firstly between members, coaches and leaders in the club, but also between the club and the local municipality.

Another factor that might be an important driver for the innovation process within the skateboarding club is the young age of the leaders and trainers. Most of the coaches and board members of the club were between 16 and 35 years old. As middle-aged men dominate organization and leadership of traditional sport, younger leadership and greater diversity among sport leaders and coaches might be an important driver and contributing factor for innovation and inclusion in sports activities. The line between a successful innovation and failure can be thin. I demonstrate the connection between the theoretical categorizations of innovation drivers and barriers and their occurrence in my empirical case in Table 4.2.

TABLE 4.2 Innovation drivers and barriers for inclusion of girls and women in skateboarding

Driver/Barrier	Innovation literature	Norwegian skateboard (empirical example)
"Top-down" innovation	• Initiated by management • Leaders of sports clubs • National sport federation	Club policies and club bylaw ("leading skateboard club for girls and women") initiated by leaders/management of the club
"Bottom-up" innovation	• Day-to-day basis • Spontaneous • Initiated by coaches/athletes	"Girl Skate" and "Girl Skate Camp" initiated by coaches and athletes
"Democratic innovation"	• User driven (e.g. members of sport clubs)	"Girl Skate" and "Girl Skate Camp" driven by coaches and athletes
Collaboration	• Between members, organizations, clubs	Collaboration with local municipality Collaboration between members of the club
Financial barriers	• Lack of material resources • Financial obstacles	Lack of economic resources to implement new skateboarding sessions for girls and women
Knowledge barriers	• Lack of necessary knowledge	Not apparent in this case study
Structural barriers	• Regulations from national and global sport organizations • Government regulations	Not apparent in this case study

As demonstrated in Table 4.2, the skateboarding club faced its own share of innovation barriers during the process of implementing their new ideas. During the interviews, leaders of the club highlighted material resources and economy as one of their toughest barriers while creating and implementing their new skateboarding activities (Arundel, 1997; Tourigny and Le, 2004; Savignac, 2006, 2008; Tiwari et al., 2007; Mancusi and Vezzulli, 2010). Without municipal funding, it is likely that their innovation story would have been one of failure instead of success. This demonstrates some of the frailty of successful sport innovations for social inclusion. While lack of economic resources was an apparent barrier for the innovation process, neither knowledge barriers nor structural barriers were apparent in my fieldwork within this skateboarding club.

Conclusion

In this chapter, I have discussed the innovation term and its possible contribution to sport studies, in particularly to the promotion of social inclusion in sport. Innovation research has grown to become a vastly large field of study. It encompasses a great body of knowledge on different types of innovation, drivers and barriers for innovation and different applications and innovation contexts. By discussing some common definitions of innovation, as well as some potential drivers and barriers for innovation, I have tried to demonstrate how this literature can be made useful in sport studies of practices of social exclusion and inclusion in sport.

What types of innovation, then, can promote social inclusion in sport? Most likely, many different types of innovation hold the potential to combat social exclusion in sport participation. Organizational innovations (e.g. innovations that change the way we organize sport activities) can promote inclusion, as the empirical example used in this chapter demonstrates. However, this is just one example in one particular sport context. It is likely that other kinds of innovations, such as social innovations and technological innovation, equally can promote inclusion in sport. For instance, the development of new and more advanced artificial limbs and prosthesis greatly contribute to the inclusion of physically handicapped groups in sport and physical activity. Another example is the development and emergence of new sports and sports activities, which might promote inclusion by appealing to previously inactive groups of the population. Further research on how, in what ways and what types of innovation can increase social inclusion in sport is needed. For future research, it will be important to investigate a variety of sport contexts and innovation processes.

Whatever the type of innovation, be it organizational, technological, social or collaborative, the aim of the innovation process must always be to change sport for the better in some way, big or small. In other words, the end goal of these innovations must be to create a somewhat more inclusive sport.

Notes

1 Bachelor's, master's and doctoral degrees.
2 Also known as the Western Roll.
3 The abbreviation P.E. will be used in this article.
4 The abbreviation NIF will be used in this article.
5 The Abbreviation NORB will be used in this article.

References

Altschuler, A. and Zegans, M. (1997). 'Innovation and public management: Notes from the state house and city hall'. In Altschuler, A. and Behn, R. (Eds.) *Innovation in American Government*. Washington, D.C.: Brookings Institution.

Anderssen, S. A., Hansen, B. A., Kolle, E., Steene-Johannessen, J., Børsheim, E. and Holme, I. (2009). *Fysisk aktivitet blant voksne og eldre i Norge – Resultater fra en kartlegging i 2008 og 2009*, Oslo: Helsedirektoratet.

Anderson, K. L (1999). 'Snowboarding. The construction of gender in an emerging sport'. *Journal of Sport Issues* 23(1): 55–79.

Arundel, A. (1997). 'Enterprise strategies and barriers to innovation'. In Arundel, A. and Garrelfs, R. (Eds.), *Innovation Measurement and Policies*. Luxembourg: EIMS Publication, European Commission, pp. 101–108.

Breivik, G. and Rafoss, K. (2012). *Fysisk aktivitet: omfang, tilrettelegging og sosial ulikhet – en oppdatering og revisjon*. Oslo: Norges Idrettshøgskole.

Baregheh, A., Rowley, J. and Sambrook, S. (2009). 'Towards a multidisciplinary definition of innovation'. *Management Decision*, 47(8): 1323–1339.

Baldwin, J. and Lin, Z. (2002). 'Impediments to advanced technology adoption for Canadian manufacturers'. *Research Policy,* 31(1): 1–18.

Baldwin, J. and Hanel, P. (2003). *Innovation and Knowledge Creation in an Open Economy: Canadian Industry and International Implications*. Cambridge: Cambridge University Press.

Behn, R. D. (2008). 'The adoption of innovation: The challenge of learning to adapt tacit knowledge. In Borins, S. (Ed.) *Innovations in Government: Research, Recognition and Replication*. Washington: Brookings Institution Press, pp. 138–158.

Booth, D. (2004). 'Surfing: From one (cultural) extreme to another'. In Wheaton, B. (Ed.) *Understanding Lifestyle Sports*. London: Routledge, pp. 94–111.

Boutroy, E., Vignal, B. and Soule, B. (2015). 'Innovation theories applied to the outdoor sports sector: Panorama and perspectives'. *Loisir et Societe,* 24–39.

Collins, M. (2014). *Sport and Social Exclusion*. Oxon: Routledge.

D'Este, P., Iammarino, S., Savona, M. and von Tunzelmann, N. (2012). 'What hampers innovation? Revealed barriers versus deterring barriers'. *Research Policy*, 41(2): 482–488.

Dougherty, D. (1992). 'Interpretive barriers to successful product innovation in large firms'. *Organization Science*, 3(2): 179–202.

Evers, A. and Ewert, B. (2015). 'Social innovation for social cohesion'. In A. Nicholls, J. Simon and M. Gabriel (Eds.) *New Frontiers in Social Innovation Research*. Hampshire: Palgrave Macmillan.

Ferriani, S., Garnsey, E. and Probert, D. (2008). 'Sustaining breakthrough innovation in large established firms: Learning traps and counteracting strategies'. In Bessant, J. and Venables, T. (Eds.) *Creating Wealth from Knowledge: Meeting the Innovation Challenge*. Cheltenham: Edward Elgar Publishing.

Fagerberg, J. (2004). 'Innovation: A guide to the literature'. In Fagerberg, J., Mowery, D. and Nelson, R. (Eds.). *The Oxford Handbook of Innovation*. Oxford: Oxford University Press.

Fuglsang, L. (2010). 'Bricolage and invisible innovation in public sector innovation'. *Journal of Innovation Economics*, 5(1), 67.

Fuller, J., Jawecki, G. and Muhlbacher, H. (2007). 'Innovation creation by online basketball communities'. *Journal of Business Research*, 60(1): 60–71.

Gjelsvik, M. (2007). *Innovasjonsledelse. Ledelse av innovasjon og internt entreprenørskap*. Bergen: Fagbokforlaget.

Goksøyr, M. (2008). *Historien om norsk idrett* [History of Norwegian Sport]. Oslo: Abstrakt Forlag.

Halvorsen, T., Hauknes, J., Miles, I. and Røste, R. (2005). 'On the differences between public and private sector innovation'. *PUBLIN Project*, Report D9.

Hartley, J. (2005). 'Innovation in governance and public services: Past and present'. *Public Money and Management*, 25(1): 27–34.

Hartley, J. (2013). 'Public and private features of innovation'. In Osborne, S. P. and Brown, L. (Eds.) *Handbook of Innovation in Public Services*. Cheltenham: Edward Elgar Publishing, pp. 44–59.

Helsedirektoratet (2015). Fysisk aktivitet og sedat tid blant voksne og eldre i Norge – Nasjonal kartlegging 2014–2015.

Howaldt, J., Kopp, R. and Schwarz, M. (2015). 'Social innovations as drivers of social change – Exploring Tarde's contribution to social innovation theory building'. In Nicholls, A., Simon, J., Gabriel, M. and Whelan, C. (Eds.). *New Frontiers in Social Innovation Research*. Hampshire: Palgrave Macmillian.

Høiland, G. and Willumsen, E. (2015). 'Innovasjon for mer integrerte tjenester: samarbeid påtvers i arbeidsinkludering' [Innovation for integrated services: Collaboration and inclusion in work] in Willumsen, E. and Ødegård, A. (Eds.). *Sosial Innovasjon – fra politikk til tjenesteutvikling [Social Innovation – from politics to public services]*. Bergen: Fagbokforlaget, pp. 213–232.

Høyrup, S. (2010). 'Employee-driven innovation and workplace learning: Basic concepts, approaches and themes'. *Transfer: European Review of Labour and Research*, 16(2), 143–154.

Iammarino, S., Sanna-Randaccio, F. and Savona, M. (2009). 'The perception of obstacles to innovation. Foreign multinationals and domestic firms in Italy'. *Revue d'Economie Industrielle*, 125, 75–104.

Johnson, R. J. (2010). 'New innovations in sports medicine: Good for the patient or good for the pocketbook?' *Current Sports Medicine Reports*, 9(4): 191–193.

Khromin, E. V., Kolychev, A. V., Subbotina, S. V. and Radostev, N. G. (2014). 'Municipal system innovations in the field of physical culture and sport: Adoption and effectiveness'. *Teoriya I Praktika Fizicheskoy Kultury*, 12: 82–85.

Kline, S. J. and Rosenberg, N. (1986). 'An overview of innovation'. In Landau, R. and Rosenberg, N. (Eds.), *The Positive Sum Strategy: Harnessing Technology for Economic Growth*. Washington, D.C.: National Academy Press.

Madanipour, A., Cars, G. and Allen, J. (2002). *Social Exclusion in European Cities: Processes, Experiences and Responses*. Oxon: Routledge.

Malina, R. M. (2006). 'Weight training in youth – growth, maturation and safety: An evidence based review'. *Clinical Journal of Sports Medicine*, 16(6): 478–487.

Malina, R. M., Bouchard, C. and Oded, B. (2004). *Growth, Maturation and Physical Activity* (2nd edition). Champaign, IL: Human Kinetics.

Mancusi, M. L. and Vezzulli, A. (2010). 'R&D, innovation, and liquidity constraints'. *KITeS Working Papers*, 30/2010. Bocconi University.

McKeown, M. (2008). *The Truth about Innovation*. London: Prentice Hall.

Mulgan, G. and Albury, D. (2003). *Innovation in the Public Sector*. London: Cabinet Office.

Mullin, B., Hardy J and Sutton W. (2007). *Sport Marketing* (3rd edition). Champaign, IL: Human Kinetics.

Murray, R., Caulier-Grice, J. and Mulgan, G. (2010). *Open Book of Social Innovation*. Available at: <www.ec.europa.eu/entrerprise/policies/innovation/policy/social-innovation> (accessed 1 December 2015).

Norges Idrettsforbund (2014). *Årsrapport*. Available at: <www.idrettsforbundet.no/globalassets/idrett/idrettsforbundet/om-nif/nif-aarsrapport-2014_enkeltsider_lr.pdf > (accessed 21 January 2016).

Numerato, D. and Baglioni, S. (2011). 'The dark side of social capital: An ethnography of sport governance'. *International Review for the Sociology of Sport*, 47 (5): 594–611.

Ommundsen, Y. and Aadland, A. A. (2009) *Fysisk inaktive voksne i Norge. Hvem er de – oghva motiverer til mer fysisk aktivitet?* Oslo: Helsedirektoratet.

Pill, S., Penney, D. and Swabey, K. (2012). 'Rethinking sport teaching in physical education: A case study of research based innovation in teacher education'. *Australian Journal of Teacher Education*, 37(8): 118–137.

Price, M. and Parker, A. (2003). 'Sport, sexuality and the gender order: Amateur rugby union, gay men, and social exclusion'. *Sociology of Sport Journal*, 20(2): 108–126.

Pyle, R., McQuivery, R., Brassington, G. and Steiner, H. (2003). 'High school athletes: Association between intensity of participation and health factors'. *Clinical Pediatrics*, 42: 8: 697–701.

Rafoss, K. and Breivik, G. (2009). 'Anleggsbruk i befolkningen: en studie av anleggstyper, aktivitetsprofiler og endring'. In Rafoss, K. and Tangen, J. O. (Eds.), *Kampen om idrettsanleggene: planlegging, politikk og bruk*. Bergen: Fagbokforlaget, pp. 53–79.

Ratten, V. (2011). 'Sport-based entrepreneurship: Towards a new theory of entrepreneurship and sport management'. *International Entrepreneurship Management Journal*, 7(1): 57–69.

Rigaux, N. (1994). 'The perception of poverty and social exclusion in Europe'. *Eurobarometer*, 40, Brussels: European Commission.

Ringuet-Riot, C. J., Hahn, A. and James, D. A. (2013). 'A structured approach for technology innovation in sport'. *Sports Technology*, 6(3): 137–149.

Ringuet-Riot, C. J., Carter, S. and James, D. A. (2014). 'Programmed innovation in team sport using needs driven innovation'. *Procedia Engineering*, 72: 817–822.

Savignac, F. (2008). 'Impact of financial constraints on innovation: What can be learned from a direct measure?' *Economics of Innovation and New Technology*, 17(6): 553–569.

Savignac, F. (2006). 'The impact of financial constraints on innovation: Evidence from French manufacturing firms'. *Cahiers de la Maison des Sciences Economiques*, 42.

Schumpeter, J. A. (1942). *Capitalism, Socialism and Democracy*. New York: Harper and Row.

Schumpeter, J. A. (1983). *The Theory of Economic Development. An Inquiry into Profits, Capital, Credit, Interest and the Business Cycle*. New Brunswick: Transaction.

Schwarz, E. and Hunter, J. (2008). *Advanced Theory and Practice in Sport Marketing*. Oxford: Butterworth-Heinemann.

Seigel, S. R., Peña Reyes, M. E., Cardenas, E. E. and Malina, R. M. (2009). 'Participation in organized sport among Mexican youth'. In Coelho Silva, M. J., Figueiredo, A. J., Elferinkgemser, M. and Malina, M. R. (Eds.). *Youth Sports Volume 1: Participation, Trainability and Readiness* (2nd edition). Coimbra: Coimbra University Press.

Speed, C. A. and Roberts, W. O. (2011). 'Innovation in high-performance sports medicine'. *British Journal of Sports Medicine*, 45(12): 949–951.

58 Anne Tjønndal

Sisjord, M. K. (2005). 'Snowboard – en kjønnet ungdomskultur'. *Tidsskrift for ungdomsforskning*, TfU 2-2005.

Spaaij, R., Magee, J. and Jeanes, R. (2014). *Sport and Social Exclusion in Global Society*. New York: Routledge.

Sport England (2001). *Making English Sport Inclusive: Equity Guidelines for Governing Bodies*. London: Sport England.

Sørensen, E. and Torfing, J. (2010). 'Samarbejdsdrevet innovation i den offentlige sektor'. *Økonomi og politikk*, 83(1), 22–33.

Sørensen, E. and Torfing, J. (2011). 'Enhancing collaborative innovation in the public sector'. *Administration and Society*, 43(8), 842–868.

Tiwari, A. K., Mohnen, P., Palm, F. C. and van der Loeff, S. S. (2007). 'Financial Constraints and R&D Investment: Evidence from CIS'. *UNU-MERIT Working Paper 2007-011*, United Nations University.

Trabal, P. (2008). 'Resistance to technological innovation in elite sport'. *International Review for the Sociology of Sport*, 43(3): 313–330.

Tourigny, D. and Le, C.D. (2004). 'Impediments to innovation faced by Canadian manufacturing firms'. *Economics of Innovation and New Technology*, 13(3), 217–250.

Ulseth, A. L. B. (2008). *Mellom tradisjon og nydannelse: analyser av fysisk aktivitet blant voksne i Norge*. Oslo: Akademisk publisering.

Turner, D. (2013). 'The civilized skateboarder and the sports funding hegemony: A case study of alternative sport'. *Sport in Society*, 16(10): 1248–1262.

von Hippel, E. (2005). *Democratizing Innovation*. Cambridge, Mass: MIT Press.

Wheaton, B. (2000). 'Just do it! Consumption, commitment and identity in the windsurfing subculture'. *Sociology of Sport Journal*. 17(3): 257–274.

Wheaton, B. (2004). 'Introduction – Mapping the lifestyle sport-scape'. In Wheaton, B. (Ed.) *Understanding lifestyle sports – consumption, identity and difference*. USA: Routledge, pp. 1–29.

Willumsen, E. and Ødegård, A. (2015). 'Innovasjon – et konsept i endring' [Innovation – a changing concept]. In Willumsen, E. and Ødegård, A. (Eds.) *Sosial Innovasjon – fra politikk til tjenesteutvikling [Social Innovation – from politics to public services]*. Bergen: Fagbokforlaget.

Willumsen, E., Sirnes, T. and Ødegård, A. (2015). 'Innovasjon innen helse og velferd – sosial innovasjon' [Innovations in health and welfare – social innovation]. In Willumsen, E. and Ødegård, A. (Eds.) *Sosial Innovasjon – fra politikk til tjenesteutvikling [Social Innovation – from politics to public services]*. Bergen: Fagbokforlaget.

Winand, M., Vos, S., Zintz, T. and Scheerder, J. (2013). 'Determinants of service innovation: A typology of sports federations'. *International Journal of Sport Management and Marketing*, 13(1–2): 55–73.

5

THE INFLUENCE OF TOTAL QUALITY MANAGEMENT IN THE INNOVATIVE CAPACITY OF MUNICIPAL SPORT FIRMS

Gastão Sousa and Maria José Madeira

Introduction

Quality is seen as a strategic factor for firms to achieve success (Reed, Lemak and Montgomery, 1996; Vijande and Gonzáles, 2008) but, in a society based on knowledge, producing high-quality products or services it is not enough (Hoang, Igel and Laosirihongthong, 2006). The basis to a sustained competitive advantage changed from quality to innovation, considering that the innovative capacity is the main factor that allows firms to achieve the desired results (Drucker, 1989; Haner, 2002; OECD, 2005).

In scientific literature there are different positions about the relationship between Total Quality Management (TQM) and innovation, in other words, it is not clear if TQM practices support (Hoang *et al.*, 2006; Vijande and González, 2008) or restrict the innovation on the company level (Adinolfi, 2003).

While "innovation" is a concept with a strong connection to the concepts of novelty, creativity and anti-conventionalism, "quality" is often associated with standardization, systemic procedures and little tolerance to risk (Haner, 2002).

Nowadays, innovation is considered as a key element in public organizations, helping these organizations to follow the technological development, to optimize their operational costs, to meet the increasing demands of customers for the quality of public services and to build a greater involvement and participation of societies (Albury, 2005; Hartley, 2005; Walker, 2006; Clark, Good & Simmonds, 2008). However, the concept of "innovation" itself is not often used in the public sector, with terms such as "reforms", "service improvement" or "restructuring" being preferred (Windrum, 2008).

Although we are in the presence of a greater concern about the implementation of new ways of management in public services, according to Potts (2009), these concerns focus on the short-term goals related to service efficiency improvement.

There is a wider understanding that public services are considered effective when the use of public resources is carried out efficiently and, that way, the improvements introduced in the management of public goods and services is totally defined as any action that makes management more efficient. This fact may be a barrier to innovation, considering the risks inherent to the innovation process (Potts, 2009).

In the Portuguese public sector the effort to implement a quality culture in several public organizations has been clear, as well as an innovation culture in public administration through various programs over several years of governing (Rodrigues, Neves & Godinho, 2003).

In the specific scope of Sports and Physical Activity, article 161 of the Portuguese Constitution, paragraph c), states that: "all Portuguese have the right to sport," and the public sport services are considered in the scope of the Basic Law on the Status of Local Government, which clearly establishes the responsibility that must be assumed by these public entities in terms of sustaining sports. For this purpose, some local governments created municipal firms in order to have a better organic adequacy to the provision of these sporting services, allowing some concepts and management models, which typically belong to the private sector, to "enter" the public sector more quickly.

To the managers of these kinds of organizations, and to the elected politicians, the lack of knowledge regarding the impact the implementation of TQM practices may have on the innovative capacity of their organizations is a factor that cannot be neglected. The decision making should be based on principles that enlighten the possible impacts of the actions that are developed and, to develop a useful theory, it is necessary to perform empiric studies illustrative of the phenomenon that occurs in the organizations.

Following this, the main aim of the current study is to analyze the connection between the TQM practices and the innovative capacity of the municipal firms. Specifically, we hope to identify: 1) the influence that TQM has in the innovative capacity of the sporting municipal firms; 2) the contribution that certain practices of TQM have in the innovative capacity of the sporting municipal firms; 3) if the innovative capacity of the firm influences the achieving of their results.

The present study is structured as follows: first it presents the connection between TQM practices and public services innovation. Based on the literature review we formulate the research proposition that will guide the empiric component of the study. The study methodology is presented and the main results are shown and discussed in the context of the relevant literature and based on the formulated research proposition. Finally, we aim to sum up the study conclusions, accentuating its limitations and suggesting new research lines that derive from this work.

Literature review

Throughout the literature review the main concepts used in the study, including TQM, innovation and innovative capacity, are classified, as well as trying to highlight the connection between TQM and innovation, aiming to formulate a research proposition, which will guide the development of the case studies considered.

Total Quality Management

Total Quality Management (TQM) was introduced in the 80s by the work of the quality leaders such as Deming, Juran and Crosby. However, as Wiklund *et al.* (2003) state, it is not easy to find a definition of TQM. In fact, in literature more descriptions than definitions are found. Many quality "gurus" do not even use that expression. Deming (1994) stated that: "The trouble with Total Quality Management – failure of TQM, you call it – is that there is no such a thing. It is a buzzword. I never use the term, as it carries no meaning."

Although it is not easy to find a widely accepted definition of TQM, there are principles that are definers and are present in the generality of studies on TQM. Thus, and according to Levis *et al.* (2008), TQM can be understood as a management philosophy fundamentally based on the participation of all members; in improving processes, products and services; transforming organizational culture in order to meet or exceed customer needs and expectations, by means of consistent leadership and continuous improvement.

The approaches to quality have evolved over the years and the new approaches do not reject what was included in the previous ones, quite the contrary. Starting with the previous approaches, new perspectives and new information were added in order to respond to new demands. Pires (2007), for example, believes that the concept of quality has evolved along several stages: Inspection, Quality Control, Quality Assurance Warranty, and finally, Total Quality, in the 90s of the last century. Although currently a new approach is proposed, Six Sigma, we cannot say that it is contradictory to the TQM approach. In fact, Cheng (2008) believes that TQM is the fundamental basis of Six Sigma. Moreover, Andersson *et al.* (2006) argue that although the definitions of TQM and Six Sigma may differ, the aim of the different concepts seems to be similar.

Therefore, companies and organizations continue to invest in TQM. One way is through self-assessment/excellence models, which are the basis for quality prizes worldwide. Wiele *et al.* (2000) state that in order for TQM to stop being a fashion (fad) and become the standard form of management, it is necessary to: 1) be clearly defined; 2) be measurable; 3) have no direct connection with short-term losses. According to these authors, self-assessment using the excellence models can be a way to meet those requirements. Indeed, underlying the Excellence Model of EFQM, the Fundamental Concepts of Excellence, which are often referred to as Total Quality Management, are found (EFQM, 2003).

Although the models of self-assessment can be viewed as a form of implementation of TQM (Lourenço, 2000) this is not just a technical system. Gregerson (1994) states that TQM is an equilateral triangle, and companies must pay attention to all three: management leadership, employee involvement and technical systems. However, to study the practical implementation of TQM, it is necessary to find what its defining dimensions are. In an extensive review of the published studies on TQM in different journals, Sila and Ebrahimpour (2002) identified 25 factors in 76 different studies.

Lenka and Suar (2008) identified: transformational leadership, orientation for the user, human resource management, organizational culture, continuous improvement and control and quality measurement, as the defining practices of TQM.

Innovation and innovative capacity

Innovation is considered as one of the most important factors of economic competitiveness (Pohlmann, 2005). Schumpeter (1934) reported the idea that development is, above all, the result of a sequence of innovations, being the entrepreneur, the agent directly responsible for such innovations.

Following this, evidence suggests that in the last decades, innovation is a concept which deserved greater attention from the scientific community and society in general, being the target of an increasing amount of theoretical and applied work, covering all the research domains, especially those related to the design of public and organizational policy measures and/or business strategies (Guimarães, 2003).

Drucker (1989) does not consider technological innovations as the most important, pointing out the fact that technology can be imported with low cost and with minimal cultural risk. On the other hand, institutions need cultural roots to grow and develop well. For Simões (1997) innovation can be characterized as a process of creation, acquisition, transfer and use of knowledge in which the emphasis cannot be placed in the exclusive activity of a group or department, but the intense and continuous collaboration between different professional and functional groups inside and outside the company.

In the literature review carried out in the field of entrepreneurial innovation, it is verified that the innovative capacity varies from company to company and it is determined by a wide and complex range of factors, as stimulator and limiter of the innovation process (Silva and Sousa, 2009). However, in this research we aim to examine whether the implementation of TQM processes influence the innovative capacity.

Connection between Total Quality Management and innovation

It is not clear if the approaches to quality management have given sufficient contribution to the solution of company problems, which include the need for flexibilization and management of smaller and smaller technology and product life cycles, and consequently, the need for continuous innovation in order for the firm to remain competitive on a global scale (Reed, Lemak and Montgomery, 1996; Haner, 2002).

There are two schools of thought regarding the connection between TQM and innovation. A group of academicians consider that TQM supports innovation, suggesting that the organizations that implement TQM practices will succeed in innovation. The other school of thought argues that TQM obstructs innovation (Hoang, Igel and Laosirihongthong, 2002).

Hoang *et al.* (2002), in a study carried out in 204 manufacturing and services companies, concluded that TQM practices have a positive connection with the novelty level and the number of new products and services, which supports the arguments of the literature that refers to the existence of a positive connection between TQM and innovation. However, not all practices associated with quality management have an impact on the innovative capacity of the company. Only three practices, namely leadership and human resources management, strategic and process management, and open organization, show a positive connection with innovation.

Vijande & González (2008), in a study that involved 93 companies from the services and manufacturing sectors of the autonomous region of Asturias in Spain, concluded that TQM is a management system that stimulates the corporate culture open or receptive to innovation. The study only involved companies with certification processes by the ISO 9001:2000 norms in order to ensure the interest of management in quality practices, as well as familiarity with the concepts used in the applied questionnaire.

By analyzing the TQM effects in innovation, Vijande & González (2008) conclude that TQM can, by itself, promote the adoption of innovations in the management systems of the analyzed companies and in the marketing function. Nevertheless, TQM effects on goods and services innovation, and on the associated processes, is mediated by the existence of a corporate culture propitious to innovation. By distinguishing between administrative innovation (which refers to any process different from the productive one) and technical innovation (that takes place in products or services or in their acquisition processes), the authors conclude that the management system seems to be, to the administrative innovation, a stronger determinant than the innovative culture itself.

This set of studies suggests that the implementation of TQM practices seems to contribute to an innovative culture in the organizations and, consequently, a higher capacity of adoption of innovations.

Contrary to the arguments that claim the existence of a positive connection between TQM and innovation, there is a current of thought that goes in the opposite direction (Wind and Mahajan, 1997; Tidd *et al.*, 1997; Slater and Narver, 1998; Kim and Marbougne, 1999, as cited in Hoang *et al.*, 2002). These authors demonstrate the fact that a high number of experiences of TQM implementation show a high discrepancy between theory and practice.

Adinolfi (2003) has also used a set of case studies in Italian and Irish hospitals, trying to evaluate the impact of the implementation of TQM practices in the performance of those organizations. The author concludes that TQM does not seem to be an instrument to promote the innovation process but it seems to be a way to identify and solve specific problems of the organization.

However, this school of thought does not totally reject the fact that some practices associated with TQM may be a stimulus of the innovative capacity of the organizations. However, they consider that this effect will always be very limited.

So, it appears that there is not a wide consensus in the scientific community about the relationship between the implementation of practices associated with TQM and innovation in the organizations, since the results of the investigation are contradictory. In this follow-up it is necessary to clarify this relationship, so we formulated the following research proposition: the use of the practices of Total Quality Management influence directly and positively the innovative capacity of local firms.

In this study, the dimensions outlined by Lenka and Suar (2008) and Sousa, Lourenço and Silva (2009) are considered as TQM practices, namely: transformational leadership, customer orientation, human resource management, organizational culture, continuous improvement and quality control and measuring. The innovative capacity is measured as a result of the innovation process covering the service innovation, the process innovation, the organizational innovation and the marketing innovation. This innovation approach is in line with previous research (Silva, 2003) and the Oslo Manual, which states that innovation is the "implementation of a product (good or service), process, marketing method or organizational methodology, new or significantly improved in management practices, organization of the workplace or the organization's external relations" (OECD, 2005, p. 46).

To sum up, we can present the basic concepts and the structure of the current study in Figure 5.1.

Methodology

The case studies are particularly useful in the analysis of complex organizational processes (Tharenou, Donohue and Cooper, 2007) and enable us to understand how or why the events occur in conditions in which the researchers have minimal control (Yin, 2003). Considering that the importance of the current investigation is specifically concerned with how TQM influences the innovative capacity of the companies, a detailed study of multiple cases, by its empirical richness, would contribute to the knowledge through theoretical development, therefore we decided to plan a research study of multiple studies cases. The selection of the

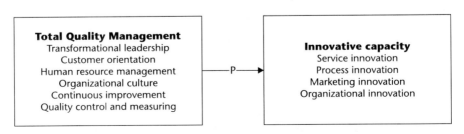

FIGURE 5.1 Basic constructs and study design

case studies was based on a replication logic in which the cases must be understood as unique experiences in relation to the theory and not as factors with statistical significance (Mele & Colurcio, 2006).

Considering the aims to be achieved by the study, the selection criteria included the following items: 1) The organizations to be studied must have existed for more than four years, which would allow a greater richness in the collected information; 2) the organizations should be in different stages of the implementation of TQM practices; 3) the geographical proximity of the organization to the researchers' workplace should allow for data collection and personal contact with the top managers with the frequency and time needed to collect the information necessary for the study development; 4) access to available information and access to the top manager of the organization should be easy, allowing data collection within the time available for the study.

This way, four municipal firms, situated in the north of Portugal, that match the first three selection criteria were identified. Through the professional knowledge of the first author of this study, phone contact with technicians or top managers of those firms was made in order to explain the scope of the study and to ask for collaboration in its accomplishment. Only three of the firms demonstrated availability to provide the information required and to be involved in the study. For privacy reasons, these municipal firms will be from now on named as EM1, EM2 and EM3.

Following this first contact, dates to conduct an interview with the top manager of each municipal firm were scheduled. Considering the complexity of the phenomenon studied, we sought to use a combination of data collection methods which allowed triangulation of the collected information, increasing the reliability of the results (Yin, 2003).

In the case of the firm EM1, a semi-directed interview was conducted, in a group situation which involved the researcher, one of the company managers, the Quality Director and the head of the swimming-pool division. The interview lasted one hour and fourteen minutes and it happened in the manager's office, recorded with their consent and later transcribed integrally.

In the cases of the companies EM2 and EM3, the same semi-directed interviews were conducted with the top managers of the organizations (Executive Administrator in the case of EM2 and the Chairman in the case of EM3). The interviews lasted one hour and thirty-four minutes and one hour and thirty-two minutes, respectively, and were recorded and later fully transcribed.

Several documents belonging to the companies involved in the study were collected, namely: statutes, business and account plans and activity reports referring to the last two years of activity, as well as several documents available on the companies' websites (news, press kits, activities description and intervention areas and flowcharts).

The qualitative data analysis software NVivo version 8 was used as an auxiliary instrument during the analysis process of the interview contents and the

66 Gastão Sousa and Maria José Madeira

TABLE 5.1 Dimensions used in the interview guide

Dimensions

Global characteristics of municipal firms and case study context

1: Total Quality Management
Concept 1 – Transformational leadership
Concept 2 – Customer orientation
Concept 3 – Human resource management
Concept 4 – Organizational culture
Concept 5 – Continuous improvement
Concept 6 – Quality control and measuring

2: Innovative capacity
Concept 1 – Service innovation
Concept 2 – Process innovation
Concept 3 – Marketing innovation
Concept 4 – Organizational innovation

documents collected in the three case studies, thus framing the codification structure from the essential concepts identified in the literature and presented in Table 5.1.

The dimensions used to inform the interview guide, which derived from the literature review, were also the basis to the assembly of the codification structure. We tried to keep this open to the inclusion of new data derived from the collected information during the interview and document research.

Results discussion

In this part of the study, an individual analysis of each case studied will be made, followed by a comparison between cases. The analysis of each case will fall upon the analysis dimensions used during the semi-directed interviews and previously presented. The implementation of TQM processes will be used as differentiating a variable of the cases, during the comparison of the results achieved in each municipal firm (to all intents, the firms were classified as "Certified," "In Certification" and "Uncertified"). However, the certification processes are not synonymous with the implementation of TQM processes, and it is understood that the use of certification shows a commitment by the organization to implementing several TQM elements. For this reason, certification is used as a differentiating variable of the case studies.

Municipal firms' characterization and study context

EM1 was created in 2003, but the current administration only began to perform their duties in 2005. Its main purpose involves the planning, administration, management and maintenance of the municipal sporting places and equipment, as well as the promotion and execution of recreational sport activities and municipal sporting programs.

EM2 was created in 2001 to manage the municipal swimming pools. The aim was to increase the service quality and to try the medium-term self-sustainability of such equipment in order to achieve balanced prices by maximizing the use of the installed capacity. Later the company will widen into other areas, extending its assistance to the management of other municipal equipment and cultural events.

Concerning EM3, the company was created in 1999 by initiative of the town hall and the objective, as the Chairman states, was:

> by that time it was clearly, not only to ensure an almost immediate future to an organization outside the municipal universe capable of managing in a more professional, expedite, active way, the wide range of sport facilities that the Town Hall was building but at the same time, which is its second action segment, sportingly dynamize the county, mainly in the areas of non-competitive sport and the promotion of services that otherwise people would not have access to.

Total Quality Management

At the time of the study, EM1 was in the final stage of the service certification process. This process lasted nearly one and a half years and appears in the follow-up of a training course for managers. As the company administrator declared:

> from that moment we thought we could really move forward quickly in a process which could standardize the company functioning, making this a real company. For that it was needed to cut some edges and we thought that the certification process would help us to improve our business (. . .) it seems that by the end of June, beginning of July, the first audit may happen.

The customer orientation has not materialized in concrete actions beyond "the usual surveys of user satisfaction" and some additional initiatives, which in the scope of the interview and the subsequent analysis of the company documents, are not clear. However, the company unveils the investment and commitment of the managers to implement a system of quality management, based on encouraging the participation of employees and in the delegation of powers. Figure 5.2, which displays the coding carried out from the transcribed interview, suggests a greater importance is given to the elements related to human resources management and transformational leadership.

The firm EM2 has had certification by the norm ISO9001:2000 since November 2004. The main reasons that led the company to start the certification

FIGURE 5.2 Number of coded references to TQM practices in municipal firm EM1

process and to integrate the quality management processes in their day-to-day are expressed by the administrator as follows:

> We had the ambition to want more, to systematize methodologies and we needed something that helped us to do it. We started with a first perspective which was the certification of some services as it was easier, but we thought it was not motivating enough, that it would not allow us to achieve the goal we intended to, which was the systematization of an organization, all focused on the different aspects of quality maximization and of value creation. That was why we decided to certify the entity as a whole by the principles of ISO9001:2000. We started and concluded the process in about ten months. We are certified for about five years . . .

During the interview, the administrator emphasized the importance that the firm gives to the people, to the human resources, as an essential way to overcome the adversities and reach success in the implementation of a culture of quality. Its leadership style is based on a total trust in sector-based leadership, avoiding the leadership overlapping and based on a continuous assessment of people, in which the concept of merit is ubiquitous, being the source of the corporate culture. There are several cases that the administrator uses to exemplify the construction of an individual organizational culture based on the valorization of the human resources merit, suggesting that it is an area of great importance and personal commitment in its leadership style.

Also in the dimension of orientation for the user, the answers of the interviewee seemed to suggest the importance that is given to this aspect. These claims are substantiated with examples such as investment and performance of training courses for employees, the selection of events, activities and other services proposed.

Following this analysis, Figure 5.3, which shows the number of elements coded from the interview with the administrator of the municipal firm EM2, seems to suggest the greater importance given to elements usually associated

FIGURE 5.3 Number of coded references to TQM practices in municipal firm EM2

with the "human" dimension of TQM, namely organizational culture, human resources management, transformational leadership and orientation for the user (Fuentes, Montes and Fernandez, 2006; Lenka and Suar, 2008). Indeed, there are a higher number of references associated with these elements than in relation to the dimension traditionally associated with regulatory and standardized affairs of TQM.

The company EM3 does not have and does not want to start any quality certification process or TQM methodology. As stated by the Chairman:

> There was a first approach, three years ago, and the opportunity to start the quality certification emerged, only on the service level, which is only the swimming pool complex. But at that time, and honestly, after asking some people and some companies involved in the certification process, the conviction we had is that these processes are extremely laborious, extraordinarily formal and that they do not add much to the organization's excellence . . .

Despite the lack of formalization in the use of TQM techniques, the Chairman says: "I think this standardized process and quality management already exists. We feel the need to systematically organize ourselves, but we do not feel the need to be certified (. . .)."

This statement, contextualized in the content of the interview, seems to suggest a deep conviction of the interviewee on a possible link between the processes of certification and TQM and the standardization of services, the systematization of the company's activities and the increase of the regulatory burden, as suggested by some authors (Adinolfi, 2003). This systematization and some patterns of functioning are seen in a positive way, namely the full explanation of the internal working rules for the workers, but the implementation of certification processes are seen as self-defeating. As shown in Figure 5.4, the Chairman of the municipal firm EM3 seems to place more emphasis on human resource management and organizational culture.

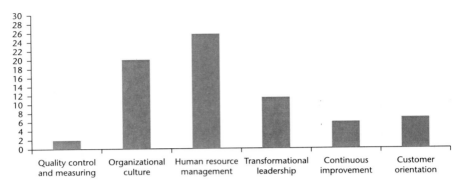

FIGURE 5.4 Number of coded references to TQM practices in municipal firm EM3

Innovative capacity

EM1 presents an innovative performance in all types of innovation (service, process, marketing and organizational) and, in the words of the administration: "A high incentive for creativity and receptivity to new service proposals and improvement of the current ones."

The implementation of quality management systems, namely the fact that the company is about to complete the certification process, appears to have allowed the delegation, the collaborators' involvement and investment in home staff, to be expressed in an environment favorable to innovation.

However, it was evident in the context of the interviewees' answers that it is in the area of innovation in services and marketing that the progress was superior. The implementation of process and organizational innovations were not mentioned in as clear a way as other types of innovation.

In company EM2 all types of innovation with concrete examples were also referred to. As in company EM1, the references to service and marketing innovations were the ones that were more clearly presented.

Finally, in company EM3 all types of innovation were presented with concrete examples. In this company, service, process and marketing innovations were more clearly presented than the innovations of the organizational type. In the last case, and considering the context of the interview, it seems that there is a concern with the maintenance of a stable organizational structure.

All municipal firms studied proved to be innovative, having introduced over the years 2008 and 2009 several innovations in their services and in their processes, marketing methodologies and organizational structure.

Case study comparison

For the purposes of this work, the municipal firms are classified as "Certified," "On Certification" and "Uncertified." As already noted above, although the certification is not synonymous with the process of TQM implementation, it is understood that its use shows an organization's commitment to many of the elements of TQM, so we use this element as a distinguishing variable between the case studies.

Therefore, we must compare the companies studied in regards to the key concepts of TQM used in the scope of this study. Figure 5.5 displays the number of coded references of the different key concepts of TQM from the interviews with the top managers of the three local companies.

As can be seen, it is in the company not certified (EM3) that a greater number of references to the concepts of organizational culture, human resources management and transformational leadership can be identified.

The certified company (EM2) has a greater number of references to the concept of orientation for the user, which may be an indicative element of the influence of the TQM practices in the customer focus of the organization.

The small number of references in the three studied cases to the concepts of control and measuring quality and continuous improvement processes were also confirmed, which may be an indicator of the lesser importance given, by the interviewees, to these elements in the process of management of their organizations. When trying to compare the references made by the interviewees to the different types of innovation (see Figure 5.6), it is verified that the certified company has

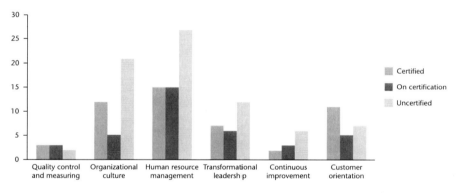

FIGURE 5.5 Comparing the number of coded references to TQM practices

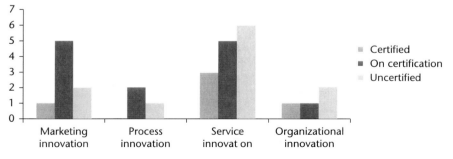

FIGURE 5.6 Number of coded references to innovation

72 Gastão Sousa and Maria José Madeira

the lowest record of the three cases studied. This fact is inconsistent with the largest number of references made to the orientation for the user from this company, it being expected that in an organization where orientation for the user is emphasized as essential the number of innovations would also be higher.

Conclusion

The analysis of the collected information allows us to conclude that the proposition of the current work, based on the literature review, was correct and seems to reveal a positive connection between the use of TQM processes and the innovative capacity of the municipal firms. The analysis of the content of the interviews with the top managers of these municipal firms emphasizes the fact that it is the leadership dimension and the human resources management that contribute the most to the innovative capacity of the companies. Quality control dimensions and continuous improvement are the ones referred to as the most difficult to implement and with less positive effects on the innovative capacity of the firm.

To the top managers of this type of organization and to the elected politician, the results of this study are useful because they demonstrate the influence of the implementation of the TQM practices in municipal firms that provide sport services.

The importance that the elements associated with human resources management, organizational culture and transformational leadership may have in the innovative capacity of organizations is a factor that cannot be neglected. The decision-making of the managers and elected politicians on the investment in TQM processes may take into account the results of the current study, enhancing the actions developed in order to increase the innovative capacity of their organizations.

For academicians, the review of the theoretical work on the influence of the processes of TQM in the companies' innovation and its application to the particular case of municipal public firms is an important contribution to the development of future studies.

The use of multiple case studies, with companies in different stages of TQM tools implementation (or those who do not choose to use them) was an interesting exercise and it allowed us to compare the different organizational realities, and may be useful for a better understanding of the phenomenon studied.

Authors that decide to develop this topic of research may find useful the use of quantitative data collection methods close by the workers and the customers of the municipal firms, allowing that way the triangulation of the information collected (Yin, 2003) and a greater reliability in the processing of those data.

References

Adinolfi, P. (2003) 'Total Quality Management in public health care: a study of Italian and Irish hospitals' *Total Quality Management*, 14 (2): 141–150.

Albury, D. (2005) 'Fostering innovation in public services' *Public Money and Management*, 25 (1): 51–56.

Andersson, R., Eriksson, H. and Torstensson, H. (2006) 'Similarities and differences between TQM, six sigma and lean' *The TQM Magazine* 18 (3): 282–296.

Cheng, J. L. (2008) 'Implementing six sigma via TQM improvement: an empirical study in Taiwan' *The TQM Journal* 20 (3): 182–195.

Clark J., Good, B. and Simmonds, P. (2008) *Innovation in the Public and Third Sectors*. NESTA Innovation Index Working Paper, accessed at <www.nesta.org.uk> on 19 August 2009.

Deming, E. W. (1994) in Romano, C., 'Report card on TQM' *Management Review*, 83 (1): 22.

Drucker, P.F. (1989) *Inovação e Gestão. Uma nova concepção de estratégia de empresa*, Editorial Presença.

EFQM (2003) *Introdução à Excelência*, EFQM, Brussels.

Fuentes, M., Montes, F. and Fernández, L. (2006) 'Total Quality Management, strategic orientation and organizational performance: the case of Spanish companies' *Total Quality Management*, 17 (13): 303–323.

Gregerson, D. (1994) in Romano, C. 'Report card on TQM' *Management Review* 83 (1): 25.

Guimarães, R. (2003) 'Aspectos institucionais da inovação e da mudança tecnológica', in Rodrigues, M., Neves, A. and Godinho, M. (eds.) *Para uma política de inovação em Portugal*, pp. 89–110, Publicações D. Quixote, Lisboa.

Haner, U. (2002) 'Innovation quality – a conceptual framework' *International Journal of Production Economics* 80 (1): 31–37.

Hartley, J. (2005) 'Innovation in governance and public services: Past and present' *Public Money and Management* 25 (1): 27–34.

Hoang, D., Igel, B. and Laosirihongthong, T. (2002) 'The impact of Total Quality Management on innovation: Findings from a developing country' *International Journal of Quality & Reliability Management* 23 (9): 1092–1117.

Lenka, U. and Suar, D. (2008) 'A holistic model of Total Quality Management in services' *The Icfaian Journal of Management Research* 7 (3): 56–72.

Levis, M., Brady, M. and Helfert, M. (2008) 'Total quality management underpins information quality management' *The Journal of American Academy of Business* 14 (1): 172–178.

Lourenço, L. (2000) 'Modelos de excelência na implementação da gestão pela qualidade total' *2° Seminário Luso-Espanhol de Economia Empresarial*, UBI, Covilhã.

Mele, C. and Colurcio, M. (2006) 'The evolving path of TQM: towards business excellence and stakeholder value' *International Journal of Quality & Reliability Management* 23 (5): 464–489.

OECD (2005) *Oslo Manual. Guidelines for Collecting and Interpreting Innovation Data*, Third Edition, OECD, Paris.

Pires, A. R. (2007) *Qualidade: Sistemas de Gestão da Qualidade*, 4th Edition, Sílabo, Lda., Lisboa.

Pohlmann, M. (2005) 'The evolution of innovation: Cultural backgrounds and the use of innovation models' *Technology Analysis & Strategic Management* 17 (1): 9–19.

Potts, J. (2009) 'The innovation deficit in public services: The curious problem of too much efficiency and not enough waste and failure' *Innovation: Management, Policy & Practice* 11: 34–43.

Reed, R., Lemak, D. and Montgomery, J. (1996) 'Beyond process: TQM content and firm performance' *Academy of Management Review* 21 (1): 173–202.

Rodrigues, M., Neves, A. and Godinho, M. (2003) *Para uma política de inovação em Portugal*. Publicações D. Quixote, Lisboa.

Schumpeter, J. (1934) *The Theory of Economic Development*, Harvard University Press, Cambridge, Massachusetts.

Sila, I. and Ebrahimpour, M. (2002) 'An investigation of the Total Quality Management survey based research published between 1989 and 2000: A literature review' *The International Journal of Quality & Reliability Management* 19 (6/7): 902–970.

Silva, M. J. (2003) *Capacidade Inovadora Empresarial – Estudos dos Factores Impulsionadores e Limitadores nas Empresas Industriais Portuguesas*, Tese de Doutoramento em Gestão, Universidade da Beira Interior, Covilhã, Portugal.

Silva, M. J. and Sousa, G. (2009) 'Determinantes da capacidade inovadora das empresas portuguesas: proposta de modelo conceptual ao nível do sector dos serviços' *Actas do 3º Congresso Nacional dos Economistas*, Lisboa, Portugal.

Simões, V.C. (1997) *Inovação e Gestão em PME*, Gabinete de Estudos e Prospectiva Económica (GEPE), Ministério de Economia, Lisboa.

Sousa, G., Lourenço, L. and Silva, M. J. (2009) 'Gestão pela Qualidade Total e Capacidade Inovadora Empresarial: Proposta de Modelo Conceptual ao nível dos Serviços Públicos de Desporto', Universidade da Beira Interior, *NECE Working Paper*.

Tharenou, P., Donohue, R. and Cooper, B. (2007) *Management Research Methods*, Cambridge University Press.

Vijande, M. and González, L. (2008) 'Efectos de la Gestión de Calidad Total en la transformación en la innovación tecnológica y administrativa' *Cuadernos de Economia y Dirección de la Empresa* 37: 33–66.

Walker, R. (2006) 'Innovation type and diffusion: An empirical analysis of local government' *Public Administration* 84 (2): 311–35.

Wiele, A. V. D., Williams, A. R. T and Dale, B. G. (2000) 'Total Quality Management: Is it a fad, fashion or fit?' *Quality Management Journal* 7 (2): 65–79.

Wiklund, H., Klefsjo, B., Wiklund, P. S. and Edvardsson, B. (2003) 'Innovation and TQM in Swedish higher education institutions – possibilities and pitfalls' *The TQM Magazine* 15 (2): 99–107.

Windrum, P. (2008) 'Innovation and entrepreneurship in public services', in Windrum, P., Koch, P. (eds.) *Innovation in Public Sector Services. Entrepreneurship, Creativity and Management*, pp. 3–20, Edward Elgar Publishers, Cheltenham, UK.

Yin, R. (2003) *Case Study Research: Design and Methods*, third edition, Sage Publications, Third Edition.

6

SPORT LEADERSHIP, PSYCHOLOGY AND INNOVATION

Vanessa Ratten

Introduction

Sport has a global reach due to its popularity and communication ability and business applications due to its monetary and social impact on global society. The importance of sport comes from its linkage with business ability to focus on competitiveness (Fletcher, 2010). There is a relationship between sport and business due to the organizational issues involved in both domains (Jones, 2002). Sport can be viewed as a business due to its organizational functions such as leadership and human resource management. The same can be seen with business as a sport due to the team work and coaching involved. This is seen in sport business analogies such as "the corporate athlete," "from the locker room to the boardroom" and "trading in the tracksuit for the pinstripe" (Fletcher, 2010, p. 140). In this chapter, I discuss the role of sport business from a leadership and psychology perspective by reflecting on what is needed to further research on this topic. I also suggest directions for future research about sport leadership, psychology and innovation.

McNutt and Wright (1995) suggest that the three common links between sport and business are: open communication, team unity and employee/player recognition. Open communication refers to the information being transferred in an honest manner (Fletcher, 2010). This helps build rapport and trust, which are important for both sport success and business performance. Team unity involves building a sense of cohesiveness amongst a group of people (Fletcher, 2010). This is important given the different types of people needed to work together in both a sport and business context. The effectiveness of people working together on certain tasks ensures that the group will perform better. Employee/power recognition involves acknowledging the functions certain people have that ensures proper workload allocation (Loehr and Schwartz, 2001). This may include focusing on motivating appropriate people to do their jobs in a certain way. This can include rewarding and congratulating people based on their achievements (Fletcher, 2010). Differentiating individuals based on merit is important for the functioning of sport and business. It may mean rewards are given in terms of monetary or psychological recognition.

Sport is a form of human expressionism with its own enjoyment and purpose (Chalip, 1992). There are three main types of sport marketing: "marketing to promote fan interest, marketing to promote sport participation, and marketing to promote consumption of consumer products via sport" (Chalip, 1992, p. 87). The marketing to promote fan interest focuses on increasing allegiance to a certain sport or team. This can include sport teams increasing their community engagement activities. Sometimes this is done by showcasing new sports in public venues. Marketing to promote sport participation involves increasing the number of times people play or view a sport. As some more traditional sports such as tennis decline in terms of participation there need to be new ways to play and view the game. CardioTennis is an example of marketing to promote greater participation in a traditionally long game. This new form of tennis combines cardio training to make the game quicker. Marketing products via sport is about how consumer goods can be advertised to sport audiences. This can include the use of new sports equipment or clothing that is worn by players. Other examples are the use of billboard advertising by companies at sport events.

In this chapter, I acknowledge that sports leadership concerns both psychological and management functions but I focus on the innovative capabilities of good managers. This lays the groundwork for building more of an innovation perspective into sports leadership studies and to develop the sport entrepreneurship field. By doing this, the focus is on innovation and entrepreneurship applications of sport leadership in the business area. The chapter explores the evolution of sport leadership by looking at how it focuses on business practices. This helps to highlight gaps in the current literature around sport leadership, which enables a model of leadership in sport entrepreneurship to develop. The goal of this chapter is to encourage more sport leadership research from an innovation and entrepreneurship perspective.

By including more emphasis on innovation within sport leadership and psychology it helps to understand the changes in the nature of sport, which are important issues for society and business. This has meant that research about sport management and innovation has grown considerably in the past decade. Scholars have examined the issue of sport leadership using mostly a psychological context with little emphasis placed on innovation. This chapter will contribute to filling the gap in the literature by discussing sport leadership in the context of psychology and innovation. As sport management is a relatively young discipline it helps to link research to the substantial literature already in existence about leadership. The purpose of this chapter is to examine sport leadership and psychology from a creativity perspective. This means discussing how sport and business have creativity evident in their practices. Potential areas for interdisciplinary collaboration between the sport, psychology and leadership management disciplines are stated. Finally, suggestions for sports marketers and potential research avenues are stated.

Literature review

Sport scientists, who include psychologists, sociologists and marketing professionals, have shown interest in understanding why individuals are motivated to be fans (Wann *et al.*, 2008). This is due to consumers being highly involved in sport due to their desire for long-term associations (Shani, 1997). This has meant that relationship marketing is used in sport as it enables consumers to be active contributors. Sport consumption is viewed by relationships such as trust, commitment, satisfaction, love, intimacy, self-connection and reciprocity. These sport consumption behaviors influence the likeliness of a person to purchase merchandise, watch media coverage and attend games.

The main motivations for becoming fans of sport are escape, economics, eustress, entertainment, family and aesthetics (Wann *et al.*, 2008). The escape motive focuses on sport as a way to direct attention from the current life situation (Smith, 1988). This means escapism is often the reason why individuals watch lifestyle sports such as surfing. The consuming of sports as a way to relax is important in society (Sloan, 1989). As more individuals live in urban areas the ability to travel to adventurous locations is more difficult so watching sport is an easier alternative. Adventure sports have been linked to the escapism motive as they provide a way for people to watch dangerous sports.

The number of people watching sport on media devices increases the value of sport marketing (Sleight, 1989). The interest of sport fans at events is an important determinant of the willingness of an organization to use sport marketing (Sloan, 1989). Sport marketing is different to other types of marketing due to the intense personal relationship people have with sport (Mullin, 1983). The ability of sport to be consumed socially means it has a social value (Yiannakis, 1989). This means that consumers identify with sport based on their psychological associations and is important in distinguishing sport as a social institution that has different characteristics to other forms of marketing (Chalip, 1992).

There are different characteristics of sports events that generate fan interest including media commentary, stadium location and environmental atmospherics. These features mean sport events have varying levels of fan interest depending on outcome and effective plays. Sport marketing can include a narrative about a theme or event that makes it more appealing to consumers (Chalip, 1987). The way sport is viewed by consumers is largely based on psychology, which is best understood from a behavioral perspective.

Sport psychology and business

Foster (2002) proposed that there are five major skills of sport psychology that impact business settings. These are mental imagery, performance routines, positive self-talk, activation control strategies and sustaining attention. Mental imagery is a sport psychology practice that can be effective when used on managers. It concerns the ability to form images in the mind with the view to putting them into practice in the future (Fletcher, 2010). This is important for athletes and business managers in terms of visualizing success. Performance routines involve preparing for a future event or activity. This may involve practicing before a special event, which requires both mental and physical training (Gordon, 2007). Positive self-talk involves saying things in a productive manner with the view to the outcome being beneficial. In sport and business, this self-affirmation is important to having goals in place that lead to a certain outcome being achieved (Fletcher, 2010). The internal voice used by athletes and managers is a psychology trait that when used in the right way has good results (Ievleva and Terry, 2008). Activation control strategies are the ability of a person to perform under certain conditions. This may mean to rest in slow periods but perform when there is competition. The ability to perform under pressure is an important part of competition in sport and business (Fletcher, 2010). Focus and sustaining attention involve looking to the long term and paying attention to a certain event. This is important when there are delays in projects that require hesitation then increased performance. In both sport and business there are times when attention needs to be paid to a project over a certain time period (Adcroft and Teckman, 2009). For some people this may involve having clarity about what they hope to achieve and the time needed for these objectives.

Organizational issues in sport include the hiring and retaining of personnel, which needs constant attention. This requires leadership in terms of strategy and functioning of a sport organization. High-performance teams will be organized well in terms of their structure (Fletcher, 2010). The principles of sport are transferrable to business due to the ability of working in a capacity to realize performance (Jones, 2002). In a study about employee well-being, Lloyd and Foster (2006) applied sport psychology principles to organizational performance. They found that mental skills used in sport psychology such as self-talk and mental imagery also help with employee well-being. This is also evident in the collaboration between sport and business, which focuses on mental toughness, job stress, burnout, life development and leadership (Gordon, 2007). These associations show how there is similar psychology used in both the sport and business contexts. The ability to perform under pressure is part of both sport and business (Fletcher, 2010). This is due to the relationships exhaustion has with outcome expectations (Jones, 2002).

Organizations try to promote an atmosphere of fun much like that used in a sport context. This means that employees have a similar type of experience to people in the sport context (Fletcher, 2010). The life-work balance is also an issue both in sport and business due to the scheduling of events. For both sport and business there needs to be leadership about the strategic direction that is undertaken. This is important for professional sport coaches who have close relationships with staff and players as part of their leadership duties. Ievleva and Terry (2008) suggest that performance psychology is used in a similar manner in both sport and business. Sometimes the leadership is focused on group cohesion and the dynamics as part of being a member of a team (Weinberg and

McDermott, 2002). Other important leadership skills are being consistent, decisive, honest, organized and trustworthy (Fletcher, 2010).

Sport leadership

Leadership is important in the sport industry due to the different types of individual styles and behaviors that exist (Peachey *et al.*, 2015). Sport leadership involves the management of individual, dyadic and group processes (Peachey *et al.*, 2015). Leadership in sport involves both on- and off-the-field coordination due to the complex relationships that exist between athletes, coaches and organizations (Peachey *et al.*, 2015). Sport leadership can be viewed as a psychological and management domain due to the different functions governed by good leaders.

In both sport and business there are common characteristics associated with being a leader. Jones and Spooner (2006) found that the most important characteristic for coaches is establishing a trustworthy and mutually respectful environment. This helps develop a supportive environment that is flexible but adds value (Fletcher, 2010). Despite the similarities between sport and business there are some key differences as noted by Ievleva and Terry (2008). These include the quick feedback based on performance in sport compared to the longer time frame for communication in business. In sports, the roles are stated clearly whereas in business they can change based on environmental factors.

The ability to interact with others and be a good listener is a hallmark of a good leader (Fletcher, 2010). Other leadership styles in both the sport and business worlds are autocratic, democratic and situational (Weinberg and McDermott, 2002). These leadership styles emphasize interpersonal skills but require different personality characteristics. Leaders that are able to communicate will usually have a clear message that enables instructions about appropriate behavior. Some leaders do this by fostering cohesion amongst team members by sharing their vision about the future (Fletcher, 2010).

Executive leaders have been described as corporate athletes due to their ability to perform and train the same way sports people do (Loehr and Schwartz, 2001). Gordon (2007, p. 273) states that "sport is one of the most obvious areas that business organizations can consult in terms of teams." The creation of a positive psychological environment is important for teams to create, unite and perform (Jones, 2002). Veach and May (2005) in a study about effective coaches found that there is a linkage between teamwork of good teams and the business world. The mind/body connection has been studied extensively in sport psychology due to its role in enhancing performance (Murphy, 1996). This mind/body research within sport has been used as a theoretical framework to advance understandings within business (Gordon, 2007). Goal-orientated businesses and sport teams share similar goal-setting initiatives to promote long-term performance (Gordon, 2007). Table 6.1 depicts the differences between sport and business leaders.

80 Vanessa Ratten

TABLE 6.1 Sport and business leadership differences

Sport leaders	Business leaders
Pick best people for teams	Hire based on skills and needs
Engage in succession training and planning	Hire when required with little planning
Engage in team coaching	Leadership training but little coaching
Team-building programs across multiple functions	Team building usually via departments
Talent identification and development	Usually only for high management positions
Manage talented athletes and help them with personal issues on an ad hoc basis	Bureaucratic human resource management of people based on guidelines
Recognize sport talent might not be related to managerial ability	Managerial role should be based on multiple personality traits

Adapted from Gordon (2007)

Sport leaders and governance

Sport leaders are involved with the daily running or the governance of their organizations (Fletcher and Arnold, 2011). More sport organizations are utilizing board members to lead and provide direction. This has been described as shared sport leadership as coaches are also board members who combine to use their expertise (Ferkins *et al.*, 2005). There has been some research about ethical decision-making of leaders due to mega-sports events having bribery and corruption scandals. In a study about ethical decision-making of leaders in the Australian Football League, Sherry and Shilbury (2009) found that the sports context and historical development affected ethical conduct. In another study about national sports governing bodies, Jones and Spamer (2011) found that most leaders have a democratic leadership style. Tomlinson (2014) discusses how governance issues are especially linked to ethics issues and corruption scandals with the Fédération Internationale de Football Association.

Due to the impact sport has in society it is important that sports leaders act ethically (Sagas and Wigley, 2014). Ethical leadership has become a growing concern for athletes in intercollegiate sport due to the link between academic freedom and sports performance (Staurowsky, 2014). Sport managers need to lead with moral responsibility due to the role sport has in a community (DeSensi, 2014). This means that often sport leaders serve as the social gauge about what is appropriate moral behavior (Peachey *et al.*, 2015). The International Olympic Committee has shown leadership in sport by introducing ethical practices such as fair-play roles (Grosset and Attali, 2011).

Leaders are normally evaluated based on the cultural context of their organizations. Most traditional studies of leadership focused on the autocratic, democratic and laissez-faire styles of leadership (Hughes *et al.*, 2012). Autocratic leaders make decisions without regard to their subordinates in a more bureaucratic way.

Democratic leaders have a more inclusive policy in terms of decisions made. Laissez-faire leaders make decisions without thinking about others in a more ad hoc way.

Leaders usually have the following key behaviors: goal-driven, facilitative and supportive (Hughes *et al.*, 2012). These behaviors normally incorporate managers leading by taking a hard or soft approach (McGregor, 1960). A hard approach follows a more bureaucratic top-down approach to making decisions. This compares to the soft approach, which is participative and reflects the concerns of other people. The contingency model of leadership effectiveness focuses on the interaction between decisions and environmental factors (Chemers, 2000). This is helpful in understanding the interaction that takes place between leaders and followers (Peachey *et al.*, 2015). In most sport contexts the coach is the leader because of their position of authority (Sage, 1973). This authority position comes from the social norms in sport respecting the decisions made by a coach for the team's benefit.

Chelladurai (1996) proposed a leadership scale for sports that incorporated multidimensional aspects of sport leadership. This leadership scale suggested that sport leaders utilize decision-making in various contexts based on group properties (Peachey *et al.*, 2015). Sport leaders can be transactional or transformational depending on their approach. Transactional leaders incorporate a reward associated with the leader-follower relationship (Bass, 1985). This means that leaders can link certain behavior to needs such as sense of belonging and achievement. As followers perform a task leaders can recognize this behavior. The alternative to transactional leadership is transformational, which incorporates a sense of change in dynamics. There has been more emphasis on transformational leadership due to the increased focus on the need for self-fulfillment and achievement of ambitions (Bass and Avolio, 1997). This has led to transformational leadership being associated with both individual needs and group performance. In the sport context, Wallace and Weese (1995) examined non-profit sport organizations and found that highly transformational leaders focused on developing between teamwork and culture-building activities. Another study by Doherty and Danylchuk (1996) found that athletic administrators had more transformational rather than transactional approaches to leadership. Some sport leadership research has focused on the role of gender due to the different behavioral traits associated with male coaches (Lovett and Lowry, 1988). A study by Doherty (1997) found that female athletic administrators had more transformational skills.

Sport leadership behavior

Sport leaders exhibit different behaviors compared to individuals in other occupational settings. This is due to sport contexts being more focused on leisure activities, group behavior and performance statistics. Branch (1990) found that leaders of athletic organizations focused more on goals than developing good relationships. There are certain skills associated with being a leader in sport. A study by Quarterman (1998) found that athletics commissioners stated skills about management as being more important than leadership ability. There is a common perception that athletic directors need to be more goal-driven rather than people-orientated. This is due to leaders in sport considering themselves more orientated toward performance rather than human resource management (Peachey *et al.*, 2015). Sport leaders' views about leadership are shaped by their work experiences (Kihl *et al.*, 2010). This is due to sport leaders needing to manage people but also administrative functions such as finance requirements. Sport leaders often get credibility from having experience as a player or athlete (Swanson and Kent, 2014). Despite the credibility associated with prior sporting success there is an increasing emphasis on education for potential sports leaders. This demonstrates the importance of possessing recent knowledge about best practices to help sport leaders (Peachey *et al.*, 2016). Table 6.2 depicts how knowledge is changing based on sport coaching attitudes shifting from the traditional to modern view.

The changing perceptions around sport coaching attitudes are changing from the increased professionalism and development of elite sport systems. Elite sport systems are defined as "the infrastructure and practices used by a sport to identify, develop and prepare athletes for international sporting success" (Böhlke and Robinson, 2009, p. 67). Due to the increased professionalization of sport, elite sport systems have grown due to their organized approach leading to the production of international athletes. There is a stereotype of athletic administrators that leaders need to show masculine traits (Burton *et al.*, 2009). In sport, leaders are viewed as having managerial capabilities but are also life-skills coordinators (Peachey *et al.*, 2015). In addition, changing modern attitudes have meant that there has been a suggestion that there are gender biases towards males as sport leaders (Molina, 2013). Despite this bias there are more female sport leaders due to the changing societal attitudes about the role of gender in sport (Claringbould and Knoppers, 2012). Regardless of gender differences, subordinates prefer leaders to be transformational in approach (Welty *et al.*, 2012). Females are under-represented in sport leadership positions. Another more modern approach towards

TABLE 6.2 Sport coaching attitudes

Traditional view	*Modern view*
Authoritarian	Participative
Coach-centered	Athlete-centered
Controlling	Empowering
Ex-player	Professionally trained coach
Hard worker	Emotionally intelligent worker
Intuitive	Strategic
Problem-focused	Results-orientated

Adapted from Beswick, 2001, and Gordon, 2007

sports leadership has been the acknowledgement that ethnicity also has an impact on sport leaders. This is due to the suggestion that there are stereotypes of sport leaders based on both their gender and ethnicity (Peachey *et al.*, 2015). In a study about Dutch football clubs, Knoppers and Anthonissen (2001) found that gender and race were used to evaluate perceptions about leadership success. The common stereotypes of sports leaders having similar cultural backgrounds has been linked to institutional racism (Bradbury, 2013).

Sport marketing implications

Sport marketing professionals need to focus on leadership in their business practices. This is due to online relationships becoming more important with sport fans that are in a competitive global market. Sport marketers should be creative with website marketing to be more interactive (Brown, 2003). This will enable sports marketers to take advantage of the information consumers and other businesses are suggesting. As sport marketers it might be helpful to understand sport psychology as a way to engage with consumers. As trends towards sport are changing it might be helpful to take a more modernist view to sport leadership.

The intention of this chapter was to discuss the role of psychology in sports using coaching and leadership examples. The different ways sport and business apply leadership practices are important for both sport marketers and business professionals. The ideas presented in this chapter will generate more discussion around innovative leadership principles from sport business that will help increase long-term outcomes. This is helpful to encourage more debate about how sport psychology can be used in business and vice versa. Both sport and business leaders can learn from each other about the way psychology can be used to increase performance.

Future research suggestions

Further research about the sport industry's use of modern leadership and psychology is needed. There is a need to understand the role leadership and innovation have in sports organizations to determine how they affect performance. A study should be conducted on why leadership on and off the sports field leads to potentially better outcomes. More research should also be conducted on leadership from the perspective of sports consumers. For example, it would be interesting to see how sports consumers view leadership on field performances by athletes. This means that research must be conducted on new ways of approaching sport from a psychology perspective. The latest online and technology developments in sport lead to a number of research possibilities. These can include the trend towards new sports using innovative technologies.

The importance of facilitating innovative leadership in sport, specifically in the areas of sports psychology, cannot be underestimated. Many sport organizations lack an understanding of leadership practices that take an innovative perspective. The study of sports leadership, psychology and innovation in terms of their impact on the growth of sport business is a field of research that deserves greater attention. Recent research suggests that there is a positive relationship between effective leadership and sport business performance but more data is required on innovative practices. This chapter suggests that for many sport business managers, particularly those in professional sports, leadership can be improved by taking a more innovative approach. Future research needs to explore how innovation within sport leadership changes the dynamics of a business. As there are different types of leadership in sport from coaches to players to support staff there are a number of interesting research possibilities.

The most value for future research is likely to come from longitudinal analysis that combines both quantitative and qualitative data about sport leadership and innovation. Future researchers could focus both on the individual and firm level to understand innovative approaches to leadership in sport. There is also a need to translate academic research about sport leadership to practice. This means that future research suggestions from academics should be applied in practice to sport firms. This would also make a stronger link between research outcomes and sport policy. As more governments and institutions are using sport policy as a way to encourage better societal outcomes it is important that governments play an active role in future sport leadership and innovation research.

Conclusion

This chapter has called to attention the need for more research to focus on the intersection of innovation and leadership in sport management. Due to the competitive nature of the sport industry there is a need to integrate the sport leadership and innovation fields. I hope this chapter has synthesized the symbiotic relationship between sport leadership and innovation as there is a lack of research in this area. There are many questions to be addressed in terms of how innovation is integrated with sport leadership and psychology. This chapter has attempted to uncover the role of sport leadership innovation by highlighting the business management aspect. This chapter has offered an analysis of sport leadership innovation and psychology, which future research can build on. Major themes in sport business leadership and psychology were provided to stimulate further research.

References

Adcroft, A. & Teckman, J. (2009). 'Taking sport seriously'. *Management Decision*, *47*(1), 5–13.

Bass, B. M. (1985). *Leadership and performance beyond expectations*. New York, NY: Free Press.

Bass, B. M. & Avolio, B. J. (1997). *Full range leadership development: Manual for the Multifactor Leadership Questionnaire* (pp. 43–44). Palo Alto, CA: Mind Garden.

Beswick, B. (2001). *Focused for soccer: Develop a winning mental approach*. Champaign, IL: Human Kinetics.

Böhlke, N. & Robinson, L. (2009). 'Benchmarking of elite sport systems'. *Management decision*, 47(1), 67–84.

Bradbury, S. (2013). 'Institutional racism, whiteness and the under-representation of minorities in leadership positions in football in Europe'. *Soccer & Society*, 14, 296–314

Branch, D. (1990). 'Athletic director behavior as a predictor of intercollegiate athletic organizational effectiveness'. *Journal of Sport Management*, 4, 161–173.

Brown, M. (2003). 'An analysis of online marketing in the sport industry: User activity, communication objectives and perceived benefits'. *Sport Marketing Quarterly*, 12(1): 48–55.

Burton, L. J., Barr, C. A., Fink, J. S. & Bruening, J. E. (2009). ' "Think athletic director, think masculine?": Examination of the gender typing of managerial subroles within athletic administration positions'. *Sex Roles*, 61(5), 416–426.

Chalip. L. (1987). 'Multiple narratives, multiple hierarchies: Selective attention varied interpretations and the structure of the Olympic program', in S.P. Kang, J. MacAloon and R. DaMatta (eds.) *The Olympics and cultural exchange*, pp. 539–576, Seoul: Hanyang University Institute for Ethnological Studies.

Chalip, L. (1992). 'The construction and use of polysemic structures: Olympic lessons for sport marketing'. *Journal of Sport Management*, 6(1), 87–98.

Chelladurai, P. (1996). *Human Resource Management in Sport and Recreation*. New York, NY: Human Kinetics.

Chemers, M. M. (2000). 'Leadership research and theory: A functional integration'. *Group Dynamics*, 4(1), 27–43.

Claringbould, I. & Knoppers, A. (2012). 'Paradoxical practices of gender in sport-related organizations'. *Journal of Sport Management*, 26(1), 404–416.

DeSensi, J. T. (2014). 'Sport: an ethos based on values and servant leadership'. *Journal of Intercollegiate Sport*, 7(1), 58–63.

Doherty, A. J. (1997). 'The effect of leader characteristics on the perceived transformational/transactional leadership and impact of interuniversity athletic administrators'. *Journal of Sport Management*, 11, 275–285.

Doherty, A. J. & Danylchuk, K. E. (1996). 'Transformational and transactional leadership in interuniversity athletics management'. *Journal of Sport Management*, 10(1), 292–309.

Ferkins, L., Shilbury, D. & McDonald, G. (2005). 'The role of the board in building strategic capability: Towards an integrated model of sport governance'. *Sport Management Review*, 8(3), 195–225.

Fletcher, D. (2010). 'Applying sport psychology in business: A narrative commentary and bibliography'. *Journal of Sport Psychology in Action*, 1(1), 139–149.

Fletcher, D. & Arnold, R. (2011). 'A qualitative study of performance leadership and management in elite sport'. *Journal of Applied Sport Psychology*, 23(1), 223–242.

Foster, S. (2002). 'Enhancing peak potential in managers and leaders: Integrating knowledge and findings from sport psychology', in R. L. Lowman (ed.), *The California School of Organizational Studies handbook of organizational consulting psychology: A comprehensive guide to theory, skills and techniques*, pp. 212–231, San Francisco, CA: Jossey-Bass.

Gordon, S. (2007). 'Sport and business coaching: Perspective of a sport psychologist'. *Australian Psychologist*, 42(1), 271–282.

Grosset, Y. & Attali, M. (2011). 'The international institutionalization of sport ethics'. *Society*, 48(1), 517–525.

Hughes, R. L., Ginnett, R. C., & Curphy, G. J. (2012). *Leadership: Enhancing the lessons of experience* (7th ed.). New York, NY: McGraw-Hill.

Ievleva, L. & Terry, P. C. (2008). 'Applying sport psychology to business'. *International Coaching Psychology Review*, 3(1), 8–18.

Jones, G. (2002). 'Performance excellence: A personal perspective on the link between sport and business'. *Journal of Applied Sport Psychology, 14*(1), 268–281.

Jones, G. & Spooner, K. (2006). 'Coaching high achievers'. *Consulting Psychology Journal: Practice and Research, 58*(1), 40–50.

Jones, G. & Spamer, M. (2011). 'A leadership styles competency framework for governing bodies in sport'. *African Journal for Physical, Health Education, Recreation & Dance, 17*(2).

Kihl, L. A., Leberman, S. & Schull, V. (2010). 'Stakeholder constructions of leadership in intercollegiate athletics'. *European Sport Management Quarterly, 10*(2), 241–275.

Knoppers, A. & Anthonissen, A. (2001). 'Meanings given to performance in Dutch sport organizations: Gender and racial/ethnic subtexts'. *Sociology of Sport Journal, 18*(1), 302–316.

Lloyd, P. J. & Foster, S. L. (2006). 'Creating healthy, high-performance workplaces: Strategies from health and sports psychology'. *Consulting Psychology Journal: Practice and Research, 58*(1), 23–39.

Loehr, J. & Schwartz, T. (2001). 'The making of a corporate athlete'. *Harvard Business Review, 79*(1), 120–129.

Lovett, J. D. & Lowry, C. (1988). 'Gender representation in the NCAA and NAIA'. *Journal of Applied Research in Coaching and Athletics, 4*, 1–16.

McGregor, D. (1960). *The human side of enterprise.* New York, NY: McGraw-Hill.

McNutt, R. & Wright, P. C. (1995). 'Coaching your employees: Applying sports analogies to business'. *Executive Development, 8*(1), 27–32.

Molina, A. (2013). 'Women in leadership at the interscholastic level'. *Interscholastic Athletic Administration, 39*(4), 22–25.

Mullin, B. (1983). *Sport marketing, promotion and public relations.* Amherst, MA: National Sport Management

Murphy, S. (1996). *The achievement zone.* New York: Putnam.

Peachey, J. W., Zhou, Y., Damon, Z. J. & Burton, L. J. (2016). 'Forty years of leadership research in sport management: A review, synthesis and conceptual framework', *Journal of Sport Management, 29*(1), 570–587.

Quarterman, J. (1998). 'An assessment of the perception of management and leadership skills by intercollegiate athletic conference commissioners'. *Journal of Sport Management, 12*(2), 146–164.

Sagas, M. & Wigley, B. J. (2014). 'Gray area ethical leadership in the NCAA: The ethics of doing the wrong things right'. *Journal of Intercollegiate Sport, 7*(1), 40–57.

Sage, G. H. (1973). 'The coach as management: Organizational leadership in American sport'. *Quest, 19*, 35–40.

Shani, D. (1997). 'A framework for implementing relationship marketing in the sport industry'. *Sport Marketing Quarterly, 6*(1), 9–16.

Sherry, E. & Shilbury, D. (2009). 'Board directors and conflict of interest: A study of a sport league'. *European Sport Management Quarterly, 9*(1), 47–62.

Sleight, S. (1989). *Sponsorship: What is it and how to use it.* London: McGraw-Hill

Sloan, L. R. (1989). 'The motives of sports fans', in J. H. Goldstein (ed.), *Sports, games and play: Social and psychological viewpoints*, 2nd ed., pp. 175–240, Hillsdale, N.J.: Lawrence Erlbaum.

Smith, G. J. (1988). 'The noble sports fan'. *Journal of Sport & Social Issues, 12*(1), 54–65.

Staurowsky, E. (2014). 'College athletes' rights in the age of the super conference: The case of the All Players United Campaign'. *Journal of Intercollegiate Sport, 7*(1), 11–34.

Swanson, S. & Kent, A. (2014). 'The complexity of leading in sport: Examining the role of domain expertise in assessing leader credibility and prototypicality'. *Journal of Sport Management, 28*(1), 81–93.

Tomlinson, A. (2014). 'The supreme leader sails on: Leadership, ethics and governance in FIFA'. *Sport in Society*, *17*(9), 1155–1169.

Veach, T. L. & May, J. R. (2005). 'Teamwork: For the good of the whole', in S. Murphy, *The sport psych handbook*, pp. 171–189, Champaign, IL: Human Kinetics.

Yiannakis, A. (1989). 'Some contributions of sport sociology to the marketing of sport and leisure organizations'. *Journal of Sport Management*, *3*(1), 103–115.

Wallace, M. & Weese, W. J. (1995). 'Leadership, organizational culture, and job satisfaction in Canadian CA organizations'. *Journal of Sport Management*, *9*, 182–193.

Wann, D. L., Grieve, F. G., Zapalac, R. K. & Pease, D. G. (2008). 'Motivational profiles of sport fans of different sports'. *Sport Marketing Quarterly*, *17*(1), 6–19.

Weinberg, R. & McDermott, M. (2002). 'A comparative analysis of sport and business organizations: Factors perceived critical for organizational success'. *Journal of Applied Sport Psychology*, *14*(1), 282–298.

Welty Peachey, J., & Burton, L. J. (2012). 'Transactional or transformational leaders in intercollegiate athletics? Examining the influence of leader gender and subordinate gender on evaluation of leaders during organizational culture change'. *International Journal of Sport Management*, *13*, 115–142.

7

A BLUE OCEAN STRATEGY IN A SPORT CONTEXT

A systematisation of literature

Elsa Regina M. Vieira and João J. Ferreira

Introduction

Kim and Mauborgne (2005b) metaphorically refer to the market as made up of two oceans, one red and one blue. The red ocean represents all the industries today in existence. The blue ocean reflects all the industries that do not yet exist and thus constitute an unexplored market where demand may be created and where there are opportunities for high levels of growth and profitability. Kim and Mauborgne (2005a) entitle their approach the blue ocean strategy.

Despite the enormous success of their book *Blue Ocean Strategy*, translated into 43 languages and with sales amounting to around 3.5 million copies, the applied research remains only very residual (Parvinen, Aspara, Hietanen and Kajalo, 2011) and that which does exist primarily makes recourse to the case study methodology (Kim, Yang and Kim, 2008; Palacios, Rodriguez, Rodriguez and Escoto, 2010; Themaat, Schutte, Lutters and Kennon, 2013; Yang and Yang, 2011). Given this situation, there is a corresponding shortcoming in the definition of a methodology for implementing the blue ocean strategy. The goal of this chapter involves setting out a systematisation of the literature on the blue ocean strategic theme, in particular on the sports sector, before then presenting a conceptual model capable of clarifying and systematising the application of this concept and thereby aiding the work of fitness/health club managers seeking to establish blue oceans.

The growth of the fitness market that integrates fitness and health clubs has proven a constant in recent years (IHRSA, 2013) and the applied research, as Garcia-Fernandez, Bernal-Garcia, Fernandez-Gavira and Velez-Colon (2014) state, has approached various areas of study, in particular: quality, satisfaction and loyalty (Afthinos, Theodorakis and Nassis, 2005; Bodet, 2009; Cheng, Hsu and Huang, 2012; Fernandéz, Carrión and Ruís, 2012; Soita, 2012), cultural organisation (MacIntosh and Doherty, 2007; MacIntosh and Walker, 2012; MacIntosh and Doherty, 2010), innovation (Yuan, Liu, Kao and Shu, 2009; Zolfagharian and

Paswan, 2008), sports facilities (Arbour-Nicitopoulos and Ginis, 2011), human resources (Koustelios, 2003; Maconachie and Sappey, 2013; Moodley and Coopoo, 2006), segmentation (Mischler, Bauger, Pichot and Wipf, 2009; Teixeira and Correia, 2009; Woolf, 2008), sociological facets (Harris and Marandi, 2002; Howell and Ingham, 2001) and others (Carvalho, Serrasqueiro and Nunes, 2013; Parrot, 1996).

However, the issues surrounding the strategic orientation of the fitness and health club sector has received little attention despite its clear relevance. According to the European report by the IHRSA (2013), in recent years the sector has experienced a difficult period in Portugal due to economic recession and the hiking of VAT from 6 per cent to 23 per cent. The strategy followed by the majority of fitness/health clubs involved adopting the same business model, with the same range of products/services, thus, the same value proposal and thereby rendering it more difficult to persuade and attract new members into facilities and with this positioning jeopardising around 70 per cent of the sector (IHRSA, 2013). However, as the IHRSA (2013) states, the sector has seen the launch of smaller-scale studios and low-cost concepts as solutions and hence opportunities would seem to exist even while needing to grasp both just what service needs delivering and how to provide value to the client. Given this gap in the literature, this study seeks to put forward a proposed conceptual model for the fitness and health club sector based upon the blue ocean strategic approach.

The chapter structure contains four sections: 1) this current section setting out an introduction to the study and establishing its pertinence and respective contribution; 2) the literature review identifying the main studies in the literature and what they have contributed to both the theme and its study; 3) presenting a conceptual model proposal for fitness and health clubs in Portugal; 4) and, finally, putting forward the conclusions and future lines of research.

Literature review

The blue ocean strategic concept

Kim and Mauborgne (2005b) state that those who strive to create blue oceans simultaneously seek out differentiation and low cost within the prevailing concept of innovating, with value that maximises the value for the consumer based on utility and the price that the companies charge their clients, whilst boosting the value returned to the company by price and cost structures.

Despite the relevance of the blue ocean strategy, the research resulting still remains only residual, Parvinen *et al.* (2011) refer to how, beyond the articles by Kim and Mauborgne, many of the articles existing are still under production, specifically: Pitta (2009), Lasen and Ward (2009) and Kim *et al.* (2008). Effectively, the research carried out as of June 2015 in the web of science core collection according to the topic "blue ocean strateg★", contained only 24 results of which six are conceptual studies (see Table 7.1), 16 are empirical studies (see Table 7.2) and two were not eligible for consideration given that they did not approach but rather only referred to the blue ocean strategy.

TABLE 7.1 Systematising the conceptual studies on the blue ocean strategy

Study	Objective	Conclusions
Kim and Mauborgne (2004)	Presenting the blue ocean strategic concept and defining its main characteristics.	The business world contains two environments denominated by the red ocean and the blue ocean. The red ocean represents all the existing industries in which competition is fierce whilst the blue ocean consists of those industries that do not yet exist. The authors carried out a study of 108 start-up companies beginning their activities and verified how the vast majority (86 per cent) still remain businesses located in the red ocean, however, they represent only 62 per cent of turnover and 39 per cent of the profits. The remaining 14 per cent are blue ocean businesses generating 38 per cent of total revenues and 61 per cent of overall profits. The authors conclude that the creation of blue oceans does not make them a synonym for technological innovation and these oceans may emerge out of the company's core business. Furthermore, the appropriate unit of analysis susceptible to explaining the creation of blue oceans and the high and sustained performance is the strategic dimension and neither the firm nor the industry. The blue ocean strategy challenges the dogma surrounding the trade-off between value and cost and simultaneously attempts to return differentiation and low cost. This thus reduces costs and simultaneously boosts the value to the purchasers and hence proves mutually beneficial to the company and its clients. The rejection of the trade-off between differentiation and low cost proves fundamental to changing strategic thought, hence, moving on from a structuralist vision to a reconstructionist perspective. The blue ocean strategy contains barriers to imitation and hence may survive for 10 to 15 years without confronting any major challenges even while blue and red ocean businesses will always coexist.

Kim and Mauborgne (2005a)	Presenting the blue ocean strategic concept; understanding the impact of the creation of blue oceans and the need for them; conveying the analytical tools for implementing a blue ocean strategy: the strategic framework, the four fields of action (the elimination, reduction, elevation and creation analytical grid) and finally tracing the characteristics of a good strategy.	Throughout the years, the structuralist vision or the determinism of the surrounding environment resulted in strategic thinking based on competition and that perceived as the market structure, as it then existed, and in which companies take up defensive positions in regards to the competition and attempt to secure competitive advantages.

Throughout the years, the structuralist vision or the determinism of the surrounding environment resulted in strategic thinking based on competition and that perceived as the market structure, as it then existed, and in which companies take up defensive positions in regards to the competition and attempt to secure competitive advantages.

Beyond the competitive strategy, there is scope for carving out a new space in the market in which competition proves irrelevant, the so-called blue ocean. Their results from quantifying the impact of the creation of blue oceans were the following: only 14 per cent of new businesses displayed characteristics in keeping with the blue ocean concept but were responsible for 38 per of turnover and 61 per cent of total profits.

Supply is outstripping demand and the standardisation of products only fosters a price war eating away at margins. Given such facts, management inherently has to pay greater attention to creating blue oceans.

The core tools required for designing a blue ocean strategy are: the strategic framework, the four fields of action and the analysis grid for elimination, reduction, elevation and creation. The definition of these four fields of action enables the reconstruction of those features valued by the acquirer within the scope of a new value curve design.

Finally, the article refers to the characteristics of a good strategy: focus, divergence and an appealing slogan.

(Continued)

TABLE 7.1 (*Continued*)

Study	Objective	Conclusions
Kim and Mauborgne (2009)	There are two distinctive visions on industrial structures interrelated with strategic actions and approaches. The structuralist vision takes the industrial organisation as its analytical model within the structure-behaviour-performance paradigm. The reconstructionist vision of strategy conveys the ways knowledge may serve in creative processes generating growth from within companies. The objectives of this article include: what is the appropriate strategic vision for each organisation? What are the essential propositions and how do these align within the framework of each strategic vision for attaining high and sustainable performance levels?	Corporate strategy development almost always begins with analysis of the conditions of the industry or environments in which the firms operate. The underlying logic here is that the strategic options of any company are limited by its environment – the structuralist vision. The blue ocean strategic framework may help in companies systematically reconstructing their industries and inverting the structure-strategy sequence in their own favour. The blue ocean strategy traces its roots to the emerging economy school, what gets termed endogenous growth with its central paradigm postulating that the ideas and actions of individual players may mould the economic and industrial panorama – a reconstructionist vision. In order to choose the appropriate strategic vision/theory, three factors require consideration: the structural conditions in which the organisations operate, their resources and capacities and the strategic mind-set. The success depends on the development and alignment of three propositions: value, profit and persons. The structuralist vision provides a choice between a strategy of differentiation and low cost across the three propositions. In the reconstructionist vision, the high performance potential stems from the three propositions combining both differentiation and low cost.
Ahlstrom, Lamond and Ding (2009)	Military history has provided a number of valuable metaphors to the management field such as positioning and the blue ocean strategy, among others. This article thus examines two episodes from twentieth-century military history taken from the First World War and the inter-war period.	Military history provides core features to strategic thinking, for example, the similarity between the blue ocean strategic concept and "island hopping" or "Leapfrogging", the military strategy employed by the Allies in the Pacific War against Japan during World War Two. The idea was to ignore the highly fortified Japanese positions and concentrate limited resources on taking strategically important islands that were nevertheless not as well defended.

Kuratko and Audretsch (2009)	The objective is to explore the various perspectives on strategic entrepreneurship. Strategic entrepreneurship proves the new term emerging in literature to represent the intersection between strategy and entrepreneurship. However, the exact nature of this concept remains undefined. In order to survey the different perspectives that this term conveys, this article sets out a general vision of the specific domains making up this concept.	All the different forms of strategic entrepreneurship involve exposure to innovations with the objective of obtaining competitive advantage. Innovation with value, which is a key concept to the blue ocean strategy, emerges here bound up with strategic renewal that seeks to redefine the relationship with the market or industry. Another concept associated with the blue ocean strategy stems from the redefinition of the domain that means striving to proactively establish a new market that others have not yet recognised.
Kim and Mauborgne (2014)	Applying the blue ocean strategic concept to leadership in order to boost employee productivity.	The main differences between conventional and blue ocean leadership are: a) focusing on the acts and activities that leaders need to deploy to stimulate motivation and achieve results, and not the personal profiles leaders need to display; b) always remaining attentive to market realities; c) distributing leadership acrosss all levels of management. The authors furthermore identify four steps to implementing blue ocean leadership: 1) observing the actual current state of their own leadership; 2) developing alternative leadership profiles and applying the elimination, reduction, elevation and creation grid to the acts and activities in which leaders invest their time and knowledge; 3) selecting the future leadership profiles; 4) institutionalising new leadership practices. Aspects for consideration in the implementation of these four steps: the senior executives lead the process; people being willing to define the actions and activities of their leaders; all levels participate in the end decision and, finally, evaluating the progress made in altering leadership. In summary, the major benefit of this integral process is trust and, consequently, spontaneous cooperation is an essential factor in the relationship between the leader and those led.

TABLE 7.2 Systematising the empirical studies on the blue ocean strategy

Study	Objective	Methodology	Conclusions
Kim *et al.* (2008)	Analysing how the company CJ-GLS managed to obtain a distinctive competitive advantage through innovative information technology that resulted in the creation of an uncontested niche in the electronic logistics market. One notable fact stems from how rapid growth did not derive from the attraction of clients from market competitors but rather from implementing a blue ocean strategy (3PL market). Hence, the objective of this study involved presenting the analytical grid of the four actions defined by the blue ocean strategy: eliminating, elevating, reducing and creating in addition to understanding how the utilisation of advanced communications and information technologies in the logistics sector drove the attainment of competitive advantage.	A case study applied to the South Korean firm CJ-GLS that developed an electronic logistics business model. The case study incorporated interviews with the CEO, the CIO, the head of logistics research, the manager responsible for the information strategy and various employees between July and September 2005.	In accordance with the blue ocean strategy, this identified the factors that the company managed to eliminate, elevate, reduce and create to attain this unexplored market. This features a comparison between the business model implemented by CJ-GLS and the remainder of companies following a red ocean strategy across the following facets: demand, competition, the trade-off between value and cost, and system alignment. This furthermore identified the factors of success and the problems implemented in the blue ocean strategy. These problems stemmed from the organisational and technological perspectives. Following an examination of the feasible and/or alternative solutions, the information strategy team held various strategic seminars to establish an efficient means of developing responses to these problems. The factors of success identified in the implementation of the blue ocean strategy are the following: a highly motivated information system team, strong leadership from senior management and an openness to innovation.

Druehl and Schmidt (2008)	Identifying the scenario of a company launching a new product and thus in this process opening up a new market and invading an existing market through the replacement of the former product by the new and low-end clients by high-end clients. Understanding that the "will to canibalise" represents a core factor both in company growth and in following any blue ocean strategy.	A case study – adopting the mobile phone industry to exemplify the entrance of a new product into a non-existing market.	The low-end invasion strategy of independent markets represents a significant extension of the invasion framework. This latter framework provides companies with an insightful means of comparing alternatives to introducing new products.
Krannich (2008)	Given the extent of organisational inertia in the field of rural sociology and in the Rural Sociology Society, this article held the objective of identifying the internal and external factors driving this situation. Based on the blue ocean strategic concept, this article discusses the actions needed to encounter intervention opportunities within the scope of rural sociology.	Case study applied to the scientific field of rural sociology and the Rural Sociology Society.	The authors identify the external and internal factors driving the current situations in the scientific domain of rural sociology and the respective society. In terms of the external factors referenced: the ageing and now reduced number of teaching staff at US universities, cutting the funding and financing available to research, the gradual disappearance of departments bearing the rural sociology name and mission, increased competition between the professional organisations representing the social science field and the transformation of the aforementioned rural societies in the US, which resulted from the merger into other sociological fields and content. As regards the internal factors referenced: the excessive organisational perspective on an applied orientation to rural society even while

(Continued)

TABLE 7.2 *(Continued)*

Study	Objective	Methodology	Conclusions
			the Society never managed to attain a large number of members from the professional field, a certain *keep to the borders* behaviour that deterred the interest and participation of some social scientists, the lack of any interconnection between the Society and the Association of American Sociology and some organisational inertia. Given these factors, the Rural Sociology Society operates in a red ocean in competition with other professional associations. In addition to ensuring its own survival in this red ocean, efforts should also focus on seeking a blue ocean. Hence, the society should also place greater emphasis on inter-disciplinarity and even trans-disciplinarity in teaching and research, both in higher education and in obtaining financing, and expanding the society beyond the scope of its research and reaching out to obtain more members, to be more inclusive and more relevant as regards its guidelines and policies for consolidated practices and establishing stronger relationships with professionals outside of the academic world and, finally, contributing towards understanding and helping resolve the main challenges confronting rural communities and persons through high-impact initiatives.

Perfetto and Woodside (2009)

The study seeks to grasp segmentation strategies for clients in accordance with the theory on extreme consumer behaviours (a few consumers are responsible for a significant proportion of consumption). Were it feasible to better understand this dimension, it might also prove possible to identify and explore blue ocean opportunities for converting non-clients into new clients and compulsive purchasers into non-purchasers. The study adopts the case of those attending casinos.

The data analysed in this study came from the DDB Needham Life Style Survey. This questionnaire approaches the demographic profile, the personality characteristics, the purchasing habits, political beliefs, opinions on current affairs and the general satisfaction with life and contains a question asking the number of times the respondent gambled in a casino in the previous year. The data applied in this study covers the years from 1993 to 1998. This study applies tree analysis and cross-classification analysis with variable stacking. A total of 20,658 research respondents were analysed over the aforementioned period.

The main conclusions are: 66 per cent belong to the non-gambling group. As regards the earnings variable, 45 per cent of non-players report low or moderate incomes. Of the most frequent gamblers, the majority have low or moderate incomes. The study also concluded that frequent casino goers (2 per cent) do exist and are responsible for almost 25 per cent of turnover. Tree analysis and cross-referenced classification analysis prove useful in showing how these players differ significantly in terms of their demographic configurations. These demographic differences result in paradoxal consumption habits.

Understanding these differences between clients and non-clients may assist in companies identifying and exploring blue ocean opportunities and informing both the industry and the government and boosting the efforts of state organisations in drafting social reform programs effectively able to attempt to control gambling-related dependence.

(Continued)

TABLE 7.2 (*Continued*)

Study	Objective	Methodology	Conclusions
Palacios et al. (2010)	The objective involves applying the blue ocean strategy methodology to the Mexican beef industry. Hence, this sought to analyse the innovation with value strategies that might enable a competitive positioning of the Mexican meat producers as global market leaders.	The methodology applied was the case study of 10 market-leading Mexican meat producers. The information came from government publications, producer associations, interviews and on-site analysis of the companies. From the information obtained, a strategic framework was set down.	In order to construct the strategic framework, this required the identification of the factors on which the companies competed. Each factor was awarded a ranking in accordance with the level of compliance. The conclusions pointed to the importance of three factors: meat quality, product presentation and market diversification. The strategic maps for the meat industry show how companies follow similar strategies although with different levels of development. The areas in which the industry invests most are: factors influencing beef quality, supply agreements with cattle breeders, product presentation, either frozen or vacuum-packed to guarantee quality and food safety, and market diversification, demonstrating consolidation in the national market, without overlooking local and regional markets and taking exports into account. Establishing policies and programs is of importance to the meat industry.

| Parvinen *et al.* (2011) | The objective involved researching the role of new mechanisms for the creation of value by the sales strategy of a company applying the creation of value and strategic marketing as the theoretical approaches. This study explores the foundations of the blue ocean strategy and categorises the ways in which this reflects on the sales-related management activities. The interconnection with performance and the influence of the surrounding environment also come in for analysis. | Data collection took place through a questionnaire sent out by e-mail to CEOs, sales and marketing directors at approximately 8,000 companies from a series of different industries in Finland and gaining a response rate of 7 per cent. Subsequently, this sample was narrowed down by excluding companies with turnover of less than €20 million to focus on companies with sufficient scale and articulated sales management processes – resulting in 168 companies. In keeping with the blue ocean strategy literature, this presented 13 dimensions to the sales management perspective. The variables applied to measure performance were: sales growth rate in comparison with the previous year and the percentage growth in operational results. The statistical methods applied were: core component analysis and cluster analysis. | Components analysis returned three factors / strategies emphasising the net construction of value, industrial transformation and commercialisation. Cluster analysis resulted in four groups relating to the blue ocean strategy approach: Group 1. *Awareness-building* (expressing the strategic intention of transforming the logic of the industry even without any activities in harmony or in relation to the client); Group 2. *Customer-specific solution orientation* (active in the customer interface, seeking BOS together with customers only when business opportunities arise); Group 3. *Enforcement-orientation* (sales activities applying a blue ocean strategy but with little or no strategic planning); Group 4. *Non-employment* (not applying the blue ocean strategy parameters in relation either to the client or to strategic planning or to sales activities). The study confirmed the benefits of implementing a blue ocean strategy for sales management. The conclusions point to the different blue ocean strategy approaches requiring selection in accordance with the context. Group 3, *Enforcement-orientation*, returns higher performance and group 4, *Non-employment*, presents surprisingly notable differentials in performance within different combinations of contexts. |

(Continued)

TABLE 7.2 *(Continued)*

Study	Objective	Methodology	Conclusions
Yang and Yang (2011)	The objective here is to expand the understanding of the "value to the client" categories. Hence, this sought to analyse and integrate the refined Kano model into the blue ocean strategy. The different "value to the client" categories contained in this approach include: client purchases, the retention of clients and margins. Thus, this study presents an integrated approach to the "creation of value" model and explains how this model may be used to select practical actions appropriate to boosting value to the client.	The methodology deployed a case study applied to an air conditioner manufacturer. The first phase consisted of interviews with 20 clients with this stage requesting these core clients suggest quality attributes. Subsequently, a total of 35 attributes were identified and presented to two internal discussion panels that then defined the 17 critical quality attributes, which were then incorporated into the questionnaire. Two types of questionnaire were designed, one with the categorisation of the quality attributes in accordance with the Kano model and the other with the level of importance attributed to the factors of quality. The questionnaires were then sent out to 1,400 random clients and 150 valid questionnaires were received.	This study found that the product may provide four types of value to the client: 1) economic value; 2) financial value; 3) psychological value and 4) creative value. The model applied conjugates the refined Kano model and the blue ocean strategy-defining attributes by the level of attention paid, by added value, for being critical, necessary, for their potential, as well as attributes to eliminate whether for monetary reasons or for resulting in client dissatisfaction. Finally, the study also considered those attributes requiring improvement or for integrating resources crucial to new products and the scope for product innovation. Subsequently, these attributes were grouped in accordance with the four blue ocean strategy fields of action.

| Wubben, Dusseldorf and Batterink (2012) | The objective is to discover an unexplored space within the European fruit and vegetable sector and evaluate the ex ante applicability of the Kim and Mauborgne blue ocean strategy. | Two research phases: First phase – six case studies, which involved in-depth interviews with both qualitative and quantitative questions. The interviewees were senior executives (two CEOs, two Board of Directors members, one President and one external strategic management professor). Second phase – applying a structured questionnaire featuring 25 questions with answers on a seven-point Likert scale and sent out to 299 companies. Response rate: 8 per cent. | The first phase returned the current strategic framework of the sector and rebuilt the market boundaries in accordance with the six strategic options contained within the blue ocean strategy. The results then confirmed that it is possible to ex ante identify an unexplored market niche that, in the case of the fruit and vegetable sector, established a combination of fruit "sweeties" attributed to fresh fruit – "Youngfruit" targeting children and adolescents. |

(*Continued*)

TABLE 7.2 (*Continued*)

Study	Objective	Methodology	Conclusions
Lindic, Bavdaz and Kovacic (2012)	Economic policies sometimes target the rapid growth of a particular sector of activity even though this objective is not always obtained. The objective of this article incorporates understanding the shortcomings to economic policies and proposing a new approach to the design of economic high-growth policies that derive directly from the business perspective. This approach studies the applicability of a business strategy – the blue ocean strategy for drafting the policies able to establish the conditions for high growth.	The empirical study stems from two case studies: companies denominated Slovenian "gazelles" (due to high growth rates) and amazon.com. As regards the Slovenian gazelles, the study spanned a questionnaire applied to 512 companies and a database. In the case of amazon.com, the study drew from various sources of information: annual business reports and accounts, press statements, blogs, audio and video recordings, the academic and management literature that features a critical vision of this company. The indicators applied for growth were: added net value per employee, sales per employee and EBIT per employee and number of patents.	The authors identify four propositions important to economic policies duly supporting high growth. Proposition 1: creating a new market niche may lead to greater growth. Proposition 2 states that blue oceans may be found in every industry and are not limited to any specific sector. Proposition 3 conveys how companies may attain high growth through pioneering value and not only through pioneering technology. Proposition 4 details how both large and small companies may attain growth through creating new spaces in the market. Results stemming from these propositions: those companies that create blue oceans grow faster and received only partial support. The results show how rapid growth is neither generated nor guaranteed by specific industries and finally, that every company, and not only small and medium-sized companies, may return rapid growth rates. The results reveal a lag between the macro level of economic policies designed to obtain high growth and the micro level of business growth. The conclusions call for a change in the focus of economic policies for specific companies, intra-industry measures for cooperation, collaboration between companies of different scales, innovation in value and the creation of uncontested markets.

Yang (2012a) | This study strove to identify the characteristics of the blue ocean strategy through the structure of its four fields of action at various hotels in Taiwan belonging to international chains.

The methodology applied was the semi-structured interview and applied to 15 hotels in Taiwan belonging to international chains. Thirty-two senior managers and executives answered the questionnaire. Data collection took place over four phases: 1) design of the interview script; 2) pre-empted delivery of the interview script to respondents; 3) application and collection of data on the blue ocean strategy; and 4) recourse to NVivo 7 software for textual coding of the interview contents.

The questions posed drew on the structure of the four fields of action in accordance with the blue ocean strategy and are as follows: 1) Which factors should the hotel industry eliminate? 2) Which factors should the industry reduce?

The results reflect the factors requiring elimination, reduction, creation and elevating by the hotel sector in Taiwan. The study findings convey how the greater the level of brand expansion, the greater their capacity to create new value for the client. Furthermore, the creation (or addition) of value to hotel services would boost sales and strengthen market share. This study concludes that all of the relevant prices, products and marketing strategies implemented by the hotels studied did emphasise key blue ocean concepts, such as innovating with value.

This qualitative study fills a gap between the theory and the practice of implementing a blue ocean strategy through the application of CRM and network theories.

The innovation component should include restructuring the market segmentation, rebranding and reformulating the pricing strategy to capture new demand.

(Continued)

TABLE 7.2 (*Continued*)

Study	Objective	Methodology	Conclusions
		3) Which factors should the industry elevate? 4) Which factors has the industry never supplied and should be supplying?	
Yang (2012b)	The main objective of this study incorporated analysis from the perspective of organisational change theory applied to intrepret the alteration in ownership of a local hotel chain in Taiwan and which subsequently underwent internal changes in terms of both corporate strategy and organisational configurations. The purposes of this study were: 1) in what way does a new CEO foster the development of change in an organisational climate and its strategic configuration; 2) understanding how the new CEO and General Director take on their leadership roles; 3) understanding how the new CEO and General Director hold the capacity for individual learning in order to adapt to the changes proposed; and 4) understanding how the new CEO and General Director generate value for the client and develop new services.	This study applied a qualitative methodology that involved the collection of data from participant observation in the field of study and subsequent in-depth interviews processed through applying the QSR NVivo software program.	This study suggested that, in the change assimilation phase: 1) the CEO should adopt a democratic approach rather than an authoritarian stance; 2) sub-cultures and conflicts may be avoided by organisational socialisation and treating opportunities equally; and 3) within the scope of organisational objectives for obtaining a blue ocean, defining two fields – reprofiling the hotel brand and fostering unique value through the provision of personalised services to clients, such as: catering for different target market segments, building historical interior designs, installations and equipment, a hotel of courtesy, an excursion through the hotel's antique collection. Finally, this concluded that the blue ocean strategic concept might be implemented within the scope of organisational change.

| Yang (2013) | This study approached new methodologies to grasp latent client needs. | The methodology incorporated an applied case study of a household appliance manufacturer, with a particular focus on the domestic air conditioner market. In order to ascertain the quality attributes, questionnaires were answered by 20 clients alongside two discussion panels with front-office members of staff. | The study developed and presented an integrated model for: 1) verifying the opportunities present for companies to improve their compliance with critical attributes with which their clients are either dissatisfied or poorly satisfied and 2) identifying and approaching the problems experienced by clients in the utilisation of products / services. |
| | The study then incorporates some of these methodologies, in particular: the refined Kano model and the four strategic actions underlying the blue ocean strategy. Applying this analytical model, companies may identify the latent needs and expectations of their clients. | The project designed four types of questionnaires: 1) the desired levels of the quality attributes; 2) the importance of quality attributes; 3) the levels of satisfaction with the quality attributes; and 4) the categorisation of attributes. These questionnaires were sent out to 1,400 clients randomly selected with 150 answers received. | Within the scope of the blue ocean strategy, this featured those attributes deemed worthy of elevating, creating, reducing and eliminating in accordance with their clients. |

(Continued)

TABLE 7.2 (*Continued*)

Study	Objective	Methodology	Conclusions
Themaat *et al.* (2013)	This article presents a framework for the development and design of a business model for the lower-class population in South Africa through utilisation of the blue ocean strategy.	Case study – the Capitec Bank considered a target market deemed irrelevant by other banks, thus identifying a blue ocean. According to the blue ocean strategy methodology, this applied the elimination, elevation, reduction and creation grid. This also involved interviews with specialists to validate the business model.	The company's returning successs in the low client earnings market segment took into account four characteristics: acceptability (utility), availability, awareness (products designed for this client type) and pricing accessibility. This study combines the different components of the business model and the strategic sequence to validate the business concept and minimise risk. Correspondingly, utility gets interrelated with the value proposal, the distribution channels and the client relationships whilst cost interacts with the key resources, activities and partners and the cost structure. Furthermore, the price component is itself a factor in the sequence and with the client component not approached by the strategic sequence. The business model for this population requires testing across two levels: covering the four core characteristics and testing the strategic sequence. The route begins by understanding the fundamental needs and demands of this segment of purchasers. The value proposition, the channels and the client interface represent the utility and form the window of opportunity. The mission for the components to this window of opportunity involve guaranteeing that the client receives utility. The price should be accessible to consumers but also enabling the companies to generate the margin and thus costs need to be low.

The infrastructural factors are the resources, activities and partners and correspond to the strategic sequence applied to the costs that simultaneously need to be lower whilst jeopardising neither the quality nor the value proposal.

In summary: the literature conveys how the low income segment may open up valuable opportunities.

The interviews highlight an important point, referred to by a majority of respondents, a company should ideally hold a position in a particular market and only afterwards approach the low-earnings segment.

Tu, Shih, Hsu and Lin (2014)	The objective is to explore the targets and scope of opportunity in the consumer market made up of the poorest socio-economic group (BOP hereafter) in Taiwan. The research adopts the concept of sustainability to discuss the characteristics of the lifestyle and the ongoing consumption of the BOP group, and establishes a norm for the strategic design of sustainable products.	The research applied both a questionnaire and interviews with specialists. The questionnaire explored to what extent sustainable product projects are accepted by people at the foot of the Taiwanese social pyramid as well as the relevant experiences, patterns of consumption and the needs of the group under study. The interviews surveyed the opinions of experts on sustainable product design.	The BOP group proves the source of strategic design innovation. The innovative design model integrates into sustainable design to balance economic development and environmental protection. The BOP group consumption characteristics and habits are exclusive and hence the needs of consumers require orientation and integrating into sustainable project design. High quality and price are the fundamental principles to developing business opportunities targeting this group and in this way cutting production costs and attracting consumers.

(Continued)

TABLE 7.2 (*Continued*)

Study	Objective	Methodology	Conclusions
		The interview structure incorporated three core dimensions: the BOP sample population, strategic design and sustainable product design. A total of 205 questionnaires were sent out with 190 valid responses received. As a statistical methodology, the research applied factorial analysis and core component analysis.	The results demonstrate that the BOP group in Taiwan constitutes a new type of poverty that requires high quality and low prices with these requisites requiring incorporation into the sustainable design development model.
Sheehan and Bruni-Bossio (2015)	This article describes how managers and consultants may now apply the strategic framework set out by Kim and Mauborgne to thoroughly test whether their company returns a low performance level. The attributes of any supply should take into account the functional needs of clients. Currently, managers have no simple tool enabling them to precisely identify those areas of the client value proposal needing improvements. Thus, the objective of this article involved presenting a tool to support managers in monitoring, diagnosing and repairing problems regarding the value proposition that the company delivers its clients.	The methodology chosen was a case study of a golf course. The first phase involved the identification of the attributes promised to members, the second phase designed the curve of the attributes delivered to members and, finally, the design of the third curve took into consideration the competition and trends in golf.	In order to diagnose and detail the client value proposal, three facets require taking into consideration: 1) the value proposal promised by the company to its target clients; 2) the value proposal that the company actually delivers to the client and 3) the future value proposal that outstrips the competition. The comparison between that promised and delivered are shortcomings in implementation. The design of the value curve needs to take into account: the competition, proceeding with an analysis of the competitive trends (Porter, PESTEL, BOS) and, finally, adding new attributes and awarding them value. In order to manage perceptions on the attributes requiring eliminating, reducing, elevating or creating, the managers may take recourse in analysing client feedback.

| Kaleta and Witek-Crabb (2015) | Understanding the correlation between the level of employee participation in the strategic management process, the type of strategy chosen and the various expressions of the growth strategy: innovation, the level of risk, ambition and clarity of vision. The study sought to ascertain the relationship between these two variables and their capacity to bring about competitive advantage. | Applying an interview survey across 150 Polish companies in 2011/12. The respondent group was stratified into three sub-groups: small companies (up to 50 employees), medium companies (between 50 and 250 employees) and large companies (over 250 employees). | The blue ocean strategy concept emerged in this study as a means of responding to dynamic business models and to saturated markets. Effectively, successful strategies are those that now render possible the creation of unexplored markets and stimulating new demand and thereby making the competition irrelevant.

The results obtained indicate the existence of positive correlations for the following variables: employee participation in strategic management and strategic growth processes, innovation strategy, ambition and a clear vision. This also clearly identified the correlation between the participation of employees in the strategic management process and the capacity to create competitive advantage. The results indicate a lack of any relationship between participation in strategic management and the level of strategic risk. |

From analysis of Table 7.1, we may conclude that a significant number of articles belong to the blue ocean strategy authors (Kim and Mauborgne) that explain the concept, present core tools for designing a blue ocean strategy and applying it to the concept of leadership within the scope of boosting employee productivity. The two articles that do not belong to Kim and Mauborgne mention the blue ocean concept but only in a superficial fashion. These facts effectively convey how the literature on the blue ocean strategy does remain very limited and thus demonstrate the potential and the need for studies focusing on this field.

Following an analysis of Table 7.2, we may conclude that there are various articles approaching the blue ocean strategy theme from an empirical perspective. These empirical articles deal with different realities: sectors of activity, supporting the definition of economic policies, supporting market demand in a determined segment of the population, applying the four fields of action methodology (eliminating, reducing, elevating and creating). Despite the diversity in the application of these empirical studies, many of them approach a particular case in which they then make a systematisation of how a particular company/sector of activity applied the four fields of action methodology and obtained a business within the scope of the blue ocean strategy.

Hence, there is an essential need for broader-reaching empirical studies, more generalist in their coverage, applied to different sectors of activity and applying multivariate methodologies. While undertaking an empirical study does not represent an objective of this current study, this does nevertheless seek to contribute to carrying out such studies through the presentation of a conceptual model proposal that aids managers seeking to systematise the blue ocean strategy to facilitate its application in practice.

Proposed conceptual model for applying the blue ocean strategy to fitness and health clubs

Kim and Mauborgne (2005b) state that the foundation of the blue ocean strategy rests on innovation with value as the focus; rather than attempting to see off the competition, it concentrates on rendering the competition irrelevant through means of generating value for both purchasers and the company and thereby entering into a new and undisputed market niche. Kim and Mauborgne (2005b) set out the principles and the core analytical structures for creating and winning blue oceans even while the presentation of these tools still requires clarification and a detailed methodology so that companies and sectors of activities may apply them in the creation of blue oceans.

Kim and Mauborgne (2005b) state how the strategic framework serves two objectives: 1) portraying the current state of competition in the known market space and 2) understanding just what consumers receive from the various competitive offers existing in the marketplace. Correspondingly, Yang and Yang (2011) deploy the refined Kano model to measure client satisfaction towards the different attributes of quality and based upon the results returned identify just which attributes to create, maintain, eliminate, elevate and reduce.

Furthermore, Chang (2011) estimates how the utility of a service to a client stems from perceived quality based upon the E-S-QUAL and E-RecS-QUAL scales that Parasuraman, Zeithaml and Malhotra (2005) put forward for the measurement of the service quality provided by websites and online stores. Hence, the model presented here also aims to identify and measure the dimensions of quality in accordance with the scale applied to sports centres from the perspective of both managers and ex-clients before then setting out the value curve displaying the positioning of the managers and former clients.

Consideration of these positionings proves extremely pertinent and encapsulates how this conceptual model seeks to serve as a contribution towards understanding whether or not there are gaps between that put forward by the managers and what the ex-clients perceive as important. Given the shortcomings returned, we become able to identify the dimensions requiring elevating, maintaining, reducing and eliminating and thus applying the four fields of action before then building a new value curve better adjusted to the expectations of the former clients and enabling managers to gain a more real awareness of what's in demand in the fitness sector. Thus, the model below (see Figure 7.1) serves as a means of support for managers attempting to systematise the blue ocean strategy methodology applied to fitness and health clubs.

Based on this new value curve, we may rebuild the boundaries of markets and establish blue oceans by deploying six strategic options to this end. The first option involves analysing all the alternative industries as companies do not only compete with organisations inside their industry but also with those that operate in other industries producing alternative products or services. In each purchasing decision, consumers make an analysis of alternatives, so it is important to think in the dimensions that are important for non-customers and that are offered by alternative industries.

The second strategic option encapsulates the identification and analysis of the strategic groups within the industry and therefore the as yet unexplored segments within the industry itself that have hitherto fallen beyond consideration.

The third option incorporates the definition of the chain of purchasers that is directly or indirectly involved in the purchase decision, hence, differentiating the purchasers that pay for the product, the users, as well as those who influence them (Kim and Mauborgne, 2005b). Where there is no overlap between these three groups, there is a need to grasp the different definitions of the chain of value.

The fourth option involves the analysis of the complementary products and services. According to Kim and Mauborgne (2005b), the solutions for finding a blue ocean business may require defining the global solution that purchasers are seeking when choosing a particular product or service.

The fifth option for discovering an unexplored market approaches the analysis of the functional or emotional stimulus provided to the purchasers. Kim and Mauborgne (2005b) refer to how industries oriented towards emotion generate

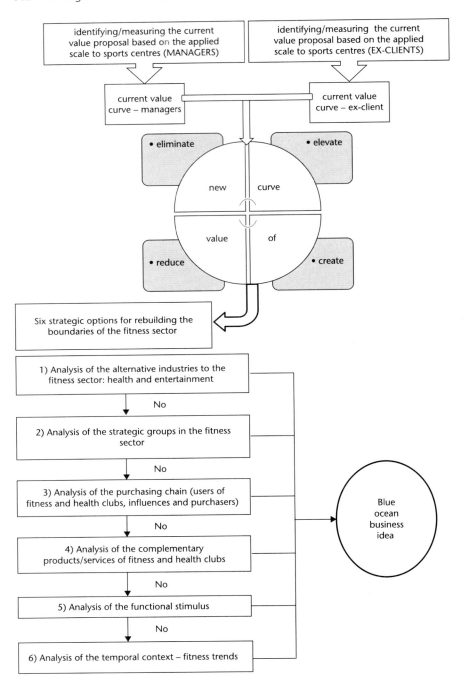

FIGURE 7.1 Blue ocean strategy conceptual strategy applied to fitness/health clubs

extras that make the price rise without improving the functionality. The elimination of these extras may result in a more simple business model, with lower costs and correspondingly cheaper prices which will satisfy consumers.

The final strategic option takes up analysis of the temporal context, thus, the capacity of the company to understand how trends will shape value to the clients and generally influence the company's business model and hence drive a more proactive stance.

Following identification of the dimensions pertinent to the former clients and cross-referencing them with each of the six strategic options, we are then able to develop a blue ocean business idea susceptible to creating more market and rendering the competition irrelevant.

Conclusions and future lines of research

There has only been a very residual amount of research on the blue ocean strategic concept and the existing outputs draw upon the considerable number of articles by the authors who originally launched the concept. The systematisation of the literature demonstrated that there are already some empirical studies applying the blue ocean concept, even while many of them are case studies of a particular example and are systematised as to how a specific company/sector of activity applied the four fields of action methodology and obtained a business within the framework of the blue ocean strategy.

The conceptual blue ocean strategy model applied to fitness/health clubs was set out within the scope of serving as a tool for understanding the value proposal from the perspectives of both managers and ex-clients and then drafting a value curve for each of these groups. Given the gaps encountered in the meanwhile, there is a need to define the dimensions for eliminating, elevating, creating and reducing and thus proposing a new value curve. Based upon this new curve that traces the dimensions relevant to launching a blue ocean business, these then need visualising in each of the six strategic options for rebuilding the boundaries to the fitness and health club sector.

The objective of the study incorporated the development of a blue ocean strategy conceptual model proposal. As such, this lacks empirical application that in itself represents one limitation. The quality dimensions underpin the construction of the value curve that serves as the means of ascertaining the core factors to the industry even while other mechanisms may also serve for the measuring of the value concept. Finally, Kim and Mauborgne (2005b) refer to how a specific sequence should prevail: utility to the purchaser, price, costs and adoption to ensure the commercial idea of the business even while the conceptual model does not extend to this sequence and thus also constitutes another limitation to this study.

Future research would benefit from applying this conceptual model to a sector of activity as a means of prospecting future business areas in markets hitherto unexplored. In this conceptual model proposal, the new value curve rests only on the categories of non-clients, that is, the ex-clients, even while Kim and Mauborgne

114 Elsa Regina M. Vieira and João J. Ferreira

(2005b) also refer to how the non-clients are those that refuse to utilise the outputs of an industry and those that have never perceived those outputs as an option. Hence, future research also needs to consider these two categories. Finally, the sequence underlying the blue ocean strategy requires testing.

References

Afthinos, Y., Theodorakis, N. D. & Nassis, P. (2005). 'Customers' expectations of service in Greek fitness centers: Gender, age, type of sport center, and motivation differences'. *Managing Service Quality*, 15(3), 245–258.

Ahlstrom, D., Lamond, D. & Ding, Z. J. (2009). 'Reexamining some management lessons from military history'. *Asia Pacific Journal of Management*, 26(4), 617–642.

Arbour-Nicitopoulos, K. P. & Ginis, K. A. M. (2011). 'Universal accessibility of "accessible" fitness and recreational facilities for persons with mobility disabilities'. *Adapted Physical Activity Quarterly*, 28(1), 1–15.

Bodet, G. (2009). 'An investigation of the influence of consumer value on service elements' contributions to satisfaction'. *Journal of Targeting, Measurement and Analysis for Marketing*, 17(3), 205–228.

Carvalho, P. G., Serrasqueiro, Z. & Nunes, P. M. (2013). 'Profitability Determinants of Fitness SMEs: Empirical Evidence from Portugal Using Panel Data'. *Amfiteatru Economic*, 15(34), 417–430.

Chang, W. L. (2011). 'A mixed-initiative model for quality-based e-services pricing'. *Total Quality Management & Business Excellence*, 22(9), 975–991.

Cheng, K. M., Hsu, C. H. & Huang, C. H. (2012). 'A study on the application of 6-Sigma on the enhancement of service quality of fitness club'. *Quality & Quantity*, 46(2), 705–713.

Druehl, C. T. & Schmidt, G. M. (2008). 'A strategy for opening a new market and encroaching on the lower end of the existing market'. *Production and Operations Management*, 17(1), 44–60.

Fernandéz, J. G., Carrión, G. C., & Ruís, D. M. (2012). 'Customer satisfaction and its relation to perceived quality in fitness centres: Calidfit scale'. *Revista De Psicologia Del Deporte*, 21(2), 309–319.

Garcia-Fernandez, J., Bernal-Garcia, A., Fernandez-Gavira, J. & Velez-Colon, L. (2014). 'Analysis of existing literature on management and marketing of the fitness centre industry'. *South African Journal for Research in Sport Physical Education and Recreation*, 36(3), 75–91.

Harris, J. & Marandi, E. (2002). 'The gendered dynamics of relationship marketing: An initial discussion of the health and fitness industry'. *Managing Leisure*, 7(3), 194–200.

Howell, J. & Ingham, A. (2001). 'From social problem to personal issue: The language of lifestyle'. *Cultural Studies*, 15(2), 326–351.

IHRSA (2013). *European Market Report: The size and scope of ... club in ... S* (Ed.). Boston, MA: International Health Racquet and ... or ...

Kaleta, A. & Witek-Crabb, A. (2015). 'Participation in the strategic management process and the expansiveness of the strategy'. *Argumenta Oeconomica*, 34(1), 61–76.

Kim, C., Yang, K. H. & Kim, J. (2008). 'A strategy for third-party logistics systems: A case analysis using the blue ocean strategy'. *Omega-International Journal of Management Science*, 36(4), 522–534.

Kim, W. C. & Mauborgne, R. (2004). 'Blue ocean strategy'. *Harvard Business Review*, 82(10), 76–84.

Kim, W. C., & Mauborgne, R. (2005a). 'Blue ocean strategy: From theory to practice'. *California Management Review, 47*(3), 105–121.

Kim, W. C. & Mauborgne, R. (2005b). *Blue ocean strategy: How to create uncontested market space and make competition irrelevant.* Boston: Harvard Business School Press.

Kim, W. C. & Mauborgne, R. (2009). 'How strategy shapes structure'. *Harvard Business Review, 87*(9), 72–80.

Kim, W. C. & Mauborgne, R. (2014). 'Blue Ocean Leadership'. *Harvard Business Review, 92*(5), 60–72.

Koustelios, A. (2003). 'Identifying important management competencies in fitness centres in Greece'. *Managing Leisure, 8*(3), 145–153.

Krannich, R. S. (2008). 'Rural sociology at the crossroads'. *Rural Sociology, 73*(1), 1–21.

Kuratko, D. F. & Audretsch, D. B. (2009). 'Strategic entrepreneurship: Exploring different perspectives of an emerging concept'. *Entrepreneurship Theory and Practice, 33*(1), 1–17.

Lasen, M., & Ward, D. (2009). 'An overview of needs theories behind consumerism'. *Journal of Applied Economic Sciences, 7*, 137–155.

Lindic, J., Bavdaz, M. & Kovacic, H. (2012). 'Higher growth through the blue ocean strategy: Implications for economic policy'. *Research Policy, 41*(5), 928–938.

MacIntosh, E. & Doherty, A. (2007). 'Extending the scope of organisational culture: The external perception of an internal phenomenon'. *Sport Management Review, 10*(1), 45–64.

MacIntosh, E. & Walker, M. (2012). 'Chronicling the transient nature of fitness employees: An organizational culture perspective'. *Journal of Sport Management, 26*(2), 113–126.

MacIntosh, E. W. & Doherty, A. (2010). 'The influence of organizational culture on job satisfaction and intention to leave'. *Sport Management Review, 13*(2), 106–117.

Maconachie, G. & Sappey, J. (2013). 'Flexing some muscle: Strategy and outcomes in the Queensland health and fitness industry'. *Journal of Industrial Relations, 55*(1), 136–154.

Mischler, S., Bauger, P., Pichot, L. & Wipf, E. (2009). 'Private fitness centres in France: From organisational and market characteristics to micromentalities of the managers'. *International Journal of Sport Management and Marketing : IJSMM, 5*(4), 426–449.

Moodley, P. & Coopoo, Y. (2006). 'Job satisfaction of self employed trainers and personal trainers employed at commercial fitness: A comparative study'. *South African Journal for Research in Sport, Physical Education and Recreation, 28*(2), 105–112.

Palacios, M. G. L., Rodriguez, M. M., Rodriguez, J. A. L. & Escoto, F. C. (2010). 'Innovation in value in the Mexican beef industry: Strategies followed by market leaders'. *Revista Mexicana De Ciencias Pecuarias, 1*(4), 417–432.

Parasuraman, A., Zeithaml, V. A. & Malhotra, A. (2005). 'E-S-QUAL – A multiple-item scale for assessing electronic service quality'. *Journal of Service Research, 7*(3), 213–233.

Parrot, D. L. (1996). 'Whose business is fitness?' *Journal of Health Care Marketing, 16*(3), 44–49.

Parvinen, P., Aspara, J., Hietanen, J. & Kajalo, S. (2011). 'Awareness, action and context-specific blue ocean practices in sales management'. *Management Decision, 49*(7–8), 1218–1234.

Perfetto, R. & Woodside, A. G. (2009). 'Extremely frequent behavior in consumer research: Theory and empirical evidence for chronic casino gambling'. *Journal of Gambling Studies, 25*(3), 297–316.

Pitta, D. (2009). 'Issues in a down economy: Blue oceans and new product development'. *The Journal of Product and Brand Management, 18*(4), 292–296.

Sheehan, N. T. & Bruni-Bossio, V. (2015). 'Strategic value curve analysis: Diagnosing and improving customer value propositions'. *Business Horizons*, *58*(3), 317–324.

Soita, P. W. (2012). 'Measuring perceived service quality using SERVQUAL: A case study of the Uganda health and fitness sector'. *International Journal of Business and Social Science*, *3*(5), 261–271.

Teixeira, M. & Correia, A. (2009). 'Segmenting fitness centre clients'. *International Journal of Sport Management and Marketing*, *5*(4), 396–416.

Themaat, T. V. L. V., Schutte, C. S. L., Lutters, D. & Kennon, D. (2013). 'Designing a framework to design a business model for the "bottom of the pyramid" population'. *South African Journal of Industrial Engineering*, *24*(3), 190–204.

Tu, J. C., Shih, M. C., Hsu, C. Y. & Lin, J. H. (2014). 'Developing blue ocean strategy of sustainable product design and development for business opportunities of BOP groups in Taiwan'. *Mathematical Problems in Engineering*, 1–23.

Woolf, J. (2008). 'Competitive advantage in the health and fitness industry: Developing service bundles'. *Sport Management Review*, *11*(1), 51–75.

Wubben, E. F. M., Dusseldorf, S. & Batterink, M. H. (2012). 'Finding uncontested markets for European fruit and vegetables through applying the blue ocean strategy'. *British Food Journal*, *114*(2–3), 248–271.

Yang, C. C. (2013). 'An analytical methodology for identifying the latent needs of customers'. *Total Quality Management & Business Excellence*, *24*(11–12), 1332–1346.

Yang, C. C. & Yang, K. J. (2011). 'An integrated model of value creation based on the refined Kano's model and the blue ocean strategy'. *Total Quality Management & Business Excellence*, *22*(9), 925–940.

Yang, J. T. (2012a). 'Identifying the attributes of blue ocean strategies in hospitality'. *International Journal of Contemporary Hospitality Management*, *24*(4–5), 701–720.

Yang, J. T. (2012b). 'Effects of ownership change on organizational settings and strategies in a Taiwanese hotel chain'. *International Journal of Hospitality Management*, *31*(2), 428–441.

Yuan, C. B. J., Liu, C. Y., Kao, K. M. & Shu, Y. C. (2009). 'Entrepreneurship and innovation process in the health industry in Taiwan'. *European Business Review*, *21*(5), 453–471.

Zolfagharian, M. & Paswan, A. (2008). 'Do consumers discern innovations in service elements?' *The Journal of Services Marketing*, *22*(5), 338–352.

8

THE RELEVANCE OF THE SOCIAL IMPACT OF SPORTS EVENTS IN THE CONTEXT OF PUBLIC FINANCING OF SPORT

David Parra Camacho, Ferran Calabuig Moreno, Juan Núñez Pomar and Josep Crespo Hervás

Introduction

In many cases the organization of large sports events requires public financing to assume its necessary investments (Maennig and Du Plessis, 2009). The demands in terms of investments on infrastructure, security and compliance with the standards raised by the Olympic Committee make public financing unavoidable in order to accommodate a sports mega-event like the Olympic Games (Matheson, 2012).

As a result, the majority of the studies carried out about these types of mega-events are focused on the economic repercussions of these events. In great measure, these studies are requested by the organizing committees or the administrations providing the public money to accommodate its celebration. It is a way to politically and publicly justify the profitability of the investments made, given their relevance. However, the social profitability, or more specifically, the studies about the social impact of this kind of sports event are not usually requested either by the organizers or the financing governments.

Some authors like Kim and Petrick (2005) emphasize at least three reasons regarding why these types of studies have been traditionally less demanded. First, the evaluations of sports events tend to focus on the economic impact as a way to promote, from a political point of view, the event amongst residents. Second, these types of impacts are harder to measure and calculate, as they are less tangible than the economic ones (Delamere, Wankel and Hinch, 2001; Getz, 1997). Third, these impacts are usually associated with negative factors such as the concerns for security and crime, alcoholism, prostitution, increased vandalism, loss of authenticity, additional costs associated with police surveillance and traffic or urban agglomeration (Deccio and Baloglou, 2002).

In this chapter, we analyze the relevance of public financing to assume the costs of these types of events emphasizing some figures related to the public costs

118 David Parra Camacho *et al.*

that derive from the reception of these events. In the second part we highlight the main aspects related to the evaluation of the social impact of sports events or "social impact assessment" (SIA).

Public financing of sports events

The public treasury tends to assume a great part of the costs that derive from the reception of sports mega-events, which have seen an increment during the last years not only because of the construction of infrastructure and facilities but also because of the associated costs of security against possible terrorist attacks. Hereunder we see the figures provided by different studies of some large sports events, underlining the Olympic Games and Football World Championships, due to the important investments necessary to be able to organize this type of event. Furthermore, we will make reference to other sports events of lesser repercussion but with high private and public outlays.

Regarding the Olympic Games, Gratton, Liu, Ramchandani and Wilson (2012) point out that some reports indicate that the investment of $51,000 million made the Sochi 2014 Olympic Games the most expensive in history. Nevertheless, Beijing is widely considered as the most expensive summer Olympic Games in history, with a figure that rises up to around $40,000 million.

What's more, Kasimati and Dawson (2009) carried out a review of the percentage of public and private financing allocated to the organization during the last editions of this mega-event. These authors stress that in the last three editions, the public financing has considerably surpassed the private one. For example, in the cases of Athens 2004, Beijing 2008 and London 2012, the contributions of the public treasury exceeded by more than 80 per cent the total expenditure of the organization.

According to Malfas, Theodoraki and Houlihan (2004), the public investment in the Barcelona Olympic Games was $6,200 million. In the case of this edition the public investment for the Olympic Games represented 67.3 per cent of the total Olympic activities (Brunet, 1995). For the Atlanta Games (1996) an investment of $2,000 million was used for projects related to the event from the announcement of the celebration of the Olympic Games (in 1990) to the spring of the year in which they were celebrated (Malfas *et al.*, 2004).

Even though the expenses related to infrastructure and facilities to accommodate these kinds of events usually represent an important part of the public expenditure, sports mega-events have the ability to bring together large multitudes that generate expenses on communication, cleaning, security or public transportation. As pointed out by Kasimati and Dawson (2009), for the Athens Games (2004) the costs associated with the construction of the sports facilities was estimated to be €3,000 million, whilst another €4,200 million was allocated to investments in different areas: transport (€1,200 million), communication (€1,200 million), security (€1,100 million) and other infrastructure (€700 million). These authors make reference to the figures of the Ministry of National

The social impact of sports events **119**

Economy (2004) to emphasize that €6,000 million was financed by the government, in other words, around 83 per cent of the total cost of organizing the event.

In accordance with Prayag, Hosany, Nunkoo and Alders (2013) a high level of investment cannot always be justified by the earnings obtained and they use as examples the expenses of the Athens Games, which were supposedly around 6 per cent of the gross domestic product of the country. Jones (2001) argues that the economic profit is often exaggerated in order to justify the use of public funds. Instead of economic profit, many cities that have hosted sports mega-events have experienced a deficit after the event (Lee and Krohn, 2013). For instance, Preuss (2004) estimates that the Organizing Committee of the Sydney Olympic Games (2000) experienced losses of more than $45 million. A recent example estimates that the Organizing Committee of the Vancouver Olympic Games (2010) also had a deficit of $48.1 million in 2008, in comparison with the $60.9 surplus obtained in 2006–2007.

If we analyze another mega-event such as the editions of the Football World Cup we verify that the public investment is also considerable. According to Baade, Matheson and Nikolova (2007), Germany spent more than €1,400 million to build and renovate 12 stadiums for the 2006 Football World Cup, with a portion of the financing of no less than 35 per cent covered by local, regional and national contributors.

Another edition of this mega-event such as the one celebrated in South Africa in 2010, organized in nine cities and ten different locations, meant a direct investment of the government of 38.3 million South African rands for the remodeling and construction of adequate infrastructure as part of a program of much larger outlay (Cottle, 2010). In spite of these imposing figures, Cottle (2010) draws attention to the fact that this sports events generated a deficit for the South African government as the fiscal income of 19,300 million rands did not even cover the public expenditure of 39,300 million rands and, therefore, did not make the mega-event profitable for South Africa. Along these lines, Tomlinson (2009) pointed out that for the celebration of the 2010 Football World Cup investments were deliberately underestimated in order to raise the possible benefits derived from the reception of the event. In the preliminary evaluation of this sports event, Cottle (2010) highlighted that the figure of public expenditure had been constantly adjusted by the South African government, increasing the initial estimate done in 2003 of 2,300 million rands to 39,900 million in 2010, which meant an increase of 1,709 per cent from the original estimate.

As indicated by Abebe, Bolton, Pavelka and Pierstoff (2014), something similar happened with the 2014 Football World Cup that took place in Brazil, from one expectation of the initial expenditure estimated at around $5,000 million to a projection of the estimated expenditure done by the Ministry of Sports of $17,000 million Brazilian reals ($10,180 million, using the exchange rates of December 31st 2010) on transport infrastructure and another 5,600 million Brazilian reals for stadiums. In the three years after the allocation of the Brazil Olympic Games, the planned expenditure on infrastructure reached 22,600 million reals ($13,290 million, using the exchange rate of October 20th 2010), meaning an increment by 165% of the expected costs fixed three years before (Abebe *et al.*, 2014). Subsequently, the Minister of Sports, Orlando Silva Jr., announced that the investment in the planned infrastructures would rise to 24,000 million reals ($15,000 million), resulting in another increase (Abebe *et al.*, 2014).

According to the website of the Brazilian Ministry of Sports, Rio 2016 predicted a budget of $14,400 million (International Olympic Committee, 2009). Abebe *et al.* (2014) state that, from that amount, half was assigned to transport-related infrastructure: $400 million to expand and improve Rio's international airport, $600 million for a bypass from Rio and other road projects in the area where most of the Olympic head offices and the Olympic Village were located, $1,310 million for the extension and improvement of capacity of regional trains and metro, $1,230 million for the development of three lines of Bus Rapid Transit that allowed the connection between the four Olympic "zones" in Rio, and $1,350 million on the trains, metro and buses (Barbassa, 2013).

Other large sports events, like the 2002 Commonwealth Games, signified an investment of £200 million on sports facilities and around £470 million on transport and other infrastructure, being the largest investment made in Great Britain when hosting a sports event before hosting the London Olympic Games (Gratton and Preuss, 2008).

In the case of the 2007–2010 America's Cup that took place in Valencia, according to the figures of a study carried out by the Valencian Institute of Economic Investigations (IVIE, 2007) about the economic impact of this event, the expenditure of public administrations rose to a number close to €3,000 million. As the report unfolds: €2,261 million corresponds to expenses (accounting those realized by direct and indirect actions) realized by the autonomous government, €410 million to Consorcio 2007 (an organization formed by the three public administrations involved in the financing of the event), €288 million of expenditure realized by the central government and around €87 million of expenditure executed by the local administration.

Due to these high expenditure numbers, developers and organizers of sports events tend to show special interest in maximizing the economic impact with the goal of justifying the important public monetary subsidies (Matheson, 2012). According to Baade and Matheson (2006) since the year 1987 until approximately 2003, 80 per cent of professional sports facilities in the United States have been substituted or have been the object of important renovation that has cost more than $19,000 million in total, being $13,600 million of public investment (71 per cent of that amount). The use of money from contributors to subsidize the decisions of professional sports' teams is justified with the conviction that such investment of public money is worthwhile, as it is compensated for by the economic activity that a professional sports team in a town generates. These explanations are often backed by studies of the economic impact that prove that the expenses of sports tourists on the host city justify the public subsidy (Gratton, Shibli and Coleman, 2006).

In the United States it is estimated that the economic profit of accommodating a Super Bowl varies between 350 and 400 million dollars. This argument was used by some of the people responsible for the organization of the NFL, in order to justify the support of citizens to vote in favor of a public investment of $325 million towards the construction of a new stadium in Arlington (Texas) that would allow hosting this event during the following ten editions (Baade, Baumann, & Matheson, 2008).

As pointed out by Matheson (2012) even if the public investment in sports infrastructure has stimulating effects on the economy, it is key to take into account the opportunity cost of capital, as reductions in other state services, increases of public debt or a rise in taxes will necessarily happen. According to this author, the best-case scenario would be a void impact of this expense on the economy because the profits that could be obtained in terms of employment are lost as a result of higher taxes or the cutback of expenses in other areas.

In this sense, Kasimati (2003) highlights that some argue that public money invested in sports events tends to come from other important sectors allocated to social well-being, such as education, health and housing. Therefore it is necessary to have the support of different interested parties or "stakeholders" bound to the celebration of the event. One of these essential groups are the politicians, who are the ones that, as a last resort, will have to decide about public investments (Preuss, 2004). This group has a fundamental role in the so-called opportunity costs, which are more decisive in developing countries due to the lack of resources to cover basic needs of the population (Rocha, 2015).

Consequently, politicians are subject to a continued evaluation of their actions by the citizens that chose them. Thus, the residents of the host country or city become another essential collective to achieve the support of this type of sports event. Having the backing of this group is indispensable for different reasons (Gursoy and Kendall, 2006): first, because they are the ones to decide about the tax increase or the parts destined for the construction of infrastructure or facilities; second, due to the fact that a satisfied population with positive predisposition is essential for the event to be a significant and enjoyable experience both for tourists and the local citizens (Hiller, 1990; Fredline, 2004; Preuss and Solberg, 2006); third, because the local support and the involvement of the population will allow extended positive impacts on the community (Deccio and Baloglu, 2002); and, fourth, to understand that the support of the residents is directly related to the reactions towards the event, being necessary to guide the efforts towards minimizing the negative impacts and maximizing the positive ones (Fredline and Faulkner, 2000; Hiller, 1990; Gursoy and Kendall, 2006).

The backing of the celebration of sports events is one of the aspects that event organizers take most into account and it is normally used as an argument to defend the candidacy (Añó, 2011). To obtain the support of this collective it is required to carry out studies before, during and after the reception of the event that enable an analysis of the social repercussion of this kind of event. The following section reviews the main concepts, theories and classifications that define this area of investigation.

Social impact of sports events

Conceptualization of the social impact of sports events

Generally, studies related to the analysis of the perception of residents or the social impact of sports events are mainly held up by the investigation of social impacts associated with tourism (Fredline, Jago and Deery, 2003). That's why the two areas of investigation share similarly the methods, the process of collecting data and the theories that serve as reference to explain the results of these studies (Deery and Jago, 2010).

It stands out how there is a lack of a specific and generally accepted definitions of what the social impacts of sports events are. A first contribution about the definition of social impact is carried out by Olsen and Merwin (1977, p. 41), which make reference to the "changes in the structure and the functioning of the order of the social patterns that take place in conjunction with an environmental, technological and social innovation or alteration."

Some authors only include within the social impacts those that cannot be encompassed in other categories like, for example, social and environmental impact, whilst others contemplate more thoroughly any impact on society or the social sphere (Fredline, 2005). In this sense, Mathieson and Wall (1982, p. 137), from the perspective of tourism, define the social impacts as the "changes in the standard of living of the residents of touristic destinations." This definition would include the economic and environmental changes within the social impacts, because the increase in the number of tourists as a result of the celebration of a large sports event increments the employment rate of the citizens, which could be considered an economic impact that, at the same time, has clear social implications. In addition, the possible damages of natural areas derived from tourism can affect the standard of living of local residents, which translates in negative social impact (Fredline, 2005). Another definition provided by the tourism context is from Hall (1992a, p. 67), which sees the social impacts as "the way in which the effects of tourism and travelling change the value system of individuals and collectives, the behavioural patterns, the community structures, the way of living and the standard of living." To sum up, we could describe the social impact of a sports event as the changes in the standard of living of residents as a consequence of the celebration of such an event.

Evaluation of the social impact of sports events: "Social Impact Assessment" (SIA)

Sports events are associated with a series of benefits that result from celebrating such an event in the organizing locations. These positive impacts or benefits depend greatly on the repercussions, the magnitude and the category of the sports event. However, the evaluation or the measurement of these benefits is usually carried out through studies of the economic impact, and to a lesser extent through studies of the social impact or studies of how the sports event is perceived by residents. This is due to the difficulty of measuring intangible aspects such as, in many cases, the benefits and social costs incurred from sports events.

The evaluation of the social impact of a sports event is fundamental to understanding how it affects the standard of living of the residents of the location where it is celebrated. The objective is to find out which aspects positively influence, and which do so negatively, to try to maximize the benefits and minimize the costs on the resident population. In this way, according to Vanclay (2003), the identification of the impacts enough in advance can, on the one hand, contribute to making better decisions about how to proceed, and on the other hand, help the development of the actions undertaken to minimize the damages and maximize the advantages of an activity or intervention specifically planned, such as a sports event.

In this way, we include in the evaluation of the social impact by Vanclay (2003, p.6) the processes directed to the "analysis, monitoring and management of the social intentional and non-intentional consequences, both positive and negative, of planned interventions (polices, programs, plans, projects) and any process of social change invoked by those interventions." In agreement with Burdge (2003), the public participation and the social impact evaluation go together, as one is in charge of publicly consulting a particular proposal or intervention and the other is in charge of knowing how such a proposal would change the lives of the affected people and community

Nonetheless, many of the contributions made about the social impact of sports events have taken place on dates close to their celebration (with some weeks or a few months in advance), during or once the event is over. These investigations provide information that, if interpreted in an appropriate manner, can become a useful tool for organizers and administrators when better managing the social impacts associated with sports events. Even though the results of the mentioned investigations can help modify the strategic lines or actions established for organizing future sports events, the outcomes, both positive and negative, of the assessed event will not likely be reoriented with the finality of improving its management. This is even more obvious if the event is not celebrated periodically in the same location, making it hard for the same city to host the celebration.

For example, Preuss (2007) emphasizes that many of the studies previously made about the celebration of a sports events focus on the analysis of the legacy that can be planned and that is tangible and positive (for instance, the expectation of the economic impact of an event), given that the intention of those requesting these studies (organizing committees) is to favor the celebration of the event. This explains the special emphasis on this type of quantifiable and foreseeable impacts, leaving aside intangible aspects such as the social impact. Along those lines, authors like Gratton and Preuss (2008) highlight the need to plan the legacy

124 David Parra Camacho *et al.*

of an event before it is celebrated, in all its dimensions, or in other words, from the initial stages of the candidacy of a city until the organization of the phenomenon. This enables the maximization of long-term positive impacts generated on the host community, affecting the improvement of their standard of living before and after its celebration.

As stressed by different authors (Kim and Walker, 2012; Zhou, 2007) there is no unified and universal criterion in the evaluation of the social impact of a particular happening, related to sports or of any other nature. Therefore, there is no standardized and universally accepted theoretical frame within the assessment of the social impact of sports events (Kim and Walker, 2012). Nevertheless, some contributions realized on this topic differentiate six evaluation dimensions: physical, economic, social, cultural, political and psychological (Gramling and Freundenburg, 1992). Table 8.1 gathers some of these mentioned contributions. Amongst them Preuss and Solberg's (2006) must be underlined, which compiles diverse proposals (see Table 8.2) classifying the potential impacts of the reception of sports events on the community in six dimensions: economic, touristic/commercial, physical, socio-cultural, psychological and political.

Similarly to the investigation about the social impacts of tourism, when evaluating the social impact of sports events it is a common method to use quantitative surveys, generally targeted at the residents of the city hosting the event (Deery and Jago, 2010). To a lower scale, in some cases techniques and methods that analyze the social impact of events from a qualitative point of view have been used, through open questions that try to gather the impressions, feelings and reactions of the citizens facing a particular occurrence.

Explanatory theories

Some scholars have exposed different theories and they seek to understand and explain the changes in the perceptions of the residents about sports events. The explanatory theories more widely used are the social representation theory and the social exchange theory.

The first theory states that citizens have a series of representations of tourism and events that define their perceptions of the generated impacts; those representations are determined by direct experiences, social interactions and other factors such as the media. This theory has been applied in different studies to explain the reactions of residents in the presence of sports events (e.g. Cheng and Jarvis, 2010; Fredline and Faulkner, 2000; Zhou and Ap, 2009).

On the other hand, the social exchange theory is most used when trying to explain the changes in the perception of residents in the face of the impacts of tourism (Ap, 1992) and, in this case, about sports events (e.g. Deccio and Baloglou, 2002; Gursoy and Kendall, 2006; Kaplanidou *et al.*, 2013; Kim, Gursoy and Lee, 2006; Prayag *et al.*, 2013; Waitt, 2003). The theory suggests that citizens have a more favorable tendency towards sports events if they consider that the expected benefits overcome the costs. Like this, those residents that take the most advantage

TABLE 8.1 Theoretical frameworks for assessing the social impact of sport events

Social impact studies	Focus of the sport events' social impact studies						
	Social	Economic	Cultural	Political	Environmental	Psychological	Commercial/Tourism
Delamere, Wankel and Hinch (2001); Dyer, Gursoy, Sarma and Carter (2007); Gursoy and Rutherford (2004)	X	X	X				
Dwyer, Mellor, Mistilis and Mules (2000)	X	X					
Gramling and Freudenburg (1992)	X	X	X	X			X
Fredline (2004); Ritchie (1984); Preuss and Solberg (2006)	X	X	X	X		X	X
Kaplanidou *et al.* (2013)	X	X		X		X	X
Ko and Stewart (2002); Prayag *et al.* (2013)	X	X	X		X		
Hritz and Ross (2010); Lee and Back (2003)	X	X			X		
Small, Edwards and Sheridan (2005)	X		X				
Llopis (2012)	X			X		X	

Source: modified from Kim and Walker (2012).

of the celebration of a sports event, because they are getting employment or improving their business, will show more positive perceptions than those who don't get any direct benefit (Fredline, 2005). What's more, it is important to consider that this is a dynamic theory and, therefore, residents can re-evaluate the exchange process and adjust their perceptions with time (Waitt, 2003).

The main difference between these two principles falls on trusting the rationality of the mind of human beings. In this way, according to Fredline (2005) the theory of social representation allows irrational reactions of residents faced with sports events based on personal and social values. In comparison, the social exchange theory assumes a rational processing of information in terms of expected costs and benefits of a sports event.

Otherwise, Eagly and Chaiken (1993) propose another theory related to the expectancy-value model that authors like Delamere (2001) and Delamere, Wankel and Hinch (2001) apply to events or festivals. Conforming to these authors there is a relationship between the importance of the residents who consider that there are certain results (value) and the degree of influence that they believe tourism has in the attainment of those results (expectancy), providing a useful explanation to understand the variations of the perceptions of residents about the derived costs and benefits of large sports events (Fredline, 2005).

Some approaches combine the use of two theories to explain the perception of residents of the impact of sports events. For example, the study by Cheng and Jarvis (2010) about GP Formula 1 in Singapore utilizes conjunctly the social exchange theory and the social representation theory. Also Kaplanidou's (2012) work combines those two theories on a conceptual level to describe the perception of residents of four different cities about the legacy of four editions of the Olympic Games. In Prayag et al.'s (2013) study, the social exchange theory and the theory of reasoned action are used.

Recently, other alternative theories have been adopted to interpret the perceptions of residents about sports events. For instance, the construal level theory expressed by Kaplanidou (2012) "proposes that the temporal distance changes people's answers towards future events, altering the way in which the people mentally represent these events" (Trope and Liberman, 2003, p. 403, cited by Kaplanidou, 2012). In spite of this theory being based on future events, the author applies this theoretical frame in the context of four past sports events, as she understands that the temporal component is the same. To justify this approach she uses support research by Dhar and Kim (2007), who suggested the existence of a connection with past assessments or opinions, because when people observe the past to make a decision, they take on a more distant perspective that involves the inspection of the general elements of the analyzed event in terms of its quality and its key characteristics.

Finally, the theory of reasoned action used by Prayag et al. (2013) explains the interrelation between the general attitude of residents towards the Olympic Games and the support of its celebration. This theory "offers that human beings are rational individuals with the ability to process information with the finality

The social impact of sports events **127**

to reach a reasonable decision about the behavior (Ajzen and Fishbein, 1980)" (Prayag *et al.*, 2013, p. 630).

Classification of the social impacts associated to sports events

The literature about the perception of residents in terms of the impacts of events tends to differentiate between positive and negative impacts or benefits and costs of the celebration of a sports event. However, the way in which citizens perceive the costs and benefits is a determinant factor that will influence if they support or oppose the event itself (Müller, 2012). This has been widely proven in numerous studies about sports events of various types (e.g. Balduck, Maes and Buelens, 2011; Deccio and Baloglou, 2002; Fredline, 2004; Gursoy and Kendall, 2006; Kaplanidou *et al.*, 2013; Lee and Krohn, 2013; Müller, 2012; Parra, Calabuig and Añó, 2013; Prayag *et al.*, 2013). Therefore, one of the tasks of the administration and organizers must be to identify and predict these impacts, aiming to minimize the negative effects and foster the positive ones (Bowdin, Allen, Harris, McDonnell and O'Toole, 2012; Fredline, 2004).

According to the classification put forward by Preuss and Solberg (2006), displayed in Table 8.2, in the following paragraphs we compile the principal impacts on the host community featured in several studies about sports events. It is relevant to bear in mind that this classification contemplates other different impacts

TABLE 8.2 Examples of the impacts of sports events

Type of impact	Positive	Negative
Economic	Increased economic activity Creation of employment Increase in labour supply Increase in standard of living	Price increase during event Real estate speculation Failure to attract tourists Better alternative investments Inadequate capital and inadequate estimation of costs of event Expensive security Over-indebtedness Increased taxes
Tourism/ Commercial	Increased awareness of the region as a travel/tourism destination Increased knowledge concerning the potential for investment and commercial activity in the region Creation of new accommodation and tourist attractions	Acquisition of poor reputation as a result of inadequate facilities Crime Improper practices or inflated prices Negative reactions from existing enterprises due to the possibility of new competition for local manpower and government assistance

Physical/ Environmental	Construction of new facilities Improvement of local infrastructure Preservation of heritage Environmental promotion Impacts on sport	Ecological damage Changes in natural processes Architectural pollution Destruction of heritage Overcrowding Unused facilities
Social/Cultural	Increase in permanent level of local interest and participation in types of activity associated with event Strengthening of regional values and traditions	Commercialization of activities which may be of a personal private nature Modification of nature of event or activity to accommodate tourism Potential increase in crime Changes in community structure Social dislocation
Psychological	Increased local pride and community spirit Increased awareness of non-local perceptions Festival atmosphere during event	Tendency toward defensive attitudes concerning host region Culture shock Misunderstandings leading to varying degrees of host/visitor hostility
Political/ Administrative	Enhanced international recognition of region and values Development of skills among planners International understanding	Economic exploitation of local population to satisfy ambitions of political elite Distortion of true nature of event to reflect elite values Failure to cope Inability to achieve aims Increase in administrative costs Use of event to legitimate unpopular decisions Legitimating of ideology and sociocultural reality Corruption

Source: Preuss and Solberg (2006, pp. 398–399)

strictly of the social scope (e.g. economic or touristic). Still, a lot of research that analyzes the social impact of sports events consults the perception of the residents about these impact categories. For this reason, the majority of the impacts regarded in this classification correspond to verified facts and other perceptions.

From the socioeconomic sphere, different positive and negative economic impacts are linked to the celebration of sports events in the communities or locations that host such events. On the one hand, the organization of sports events can mean positive socioeconomic impacts like those associated with new fiscal revenue for the administration, creating employment opportunities and other sources of income (Deccio and Baloglou, 2002; Getz, 1997; Hall, 1989). Besides, they can attract new investors and increase the trade and business of the city or region (Ritchie, 1984).

On the other hand, sports events also imply a series of negative repercussions related to the poor management of public investment, price inflation and tax increases that finance the infrastructure and facilities necessary for the event and the city (Deccio and Baloglou, 2002; Gursoy and Kendall, 2006; Solberg and Preuss, 2007). Additionally, Malfas *et al.* (2004), referencing Hall and Hodges (1998), point out that large sports events can affect the housing market and the land value, since the construction of new infrastructure connected to the event could lead to the expropriation of land and the moving of housing, at the same time it can result in a rise in housing and rental prices. As a last resort, this aspect could bring on a negative impact on the low-income inhabitants of these areas. Other negative economic impacts are the "hidden costs" related to the police and security costs or those dedicated to cleaning and hygiene of the facilities where the event is situated and its surroundings (Collins, Flynn, Munday and Roberts, 2007; Añó, 2011).

Differently, the touristic and commercial impact is tied to the economic impact as affirmed by Malfas *et al.* (2004, p. 212):

> the economic contribution of large sports events is mainly thought in terms of the possibilities offered to increment the conscience of the city or region as a touristic destination and the knowledge of the investment and commercial activity opportunities in the region.

Consequently, this type of phenomenon can attract investors and visitors, and, thus, contribute to the creation of new job positions and the economic growth of the city or region. Plus, large sports events can develop the tourism industry in a destination by increasing the affluence of tourists, the duration of their stay and their expenditure (Barker, Page and Meyer, 2002; Getz, 1997).

Furthermore, large sports events can add to urban regeneration by constructing new infrastructure and facilities for the city. In this way, several authors (e.g. Fredline and Faulkner, 2000; Kim *et al.*, 2006; Mihalik and Simonetta, 1999; Ritchie and Aitken, 1984; Smith and Fox, 2007) indicate that the real impact or legacy in the physical area or sustainable urban regeneration must be oriented to the usage of those infrastructures and facilities after the event. As a model, Hiller (2006) mentions that facilities constructed for the celebration of large sports events like the Olympic Games (for example: cycle tracks, stadiums, speed skating rinks, etc.) could serve to continue hosting sports competitions or as training centers, even though they have to be adapted and inspected constantly to comply with world standards. Moreover, large sports events most often develop infrastructures that are not directly related to the event, including leisure facilities, shopping malls and open spaces, with the purpose of improving the physical appearance of the host city or region (Malfas *et al.*, 2004).

All the same, Smith and Fox (2007) stress that cities are posed with a big dilemma when they organize a large sports event which consists, on one side, of the physical legacy resulting from the construction or improvement of infrastructures and facilities and, on the other side, of making sure that the money and resources invested are not wasted on unnecessary amenities. These authors cite as examples, first, the case of the 1996 Atlanta Olympic Games in which most of the infrastructure was temporary hence the physical legacy was limited in that sense and, second, the case of the 2004 Athens Olympic Games, with 95 per cent of the facilities being permanent.

From an environmental point of view, sports institutions, teams and organizations that sponsor such events recognize the need to better understand the environmental impact of the activities and the events that represent them (Collins, Jones and Munday, 2009). Large sports events have a potential impact on local ecosystems, on the use of irreplaceable natural capital and on the contribution of carbon emissions linked to climate change (Collins *et al.*, 2009; Jones and Munday, 2008).

On the one hand, we can emphasize the positive impacts, such as the possibility that sports events can help preserve the environment and the local heritage by guaranteeing its sustainability (Deccio and Baloglou, 2002; Getz, 2007), for example contributing to the development of strategies to plan and control pollution and recycling (Allen, O'Toole, McDonnell and Harris, 2005). In addition, they can serve as a starting point towards improving the level of conscience of citizens regarding the environment (Kim *et al.*, 2006). For instance, in Jin, Zhang, Ma and Connaughton's (2011) study it was found that residents agreed with the fact that the celebration of the 2008 Beijing Olympic Games had helped improve the quality of the air and the water, to better use energy resources, to develop a more comfortable public transport, to increase the green coverage rate, to improve the management of industrial pollution and solid residues and to improve environmental education.

On the other hand, the negative impacts at an environmental level are related to noise pollution, problems in traffic, destruction of the environment and natural areas or the accumulation of residues (Barker *et al.*, 2002; Collins *et al.*, 2007; Dwyer, Mellor, Mistilis and Mules, 2000; Faulkner and Tideswell, 1997; Kim *et al.*, 2006; Ritchie, Shipway and Cleeve, 2009), changes in land use, pollution of beaches, rivers, lakes or the damage of historical and cultural patrimony (Kim *et al.*, 2006). Additionally, Malfas *et al.* (2004) highlight the negative impacts on the environment correspondent to the temporary nature of some structures or facilities made to cover the needs of the event. In this sense, they reference Lenskyj (2000) who states that the transitoriness of infrastructure built for four sports in the Atlanta Olypmic Games that were demolished once the event was over was due to their limited usage by the local community. This has negative consequences on the sustainable ecological development, as elimination practices of those materials that cannot be recycled must be carried out (Malfas *et al.*, 2004).

Another group of important repercussions that result from the reception of sports events refers to the socio-cultural aspects. Within this group we must bring

The social impact of sports events **131**

attention to the contributions of numerous investigators that have identified several positive and negative impacts (e.g. Deccio and Baloglou, 2002; Fredline and Faulkner, 2000; Kim *et al.*, 2006; Parra, Calabuig, Añó, Ayora and Núñez, 2014; Ritchie *et al.*, 2009; Waitt, 2003). Some of the positive impacts of the category are associated with the opportunities granted by sports events of getting to know new people, incrementing the pride of the residents, to help understand and comprehend other cultures, to strengthen traditions and cultural values, as well as to develop a sense of national identity (Cheng and Jarvis, 2010; Fredline and Faulkner, 2000; Kim *et al.*, 2006; Malfas *et al.*, 2004; Waitt, 2003; Zhou and Ap, 2009). Moreover, sports events are portrayed as a unique opportunity to entertain local citizens and to improve the leisure possibilities of a city (Fredline, 2005).

Furthermore, reference has to be made to the likelihood that the organization of large sports events acts as a wake-up call to increment the interest of residents for the practice of sports activities, contributing to the improvement of the standard of living of those individuals (Malfas *et al.*, 2004). Nevertheless, there is not a unanimous consensus around this particular repercussion of sports events as different sources (e.g., Coalter and Taylor, 2008; EdComs, 2007; Murphy and Bauman, 2007; Veal and Frawley, 2009; Weed, Coren and Fiore, 2009) fix on the lack of confirmed evidence supporting that large sports events increase the level of participation in physical and sports activities amongst local residents. However, the demonstration effect of these events has a high potential to increment the frequency of participation of those that already take part in physical activities (Weed *et al.*, 2009) and acts as a catalyst to promote sports activities in the local community, which may have long-term consequences improving the physical conditions and health levels (Fredline, 2005).

Conclusively, as part of the sports repercussions, sports events can contribute to the construction of new sports facilities or improve existing ones, as well as increment the support of sports clubs, promoting local sports and granting new opportunities to young athletes (Gratton, Shibli and Coleman, 2005). However, Weed *et al.* (2009) state that the potential legacy of facilities is specially related to the impact on the participation of children and youth, with results that can vary depending on the event, pointing out evidence of a negative legacy if the local amenities are not located in a convenient area or targeted to the appropriate audience (EdComs, 2007). Likewise, Brown and Massey (2004) suggested, in their study about the 2002 Commonwealth Games, that the construction of new sports facilities benefited more elite athletes than the local residents of the city hosting the event.

On the contrary, the negative socio-cultural impacts relate to the alteration of how the city normally functions (Dwyer *et al.*, 2000; Faulkner and Tideswell, 1997) and how residents live or the restriction of access to public spaces and facilities (Fredline, 2005). This can lead to conflict between residents and visitors and a possible displacement of local citizens towards other places to avoid the mass use of the facilities by tourists during the time of the event (Bull and Lovell, 2007;

132 David Parra Camacho *et al.*

Fredline, 2004). Other negative impacts make reference to the congestion and traffic problems (Añó, Calabuig and Parra, 2012; Cegielski and Mules, 2002; Kim and Petrick, 2005; Kim *et al.*, 2006; Mihalik and Simonetta, 1999; Ohmann, Jones and Wilkes, 2006; Zhou, 2010), vandalism, the rise of crime rates, prostitution and inappropriate behaviors like excessive alcohol or drug consumption (Barker *et al.*, 2002; Cheng and Jarvis, 2010; Collins *et al.*, 2007; Dwyer *et al.*, 2000; Kim and Petrick, 2005; Kim *et al.*, 2006; Mihalik and Simonetta, 1999; Ohmann *et al.*, 2006).

At a psychological level there are different positive consequences of hosting sports events. Many researches include these impacts within the socio-cultural category due to their connection to other social aspects. Yet, following the classification by Preuss and Solberg (2006), displayed in Table 8.2, these impacts are considered as their own category. As a result, some positive aspects emphasized by numerous authors are related to the improvement of the residents' pride and the sense of belonging and identification in the community (Añó, Calabuig, Ayora, Parra and Duclos, 2014; Calabuig, Parra, Añó and Ayora, 2014; Fredline, 2004; Mihalik and Simonetta, 1999; Waitt, 2003; Zhou and Ap, 2009). As an example, in Mihalik and Simonetta's (1999) study about how residents perceived the benefits and costs of the Atlanta Olympic Games and in Ritchie and Aitken's (1984, 1985) study about the 1988 Calgary Winter Olympics, it was observed that the citizens' perceptions of the benefits were related more favorably to the pride of belonging to the city hosting the event than to the economic benefits. On top of that, Gursoy and Kendall's (2006) studies stress the importance of these psychological benefits as they can help tolerate or accept in a less dramatic manner negative socio-economic impacts (e.g. high public investment).

Along those lines, Kaplanidou *et al.* (2013) highlight different studies that state that psychological benefits are, on many occasions, the most valued amongst residents after the event (Kaplanidou, 2012; Kim and Petrick, 2005; Kim *et al.*, 2006). These authors quote the results found in the study by Kaplanidou (2012) carried out in 2010 about the perception of residents regarding the impact of the Olympic Games two, six, ten and fourteen years after their celebration. In her research she found out that Atlanta residents saw pride as one of the most important legacies of the Olympic Games in order to improve the standard of living, whilst in the case of Sydney residents the global awareness of Australian culture and the pride were also legacies that stood out as highly relevant.

Other psychological impacts relate to the festive ambience generated in the host community during the celebration of these events (Fredline, 2005; Jones, 2001; Preuss and Solberg, 2006; Waitt, 2003). For instance, in Ohmann *et al.*'s (2006) study on the social impact of the 2006 Germany Football World Cup, residents stressed the great festive environment and the enthusiasm of fans around the celebration of the event. Waitt (2003) also acknowledges, in his study about the social impact of the 2000 Sydney Olympic Games, that the degree of enthusiasm of residents because of the event was quite high, especially in the year of its celebration. The reception of a large sports event creates a festive ambience in

The social impact of sports events **133**

involving participation from residents and tourists, it being the joint participation and the urban life that allows the existence of the festive atmosphere in the host city (Preuss and Solberg, 2006). In fact, residents are an essential group in creating the mentioned positive atmosphere when they attend the event as spectators and interact with tourists and visitors. Moreover, event promoters tend to organize parties and different activities complementary to the event seeking to increase the excitement (Kim and Walker, 2012).

Some negative impacts at a psychological level are associated with the possibility that residents may adopt a defensive attitude towards the city, location or region hosting the event, as well as the possibility of misunderstandings that can lead to conflict or hostilities between residents and visitors (Preuss and Solberg, 2006).

Impacts at a political and administrative level are related to the city's image enhancement and its international recognition (Jeong and Faulkner, 1996) or the ability of the location to organize large sports events. These aspects are positive impacts that acknowledge the administrative and political aptitudes of the city to embrace large international ceremonies. In addition, they allow the organizers to develop, gain experience and improve their abilities to organize future sports events (Malfas *et al.*, 2004). In this way, Chalip (2006) shows that the final objective of events is not only to evaluate the impact of the event but also to take advantage of the learning opportunity to better face the organization of future happenings.

The aspects related to the enhancement of the image and international recognition of the city hosting the event are usually the most valued by residents in many of the investigations of this scope of research (e.g., Balduck *et al.*, 2011; Cegielski and Mules, 2002; Kim and Petrick, 2005; Mihalik and Simonetta, 1999; Parra, Añó, Ayora and Núñez, 2012; Zhou, 2010).

At a political level, the reception of large sports events like the Olympic Games is an opportunity for governing bodies to improve their image, prestige and political career (Hall, 1992b; Fredline, 2004). Malfas *et al.* (2004) reference Ritchie (1984), who calls this phenomenon a factor of micro-politics, which allows politicians to improve their public relations with international sports authorities and with the commercial organizations that participate in the event. In this sense, they use the case of the President of the Organization Committee of Sydney 2000 as an example, when he retired from politics after the Games to, later, work in the International Olympic Committee. Also, large sports events can promote and improve the image of certain political ideologies (Hall, 1992b; Roche, 2000; Zhou, 2007).

Conversely, within the negative impacts at a political and administrative level we have to highlight the possible use of the event as a propagandistic tool to influence the opinion of the residents (Hall, 1992b; Shone and Parry, 2001; Zhou, 2007). Furthermore, one must emphasize the likelihood that economic exploitation of the local residents may happen in order to satisfy the ambitions of the political elite, distorting the nature of the event to reflect certain political values (Preuss and Solberg, 2006) and imbalances in the distribution of benefits from the event may take place (Bowdin *et al.*, 2012; Hall, 1992b; Zhou, 2007). This can lead to conflicts, the formation of protest and collectives opposed to the event from the local residents' side, which can complicate the success of the event itself (Fredline, 2004).

Another negative consequence would be linked to the conflict of political interests that can favor those in power (Fredline, 2004). In this way, Malfas *et al.* (2004) point out that the organizing committees of large sports events frequently include political representatives that serve as their members or even as presidents, possibly being under contradictory pressures to present, on one side, the interests of contributors and, on the other side, the for-profit interests.

Conclusion

Large sports events require important economic investments with a percentage normally financed by the public administrations with regards to the construction or renovation of facilities and infrastructure, security, cleaning, etc.

The relevance of the public spending carried out on this kind of event makes it unavoidable to consult the citizens' opinions in order to know to what extent they support the celebration of the event. Even though in the majority of candidacies of large sports events it is normal to take into consideration if the residents support the celebration, studies that deeply analyze the social impact before, during and after the event takes place tend to be rarely requested by administrations and organizers, who prioritize those of an economic nature.

Most administrations and organization committees usually request studies that prove the economic impact of hosting large sports events to demonstrate their profitability. However, this type of event can surpass the costs and structural capacities of host cities, making it necessary to undertake important investments to respond to the specific organizational demands of the events themselves. Because of this, as highlighted by Matheson (2012), local administrations should take into account that a consistent strategy to celebrate sports events of smaller scale can provide greater net profits than a strategy focused on mega events of large dimensions but less frequency.

Likewise, the analysis of the social impact of events must be considered by the administrations as equally or more relevant than the economic impact. Among other reasons, social sustainability and viability of the event depend on the support of the citizens of the host city. Consequently, knowing and identifying the social impacts will allow improvements in the planning and management of sports events in all its phases.

At present there is not a theoretical frame with broad consensus about the social impacts of sports events, but classifications of the possible impacts derived from their celebration in host communities do exist. The consistency with other areas of investigation like tourism, as sports events are a phenomenon of especial touristic relevance, makes it possible for an important overlapping of both fields of research to exist. As a result, the majority of the scientific contributions realized in this area have focused on the use of scales, adapted from investigations carried out in the context of tourism, as well as explanatory theories that analyze and interpret the perceptions of residents about the impacts of certain sports events.

To attain the support of residents it is essential for a positive social exchange to take place, in which the residents consider that the benefits exceed the costs associated with the celebration of the event. This is one of the principles of the social exchange theory that has served as a support to the majority of the studies that assess the social repercussion of sports events.

In any case the assessment of the social impact of sports events must be taken into account in the integral analysis of this type of happening as they affect in a greater or lesser measure the standard of living of residents. If anything, this is more important when public money is invested to host such an event or when there is a redistribution of public income that would be otherwise destined for other areas influencing the social well-being of the community.

References

Abebe, N., Bolton, M. T., Pavelka, M. & Pierstoff, M. (2014). *Bidding for development: How the Olympic bid process can accelerate transportation development.* New York: Springer.

Ajzen, I. & Fishbein, M. (1980). *Understanding attitude and predicting social behaviour.* Englewood Cliffs, NJ: Prentice-Hall.

Allen, J., O'Toole, W., McDonnell, I. & Harris, R. (2005). *Festival and special event management* (3rd ed.). Milton, Australia: John Wiley & Sons.

Añó, V. (2011). *La organización de eventos y competiciones deportivas.* Valencia: Universidad de Valencia.

Añó, V., Calabuig, F., Ayora, D., Parra, D. & Duclos, D. (2014). 'Percepción social de la importancia, el impacto y los beneficios esperados de la celebración de los Juegos Mediterráneos de Tarragona en 2017'. *Revista de Psicología del Deporte, 22*(2), 321–329.

Añó, V., Calabuig, F. & Parra, D. (2012). 'Impacto social de un gran evento deportivo: el Gran Premio de Europa de Fórmula 1'. *Cultura, Ciencia y Deporte,* 7(19), 53–65.

Ap, J. (1992). 'Residents' perceptions on tourism impacts'. *Annals of Tourism Research, 19*(4), 665–690.

Baade, R., Baumann, R. & Matheson, V. (2008). 'Selling the game: Estimating the economic impact of professional sports through taxable sales'. *Southern Economic Journal,* 74(3), 794–810.

Baade, R. & Matheson, V. (2006). 'Have public finance principles been shut out in financing new stadiums for the NFL?' *Public Financing and Management, 6*(3), 284–320.

Baade, R., Matheson, V. & Nikolova, M. (2007). 'A tale of two stadiums: Comparing the economic impact of Chicago's Wrigley Field and U.S. Cellular Field'. *Geographische Rundschau International Edition, 3*(2), 53–58.

Balduck, A., Maes, M. & Buelens, M. (2011). 'The social impact of the Tour de France: Comparisons of residents' pre- and post-event perceptions'. *European Sport Management Quarterly, 11*(2), 91–113.

Barbassa, J. (2013). 'A river runs over with it'. Available at: <www.latitude.blogs.nytimes.com/2013/07/18/ariver-runs-over-with-it/?src=xps>.

Barker, M., Page, S. J. & Meyer, D. (2002). 'Modelling tourism crime: The 2000 America's Cup.' *Annals of Tourism Research*, *29*(3), 762–782.

Bowdin, G., Allen, J., Harris, R., McDonnell, I. & O'Toole, W. (2012). *Events management* (3rd ed). Oxford: Elsevier.

Brown, A. & Massey, J. (2004). *The sports development impact of the Manchester 2002 Commonwealth Games: Post Games Report*. London: UK Sport.

Brunet, F. (1995). 'An economic analysis of the Barcelona '92 Olympic Games: Resources, financing and impact'. In M. De Moragas & M. Botella, (eds.), *The keys to success: The social, sporting, economic and communications impact of Barcelona' 92* (pp. 203–237). Barcelona: Centre d'Estudis Olimpics de l'Esport, Universitat Autónoma de Barcelona.

Burdge, R. J. (2003). 'The practice of social impact assessment background'. *Impact Assessment and Project Appraisal*, *21*(2), 84–88.

Bull, C. & Lovell, J. (2007). 'The impact of hosting major sporting events on local residents: An analysis of the views and perceptions of Canterbury residents in relation to the Tour de France 2007'. *Journal of Sport Tourism*, *12*(3), 229–248.

Calabuig, F., Parra, D., Añó, V. & Ayora, D. (2014). 'Análisis de la percepción de los residentes sobre el impacto cultural y deportivo de un Gran Premio de Fórmula 1'. *Movimento*, *20*(1), 261–280.

Cegielski, M. & Mules, T. (2002). 'Aspects of residents' perceptions of the GMC 400-Canberra's V8 supercar race'. *Current Issues in Tourism*, *5*(1), 54–70.

Chalip, L. (2006). 'Towards social leverage of sport events'. *Journal of Sport & Tourism*, *11*(2), 109–127.

Cheng, E. & Jarvis, N. (2010). 'Residents' perception of the social-cultural impacts of the 2008 Formula 1 Singtel Singapore Grand Prix'. *Event Management*, *14*(2), 91–106.

Coalter, F. & Taylor, J. (2008). *Large Scale Sports Events: Event Impact Framework*. Report to UK Sport. London: UK Sport.

Collins, A., Flynn, A., Munday, M. & Roberts, A. (2007). 'Assessing the environmental consequences of major sporting events: The 2003/04 FA Cup Final'. *Urban Studies*, *44*(3), 457–476.

Collins, A., Jones, C. & Munday, M. (2009). 'Assessing the environmental impacts of mega sporting events: Two options?' *Tourism Management*, *30*(6), 828–837.

Cottle, E. 2010. *A preliminary evaluation of the impact of the 2010 FIFA World Cup™ in South Africa*. SHA, Zurich. Available at: <www.sah.ch/data/D23807E0/Impactassessment FinalSeptember2010EddieCottle.pdf>.

Deccio, C. & Baloglu, S. (2002). 'Non-host community resident reactions to the 2002 Winter Olympics: The spillover impacts'. *Journal of Travel Research*, *41*(1), 46–56.

Deery, M. & Jago, L. (2010). 'Social impacts of events and the role of anti-social behaviour'. *International Journal of Event and Festival Management*, *1*(1), 8–28.

Delamere, T. A. (2001). 'Development of a scale to measure resident attitudes toward the social impacts of community festivals, part II: Verification of the scale'. *Event Management*, *7*(1), 25–38.

Delamere, T. A., Wankel, L. M. & Hinch, T. D. (2001). 'Development of a scale to measure resident attitudes toward the social impacts of community festivals, part I: Item generation and purification of the measure'. *Event Management*, *7*(1), 11–24.

Dhar, R. & Kim, E.Y. (2007). 'Seeing the forest or the trees: Implications of construal level theory for consumer choice'. *Journal of Consumer Psychology*, *17*(2), 96–100.

Dwyer, L., Mellor, R., Mistilis, N. & Mules, T. (2000). 'A framework for assessing "tangible" and "intangible" impacts of events and conventions'. *Event Management*, *6*(3), 175–189.

The social impact of sports events **137**

Dyer, P., Gursoy, D., Sharma, B. & Carter, J. (2007). 'Structural modelling of resident perceptions of tourism and associated development on the Sunshine Coast, Australia'. *Tourism Management*, *28*(2), 409–422.

Eagly, A. H. & Chaiken, S. (1993). *The psychology of attitudes*. Orlando: Harcourt Brace Jovanovich.

EdComs (2007). *London 2012 legacy research: final report*. DCMS.

Faulkner, B. & Tideswell, C. (1997). 'A framework for monitoring community impacts of tourism'. *Journal of Sustainable Tourism*, *5*(1), 3–28.

Fredline, E. (2004). 'Host community reactions to motorsport events: The perception of impact on quality of life'. In B. W. Ritchie & D. Adair (eds.), *Sport tourism: Interrelationships, impacts and issues* (pp. 155–173). Clevedon, Reino Unido: Channel View Publications.

Fredline, E. (2005). 'Host and guest relations and sport tourism'. *Sport in Society*, *8*(2), 263–279.

Fredline, E. & Faulkner, B. (2000). 'Host community reactions: A cluster analysis'. *Annals of Tourism Research*, *27*(3), 763–784.

Fredline, L., Jago, L. & Deery, M. (2003). 'The development of a generic scale to measure the social impacts of events'. *Event Management*, *8*(1), 23–37.

Getz, D. (1997). *Event management and event tourism*. New York: Congizant Communication Corporation.

Getz, D. (2007). *Event studies. Theory, research and policy for planned events*. Burlington: Butterworth-Heinemann.

Gramling, R. & Freudenburg, W. R. (1992). 'Opportunity, threat, development, and adaptation: Toward a comprehensive framework for social impact assessment'. *Rural Sociology*, *57*(2), 216–234.

Gratton, C. & Preuss, H. (2008). 'Maximizing Olympic impacts by building up legacies'. *The International Journal of the History of Sport*, *25*(14), 1922–1938.

Gratton, C., Liu, D., Ramchandani, G. & Wilson, D. (2012). *The global economics of sport*. London: Routledge

Gratton, C., Shibli, S. & Coleman, R. (2005). 'Sport and economic regeneration in cities'. *Urban Studies*, *42*(5–6), 985.

Gratton, C., Shibli, S. & Coleman, R. (2006). 'The economic impact of major sports events: A review of ten events in the UK'. *The Sociological Review*, 54, 41–58.

Gursoy, D. & Kendall, K. W. (2006). 'Hosting mega events: Modeling locals' support'. *Annals of Tourism Research*, *33*(3), 603–623.

Gursoy, D. & Rutherford, D. G. (2004). 'Host attitudes toward tourism: An improved structural model'. *Annals of Tourism Research*, *31*(3), 495–516.

Hall, C. M. (1989). 'Hallmark tourist events: Analysis, definition, methodology and review'. In G. J. Syme, B. J. Shaw, D. M. Fenton, D. M., & W.S. Mueller (eds.), *The planning and evaluation of hallmark events* (pp. 3–40). Sydney, Australia: Avebury

Hall, C. M. (1992a). 'Adventure, sport and health tourism'. In B. Weiler & C. M. Hall (eds.), *Special interest tourism* (pp. 141–158). London: Belhaven Press.

Hall, C. M. (1992b). *Hallmark tourist events: impact, management, and planning*. London: Belhaven Press.

Hall, C. M. & Hodges, J. (1998). 'The politics of place and identity in the Sydney 2000 Olympics: "Sharing the spirit of corporate capitalism" '. In M. Roche (ed.), *Sport, popular culture and identity* (pp. 95–112). Aachen: Meyer & Meyer.

Hiller, H. H. (1990). 'The urban transformation of a landmark event: The 1988 Calgary Winter Olympics'. *Urban Affairs Quarterly*, *26*(1), 118–137.

Hiller, H. H. (2006). 'Post-event outcomes and the post-modern turn: The Olympics and urban transformations. *European Sport Management Quarterly*, *6*(4), 317–332.

Hritz, N. & Ross, C. (2010). 'The perceived impacts of sport tourism: An urban host community perspective. *Journal of Sport Management*, *24*(2), 119–138.

International Olympic Committee (2009). *Report of the 2016 IOC Evaluation Commission – Games of the XXXI Olympiad. 02 sept. 2009.* Available at: <www.olympic.org/Documents/Reports/EN/en_report_1469.pdf>.

Jeong, G. H. & Faulkner, B. (1996). 'Resident perceptions of mega-event impacts: The Taejon international exposition case'. *Festival Management & Event Tourism*, *4*(1–2), 3–11.

Jin, L., Zhang, J. J., Ma, X. & Connaughton, D. P. (2011). 'Residents' perceptions of environmental impacts of the 2008 Beijing Green Olympic Games'. *European Sport Management Quarterly*, *11*(3), 275–300.

Jones, C. (2001). 'Mega-events and host region impacts: Determining the true worth of the 1999 Rugby World Cup'. *International Journal of Tourism Research*, *3*(3), 241–251.

Jones, C. & Munday, M. (2008). 'Assessing the impact of a major sporting event: The role of environmental accounting'. *Tourism Economics*, *14*(2), 343–360.

Kaplanidou, K. (2012). 'The importance of legacy outcomes for Olympic Games four summer host cities residents' quality of life: 1996–2008'. *European Sport Management Quarterly*, *12*(4), 397–433.

Kaplanidou, K., Karadakis, K., Gibson, H., Thapa, B., Walker, M., Geldenhuys, S. & Coetzee, W. (2013). 'Quality of life, event impacts, and mega-event support among South African residents before and after the 2010 FIFA World Cup'. *Journal of Travel Research*, *52*(5), 631–645.

Kasimati, E. (2003). 'Economic aspects and the Summer Olympics: A review of related research'. *International Journal of Tourism Research*, *5*(6), 433–444.

Kasimati, E. & Dawson, P. (2009). 'Assessing the impact of the 2004 Olympic Games on the Greek economy: A small macroeconometric model'. *Economic Modelling*, *26*(1), 139–146.

Kim, H. J., Gursoy, D. & Lee, S. B. (2006). 'The impact of the 2002 World Cup on South Korea: Comparisons of pre- and post-games'. *Tourism Management*, *27*(1), 86–96.

Kim, S. S. & Petrick, J. F. (2005). 'Residents' perceptions on impacts of the FIFA 2002 World Cup: The case of Seoul as a host city'. *Tourism Management*, *26*(1), 25–38.

Kim, W. & Walker, M. (2012). 'Measuring the social impacts associated with Super Bowl XLIII: Preliminary development of a psychic income scale'. *Sport Management Review*, *15*(1), 91–108.

Ko, D. & Stewart, W. P. (2002). 'A structural equation model of residents' attitudes for tourism development'. *Tourism Management*, *23*(5), 521–530.

Lee, C. & Back, K. (2003). 'Pre- and post-casino impact of residents' perception'. *Annals of Tourism Research*, *30*(4), 868–885.

Lee, S. & Krohn, B. D. (2013). 'A study of psychological support from local residents for hosting mega-sporting events: A case of the 2012 Indianapolis Super Bowl XLVI'. *Event Management*, *17*(4), 361–376.

Lenskyj, H. J. (2000). *Inside the Olympic industry: Power, politics and activism.* New York: State University of New York.

Llopis, R. (2012). 'Repercusiones y efectos sociales de los mega-eventos deportivos. Acotaciones teóricas y evidencia empírica'. In R. Llopis (ed.), *Mega-eventos deportivos: perspectivas científicas y estudios de casos*, (pp. 97–134). Barcelona: Editorial UOC.

Maennig, W. & Du Plessis, S. (2009). 'Sport stadia, sporting events and urban development: International experience and the ambitions of Durban'. *Urban Forum*, *20*(1), 61–76.

Malfas, M., Theodoraki, E. & Houlihan, B. (2004) 'Impacts of the Olympic Games as mega-events'. *Municipal Engineer*, *157*(3), 209–220.

Matheson, V. (2012). 'Efectos de los principales mega-eventos deportivos en las economías locales, regionales y nacionales'. In, R. Llopis (ed.), *Mega-eventos deportivos: perspectivas científicas y estudios de casos*, (pp. 53–74). Barcelona: Editorial UOC.

Mathieson, A. & Wall, G. (1982). *Tourism: Economic, physical and social impacts*. London: Longman.

Ministry of National Economy (2004). *Budget Deficit in Greece*. Statements of Vice Minister Petros Doukas (August 4), Athens.

Mihalik, B. J., & Simonetta, L. (1999). 'A midterm assessment of the host population's perceptions of the 1996 Summer Olympics: Support, attendance, benefits, and liabilities'. *Journal of Travel Research, 37*(3), 244–248.

Müller, M. (2012). 'Popular perception of urban transformation through mega-events: Understanding support for the 2014 Winter Olympics in Sochi'. *Environment and Planning C: Government and Policy, 30*(4), 693–711.

Murphy, N. & Bauman, A. (2007). 'Mass sporting and physical activity events – are they "Bread and Circuses" or public health interventions to increase population levels of physical activity?' *Journal of Physical Activity and Health, 4*(2), 193–202.

Ohmann, S., Jones, I. & Wilkes, K. (2006). 'The perceived social impacts of the 2006 World Cup on Munich residents'. *Journal of Sport and Tourism, 11*(2), 129–152.

Olsen, M. & Merwin, D. (1977). 'Towards a methodology for conducting social impacts assessments using quality of life indicators'. In K. Finsterbusch & C. Wolf, (eds.), *Methodology of social impact assessment*. Pennsylvania: Dowden, Hutchinson & Ross.

Parra, D., Añó, V., Ayora, D. & Núñez, J.M. (2012). 'Percepción social sobre la repercusión de un evento deportivo'. *Journal of Sports Economics and Management, 2*(1), 34–51.

Parra, D., Calabuig, F. & Añó, V. (2013). 'Relación entre el apoyo a la acogida de un evento deportivo y la percepción de los residentes sobre el impacto socio-económico'. In P. Burillo, J. García, B. Pérez & J. Sánchez (eds.), *Reinventando la Economía del Deporte* (pp. 39–42). Madrid: Gráficas Lid.

Parra, D., Calabuig, F., Añó, V., Ayora, D. & Núñez, J. M. (2014). 'El impacto de un evento deportivo mediano: percepción de los residentes de la comunidad de acogida'. *Retos: Nuevas tendencias en Educación Física, Deporte y Recreación*, 26, 88–93.

Prayag, G., Hosany, S., Nunkoo, R. & Alders, T. (2013). 'London residents' support for the Olympic Games: The mediating effect of overall attitude'. *Tourism Management, 36*, 629–640.

Preuss, H. (2004). 'Calculating the regional economic impact of the Olympic Games'. *European Sport Management Quarterly, 4*(4), 234–253.

Preuss, H. (2007). 'The conceptualisation and measurement of mega sport event legacies'. *Journal of Sport & Tourism, 12*(3–4), 207–228.

Preuss, H. & Solberg, H. A. (2006). 'Attracting major sporting events: The role of local residents'. *European Sport Management Quarterly, 6*(4), 391–411.

Ritchie, J. R. B. (1984). Assessing the impact of hallmark events: Conceptual and research issues. *Journal of Travel Research, 23*(1), 2–11. doi:10.1177/004728758402300101

Ritchie, J. R. B. & Aitken, C. (1984). 'Olympulse I: The Research Program and Initial Results'. *Journal of Travel Research, 22*(1), 17–25. doi:10.1177/004728758702600104

Ritchie, J. R. B. & Aitken, C. (1985). 'Olympulse II: Evolving Residents Attitudes toward the 1988 Olympic Winter Games'. *Journal of Travel Research, 23*(3), 28–33. doi:10.1177/004728758502300306

Ritchie, B. W., Shipway, R. & Cleeve, B. (2009). 'Resident perceptions of mega-sporting events: A non-host city perspective of the 2012 London Olympic Games'. *Journal of Sport & Tourism, 14*(2), 143–167.

Rocha, C. M. (2015). 'Support of politicians for the 2016 Olympic Games in Rio de Janeiro'. *Leisure Studies, 35*(4), 487–504.

Roche, M. (2000). *Mega-events and modernity: Olympics and expos in the growth of global culture.* London: Routledge.

Shone, A. & Parry, B. (2001). *Successful event management, a practical handbook.* London: Continuum.

Small, K., Edwards, D. & Sheridan, L. (2005). 'A flexible framework for evaluating the socio-cultural impacts of a (small) festival'. *International Journal of Event Management Research, 1*(1), 66 –77.

Smith, A. & Fox, T. (2007). 'From "event-led" to "event-themed" regeneration: The 2002 Commonwealth Games. *Urban Studies, 44*(5–6), 1125–1143.

Solberg, H. A. & Preuss, H. (2007). 'Major sport events and long-term tourism impacts'. *Journal of Sport Management, 21*(2), 213–234.

Tomlinson, R. (2009). 'Anticipating 2011'. In U. Pillay, R. Tomlinson & O. Bass (eds.), *Development and dreams: The urban legacy of the 2010 Football World Cup.* Cape Town: HSRC Press.

Trope, Y. & Liberman, N. (2003). 'Temporal construal'. *Psychological Review, 110*(3), 403–421.

Valencian Institute of Economic Investigations (2007). *Impacto económico de la 32a America's Cup Valencia 2007.* Valencia: Instituto Valenciano de Investigaciones Económicas.

Vanclay, F. (2003). 'International principles for social impact assessment'. *Impact Assessment and Project Appraisal, 21*(1), 5–12.

Veal, A. & Frawley, S. (2009) *'Sport for All' and Major Sporting Events.* Sydney Australian Centre for Olympic Studies, UTS: Sydney.

Waitt, G. (2003). 'Social impacts of the Sydney Olympics'. *Annals of Tourism Research, 30*(1), 194–215.

Weed, M., Coren, E. & Fiore, J. (2009) *A systematic review of the evidence base for developing a physical activity and health legacy from the London 2012 Olympic and Paralympic Games.* Canterbury: SPEAR.

Zhou, J. Y. (2007). *Government and residents' perceptions towards the impacts of a mega event: the Beijing 2008 Olympic Games.* (Doctoral thesis). School of Hotel and Tourism Management, The Hong Kong Polytechnic University.

Zhou, J. Y. (2010). 'Resident perceptions toward the impacts of the Macao Grand Prix'. *Journal of Convention & Event Tourism, 11*(2), 138–153.

Zhou, J. Y. & Ap, J. (2009). 'Residents' perceptions towards the impacts of the Beijing 2008 Olympic Games'. *Journal of Travel Research, 48*(1), 78–91.

9

SPORT ENTREPRENEURSHIP AND COMMUNITY DEVELOPMENT IN JAPAN

Isao Okayasu and Duarte B. Morais

Introduction

Sport has produced several effects on communities. Effects of sport on the community are not only economic, but social, such as enhancing community ties and identities. With an aging society, the Japanese government has focused on sport-related communities for regional residents and tourists. This chapter will examine two aspects of sport entrepreneurship and, in particular, micro-entrepreneurship in Japan through face-to-face or telephone semi-structured interviews.

First, this paper examines community sport organizations. This type of sport organization has the purpose of promoting physically and mentally healthy lives in its community. And the Japanese government has promoted comprehensive community sport organizations for its residents. However, these types of organizations have some problems, including financial management. Community sport organizations need to consider and understand sport entrepreneurship methods.

Second, we will focus on sport entrepreneurship and inbound tourism. Regional communities, in particular, face social problems such as isolation of the elderly within an aging society. In many of these regions, there are natural areas which have big potential for attracting sport tourists with trekking, rafting and so on. And some foreign entrepreneurs have started nature-tourism-related businesses in these regions. This chapter will focus on a commercial rafting company and its operations in a regional setting as a foreign-owned business. Regional areas can generally be an exclusive society. This chapter investigates how they solved some of these regional community barriers.

Sport environment in Japan

Japanese society has tended to expect a relationship between sport and social development. Tokyo will host the Summer Olympic and Paralympic Games in 2020. And, Japan will host the Rugby World Cup in 2019. In addition, Kansai area, where Osaka, Kyoto and Kobe are located, will host the World Masters Games in 2021.

In these circumstances, community sport and sport tourism in Japan have changed their management. Both have become more entrepreneurial with more self-management and self-organization. According to the basic plan for the promotion of sport in Japan (2001 ~ 1010), comprehensive community sport clubs are an important part of improving the sport situation and bringing about a lifelong sports society.

Historically, Japanese community sports clubs have organized both school and business organizations. Kawanishi (2003) noted that schools and business organizations provided opportunities to improve competitive abilities and enrich sports activities.

However, the Japanese economy has slackened and sport in Japan has been affected by a decrease in the number of sport teams in businesses and a shortage of financial resources. Yamaguchi (2006, p. 42) noted that "The traditional Japanese sport system is now facing a number of difficulties. The training of athletes has been conducted separately during different stages in life at school, in the community, and at the workplace."

Under these circumstances, the Ministry of Education, Culture, Sports, Science and Technology (MEXT) kicked off a comprehensive community sports club project. This type of club was launched to be available to people of all ages from children to elderly and all levels of skill from beginners to top-level athletes. Kurosu (2003) explained that this type of community sport club has organized regional residents. Community sport clubs found it necessary for their members to manage and be independent from public sector financial resources and philosophies. Namely, community sport organizations in Japan have shifted to independent management styles in order to meet the needs of the community.

The new type of community sport clubs that were launched are shown in Figure 9.1. Around 3,200 clubs have been organized and around 250 clubs have been prepared in 2014. In addition, according to a report on comprehensive community sport clubs, there are around 650 clubs with corporate status such as NPO.

Historically, tourism was a very popular activity in Japan. Takada & Ishimori (1993) noted that about 1 million passersby went through the *Tokaido*, which was an important 500 km route that connected Edo (modern-day Tokyo) to Kyoto. However, the Tokugawa shogunate government during this Edo era prohibited foreigners from entering Japan and any Japanese from leaving the country under penalty of death.

In December 2006, the Japanese government launched Tourism Nation Promotion Basic Law. This law set four basic policies. One of the policies was "Promotion of International Tourism", which calls for an increase in inbound

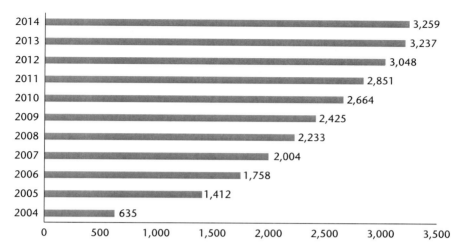

FIGURE 9.1 The total number of comprehensive community sport clubs

Resource: The actual condition survey of comprehensive community sport clubs: Overview by Ministry of Education, Culture, Sports, Science and Technology-Japan

tourism. Figure 9.2 shows that tourism in Japan has been imbalanced in the long term between inbound and outbound tourists. The Japanese government has been trying to correct this imbalance with a strategy of enhancing the Japanese tourism industry. Japan has some unique attractions such as traditional architecture and natural scenic beauty.

In terms of Japanese travel overseas, approximately 13 million Japanese people traveled abroad in 2003. On the other hand, the number of inbound tourists visiting Japan had remained stagnant until 2003, as shown in Figure 9.2. Under these circumstances, the Japanese government launched the "Visit Japan" campaign in 2003 to promote inbound tourism. However, Japan has a big problem in promoting more inbound tourism. It is language. Okayasu *et al.* (2012) pointed out the importance of speaking English in Japanese tourism services. In addition, hardware and soft content enhance the experience for tourists as Nogawa noted (2007).

Sport tourism can help increase the number of inbound tourists. Japan has some attractive sports for foreign tourists. This includes spectator sports such as professional baseball, football and sumo. On the other hand, there are participation sports such as skiing, trekking and rafting.

According to a consumer report regarding inbound tourists from January to March of 2015, 10 per cent of the tourists reported participating in skiing/snowboarding. However, 20 per cent responded that they expected to participate in skiing/snowboarding on their next visit to Japan. This may show possibilities for increasing winter season sport tourism.

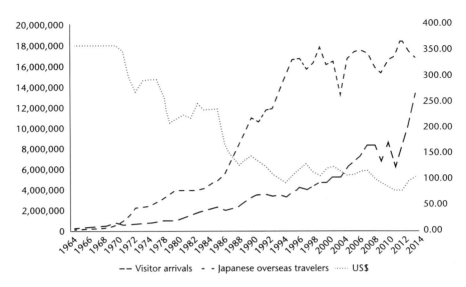

FIGURE 9.2 The number of inbound/outbound tourists and the rate of Japanese yen to US dollars

Resource: Visitor arrivals, Japanese overseas travelers by years by the Japan National Tourism Organization

Social development through community sport organizations

Sport is a culture which has grown together with the development of human society (Ikeda, *et al.*, 2003). Long and Sanderson (2001) noted the possibilities of what sport can do for a community. They pointed out its contributions of leisure, recreation, community participation, enhancement of confidence and self-esteem, reduction in crime, encouraging community pride and so on.

As we noted, the Japanese government launched a policy for a new type of community sport organization. It was named comprehensive community sport club in 2003. An example of such a community sport club is the sport club in Hatsukaichi, which started a junior soccer team in 1998. In the following year, it started a junior tennis club. The club has also received its NPO certification from the local prefecture. The number of club members was about 900 in November of 2015. The youngest member is two years old, and the oldest member is 83 years old.

The purpose of this club is "to make a good community where everyone can enjoy sporting activities" (Hatsukaichi Sport Club, n.d.). The vision of this club is stated in the following three ideas: 1) To create a great club environment for children to the elderly as a symbol of community; 2) Have training strategies for top athletes; 3) Plan a sport fund that supports social welfare in the community. The concept is outlined in Figure 9.3.

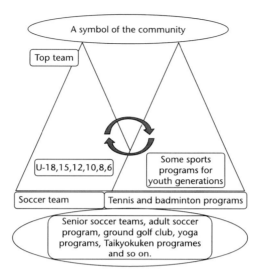

FIGURE 9.3 The image of the sport club in Hatsukaichi City
Modified with original concept from official website

According to the founder, the club would like to promote social aspects of community development through the sport club. Public fields are used for some of the club's top teams and junior soccer teams. Elderly participants in yoga and Tai Chi use a room in a community center. The club maintains a good relationship with other local organizations. In addition, the club has a club house where staff and members can communicate. This club house is also used for sport programs. This club house is supported by the Sport Promotion Fund and the Lottery Department by Japan Sport Council. This fund helps enhance the development of community sport entrepreneurship in Japan.

Table 9.1 shows an analysis of skills/experience in the sport club of Hatsukaichi. The club has access to good staff and workers with useful skills and experience from within the community. Some of the residents in the community volunteer and assist with the management of the club, which has been very helpful. The

TABLE 9.1 An analysis of skills/experience in the Sport Club of Hatsukaichi

Useful skills/experience	Missing skills/experience
SKILLS	SKILLS
Human network	Management of public field
EXPERIENCES	EXPERIENCES
History since 1998	Consortium of management in public field

founder of the club has been living in the community for about 30 years. The club has been around for 20 years. When he first came to the community, there was no network of sport club workers. As he built various programs, he also built up a human resource network of sport club workers.

On the other hand, the founder previously didn't have an opportunity to be part of a designated manager system of public facilities. Under such an arrangement, plans were made to hold a kids' futsal school program weekly, making use of a hospital facility near the club. The community sport club and the hospital are looking into possible sport programs for the disabled, such as soccer for amputees. These types of collaborations can enhance community welfare and social inclusion.

Japanese society faces a low birthrate coupled with a high life expectancy. In these circumstances, community sport clubs are one of the key factors in community sport promotion. The number of children participating in community teams has fallen. The founder of the community sport organization could have consolidated some of the teams but decided against it, because he wanted to keep offering different choices for the children. His club has a higher fee than other local clubs, but hires good coaches and competes for championships.

In order to provide diverse choices to society and communities, economically and skills-wise, clubs need to be offered at multiple price points, from low fees to high fees, and also at multiple levels from recreational to top-level athletes.

Social development through commercial rafting companies

A pioneer of sport tourism in the Niseko area

Japan has attractive mountains and forests. However, these sites and Japanese sport tourism have structural problems. According to Harada (2009), local sightseeing sites did not have enough sporting infrastructure and programs to attract many tourists.

Japanese sport culture has not popularized these types of outdoor sport programs as leisure activities. At the start of the Outdoor Sport Programs Company, many were skeptical about community development through an outdoor sport program, partly due to the Japanese inexperience with rafting and kayaking as leisure activities. Some athletes were involved with canoe slalom, wildwater and so on – but those types of leisure activities were not popular in Japan.

Sport entrepreneurs will likely focus on both local community residents and visitors. They will likely have to build their business model on both. For example, a rafting company should seek local schools and groups to come on trips, as well as outside visitors. A martial arts academy will have regular local students and will also likely organize competitions that attract outside teams to visit the region during weekends.

The research asked two key people three questions about sport entrepreneurship and outdoor sport activities for people in the community and outside visitors by semi-structured interviews face to face or by telephone. 1) How did you build an outdoor sport company? 2) What were some of the difficulties of being a foreign manager? 3) How can sport entrepreneurship benefit society? The outdoor sport field, in particular?

The founder built the Outdoor Sport Programs Company in the Niseko area located in the north part of Japan in 1996. He has helped develop sport tourism in the Niseko area, which is a popular summer activity area for trekking, kayaking and rafting. In addition, he promotes to Australian and New Zealand skiers, encouraging them to visit the region. He was selected as "tourism charisma" in 2004, a first for a foreigner, by the Japan Tourism Agency and also serves on a number of public boards and committees related to sport tourism.

When he built the company, the Niseko area was stagnant in its tourism promotion. His activities triggered the making of community brands in the area, which includes the Outdoor Sport Holy Land in the Hokkaido prefecture. He could not have imagined a greater success at the beginning of his company. And his perspective and communication with local organizations led to the making of a community brand and busy tourism seasons for the area. An analysis of skills/experience in the Outdoor Club of Niseko is outlined in Table 9.2.

This area is famous among tourists from Australia and East Asian countries for its good snow conditions. The founder noted that about 96 per cent of the participants in the winter season programs were foreign (NAC Niseko Adventure Centre, 2016). In particular, Oceanian and South east Asian tourists were the main guests of his company's programs during the winter. This situation has been going on throughout the entire Niseko area. According to a Niseko town report, the numbers of summer and winter season tourists in the town have been similar. Historically, this area was famous for its good snow, and winter tourism was bigger than summer tourism. However, after rafting in the Niseko area was popularized, there were more summer tourists than winter tourists beginning in 1999. The reputation of the quality of the snow and the resorts at Niseko spread among foreign tourists in the 2000s, and the numbers of tourists in the summer and winter are now almost equal as Figure 9.4 demonstrates.

TABLE 9.2 An analysis of skills/experience in the Outdoor Club of Niseko

Useful skills/experience	**Missing** skills/experiences
SKILLS	SKILLS
Branding	**Language skill of Japanese staff**
EXPERIENCES	EXPERIENCES
History from 1996	**Balance of customer numbers in each season**

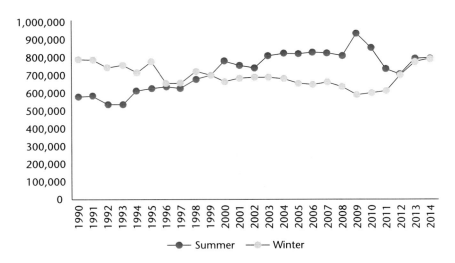

FIGURE 9.4 The number of tourists in summer and winter season at Niseko Town

Resource: The report of Niseko town

Multi-organizer of outdoor sport programs in the Minakami area

The founder is a rafting company owner in Japan and lives Minakami town, which is about three hours from Tokyo. Traditionally, this area was a popular spa resort in Japan. However, the number of outside visitors had been declining in recent years. Some outdoor sport programs such as rafting, trekking and snowboarding have attracted outdoor lovers. This study explores the relationship between outdoor sport and social entrepreneurship.

First, the founder created an original outdoor sport programs company in 1995. Before becoming an owner, he worked at another rafting company as a guide and operations manager in Japan. When he founded a new company in Minakami, he faced challenges in communicating with local organizations in the tourism industry, and the residents. He is now a participating member of a local community committee on tourism. He has incorporated the ways tourism was promoted in Queenstown, New Zealand, his hometown, in the Minakami area to formulate a new approach to tourism development in the local town.

Second, outdoor sport programs have some risks due to the natural environment. And it's not possible to completely eliminate all risks related to outdoor recreational activities. In addition, the Japanese have different attitudes and behaviors regarding outdoor recreational activities and their potential risks than Western participants. Commercial companies and guides need to consider these differences.

Third, social sport entrepreneurship faces challenges within regional areas. The founder noted the need for communication with local organizations and related private companies and the need for building trust through a business relationship in order to increase business for outdoor sport programs. His company has some winter sport programs such as skiing and snowboarding. However, he did not have good connections with the local ski and snowboard organizations. A staff member, who was a rafting guide, from a winter resort organization introduced him to the program coordinator of a ski resort. He knew this staff member and had a good connection through an old acquaintance. As previously mentioned, the Japanese government had launched an inbound tourism promotion. Local governments have paid attention to this tourism policy. However, many local areas do not have good programs for inbound tourism. Foreign social entrepreneurs can make great use of an inbound tourism promotion for regional areas. But, local governments do not have good connections with foreign social sport entrepreneurs and have not built a solid relationship with them. Despite these circumstances, the founder has secured a chance to communicate with the local government and resort companies. Table 9.3 shows a summary of his useful and missing skills and experiences. He has managed so far using his strengths. He is studying Japanese business customs and other areas in which he is weak. The local residents have come to gradually understand his passion for outdoor sport and Japanese community development.

Figure 9.5 shows the number of guests at the Outdoor Sport Program Company from 2008 to 2014. Minakami town, like many other Japanese regional towns, faces a decrease in tourists and residents and the accompanying social problems. In these situations, some outdoor sport programs may be a part of the solution to these problems. With the exception of a decrease in the number of international guests following the 2011 earthquake, the company data shows an increase in international tourists and tourism in general. This increase is due to, in large part, foreign social sport entrepreneurship.

Figure 9.6 shows that over half of the foreign guests visiting were from Australia. As reflected in these statistics, Japanese outdoor sport sites have attracted Australian tourists. This has been going on for the last 10 years. On the other hand, the program was not popular with tourists from Asian countries. These results show what can be possible with international program planning by sport entrepreneurs in Japan and can lead to further consideration of outdoor sport programs in relation to community development and foreign tourism.

Sport entrepreneurs will likely focus on local community residents and visitors, with sport tourism being a key factor. According to the website of the Rafting

TABLE 9.3 An analysis of skills/experience in the Outdoor Club of Minakami

Useful skills/experiences	Missing skills/experiences
SKILLS	SKILLS
New marketing strategy	Japanese customs
EXPERIENCES	EXPERIENCES
Outdoor activities in the world	Community business

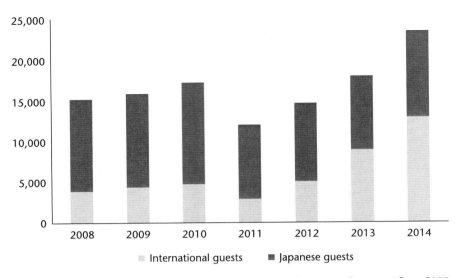

FIGURE 9.5 The number of guests at the Outdoor Sport Programs Company from 2008 to 2014

Resource: Original data from the Outdoor Sport Programs Company in Minakami

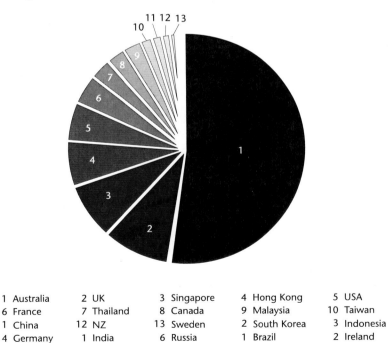

1 Australia	2 UK	3 Singapore	4 Hong Kong	5 USA
6 France	7 Thailand	8 Canada	9 Malaysia	10 Taiwan
11 China	12 NZ	13 Sweden	2 South Korea	3 Indonesia
4 Germany	1 India	6 Russia	1 Brazil	2 Ireland

FIGURE 9.6 The number of foreign guests at the Outdoor Sport Programs Company in 2014

Resource: Original data of Outdoor Sport Programs Company in Minakami

Association in Japan about 50 companies have received certification from this association. Rafting in Japanese regional communities can contribute to social and economic enhancement in those areas. On a related note, the International Rafting Federation has announced that the 2017 World Championship will be held in Miyoshi of Tokushima prefecture in Japan. Miyoshi city also faces a declining birthrate and an aging society. According to the master plan by the city (N.D.), the population of those over 65 years old was up 2,501, or over 25 per cent, from 11,385 over 20 years. The rafting championship can be an opportunity to get more rafters and help with the development of the region.

The possibility to enhance sport entrepreneurship in Japan

Social entrepreneurship can be a part of a solution for the two foreign entrepreneurs introduced in this section, who are working to build good relationships with their communities and helping them grow through outdoor sport activities. These people encounter some friction with the regional communities due to differences in culture and thinking. These problems may also be encountered by a Japanese entrepreneur, someone who perhaps moved to the area after marriage and is also not a local. According to Lebra (1976), Japanese people tend to evaluate and engage with *soto*, or outside or public, very differently from how they evaluate and engage with *uchi*, or inside or private, Thus, foreign and non-local entrepreneurs may face disadvantages in their work. However, Japanese society has been gradually changing to better understand "outsiders." There's a theory in Japan that *wakamono* (young people), *yosomono* (outsiders), and *bakamono* (idiots) are needed to revitalize regional areas. Japanese communities want a better understanding of and solutions for problems such as depopulation and economic recessions. As Aldrich (2005) notes, communities can enhance ties between socially different people through experiencing diversity.

Japan has had to deal with various natural disasters like the Great East Japan earthquake of 2011 and its various effects such as the nuclear power plant meltdowns. These incidents have created new social problems and challenges which may require alternative ways and solutions to increase the quality of life for those affected. Kono (2014) indicated that leisure can have a significant meaning and role in improving the quality of life for those affected by disasters. Ratten (2011) noted that sport entrepreneurs provide social capital by taking advantage of technological innovations for business ventures. In addition, sport entrepreneurs foster social capital and community networks in sport tourism and community sport. And sport entrepreneurship can help solve some community issues. This leads to Hoye *et al.*'s (2015) finding that involvement in sport organizations is associated with increased levels of social connections. In addition, Hitt and Reed (2000) note that the new, smaller entrepreneur is flexible. Therefore, a sport entrepreneur would have the ability to adjust to social situations and changes and be a catalyst for sport promotion in the community.

References

Aldrich, H. E. (2005) 'Entrepreneurship'. In Smelser, N. & Swedberg, R. (Eds.), *Handbook of Economic Sociology* (pp. 451–577), Princeton, NJ: Princeton University Press.

Hatsukaichi Sport Club (n.d.) 'For Hatsukaichi Sports Club (concept)'. Retrieved from <www.hatsukaichi-fc.com/concept.html> (accessed July 17, 2016).

Hitt, M. A. & Reed, T. S. (2000) 'Entrepreneurship in the new competitive landscape'. In Meyer, G. D. & Heppard, K. A. (Eds.). *Entrepreneurship as strategy: competing on the entrepreneurial edge* (pp. 23–48). London, UL: Sage Publications.

Harada, M. (2009) 'Tourism no rekishiteki haten' [The historical development of tourism]. In Harada, M. & Kimura, K. (Eds.), *Sport/Health tourism* (pp. 3–28), Tokyo, Japan: Taishukan shoten.

Hoye, R., Nicholson, M. & Brown, K. (2015) 'Involvement in sport and social connectedness'. *International Review for the Sociology of Sport*, 50(1) 3–21.

Ikeda, M., Yamaguchi, Y. & Chogahara, M. (2003) 'Japan: Sport for all in lifelong perspectives of health and fitness'. In DaCosta, L. & Miragaya, A. (Eds.), *Sport for all* (pp. 89–108). Oxford, UK: Meyer & Meyer Sport.

Kawanishi M. (2003) 'Future of community sport clubs in Japan: Expectations of their role in creating communities'. *International symposium on the promotion of community sports clubs and club life*. Research proceedings, 404–407.

Kono, S. (2014) 'The relationships between leisure experiences and psychological recovery from disaster: A case study of the Great East Japan Earthquake and tsunami'. *Master thesis*, University of Illinois

Kurosu, M. (2006) 'Sougougata chiki sport kurabu no resou to genjitu'. In Kiku, K., Shimizu, S., Nakazawa, M. & Matsumura K. (Eds.), *Gendai sports no perspective* (pp. 118–137), Tokyo, Japan: Taishukan shoten.

Lebra, T. S. (1976) *Japanese patterns of behavior.* University of Hawaii Press, Hawaii.

Long, J. and Sanderson, I. (2001) 'The social benefits of sport: Where's the proof?' In Gratton, C. and Henry, I. (Eds.), *Sport in the city* (pp. 187–203), London, UK: Routledge.

Ministry of Education, Culture, Sports, Science and Technology-Japan (n.d.) 'The actual condition survey of comprehensive community sports club: Overview'. Retrieved from: <www.mext.go.jp/component/a_menu/sports/detail/__icsFiles/afieldfile/2015/03/19/1234682_11.pdf> (accessed July 17, 2016).

Miyoshi City (n.d.) 'Miyoshi-shi toshi keikaku master plan' [The masterplan of Miyoshi city urban planning] Retrieved from <www.city-miyoshi.jp/docs/2013073100025/files/1syou.pdf> (accessed July 17, 2016).

NAC Niseko Adventure Centre (2016) 'NennkanSankasya report' (Annual report in 2015).

Niseko (2016) 'By the numbers', Retrieved from <www.town.niseko.lg.jp/machitsukuri/files/suujide-miru-niseko.pdf> (accessed July 17, 2016).

Nogawa, H. (2007) 'Sport tourism no Management' [Management of sport tourism], *Journal of Health, Physical Education and Recreation*, 57(1), 39–43.

Okayasu, I., Ito, E., Watanabe, Y. & Nogawa, H. (2012) 'Inbound leisure and sport tourism to Japan'. *Inaugural International Academy of Sportology*, 132–137.

Ratten, V. (2011). 'Social entrepreneurship and innovation in sports'. *International Journal of Social Entrepreneurship and Innovation*, 1(1), 42–54.

Takada, M. & Ishimori, S. (1993) *The beginning of new tourism.* Tokyo Japan: PHP.

Yamaguchi, Y. (2006) 'Integration and sport for all: The Japanese perspective'. *TAFISA Magazine*, 41–44.

10

COHERENCE, THE BEGINNING AND END OF EVERYTHING

Marco Arraya

Introduction

The sports industry essentially comprises entrepreneurs that create and develop several types of organization,[1] some of which are for-profit and non-profit (gymnasiums, amateur clubs, equipment producers), and also, non-profit with public interest (clubs with public utility status and regulatory entities). All of them are involved in the supply of sporting products and/or services, which make use of resources that should serve to benefit their members and the communities they belong to.

Today, sports as an activity can be divided into three large segments:

1) wellness with users[2] – this includes those that have privileged health and well-being;
2) competition – those who seek victory and overcoming their peers. This is one of the most visible sides of the sports industry. This involves the promotion of professional athletes and teams, whose business model is based on revenue generation from match-day tickets, broadcasting and commercials, amongst other things;
3) Finally, the entire segment of sporting equipment. This particular segment employs the highest number of people.

As a matter of fact, since ancient Athens and Rome, sport has been based on competition and the struggle for the resources that facilitate victories. However, substantial differences between competitors with disproportional features and capabilities make the competition unattractive to all stakeholders, from the audience to the athletes. Therefore, a feature of the segment directed to competition is the need for a certain degree of balance between competitors, in order to have a vibrant and emotional product which is unifying to the public.

The role of the entrepreneur in sports has ever more to do with his/her proactiveness, innovation, knowledge and risk-taking (Holt, Rutherford and Clohessy, 2007; Ratten, 2011), in order to create sportive, economic development, and in the long run, value. Attracting investors, resources, consumers, audiences and media coverage consistently requires a clarity and coherence of strategic activities from the entrepreneur in the management of resources, capabilities and business culture. This is the topic we will cover in this chapter.

The entrepreneur's design

The entrepreneur develops actions in order to face environmental factors, and also build a competitive advantage in the face of competition to the established ideas. In the sports industry, the entrepreneur can reach that advantage by capturing strategic resources which are valuable, rare, non-imitable and which involve organizational support (the VRIO framework, Barney, 1991, 1995), in order to subsequently transform them into a system of abilities and, consequently, into products and/or services which potential customers desire (Barney and Hesterly, 2009; Leinwand and Mainardi, 2011).

The value of a resource is associated with the degree to which it enables the organization "to conceive of and implement rare strategies that improve its efficiency and effectiveness" (Barney, 1991, p. 101). In the case of sports, the resources can be financial, related to skills and knowledge, contracting of human resources, sponsoring opportunities, visibility in the media, users or athletes, clients, partners and fans, experience in market participation, equipment or facilities, amongst many others. In turn, access and the efficient use of these resources can lead to success in sports competitions or to greater profits/income due to the increase of the presence of fans at competitions, the increase of sales of sporting goods or the greater attendance of users at sports facilities in the leisure segment.

However, for resources to improve performance, they need to be combined with each other, and also cooperate with the capabilities creating a system (Barreto, 2010; Leinwand and Mainardi, 2011; Newbert, 2007). This capabilities system is born from what the entrepreneur is really good at, and then develops and reinforces those capabilities until they're best-in-class. These capabilities support the entrepreneur's strategic purpose to deliver an adequate product or service to customers (Leinwand and Mainardi, 2010).

If we associate the entrepreneur's profile,[3] the market and the target customer, various "fields of activity or game" arise, that is, what McGrath (2013, p. 14) called the arena: "an arena is a combination of a customer segment, an offer, and a place in which that offer is delivered."

The entrepreneur will then have to choose the "way to play" – or "where to play" and "how to win", which is the position in the market – the right to sell his/her "fit product or service", if he/she wants to get the "right to win" (Favaro,

Rangan and Hirsh, 2012; Leinwand and Mainardi, 2011). This choice or decision will maximize (or not) the value in the long term (Favaro *et al.*, 2012).

Mainardi and Kleiner (2010) defined the "right to win" as:

> the ability to engage in any competitive market with a better-than-even chance of success – not just in the short term, but consistently. The right to win cannot be taken for granted. It must be earned. You earn it by making a series of pragmatic choices that align your most distinctive and important capabilities with the way you approach your chosen customers, and with the discipline to offer only the products and services that fit.

"Where to play" specifies the target customer in terms of clients and the needs to be met. To define the target market is necessary to consider the clients with greater possibility of purchasing the products or services of the organization. For this, it is necessary to know:

1) where the target clients are (location);
2) how they purchase (through which channels);
3) who they are (demographics and other characteristics);
4) when they purchase;
5) what they purchase; and
6) for whom they purchase.

To aim at a target market does not mean that one has to exclude people that do not fit the base purchase criteria defined by the entrepreneur; however, one should focus the message about the products and services which are more liable to be purchased.

"How to win" states the value proposal that will distinguish the offer from the organization in the eyes of its target clients, along with its abilities to provide an advantage in the supply of the value proposal. The entrepreneur has to make a choice due to the fact that there is at least one way to win in all markets, but not all participants manage to win in any market. A good choice allows earning the right to win in the selected target-market.

"Fit product or service" is probably the key element of this trilogy for an obvious reason: because, they are the only ones which generate income. For a product/service to be fit, it must be coherent, aligned with the entrepreneur's DNA, organizational culture, "way to play" (market approach), resources available and, most of all, with the capabilities system.

The "way to play" ("where to play" and "how to win"), the fit product/ service and the capabilities system should merge in a coherent manner (Leinwand and Mainardi, 2011). This symbiosis and practical implementation is part of an integrated, continuous, never-ending process which requires subsequent re-evaluation and overhaul.

The influential elements of the entrepreneurial options

The entrepreneur faces numerous options of "way to play". Knowing which is the right choice is his/her challenge, and the option chosen will mark the present and the future. During the decision-making process, the pertinent questions regarding sustainability and short-term profitability arise. Maximizing the long-term value is to never stop looking at options of greater value, and also not forgetting the day of today, since the economic value takes into consideration the growth and profitability (today and the future), the risk and the reward.

This enormous challenge finds several elements along the way that mould the decision and the execution to take; we will approach those that we consider most pertinent.

The entrepreneur aiming for goals and objectives must deal with *environmental factors*. As Daft (2010) mentions, the environmental factors are comprised of all the factors that surround him/her, and affect him/her. These also can be divided into two categories: general and specific. The general environmental factors include elements that do not have a direct effect over the day-to-day operations of the organization, but still influence them. The environmental factors in general include the economy, technology, politics, social and cultural forces and demographics. The specific environmental factors include agents external to the organization, which Daft (2010) identifies as stakeholders.[4]

The environmental factors and the sports organizations are in constant exchange of information, that is, they are an open system (Campbell, 1997) that interacts in the collection, absorption and management of resources.

The influence of environmental factors in the entrepreneur's initiatives and events seems clear, therefore, understanding the environmental factors and carefully monitoring their effects allows the perception, interpretation, adaptation, redirection or formulation of new products and services. As a matter of fact, the entrepreneur does not have control over the main condition required for the survival of his/her initiative/event – the revenue/profit. The source of profits is an external resource, and as such, it depends on the environment. This comprises elements that are difficult to control; however, there is always the chance of influencing them. Therefore, survival of the initiative or event depends not only on internal adjustments, but mainly on adjustments and adaptations to the external environment.

In most arenas of the sports industry, the entrepreneur, in order to become adaptive, needs to:

1) understand what happens in the external environment;
2) be flexible and able to adjust and adapt quickly;
3) be open to new ideas;
4) learn by experiences;
5) be quick in his/her replies.

Coherence, the beginning and end of everything **157**

However, in a dynamic environment, he/she needs to have a strong ability to: a) anticipate the organizational and environmental reconfigurations; b) solve problems; c) administer difficulties and crisis. In sports, what "today is the truth, tomorrow can be a lie".[5] Therefore, the adjustments and adaptations[6] are an essential process for success.

On the other hand, there is an invisible force originating from the *entrepreneur's genes (DNA)* and related interaction with the available human resources, which influences the organization (or firm), contributing to the posture, the behaviour and the decisions of the entrepreneur or the staff, and above all, it builds a work culture for the team. The organization, just as the human being, results from the association of the genetic load or static set of genes that comprise it, which is called the genotype. On the other hand, the result from the action of environmental factors over living beings, or the dynamic set of their observable characteristics, is called the phenotype. The genotype influences the phenotype, which is the set of variables conditioned by the genes.

According to Neilson & Estupiñán (2014), the entrepreneur/organization's phenotype should be made up of four pairs of building blocks: 1) decision rights and norms (what people think is the right way to behave); 2) motivators and commitments (the promises people feel motivated to keep); 3) information and mind-sets[7] (deeply held attitudes and beliefs) and; (4) structure and networks (connections among employees outside the formal structure). These building blocks influence the ways human resources think, feel, communicate, behave, and the way they combine determines an organization's fitness for execution. This means that, if the organization wants a solid execution, it should consider the building blocks as a whole and not individually (Neilson & Estupiñán, 2014), that is, balanced and coherent.

The entrepreneur/organization must be regarded as an open system, because, it is "characterized by an assemblage or combination of parts whose relations make them interdependent [. . .] the interactions between parts in the system become more complex and variable" (Scott, 2003, p. 77). The entrepreneur/organization interacts with the environmental factors by exchanging energy, knowledge, and should consider the interrelationships of people (external and internal), processes, inputs and outputs, goals, learning, assessment and evaluation and of course, decisions – and design organizational actions accordingly (Gabor, 2010; Scott, 2003). Organizations – regardless of size – are complex, ever-changing and must be capable of learning and adapting to unexpected developments (Ackoff, 1981; Gabor, 2010; Pellissier, 2008). This adaptation must be based in experimentation and trial-and-error learning (Gabor, 2010) (see Figure 10.1).

This means that the organization, in the first instance, is the result of the symbiosis of the genes of the entrepreneur and the human resources (staff) that constitute it, not being a "better" genotype. The creation of a value concept cannot be applied to the genotype without specifying the environmental factors. That is, a genotype is good or bad depending on the environment; an environment is

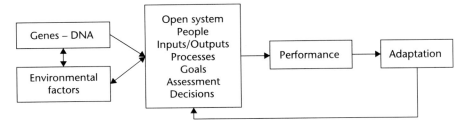

FIGURE 10.1 DNA, environmental factors, performance and adaptation

good or bad depending on the genotype. The interaction of the two is close, complex, and non-linear. Here are two examples: 1) the manager of a sports club can be good or bad according to his adaptation to the club's stakeholders; 2) a sports club with a poor performance in one sport, when it decides to transfer its focus and resources to another sport may become a successful club. This same characteristic (resource) can be a larger or lesser quality depending on the context. However, the effect of the pair gene/environment over the phenotypical dynamic is unpredictable.

No organization inherits a "gene for higher performance", but a genotype which, as a whole, conditions the taking of decisions and a certain level of performance in complex interaction with the environmental factors. The potential is determined genetically, and the capacities or skills expressed are derived from the phenotype. It is relevant to mention that, the organization is a whole and not the sum of the parts which can be changed independently from one another (Pellissier, 2008). The organization as an open system requires coherence and:

> understanding of how all the parts fit together as a whole; it also depends on an intimate understanding of the parts themselves. This is because, change in any part of the system or in its outside environment – including the other systems to which it is connected – can produce profound ripple effects.
>
> *(Gabor, 2010)*

All stakeholders should learn how the organization works, to develop its innovation, processes, communication and most of all to improve it.

In order to increase complexity, besides the DNA and the environment, there is a third variable: *contingency*. The stochastic variation – patterns that appear through random events – is an intrinsic part of the development procedures, and its importance will depend on its management and the so-called emerging strategies.[8]

The sports industry has two basic characteristics that make contingency a "way of life": the *sensitive dependence on initial conditions* or *butterfly effect,* and the *non-linear system*. The influence of these characteristics is essentially at the level of the sequence of events inside and outside of the organization, which will guide the organizational dynamic.

The *sensitive dependency of initial conditions* refers to almost imperceptible differences that lead to a succession of reactions, causing behaviour and a result that is completely different from what is expected. The *non-linear system* has to do with external environmental factors that cause changes and alterations without producing an effect-type cause effect, but amplify the final result. These two characteristics justify stating that: in the sports industry, small causes can lead to large effects, via a succession of chained events, making it hard to make previsions, being part of the batch of factors that reinforce that, "the truth of today, can be a lie tomorrow".

A good example of the butterfly effect and non-linear system occurred in Nazaré, Portugal, in November 2011. Until that date, Nazaré was a small fishing village on the Atlantic coast with some summer tourism activity. In November 2011, a surfer event changed the life of Nazaré. The American surfer Garrett McNamara, surfed a record-breaking giant wave: 23.8 m (78 feet) from trough to crest, and entered the Guinness World Records. After this event, the surfer tribe started to come to Nazaré, thereby improving the village's way of life and income. In October 2013, the Brazilian surfer Carlos Burle surfed another wave that is currently being scrutinized as possibly the largest wave ever ridden.

Today, Nazaré has a good rate of tourist occupations during the whole year due to surf. This episode is instructive on how a sequence of small events can change the life of a community. The break down of this is that:

1) one athlete imagined a challenge and prepared to beat it;
2) he chose a spot with no recognized history;
3) on the day of the challenge the weather and nautical conditions were ideal;
4) the athlete and his amphibious team managed to ride the best wave of the day;
5) the athlete had an amazing performance; and lastly,
6) the media were invited and publicized the news around the four corners of the world, thereby motivating other world-renowned surfers and surf lovers to challenge the, now called, Nazaré Canyon.

The product/service that the entrepreneur will place on the market is always subject to the complexity of numerous factors, improving even more the capacity for adaptation and innovation of the organizational culture.

The *organizational culture* can be seen as collective cognition being demonstrated in traditions, habits, execution of procedures, ability of thought, knowledge management and in other tangible manifestations of an organization (Collins and Porras, 2004). As previously mentioned, the organizational culture has as its basis the entrepreneur's DNA and the organization's human resources; never forgetting the influence of environmental factors (as mentioned by Ortega y Gasset: "I am I and my circumstance") and the stakeholders. However, the greatest contribution is from the entrepreneur or leader of the organization, due to his unique form of leadership, motivation and management of personnel and situations. When consolidated, the culture can be seen as a competitive differentiator, in virtue of its causal ambiguity not allowing replication. The culture influences the style of thinking and consequently establishes the premise for the decisions of people. On the other hand, it can influence the commitment and encourage the behaviour of the organization, favouring or hindering adaptations and changes in strategy. The sports industry forces an organizational culture in which the flexibility, the "open spirit", the speed of adjustment and adaptation to the reality of the moment are always present.

In the face of the above, and in order to define the bases of the entrepreneur's design, it is useful to consider the principles proposed by Geus (1997):

1) Sensitivity towards the environmental factors – capacity to learn and adjust.
2) Cohesion and identity – the skills to build a community/work team with personality, vision and purpose.
3) Tolerance and decentralization – the skill to build relationships.
4) Conservative management of financial resources.

In the understanding of Geus, by following these principles, there is a possibility for perpetuity. In virtue of emphasizing the knowledge in contrast with economic greed, in privileging human resources, having the capability of learning and creating their own processes and goals.

After considering the environmental factors, the genes, the organization as an open system in which the butterfly effect and non-linearity are determinants, the culture, and the principles of Geus, we are in condition to perform and answer the entrepreneur's three main questions (Favaro *et al.*, 2012):

1) Who is the target customer ("where to play") for our idea or event?
2) What is the value proposition ("how to play") to that customer?
3) What are the essential capabilities needed to deliver that value proposition?

The answers for these three questions should be clear and coherent. The entrepreneur may have the perfect DNA for the prospective business, a fantastic vision and mission, unambiguous goals and an ambitious business plan with many actions under way, but without these answers he or she won't really have a strategy.

Customer target identification ("where to play")

It's difficult to solve the needs of the entire world with a single product/service, and if we aim to attract everyone, maybe we will have a "freak out"! This means that, the formula "less=more=better" is true in marketing for new businesses.

To identify the target-client is to know very well the potential client, develop a deep understanding of his/her needs, yearnings and expectations, that is, focus

Coherence, the beginning and end of everything **161**

Demographics	**Psychographics**
Gender Age Location Occupation Marital status Education Income levels	Personality Attitudes Values Lifestyle Behaviour Hobbies/Interests

Why to buy?	**What are the purchase methods?**
Physiological need (health) Social or emotional need Pressure of the family budget Professional obligation	In store Online shop By phone Spontaneous or rational purchase

Investment in shopping habits	**Organization recognition**
Expenses budget Spend in accordance with the opportunity	Benefits of the product/service Price-quality relationships or value Customer support

Decision questions
Are there enough people that fit product or service criteria?
Will the chosen target really benefit from this product/service?
Will people see a need for our product/service?
Do we really understand what drives the chosen target to make decisions?
Can they afford our product/service?
Can we reach them with our message?
Are they easily accessible?

FIGURE 10.2 Customer target identification variables

on a client's profile. By knowing the target-client, the entrepreneur will develop abilities and use the resources available in a more efficient manner, due to the fact that he or she is focused on a specific group of people. To define the target-client is therefore to know everything you can about the individual or group under analysis, what he/she does, thinks, values, acquires; in order to attract him/her to purchase the products and services of the organization.

Each entrepreneur should build and obtain answers to a series of questions. With the information gathered and analyzed, he will identify and create products and services which will meet the needs of his target-client and create an unforgettable emotional experience (see Figure 10.2).

Customer value proposition ("how to win")

The most common definition of "value" is based on the quality-price ratio of a product/service or in the difference between the perceived benefits and costs (Anderson and Narus, 1998). The value arises when the attributes of the product/service (design, maintenance, customer support, etc.) meet the specific needs or problems of the client. In turn, the proposal of value described as the offer of products/services of an organization, is different than the one of its competitors, and thus explains the client's motive for purchase (Anderson, Narus and Rossum, 2006). The value proposal is focused on the client and on how the organization satisfies the explicit and implicit needs, solves problems, contributes to the life of the client and still defines the focus on the performance, in better service to clients, in a profitable way (Lindic and Marques da Silva, 2011).

The value proposal should have a goal: to provide benefits that help solve the target-client's constraints in a different and sustainable fashion in comparison to the competitors. Thus, the value proposal is not about the resources of the organization nor the *portfolio* of products/services, but rather about the client's experience in terms of satisfaction of needs and desires.

Clients tend to evaluate the value proposal based on the following formula: value = benefits = costs (Anderson and Narus, 1998). The "value" perception comprises of two complementary concepts, the perceived benefit and the perceived costs.

The *perceived benefit* is wrongly compared to the characteristics and features of products. It so happens that clients don't buy these two things; what they buy are the benefits that a product provides. The benefit of a product/service consists of the needs it will meet and that which the client values. During the decision-making process, clients can compare the characteristics of a product/service with the competitors', but the decision-making normally has as a base the benefits offered, especially those that allow exceeding the initial expectations. The perceived costs refer to the combination of the product/service's nominal price and the other related costs (time, risk, opportunity, research, effort, etc.), with its acquisition and consumption.

When the benefits offered by the product/service and the client's experience exceed the perceived costs, the organization meets or exceeds the client's expectations and added value. When, however, the costs exceed the benefits, the product/service falls short of the client's expectation and the organization destroys value for the client (Lindic and Marques da Silva, 2011).

These two concepts – benefit and cost – form the value perceived by the client; as such, the greater the perceived benefits and the smaller the perceived costs, the greater the value perceived by the client will be. However, it is important to mention: 1) the value is specific for a determinate reality, because the time, convenience, perceived risks, among others, are factors that vary from organization to organization, and from individual to individual; 2) the value is defined by its client; that is, the benefits and costs perceived are those in the eyes of the client, not those of the entrepreneur.

Success in the market comes from the conjunction between the value proposal for the client and the satisfaction of his needs. To identify the target-client and understand him focuses the offer, creating conditions to provide an amazing experience for the client, placing the product/service in the value perspective. Once the entrepreneur understands and focuses on the client, this allows him/her to make more intelligent choices about how to create and develop a capabilities

Coherence, the beginning and end of everything **163**

system, and where to allocate the available resources for the development of new products/services and in the sale of the current ones (Ambrosini, Bowman and Collier, 2009; Leinwand and Mainardi, 2011).

Resources and capabilities

All entrepreneurs/organizations have points in common and they all diverge in the moment of truth. The specific environmental factors, the DNA of the leaders, the organizational culture, the different management decisions and choices made, make them unique. The developmental stage and the performance culture mould the characteristics of each entrepreneur/organization, making them specific, that is, peculiarly competent (or incompetent) to do a specific type of work (Selznick, 1960).

The efficient symbiosis of resource management and the creation of capabilities is the formula for seeking competitive advantage, where the resources are the means to solve a problem or to reach a goal, that is, the productive assets and capabilities of the entrepreneur/organization are what he/she/it does, that is, multifunctional combinations of technology, processes, skills and mind-sets, which work in synergy to solve certain problems or perform certain functions in order to stand out from the competition and consistently provide value for its target-clients (Ambrosini *et al.*, 2009; Andersén, 2011). Resources alone do not confer competitive advantage; they have to work in cooperation with the capabilities, thereby creating a capabilities system (Leinwand and Mainardi, 2011). The capability is the essence of superior performance. Figure 10.4 shows the hierarchy of DNA/culture, resources, capabilities, strategy and competitive advantage and coherence.

In order to have a broader vision of *resources*, it is useful to identify the two large groups of resources: the *tangible* and the *intangible*. However, the main goal of the identification and analysis of resources is not its value as "assets", but to understand its potential in the creation of competitive advantage. According to Penrose (1959, p. 85), "there is a close relation between the various kinds of resources with which a firm works and the development of ideas, experience, and knowledge of its managers and entrepreneurs".

Tangible resources – financial resources and physical assets – are the easiest to identify and assess, due to the fact that they are mirrored in the organization's financial demonstrations. The same is not true for the resources regarding organizational capabilities; these have to be assessed by means of efficiency indicators. Hence, after obtaining precise information about the tangible resources of the organization, we can explore the creation of additional value from them. This requires approaching a fundamental issue: which opportunities exist in the monetization – operational synergies, development of new offers, cooperation with other entities and cost control – of their use?

The majority of researchers in management consider intangible resources as more valuable than the tangible ones. Intangible resources are underlined as employees with varying degrees of skill, who meet a wide range of activities, tasks and functions with their knowledge, experience and effort, in the service of the common good (Arraya, 2014). Many of these employees represent a substantial investment by the entrepreneur, and when their efficiency, productivity and motivation decrease, or in the worst-case scenario, their exit is recorded from the work group, this is like losing financial capital (Penrose, 1959).

However, the capacity of employees to harmonize their efforts and integrate their different skills does not depend only on their will and knowledge, but specifically on the organizational context. The organizational context is determined by a fundamental intangible resource: the organizational culture.

The brands and intellectual property – patents, copyright, commercial secrets, technological resources and registered trademarks – are a form of reputation assets, whose value is in the trust that they instil in the target-client. This value is reflected in the price difference that the clients are willing to pay for a product from a brand when compared to an unknown brand. On the other hand, the reputation can be the reliably hinged between the entrepreneur and the stakeholders.

One of the main strategic decisions of the entrepreneur/organization is to decide which resources should be developed and acquired. It is up to him/her to invest in analysis, selection, acquisition or development of the necessary resources for the product/service to have good acceptance in the market. Therefore, the resources should provide value to the target-client and also create a competitive advantage; otherwise, they are not useful to the idea/event. Following this context, Barney (1991) labelled the major resource elements as the VRIO framework:

- **V**aluable; the resource must be capable of allowing an organization to increase value to customers and to take advantage of opportunities and minimize threats;
- **R**are; a valuable resource must be held and explored by few players, otherwise, any possible advantage generated will be a commodity (Barney & Zajac, 1994);
- **I**nimitability; if a valuable and rare resource is easily imitable, all players would promptly copy it and the advantage would be gone;
- **O**rganization; competitive advantage stems from the way players manage and interconnect their strategic and ordinary resources by exploiting organizational processes and routines in search of quality products/services (Pan, Tan, Huang and Poulsen, 2007; Warnier, Weppe and Lecocq, 2013).

These elements become keys to comprehending competitive advantage and they are explored below.

The more elements a resource has, the greater the potential for a competitive advantage. However, the resource *per se* remains an "input" until it is used and produces an "output". Hence, the same resources, when used differently or in different combinations, provide different outputs (Barney and Hesterly, 2009).

However, the specificity of a bundle of resource/value combination may positively impact one organization's competitive position, and may have no impact on that of another. According to Warnier *et al.* (2013, p. 1362), an organization has two kinds of resources, *strategic* and *ordinary*:

> a strategic resource is a rare resource on the market, generally perceived as positive in terms of performance, i.e. with an expected level of productivity that is greater than its cost (acquisition or development). Such a resource is considered a potential source of rents [. . .] an ordinary resource is a common resource on the market, generally perceived as neutral in terms of performance, i.e. with an expected level of productivity equivalent to its cost (acquisition or development). Such a resource is considered, at best, as ensuring competitive parity.

The resource heterogeneity allows some competitors to own more strategic resources than others, and because strategic resources induce rents, a competitor that owns them can develop or expand competitive advantages (Hoopes, Madsen and Walker, 2003). The ordinary resources constitute an organization's assets, and due to their regular use and universal nature, may appear as commodity resources in which "productivity is equal to the cost of their acquisition or development" (Warnier *et al.*, 2013, p. 1361).

The configuration of strategic and ordinary resources guarantees the superior organization's performance. This resource configuration is defined as a dynamic open system evolved from the orchestrated ordinary and strategic resources (Hafeez, Zhang and Malak, 2002; Warnier *et al.*, 2013) connected with a holistic behaviour. This means, the organization should concentrate its efforts and focus on the bundles of embedded resources that create a source of competitive advantage (Black and Boal, 1994).

Management authors have identified four to six categories of strategic resources that organizations use to plan and execute their strategies. These are: financial, physical, human and organizational capital (Barney and Arikan, 2001; David, 2011); technological capabilities (Arraya, 2014; Lichtenstein and Brush, 2001); social capital resources (Arraya, 2014; Ireland, Webb and Coombs, 2005) (see Table 10.1).

However, to make the best use of the available resources, the entrepreneur/organization requires *capabilities*. A capability is something the entrepreneur/organization makes better than the competitors and has customer value. It's more than an activity or a function: it is the interconnection of cross-functional combinations of technology, people, leadership, human resources management, tools, processes, skills, knowledge, financial resources management and mindsets that work together synergistically, and enable the entrepreneur/organization to outmaneuver rivals on some important measures (Divakaran, Neilson and Pandrangi, 2013; Leinwand and Mainardi, 2010; Schreyögg and Kliesch-Eberl, 2007).

166 Marco Arraya

TABLE 10.1 The VRIO framework elements

Attributes	Description	Sports Example "a hypothetical soccer academy"
Value	Value refers to the importance of a resource relative to performance, i.e., a resource has value only if it contributes to a competitive position. According to Barney and Hesterly (2009, p. 69), the spirit of value can be found by responding to the following question: "*Do resources and capabilities enable a firm to exploit an external opportunity or neutralize an external threat?*"	Recognition. The ability to attract young players with high potential and financial support. There is a relationship between success in sports and various organizational outcomes.
Rareness	Not all features can be valuable sources of competitive position, because most competitors obtain the same resources in a given sector. To have the potential competitive position, the entrepreneur must implement an effective strategy of valuable resources, but "rare", so that other competitors are unable to replicate the strategy due to lack of resources, i.e., the smaller the percentage of competitors who possess the resource, the more rare it becomes. According to Barney and Hesterly (2009, p. 75) the spirit of this element can be best understood by answering the following question: "*How many competing firms already possess particular valuable resources and capabilities?*"	Continuity of excellent coaches. Scouting efficiency. Media exposure.
Imitability	Valuable and rare resources have the potential to create competitive positions; however, they must have another attribute: the inimitable, i.e. difficult to copy, replicate or obtain. Barney and Hesterly (2009, p. 76) pose it: "*Do firms without a resource or capability face a cost disadvantage in obtaining or developing it compared to the firms that already possess it?*" They also mention the following reasons as "sources of costly imitation" (p. 78): history and knowledge (conditions that allow the entrepreneur to possess the resource in the first place), ambiguity (competitors find it difficult to understand why the competitive position exists), complexity (it is difficult for the competition to develop certain intangible resources that help to create a capability system) and patents (the competition is legally prevented from acquiring or developing the resource).	Identifying the relevant variables, e.g. infrastructures, characteristics of players, continuity of coaching staff, campus location, etc. Their ambiguity and complexity would be exceptionally difficult, if not impossible to replicate. The intangible factors of the academy's culture, leadership and knowledge are difficult to measure.

Organization	Organization is necessary to take advantage of a valuable, rare and not easily imitated resource. Organization refers to the organizational intangible or tangible variables, including systems (intangible), structures (tangible), policies (tangible), leadership and culture (intangible). Essentially, the entire entrepreneur team must function in an effective, efficient manner to capitalize upon a valuable, rare, and not easily imitated resource. Barney & Hesterly (2009, p. 81) ask: *"Is the firm organized to exploit the full competitive potential of its resources and capabilities?"*	Variables such as leadership, decision-making, organizational culture, infrastructure and financial incomes/outcomes should be focused on continuous improvement.

On the other hand, capabilities that allow an entrepreneur/organization to be distinctive from competitors and consistently deliver value to chosen target customers are difficult to create, and difficult to acquire. As such, he/she/it must do a combination of capabilities – the capabilities system – which consist of three to six unique capabilities. What makes them into a system is that they are mutually reinforcing, turning them into more than the sum of their individual parts. True capabilities systems are very difficult to replicate (Divakaran *et al.*, 2013; Leinwand and Mainardi, 2011).

While many resources are tangible assets, the capability, by its very nature, is intangible, and can be found in organizational structures, routines, productive and management processes (Ambrosini *et al.*, 2009). The capability represents the organizational capital in the form of leadership, experience, skills and know-how (technical), allowing that people can do their assignments well in a group or individually (Fuchs, Pais and Shulman, 2013).

A capabilities system is something specific that encompasses three to six capabilities that mutually reinforce themselves, and that are organized in order to support and drive the entrepreneur/organization strategy – integrating people, processes and technologies – in order to produce a value proposal to the target-client. These capabilities are not part of those that ensure the basic activity of the organization such as, for example, legal and fiscal fulfilment, operations and resources for management of installations. Instead, they are differentiating and complementary, working in tandem, reliably in the consistent production/delivery of a specific result, in support of the strategy and market position, i.e. they are distinctive. These systems are complex, multifunctional, intimately connected to the identity of the entrepreneur/organization and consume a lot of investment and attention in their construction and maintenance. Once tuned, they drive the entrepreneur/organization within the market, in order to create value and provide distinction and proficiency in their products/services.

168 Marco Arraya

The capabilities system – besides its three or six distinctive capabilities – should consider the innate qualities of an entrepreneur/organization that distinguish he/she/it from all others – its operational processes, culture, relationships. They are built up slowly but surely, decision by decision, continually reinforced through organizational practices and commitments, and finally ensuring that the right individuals are placed in the right jobs (Collins, 2001; Leinwand and Mainardi, 2011).

A good example of a capabilities system is a hypothetical soccer club that transforms a simple game into an attractive show (content offer), in the sale of *merchandising* (products), in the relationship of management with fans and affiliates (clients) and in presentation to the media (international sale of television rights and institutional communication).

The identification process for basic and distinctive capabilities can start in several ways, but the three most common are: 1) via a classification of all capabilities according to the function; 2) via an analysis of the value chain[9] that divides the organization into small sequential activities; or 3) the entrepreneur/organization can figure out which capabilities have the furthermost potential to perform, by benchmarking their competitors, and developing or adapting to their reality, thereby giving them a competitive position.

The resources and capabilities need to be evaluated considering two fundamental criteria:

1) Which are the most important resources and capabilities in the conquest of the competitive advantage and coherence?
2) Where are our strong and weak points in comparison to the competitors'?[10]

Coherence and competitive advantage

The idea of coherence management is a central theme in this chapter, and starts to have some attraction in the business world. Our understanding of *coherence* is a logical, orderly and consistent relation of parts to the whole (Doucet, Saha, Gøtze and Bernard, 2009).

The coherent entrepreneur/organization must be based on he/she/its gene for an effective and efficient, and well understood operation and execution (Doucet *et al.*, 2009). In reality, coherence is a way to design a framework to look at performance, where everyone is aligned, and realizes the link between their ideals and the processes with the customer.

A coherent entrepreneur/organization is structured to take advantage of the social networks' and processes' complexity, allowing information to flow as freely as possible, collaboration – working for a common objective – and cooperation – sharing freely – flows both ways, promoting and encouraging coherent actions and affording collaborators the space to make sense of it, and share their experiences and knowledge (Lissack and Roos, 1999). These elements afford agility – entrepreneur/organization's ability to manage change – because, the designs are coherent and collaborators understand and practise the right things (Collins, 2001; Doucet *et al.*, 2009); and assurance – stakeholders control, confidence and fidelity – is gained through learning and knowledge that allow the right decisions, design the right processes and execute at peak proficiency (Doucet *et al.*, 2009).

The entrepreneur/organization becomes coherent only when his/her/its capabilities system is deliberately chosen and implemented to support the "way to play" – strategic purpose – and is aligned with the fit product/service portfolio, and the entrepreneur/organization can provide clear answers to the following questions (Leinwand and Mainardi, 2010):

- How are we going to face the market? The entrepreneur/organization should have a clear understanding of how they create value for customers.
- What capabilities do we need? The locomotive of value creation is a system of three to six capabilities that mutually allow the entrepreneur/organization to deliver his/her/its value proposition successfully.
- What are we going to sell, and to whom? Coherent entrepreneurs/organizations build his/her/its product/service portfolios so that every offering is aligned with the capabilities system and the "way to play". Products/services that require different capabilities are removed from the mix. The environmental factors and market are recurrently scanned for new opportunities that leverage the capabilities system.

Coherent entrepreneurs/organizations build deep, scalable knowledge and expertise in just a few areas and arenas; he/she/it aligns and quickly moves his/her/its strategy and day-to-day decision-making to take advantage of them (Leinwand and Mainardi, 2010; McGrath, 2013).

According to Leinwand & Mainardi (2011), coherency creates value in four ways:

1) It contributes to greater effectiveness because the entrepreneur/organization can focus on their distinctive capabilities and continually improve what truly matters.
2) Coherence produces efficiencies of scale because the entrepreneur/organization can deploy the same capabilities across a larger array of products and services.
3) Coherence focuses strategic investment on what matters because the entrepreneur/organization will just research and develop projects that enhance his/her/its position. He/she/it invests direct capital, time and talent to activities that make a difference to customers.
4) Coherence creates alignment between strategic intent and operations decision-making, and because of that, all collaborators understand what is important, thereby executing better and faster (see Table 10.2).

TABLE 10.2 The coherency diagnostic

Can the entrepreneur/organization state it?	*Does the entrepreneur/organization live it?*
Way to play	
Is the entrepreneur/organization clear about how he/she/it chooses to create value in the marketplace?	Is the entrepreneur/organization investing in the capabilities that really matter to his/her/its "way to play"?
Capabilities system	
Can the entrepreneur/organization articulate the three to six capabilities that describe what he/she/it does uniquely better than anyone else?	Do all entrepreneur/organization businesses draw on this superior capabilities system?
Has the entrepreneur/organization defined how they work together in a system?	Does the entrepreneur/organization structure and operating model support and exploit it?
	Does the entrepreneur/organization performance management system reinforce it?
Product & service fit	
Has the entrepreneur/organization specified his/her/its product and service "sweet spot"?	Do most of the products and services the entrepreneur/organization sells fit the capabilities system?
Does the entrepreneur/organization understand how to leverage the capabilities system in new or unexpected areas?	Are new products and acquisitions evaluated on the basis of their fit with the way to play and capabilities system?

Adapted from Leinwand & Mainardi (2010)

The term *competitive advantage* is used when the organization has a system of capabilities and resources whose manipulation, coordination and development allow it to perform a strategy at a performance level that is higher than the competition, thereby obtaining greater client retention, profitability and value to the stakeholders.

The symbiosis between resources and capabilities system should highlight the benefits that the target-client receives when he does "business" with the entrepreneur/organization. However, upstream may include: access to natural resources, to highly trained and qualified human resources, new technologies, manufacturing processes, innovation, business model, knowledge of the target-client, distribution network, client support, product/service portfolio, reputation, location, cost structure, amongst others. The stronger the competitive advantage is, the harder it is for competitors to neutralize it; and its source is rare/scarce, relevant and, if possible, inimitable.

When the target-client buys a product/service, he intends to acquire a benefit, such as, making his/her life simpler, healthier, or making him/her feel better about himself. An example could be the competitive advantage of a pool with a cleaning and disinfection procedure for the water in the tank, with high-performing natural hypo-allergic products. Different users can see different benefits:

i) users with allergies or concern regarding chemical products will appreciate the physical and emotional improvement;
ii) parents may feel that their children are more protected;
iii) environmentalists will be pleased with environmental sustainability.

Thinking how the products/services can benefit the target-client will contribute to identifying the competitive advantage:

1) what the fundamental resources and capacities to the design of the product or service are;
2) it should reflect the competitive strength of the organization (for example, quality of service);
3) preferably original/unique;
4) clear and simple;
5) flexible and agile, in order to reinvent itself in face of the competitors;
6) supported by a permanent market research;
7) to highlight the benefits for the target-client, instead of being proud of his/ her own "business".

Amongst the several types of competitive advantages, two are highlighted: the *comparative advantage* and the *differential advantage*. The comparative advantage, or cost advantage, is the capacity to produce a good or service at a smaller cost than the competition, which allows selling the products/services at a lower price or generating a larger margin in sales than the competition. The differential advantage happens when the products/services differ from their competitors and are recognized as better by the target-client.

However, the competitive advantage is not sustainable because, the "technological disruptions, upstart competition, shifting capital flows, new regulatory regimes, political changes, and other facets of a chaotic and unpredictable business environment" (Mainardi and Kleiner, 2010) make it transient. According to McGrath (2013b, p. 67), the notion of a transient competitive advantage is about responding to customers' "jobs to be done" in an arena that forces the product/service life cycle stages to be smaller and more flexible, and the entrepreneur/organization should have a deeper understanding of the early and late stages – launch and reconfigure or disengagement (see Figure 10.3).

Conclusion

The entrepreneur that creates an idea or successful organization has a clear, unequivocal and agile "idea of how to win". Success does not happen by accident or luck. Just like an athlete when facing a challenge would assess the possibilities

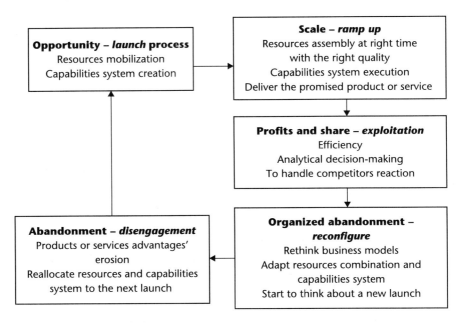

FIGURE 10.3 The life cycle stages
Adapted from McGrath (2013b)

and opportunities, train and compete, the entrepreneur seeks and builds a strategy based on his strongest abilities and the market opportunities. Usually, this means choosing a direction, and not just following others. This is a difficult decision, especially in a sector such as the sports industry, with quick evolution and with many arenas. However, when the entrepreneur/organization's options are clear and consistent about the "where to play", "how to play", and the "product/service fits", the "right to win" will be consistent and coherent.

Thus, the entrepreneur/organization coherency includes (Barreto, 2010; Collins, 2001; Divakaran et al., 2013; Leinwand and Mainardi, 2011):

1) To clearly identify the target-client. The entrepreneur/organization must choose the appropriate arena to their DNA, culture, resources and capabilities.
2) To identify the value proposal for the target-client, and to determine which are the specific benefits to highlight and obtain differentiation in the market. The entrepreneur/organization must have a clear and differentiated way of creating value for its customers, this means, he/she/it needs to choose how to distinguish. For example, as innovators continuously introducing new products and services, or as value providers offering their products or services at an attractive price point.
3) To create a capabilities system – things the entrepreneur/organization does exceptionally well that are central to its ability to perform, and hard to

replicate – that clearly defines and establishes the operating model required for delivering the value proposition to the target customer. These capabilities are cross-functional combinations of technology, processes, skills, and mindsets that work together synergistically; and they enable the entrepreneur/organization to stand out from competitors, and consistently provide value for its chosen customers that no one else can match.

4) To create a distinctive and coherent corporate identity which is a fundamental enabler of strategy and a source of competitive advantage. This corporate culture attracts customers and other stakeholders, and is grounded in internal capabilities – things the entrepreneur/organization can do with distinction – and in market realities – the games which the entrepreneur/organization chooses to play.

5) To guarantee collaborators' involvement and participation, which are critical for creating and maintaining learning and adaptive capabilities.

6) The resources and capabilities should be constantly updated or renovated in order to allow maintaining the competitive advantage in relation to competitors.

A consistent, coherent and successful entrepreneur/organization has an organizational design and capabilities system according to their DNA and culture. The right organizational design can lead to success and enables the strategy's execution. Nevertheless, being clear and consistent about "where to play" and "how to win" are necessary steps towards building a coherent strategy – the "right to win" – where all the parts fit well together, making a superior whole. The "right to win" also provides the necessary starting point for the improvement of the organizational design process. Since the entrepreneur/organization's DNA and culture are unique, the right organizational design is also unique, even within the same industry; this means improvement as a learning process is also unique. The four building blocks of the competitive advantage and coherency are always dependent on the execution, and there is a strong correlation between the entrepreneur/organization's gene and how well he/she/it executes the chosen strategy. Finally, the competitive advantage, coherency, and execution are not self-sustaining; a successful entrepreneur/organization must continuously work and learn to stay at the top of its game.

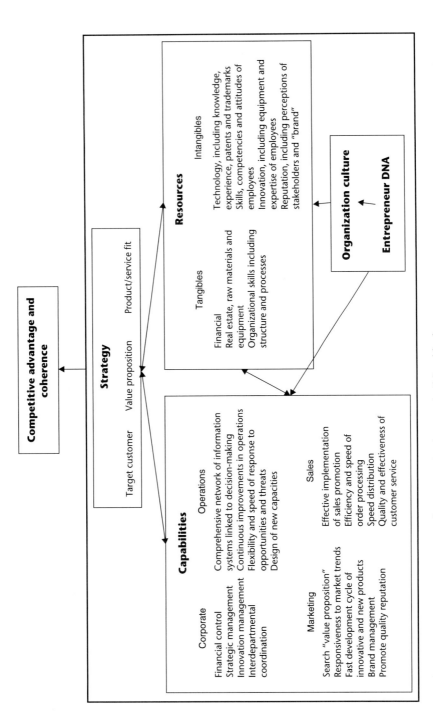

FIGURE 10.4 The four competitive advantage and coherence building blocks

Notes

1 In this chapter the term "organization" is understood as a group of people who work for the same goal such as a team or company (in abstract).
2 In this chapter the terms consumer, client and user mean the same: person that usually frequents the same location, person requesting services against payment or person purchasing something.
3 We understand the "entrepreneur profile" as the symbiosis of its DNA and corporate culture.
4 According to Connor, McFadden and McLean (2009, p. 13) "stakeholders can be defined as any individual, group or body who has an interest in the organisation's success. Stakeholders are not confined to owners or shareholders but include employees, suppliers, customers, unions, government (local, central and agencies) and partner organizations."
5 This expression originates from the Portuguese sports leader Pimenta Machado (Guimarães, Portugal, 1950).
6 The term adaptation should be used when the structural/functional changes happened irreversibly with possibility of transfer to future generations due to its adaptative value for the species. While, adjustment is a temporary situation.
7 In the theory of decision and in the general theory of systems, the *mind-set* is a set of assumptions, methods or notes accepted by one or more people that motivates them to continue adopting or accepting previous behaviours, choices, or tools. This phenomenon is also sometimes described as "mental inertia", "group thought" or a "paradigm", and it is often difficult to neutralize its effects over the analysis and decision-making processes.
8 Emergent strategy comes from Mintzberg (1978), and according to Moore (2011) "is the view that strategy emerges over time as intentions collide with and accommodate a changing reality. Emergent strategy is a set of actions, or behaviour, consistent over time, 'a realized pattern [that] was not expressly intended' in the original planning of strategy. Emergent strategy implies that an organization is learning what works in practice."
9 The subject of the value chain was started by Porter (1985) and is focused on manufacturing organizations. In 1998, the authors Stabel and Fjeldstad presented the "value shop", which is focused on the solution of problems in the organization being strongly associated with the reputation. Stabel and Fjeldstad (1998) evolve to the "value network" which is aimed at intermediation between consumers and groups of consumers that should have good relationships among themselves and, lastly, the one that better adapts to the sports organization, the "value creation".
10 The assessment of strengths and weaknesses is extremely useful to the organization. The tools most often used are: SWOT analysis, PEST analysis and the competitive strengths of Porter. However, this subject will not be approached in this chapter.

References

Ackoff, R. L. (1981). *Creating the Corporate Future: Plan or Be Planned For*. John Wiley & Sons: New York.
Ambrosini, V., Bowman, C. & Collier, N. (2009). 'Dynamic Capabilities: An Exploration of How Firms Renew Their Resource Base'. *British Journal of Management*, 20(1), pp. 9–24.
Andersén, J. (2011). 'Strategic Resources and Firm Performance'. *Management Decision*, 49 (1), pp. 87–98.
Anderson, J. C. & Narus, J. A. (1998). 'Business Marketing: Understand What Customers Value'. *Harvard Business Review*, 76(6), pp. 53–65.

Anderson, J. C., Narus, J. A. & Rossum, W. (2006). 'Customer Value Propositions in Business Markets'. *Harvard Business Review,* 84(3), pp. 1–8.

Arraya, M. (2014). 'O efeito da alostasia nas organizações e no desempenho: o caso das organizações desportivas'. *Revista Intercontinental de Gestão Desportiva,* 4 (1), pp. 13–70.

Barney J. B. & Arikan A. (2001). 'Resource-based View: Origins and Implications'. In *The Blackwell Handbook of Strategic Management,* Hitt M., Freeman R., Harrison J. (eds.) Blackwell: Malden, MA.

Barney, J. (1991). 'Firm Resources and Sustained Competitive Advantage'. *Journal of Management,* 17 (1), pp. 99–120.

Barney, J. (1995). 'Looking Inside for Competitive Advantage'. *The Academy of Management Executive,* 9(4), pp. 49–61.

Barney, J. & Zajac, E. J. (1994). 'Competitive Organizational Behavior: Toward an Organizationally-based Theory of Competitive Advantage. *Strategic Management Journal,* 15 (S1), pp. 5–9.

Barney, J. B. & Hesterly, W. S. (2009). *Strategic Management and Competitive Advantage: Concepts and Cases* (3rd edition). Prentice Hall: Upper Saddle River, New Jersey.

Barreto, I. (2010). 'Dynamic Capabilities: A Review of Past Research and an Agenda for the Future'. *Journal of Management,* 36(1), pp. 256–280.

Black, J. A. & Boal, K. B. (1994). 'Strategic Resources: Traits, Configurations and Paths to Sustainable Competitive Advantage'. *Strategic Management Journal,* 15(S2), pp. 131–148.

Campbell, A. (1997). 'Stakeholders: The Cause in Favour'. *Long Range Planning.* 30 (3), pp. 446–449.

Collins, J. (2001). 'Good to Great'. *Fast Company,* October. Available at: <www.fastcompany .com/43811/good-great> Date accessed: 21 Aug. 2015.

Collins, J. C. & Porras, J. I. (2004). *Built To Last: Successful Habits of Visionary Companies.* Harper Business Essentials.

Connor, G., McFadden, M. & McLean, I. (2009). *Organization Design.* Available at: <www.cipd.co.uk/NR/rdonlyres/8C5DA6D7-99B5-41F2-859A-E2DF80539C5C/0/ 978184398132_sc.pdf> Date accessed: 10 Aug. 2015.

Daft, R. L. (2010). *Organization Theory and Design* (10th ed.). Cengage Learning: Mason, OH: South-Western.

David, F. R. (2011). *Strategic Management: Concepts and Cases* (13th edition). Pearson Education: Upper Saddle River, New Jersey.

Divakaran, A., Neilson, G. L. & Pandrangi, A. (2013). 'How to Design a Winning Company'. *Strategy+Business, Strategy & Leadership.* Issue 72. Available at: <www. strategy-business.com/article/00194> Date accessed: 15 Aug. 2015.

Doucet, G., Saha, J., Gøtze, P. & Bernard, S. A. (2009). 'Coherency Management: Using Enterprise Architecture for Alignment, Agility, and Assurance'. *Journal of Enterprise Architecture,* 4(2), pp. 9–20.

Favaro, K., Rangan, K. & Hirsh, E. (2012). 'Strategy: An Executive's Definition'. *Strategy+Business, Strategy & Leadership.* Issue 67. Available at: <www.strategy-business. com/article/cs00002> Date accessed: 01 Aug. 2015.

Fuchs, S., Pais, G., & Shulman, J. (2013). 'Building Superior Capabilities for Strategic Sourcing'. *Insights & Publications,* McKinsey & Company, May. Available at: <www. mckinsey.com/insights/operations/building_superior_capabilities_for_strategic_ sourcing> Date accessed: 21 Aug. 2015.

Gabor, A. (2010). 'Seeing Your Company as a System'. *Strategy+Business, Strategy & Leadership.* Issue 59. Available at: <www.strategy-business.com/article/10210> Date accessed: 13 Aug. 2015.

Coherence, the beginning and end of everything **177**

Geus, Arie de. (1997). 'The Living Company'. *Harvard Business Review*, March/April, winner of the McKinsey Award.

Hafeez, K., Zhang, Y. & Malak, N. (2002). 'Determining Key Capabilities of a Firm Using Analytic Hierarchy Process'. *International Journal of Production Economics*, 76(1), pp. 39–51.

Holt, D., Rutherford, M. & Clohessy, G. (2007). 'Corporate Entrepreneurship: An Empirical Look at Individual Characteristics, Context, and Process. *Journal of Leadership & Organizational Studies*, 13(4), pp. 40–54.

Hoopes, D. G., Madsen T. L. & Walker, G. (2003). 'Guest Editors' Introduction to the Special Issue: Why is there a Resource-based View? Toward a Theory of Competitive Heterogeneity'. *Strategic Management Journal*, Special Issue 24(10), pp. 889–902.

Ireland, R. D., Webb, J. W. & Coombs, J. E. (2005). 'Theory and Methodology in Entrepreneurship Research'. In D. Ketchen and D. D. Bergh (Eds.), *Research Methodology in Strategy and Management*, 2, pp. 1–32.

Leinwand, P. & Mainardi, C. (2010). 'The Coherence Premium'. *Harvard Business Review*. June, pp. 86–92.

Leinwand, P. & Mainardi, C. (2011). 'Sustainable Success: Winning Through Capabilities'. *Business Strategy Review*, 22(2), pp. 64–67.

Lichtenstein B. & Brush, C. (2001). 'How do "Resource Bundles" Develop and Change in New Ventures? A Dynamic Model and Longitudinal Exploration'. *Entrepreneurship: Theory and Practice,* 25 (3), pp. 37–59.

Lindic, J. & Marques da Silva, C. (2011). 'Value Proposition as a Catalyst for a Customer Focused Innovation'. *Management Decision*, 49 (10), pp.1694–1708.

Lissack, M. & Roos, J. (1999). *The Next Common Sense – Mastering Corporate Complexity Through Coherence*. Nicholas Brearley Publishing: New York.

Mainardi, C. & Kleiner, A. (2010). 'The Right to Win'. *Strategy+Business. Strategy & Leadership*. Issue 61. Available at: <www.strategy-business.com/article/10407?gko=19c25> Date accessed: 03 Aug. 2015.

McGrath, R. G. (2013). *The End of Competitive Advantage: How to Keep your Strategy Moving as Fast as your Business*. Harvard Business Review Press: Boston, MA.

McGrath, R. G. (2013b). 'Transient Advantage'. *Harvard Business Review*, June, pp. 62–70.

Mintzberg, H. (1978). 'Patterns in Strategy Formulation'. *Management Science,* 24(9), pp. 934–948.

Moore, K. (2011). 'Porter or Mintzberg: Whose View of Strategy Is the Most Relevant Today?' *Forbes*. Available at: <www.forbes.com/sites/karlmoore/2011/03/28/porter-or-mintzberg-whose-view-of-strategy-is-the-most-relevant-today/> Date accessed: 13 Aug. 2015.

Neilson, G. L. & Estupiñán, J. (2014). 'The 10 Principles of Organizational DNA'. *Strategy+Business, Organizations & People*. October. Available at: <www.strategy-business.com/blog/The-10-Principles-of-Organizational-DNA> Date accessed: 1 Aug. 2015.

Newbert, S. L. (2007). 'Empirical Research on the Resource-based View of the Firm: An Assessment and Suggestions for Future Research. *Strategic Management Journal*, 28(2), pp. 121–146.

Ortega y Gasset, J. (1914). *Meditaciones del Quijote*. Catedra Letras Hispanicas.

Pan, S. L., Tan, B. C. C., Huang, J. & Poulsen, B. (2007). 'The Development Paths of Non-strategic Capabilities. *European Management Journal*, 25(5), pp. 344–358.

Pellissier, R. (2008). 'A Conceptual Framework for the Alignment of Innovation and Technology'. *Journal of Technology Management & Innovation*, 3(3), pp. 67–77. Available at: <www.jotmi.org/index.php/GT/article/view/art88> Date accessed: 13 Aug. 2015.

Penrose, E. (1959). *The Theory of the Growth of the Firm*. OUP: Oxford.

Porter, M. (1985). *Competitive Advantage: Creating and Sustaining Superior Performance*. New York: Free Press.

Ratten, V. (2011). 'Sport-based Entrepreneurship: Towards a New Theory of Entrepreneurship and Sport Management'. *International Entrepreneurship and Management Journal*, 7(1), pp. 57–69.

Schreyögg, G. & Kliesch-Eberl, M. (2007). 'How Dynamic Can Organizational Capabilities be? Towards a Dual-process Model of Capability Dynamization'. *Strategic Management Journal*. 28 (9), pp. 913–933.

Scott, W. R. (2003). *Organizations: Rational, Natural, and Open Systems* (5th ed.). Prentice Hall: Upper Saddle River, NJ.

Selznick, P. (1960). *The Organizational Weapon: a Study of Bolshevik Strategy and Tactics*. Free Press: Glencoe, IL.

Stabel, C.B. & Fjeldstad, O.D. (1998). 'Configuring Value for Competitive Advantage: On Chains, Shops and Networks', *Strategic Management Journal*, May: pp. 413-432.

Warnier, V., Weppe, X. & Lecocq, X. (2013). 'Extending Resource-Based Theory: Considering Strategic, Ordinary and Junk Resources'. *Management Decision*, 51(7), pp. 1359–1379.

11

SPORT, INNOVATION AND PUBLIC POLICY

Vanessa Ratten

Introduction

Sport is embedded in common culture because of the communal traditions associated with sport and is considered a democratic cultural activity because it transcends social barriers (Hughson *et al.*, 2004). Innovation is a feature of sport but is less recognized in the public policy area as a fundamental way for governments to interact with technological advancements. This is despite innovation being referred to as an important area of sport policy due to its impact on societal advancement. Sport policy can make a significant contribution to the innovation management discipline due to the variety of ways sport continually changes and adapts from societal change. In addition, studies about sport innovation can contribute to the sport policy discipline as there is little research about how innovative policy-making is conducted in sport and how policy spills over from sport innovations. This means that sport innovation can serve as the initiation for the development of policy aimed at introducing new things to the practice of sport. The challenge for sport policy is to accept that there is an inherent innovative capability of sport, which ensures continual change. Sport policy links to other policy areas including education, health and tourism, which makes it important to focus on innovative capabilities of sport services.

Sport is viewed as a low-cost but highly visible way to influence public policy. Often sport is used as a low risk way to bring culturally and politically different countries together. This has led to more innovative sport policy aimed at encouraging initiatives such as sport for peace and sport for development (Levermore, 2008). Sport policy is distinctive due to its cultural identity, economic application and diplomatic capabilities in the way individuals engage with sport. (Houlihan *et al.*, 2009). This has meant that sport often has stories associated with it from participating or fan engagement due to sport's positive impact on community integration and social well-being. Sport policy is emotional due to individuals' involvement or attachment to the sport, team, athlete or arena. The practice of sport policy means that government interventions can be innovative and bring about social change. A necessary part of sport policy has been the role of politics and this is closely linked to innovation. Sport is part of politics as it is a cultural leveller and proponent of equality (Hughson, 2004). This has led to sport taking its place within town planning because of its links to municipal authorities concerned with building sports grounds (Hughson, 2004). In addition, politically motivated sport interest groups have increasingly become concerned with civic planning and negotiating with extensions of existing sports services.

Sport policy impacts people in different ways depending on whether a person is an athlete, team player, spectator, volunteer, employee or manager. Sport innovation policy offers potential to integrate a multi-disciplinary perspective to the role of innovation in sports. There has been an increase in interest about public sector sport policy, especially in terms of how government action affects societal change (Houlihan, 2005). Despite the increased interest in sport policy in terms of the environment, community building and economic impact, the role of innovation in terms of sport public policy is limited. This is despite policy being influenced by cultural, demographic, international, economic and political change that affects its development (Cerny, 1995). The involvement of the government and state is an important part of sport policy and helps combine innovation into political discussion. Houlihan *et al.* (2009) discuss how sport policy has integrated the role of the state in affecting cultural and historical events. This means that cultural processes shaped by social trends influence how the state and government affect sport. Sport policy can be conducted taking a "bottom-up" approach to incorporate individuals such as coaches and teachers (Houlihan, 2005). This enables policy to be developed on a more practical level by taking an experiential approach to the sports context. Some policy utilizes the interests of sport development authorities including local councils to encourage innovative programs using community facilities. However, the entrenched political interests represented in some sport policies can make it hard to be innovative.

Policy for the development of sports innovations can take a cultural perspective, which is influenced by traditions. This is due to sport policy having transitioned from being a distinct area of policy into being incorporated into cultural policy (Hughson, 2004). The purpose of this chapter is to highlight the increasing role innovation is playing in the development of sport policy. We aim to show that innovation is represented in sport but also through government interventions. The issues around sport policy innovation are discussed in terms of advancing societal and technology change influencing sport.

The role of this chapter is to link innovation with sport policy by envisioning a more dynamic understanding of contemporary policy trends. This chapter argues that sport is part of innovation policy due to the role sport has within business, society and culture. Sport has both a unifying and dividing role in policy

Sport, innovation and public policy **181**

debates. This has led to sport and innovation being popular topics in both policy and research, which this chapter discusses in terms of sport innovation policy. Drawing on contemporary cultural policy linking sport to society, the main part of this chapter describes the possibilities of sport innovation being a distinct area of policy. During policy discussions most governments incorporate sport as a societal good, but this has changed with the commercialization of sport services. For sport to achieve its policy objectives, innovation can be utilized to provide an alternative approach. There are indications that sport innovation policy is needed to challenge traditional policy relationships in order to increase innovation in society.

Literature review

Stories accompanying policies help to show the impact of government intervention on community life (Fischer, 2003). An innovation perspective of policy can enhance our understanding about the role of governments in a sport context. This will help to build a better understanding about how innovation influences sport policy-making. Innovation in sport policy incorporates political change due to there being an increased interest in the role of the government in terms of promoting innovative policy. This can be seen in government intervention in building innovative sport stadiums and encouraging innovative ways to link sport to community projects. In addition, more government investment has been focused on innovative sports facilities that use sustainable products in order to encourage better environmental policy initiatives.

The role of the government in sport leads to questions about the motives of state agencies in policy initiatives (Houlihan *et al.*, 2009). The approach of government towards sport means issues about practical relevance are raised. Governments need to assess the extent of their sport policies by analyzing their innovativeness. Some governments perceive sport as having a strong case for intervention due to its role in policy debate. This has led to there being numerous ways that governments can change behavior with sport policy (Houlihan *et al.*, 2009). Hood (1983) suggests that there are inducements from financial to special which influence individuals to comply with government policy. Sanctions are another way governments can impose their policies due to the legal ramifications of this behavior. Other mechanisms include education initiatives that share information about the positive aspects of the sport policy (Houlihan *et al.*, 2009).

Houlihan (2005) discusses how there are independent variables in sport processes that impact policy decisions. Factors influencing sport policy include contextual, processual and specific (Houlihan, 2009). Contextual factors concern the culture and funding that is given to sport (Oakley and Green, 2001). This can include both financial and non-financial resources that help create an entrepreneurial ecosystem so sport can be developed. Culture can take a variety of forms but it is often embedded in media, which includes promotional activities, marketing and sponsorship (Digel, 2002). Processual factors involve the development of sport from its conception to performance (Houlihan, 2009). This process involves a number of steps from talent scouts, recruiting of players and coaches to performance management (Digel, 2002). The processes may change depending on whether the sport is elite, amateur, local or international. In terms of sport policy development, processual factors are important in evaluating funding and regulatory frameworks. An integrated approach to policy development is often favored as it helps to access policies for innovations occurring in sport contexts from new technologies to better equipment.

Specific factors regarding sport policy are more orientated to the specific sport or geographical place the sport is played. Examples of specific factors include sports medicine, which has been a growth area for policy analysis due to the innovative treatments becoming available for athletes. Doping cases in elite sport have become more common and international sport policy has developed to cope with this increase. The increased internationalization of sport, which has been made possible by mobile technology, has also led to specialized policies being developed. Some sports have innovated on a pay-per-view policy including Ultimate Fighting Championship events in which global viewers watch the event live. Other sports such as the Titans of Mavericks surfing event in San Francisco have banned spectators and instead filmed the event as a movie.

Sport innovations have also been in conjunction with different training regimes being utilized by elite athletes. This has meant there has been more elite facility development for certain sports that aim to increase performance (Green and Houlihan, 2005). This includes using different training facilities to help develop athlete endurance and increase performance. At the elite level there has been an increase in governmental intervention in sport policy (Green and Houlihan, 2005). This has been the result of changing governments and the priority they give to elite sport organizations. At the domestic level there has also been more government intervention of high-performance sport facilities to specialist sport technology services. This elite sport policy has resulted from the experience of elite athletes in terms of their on-the-field performance but also their appeal in the marketplace.

Many countries focus on innovation through sport by highlighting sustainability initiatives as the way to link sport to the environmental issues that consumers are involved with. This has led to outdoor sports fields and natural resources being preferred by some governments who utilize policy about physical education to encourage innovative programs. Examples of these sport policies include charity events and increased recognition about sport in lifestyle choices. Houlihan and White (2002) discuss how governments have implemented policies to increase mass participation in sport due to health and economic reasons. Governments see sport as a way to connect with their electorates by ensuring that there is social welfare and increased quality of life for individuals.

Education is a key way governments influence behavior, especially in the sport context as individuals learn about potential ramifications of playing or being involved in sport. Other ways behavior is changing through government policy

Sport, innovation and public policy **183**

are exchange, love and threats (Boulding, 1990). By exchanging information individuals can learn about better ways to participate in sport. Many individuals love their sport teams or playing a sport due to their emotional attachment. Threats about inappropriate behavior at sports events can be about match fixing or physical inequalities amongst athletes.

Boulding's (1990) approach for the way governments make change based on behavior is based on integrative outcomes. These outcomes influence sport policy decisions, which have a number of different impacts on communities, individuals and organizations (Houlihan *et al.*, 2009). The main types of policies are distributive, redistributive, regulatory and constituent. Distributive policies mean allocating funding to sports based on equity principles. This can be in the form of funding different types of sports based on demand. Redistributive policies means funding less socio-economically advanced regions to encourage sport. Regulatory policies involve mandatory ways sport is played and viewed by society. Due to the increased number of technological innovations in society such as mobile sport betting, governments are innovating in the way they regulate. New sports such as kitesurfing are also influencing regulatory policy from imposing boundaries on where and when the sport can be conducted.

Constituent policy involves the restructuring of institutions (Houlihan *et al.*, 2009). Other types of policy are aimed at the grassroots level so that communities become involved with government intervention. In sports, grassroots policy can be seen as local sports clubs petitioning for new fields. The way governments intervene in sports can be viewed as hard or soft power. Hard power involves regulatory policies that take a specific approach to the way sport is viewed in society. This includes geographic areas sport can be played or the times sport can be watched. Soft power involves coercing people to engage in certain behavior (Nye, 2008). This can include suggesting appropriate behavior based on outcomes that are the best for society (Houlihan *et al.*, 2009). In the sport context, soft power might involve suggesting better use of resources such as water, electricity and materials on the field and in clubhouses.

Policy analysis

In the policy analysis literature there are two major types of policy: analysis of policy and analysis for policy (Houlihan *et al.*, 2009). Analysis of policy involves examining the positive and negative influences of changes implemented by the government. It may also include studies focused on the economic and social impact of sport to see whether the decisions resulted in appropriate outcomes. The analysis of sport policy includes suggestions for future innovations that can be made and might mean examining how the change has resulted in better outcomes or increased fan involvement.

Analysis for policy is more orientated towards advocating certain regulations or approaches to take. This involves looking at sport policy in terms of changing societal involvement with sport. The analysis for sport policy can involve focusing on different stakeholders and how they view sport. For some, this includes developing a close relationship between government, sport authorities and the community. Some view the analysis for policy as being inspirational rather than practical due to sport's spiritual conceptualization in the mind of some individuals. This can be seen in the development of sport stadiums for mega-sport events such as the World Cup that needed government intervention after the event to make the stadiums useful for the community. Houlihan *et al.* (2009, p. 6) state that sport policy can be for other reasons as "prominent non-sport objectives include economic development and regeneration, civic boosterism, social control, the development of social capital and a variety of diplomatic objectives, while sport-related objectives give varying emphasis to improved elite performance, growth/school spirit and increased participation."

Cultural significance of sport

The cultural significance of sport in a country affects government policy aimed at both the commercial and social sector. Governments can introduce policy to promote certain individual and institutional conduct rather than governing this action (Raco and Imrie, 2000). This is similar to the view that governments should seek social order by harnessing their choices rather than mandating certain behavior. Sport policy can increase autonomy in society by empowering institutions. This is viewed as a better way to influence public policy debate when sport is viewed as both a professional and amateur activity. Depending on the cultural significance of sport in a country, governments can intervene in varying degrees.

A key role of sport policy is to foster better social relations and well-being in society. This can be done be seeing sport as an enjoyable activity that all people regardless of social status can be involved in. Citizens around the world are increasingly becoming interested in public policy decisions. Sport policy can be viewed in terms of deliberate democracy as it encompasses the role athletes, teams and consumers have in the policy process (Kihl *et al.*, 2007). Deliberative democracy is when there is a system of representative government. Thibault *et al.* (2010, p. 278) view deliberate democracy in the context of sport policy as "open public debate and the direct participation of the people themselves in decision making." This means that policy and politics should be based on the views of the people. Deliberate democracy is different depending on the country context and the role of public policy in society. These differences are seen in developing or emerging economies that may have different political conditions affecting sport policy.

Culture is organic as it changes with society based on customs and leisure activities of people (Eliot, 1948). Some cultures are focused on the pastimes of people that are handed down through generations. Culture is constantly being remade based on traditions altering from changes in the environment (Williams, 1958). Some sports are seen as a surrogate religion and sports stadiums as places of worship (Hughson, 2004). This is due to sport and religion having similar customs due to the linkage with rituals (Bale, 1993). In addition, sport has a spiritual appeal to people due to the aspirational role teams and athletes play in society. Often policy makers capitalize on the spiritual and religious association with sport to put forward better government policies. Bale (1993) discusses how there are strong emotions associated with sports grounds. This means that the love of sport places affects policy plans. Sports stadiums are sacred places that are nurtured by individual feelings (Bale, 1991).

International policy

International sport policy needs to be inclusive to give all stakeholders a position at the negotiation and decision-making table (Katwala, 2000). There are many different stakeholders from sports organizations influencing policy and these include athletes, coaches, managers, officials and volunteers (Thibault *et al.*, 2010). In the international environment, stakeholders interested in sport policy include media, sponsors, government authorities and non-government organizations. For international sport organizations policy needs to include a collaborative, open and multi-stakeholder approach (Katwala, 2000).

Increasingly, sport policy is becoming more similar internationally as domestic sport bodies have similar characteristics to their global counterparts. This is evident in policy changing from being developed based on political boundaries to incorporating more national and global agendas (Houlihan, 2009). The concept of supra-national policy networks gained prominence as domestic politics were affected by external environmental trends (Andersen and Eliassen, 1993). Supra-national policy incorporates provisions aimed at coordinating policy in a more holistic manner. This is important since there are policies at the global level that provide mechanisms for regulating the operation of sporting bodies. Supranational regulations as instruments monitoring the trade of firms based on certain social and welfare objectives. Houlihan (2009) describes supra-national sport policies in terms of rights to work in sport and helping regulate global players. This is important as more international sports federations shape sport policy.

International sport agencies include the International Association of Athletic Federations (IAAF) who utilize sport policies to encourage more equality between developing, transition and developed countries. This has led to sport policy being changed from development at the government level to focusing more on the commercial applications. This has coincided with the commercialization of sport from amateur events to professional activities (Silk *et al.*, 2005). Sport is now viewed as a brand that can transcend national boundaries but has mass market appeal.

Policy analysis is often viewed from an international perspective due to the technology and societal changes that affect everyday life. International sport institutions such as the International Olympic Committee have affected sport policy in terms of governance and athlete conditions (Houlihan, 2009). The

186 Vanessa Ratten

increasingly global nature of sport has led to policy being developed on an international basis so that there is consistency in rules and frameworks. As global sport businesses have become more prevalent there is more emphasis on policy that makes sense for an international audience rather than a purely domestic market. Increasingly, sport policy has been led by international government organizations that are concerned primarily with sport in terms of how to monitor that integration of innovation into sport. This has coincided with more emphasis from governmental bodies such as the European Union implementing policies to affect societal change in sport. Recent examples of this have been the European Union introducing policies to include a minimum number of females on sport boards to increase gender equality. The increased international emphasis on sport policy has prompted more interest in the role of sport in society.

Sport policy and innovation ecosystems

Policy around sport has altered as governments have become bigger and more regionally focused. This governmentalization refers to the shift in responsibilities to a state authority (Houlihan, 2009). This can been seen in the management of sport services that were previously viewed as societal goods but now are seen as revenue-raising concerns. The state has accrued more power in the delivery of sport services as sport has become ingrained in the politics of governments and seen as a reflection of good performance. For some governments, the way politicians decide their policy preferences depend on community concerns (Fischer, 2003). Sports groups often form special societies to promote their vested interests. The capacity of governments to find acceptable solutions for sports groups depends on the value and beliefs seen as being important in society.

Hughson (2004, p. 323) states that "sport offers an emotive, highly discernable and almost tangible means of civic and/or regional identity." This has led to there being a link between sport and social policy due to the trends occurring in society regarding viewing sport as necessary for social welfare (Houlihan, 2009). The policy ambition for sports is influenced by grassroots and elite organizations (Hughson, 2004). Governments have had a number of policies aimed at restructuring semi-independent sport authorities (Hughson, 2004). This restructuring is viewed as changing the organizational system to make it more competitive.

Stam (2015) discusses how innovation is recognized in policy analysis as a way to increase growth and entrepreneurship. There has been a change in the way sport policy is viewed based on the way innovation leads to new business creation. The traditional view of policy was from an economic system analysis that focused on value creation (Stam, 2015). This has changed due to contemporary views that economic systems are complex and need to incorporate innovative approaches. Government intervention is usually viewed as a way to change unbalanced markets instead of a way to encourage innovation. The inability of a market to perform efficiently may lead to government intervention focusing on innovation (Jacobs and Theeuwes, 2005). Some government intervention constrains rather than promotes innovation (Nooteboom and Stam, 2008). There is a necessity in a market to induce innovation because of the complexity of the economic system.

A recent policy framework is the innovation systems approach, which recognizes the role of cooperation by knowledge exchange (Stam, 2015). Cooperation meaning the integration of organizations, individuals or communities into a competitive marketplace has become more popular especially with the knowledge economy. This informal interaction in the knowledge economy is facilitated by different forms of knowledge being shared. The innovation systems approach highlights how the lack of knowledge encourages stakeholders to share information to create change. This leads to stakeholders in the innovation system working together to create mutually beneficial outcomes.

Another recent approach to policy analysis is the entrepreneurial ecosystem approach (Stam, 2015). This approach incorporates innovation but stresses the role of leaders embedded in society that instigate change. In entrepreneurial ecosystems, the environment is conducive to facilitating innovative behavior that spills over to other areas. The entrepreneurship involves building opportunities for creativity to develop. These opportunities are facilitated by entrepreneurship being explored and evaluated depending on the market (Shane and Venkataraman, 2000). The exploitation of new ideas helps create an ecosystem for furthering innovation initiatives.

In environments conducive to the development of entrepreneurial ecosystems there are productive forms of entrepreneurship, which result from innovative activity (Stam *et al.*, 2012). As entrepreneurship can take a variety of forms from social, international and corporate, it is important that this diversity be included within an ecosystem that has a sport focus. In a sport ecosystem, entrepreneurship is defined broadly as innovative capabilities derived from productive associations. Stam (2015, p. 1761) states "the entrepreneurial ecosystem concept emphasizes that entrepreneurship takes place in a community of interdependent actors." This means that the context for entrepreneurship is important as it enables sports systems to develop. There has been increased interest in entrepreneurial systems as a way to incorporate innovation systems theory to emerging research focusing on entrepreneurship (Acs *et al.*, 2014). The social element of entrepreneurship is a component of environmental factors influencing the way entrepreneurship occurs (Levie *et al.*, 2014).

Innovation systems are sometimes referred to as clusters, districts or regions due to the concentration of activity located in these areas (Sternberg, 2007). Another way to view innovation systems especially in the sport context is by explaining them in terms of learning environments that integrate society with change. The focus in entrepreneurial ecosystems is on individuals who interact with the business environment (Stam, 2015). Entrepreneurship policy has focused more on leadership rather than government intervention (Feld, 2012). This is due to entrepreneurship considering business rather than government policy being the key element of the innovation systems. The entrepreneurship ecosystem incorporates leaders who supervise change and who provide information about future directions (Stam, 2015). This means that there is a constant flow of knowledge related to opportunity recognition being filtered via the sport ecosystem. Sport policy makers are also key stakeholders in entrepreneurial ecosystems due to their ability to link government authority to market need. In order for ecosystems to develop they need to incorporate culture, finance, human capital, markets, policy and support (Isenberg, 2011). In the sport context, culture is evident in the way sport is perceived based on societal attitudes. Some cultures have more emphasis on sports than others due to the lifestyle of citizens. Finance is important to facilitate sport and this occurs when governments invest in sports precincts. Some governments see financing of local sports clubs or building better sports facilities as part of their political duties. Human capital in sport is developed by governments supporting athlete welfare and the development of sports authorities. Talent management in sport is important especially for global sports organizations that want to attract and retain the best sport personnel. To do this, policy aimed at encouraging certain sports clubs to move to a different geographic area is introduced.

Markets in entrepreneurial ecosystems concern building a competitive basis for sports teams that enable global best practice. Sport policy concerns thinking about the other ecosystem elements to see how they can be changed. Support can be in the form of information and resources that enable sport to be directed towards a particular outcome. Zhang and Li (2010) discuss support in terms of service intermediaries who encourage better participation. There has been a shift in entrepreneurship policy from being regionally focused to more of an ecosystem approach that transcends geographical boundaries (Thurik *et al.*, 2013). The entrepreneurial ecosystem approach stresses that activity occurs in a complex manner with interdependencies developing on an ad hoc basis, which are particularly evident in sports contexts. Table 11.1 depicts the sport entrepreneurial ecosystems participants by stating the sport element and related components.

TABLE 11.1 Sport entrepreneurial ecosystem participants

Sport element	Components
Cultural support	Athlete role models, sport team success, positive sport environment
Education and training	Physical education, kinesiology training, sport psychology
Funding and finance	Fan engagement, private equity, sport ventures
Government and regulation	Sport business, tax incentives, stadium infrastructure, telecommunications, transport
Human capital	Team management, technical website talent, sport outsourcing
Universities	Sport research, commercialization, training
Workforce and markets	Sport companies, international marketing, sport branding

Developed from Stam (2015)

Sport, innovation and public policy **189**

Entrepreneurial ecosystems are important to sport in order to build community spirit. Human capital and workforces help grow an ecosystem by encouraging sport-related activities to foster further innovation. The success of ecosystems depends on how sport components such as universities and the government incorporate public/private partnerships. This includes institutional structures such as educational providers that foster community engagement (Acemoglu *et al.*, 2005). For sport policy to be successful there needs to be communication from the government to relevant sports authorities. Public authorities can intervene in sport to make it more accessible for the community. The public sector can intervene in sport policies to increase the collaboration between voluntary and commercial organizations (Puig *et al.*, 2010).

Future research suggestions

Future research agendas about sport innovation policy can facilitate further understanding about policy and how it is impacted by innovation. There is a need to analyze the role of innovation, government and the state in influencing the development of sport. Due to the financial and societal impact sport has in the community it is important to reflect on the role of state intervention in sport (Houlihan, Bloyce and Smith, 2009). This chapter presents an important step in understanding the role innovation plays in sport policy. Some governments have utilized innovations to ensure sport policy is linked to market trends. Future research on sport innovation policy could include interviews with multiple stakeholders who view innovation in different ways. This would help provide clarification on the role of innovation in sport policy and its impact on sport development. More research on innovation in sport policy may lead to better political outcomes for all stakeholders.

There is a shortage of detailed policy analysis emphasizing sport changes from innovation. Research that focuses on longitudinal analysis of innovations in sport would be welcome. In addition, research that explains how innovation impacts sport policy would be a useful addition to the literature. Sport policy is affected by innovation changes in other areas such as technology and education and varies by country depending on the perception of sport in the culture. Some governments view sport as a necessity and a basis for economic activity whilst others are less concerned with sport. More research taking an interdisciplinary perspective to sport innovation policy is required. It is hoped the entrepreneurial ecosystem approach utilizing the innovation systems theory will be further explored in future research.

References

Acemoglu, D., Johnson, S. and Robinson, J. A. (2005) 'Institutions as a fundamental cause of long-run growth', in: P. Aghion and S. Durlauf (eds.) *Handbook of Economic Growth*, Amsterdam: Elsevier, pp. 386–472.

Acs, Z. J., Autio, E. and Szerb, L. (2014) 'National systems of entrepreneurship: Measurement issues and policy implications', *Research Policy*, 43(3): 476–494.

Andersen, S. S., and Eliassen, K.A., eds., (1993) *Making Policy in Europe: The Europeification of National Policy-making*, London: Sage.

Bale, J. (1991) 'Playing at home: British football and a sense of place', in: J. Williams and S. Wagg (eds.) *British Football and Social Change,* Leicester: University Press: Leicester, pp. 130–144.

Bale, J. (1993) *Sport, Space and the City*, London: Routledge.

Boulding, K. E. (1990) *Three Faces of Power*, Newbury Park, CA: Sage.

Cerny, P. (1995) 'Globalisation and the changing logic of collective action', *International Organisation*, 48(4): 595–625.

Digel, H. (2002) 'A comparison of competitive sports systems', *New Studies in Athletics*, 17(1): 37–49.

Eliot, T. S. (1948) *Notes towards a Definition of Culture,* London: Faber & Faber.

Feld, B. (2012) *Startup Communities: Building an Entrepreneurial Ecosystem in Your City*, New York, NY: Wiley.

Fischer, F. (2003) *Reframing Public Policy: Discursive Politics and Deliberative Practices*, New York: Oxford University Press.

Green, M. and Houlihan, B. (2005) *Elite Sport Development: Policy Learning and Political Priorities*, London: Routledge.

Hood, C. (1983) *The Tools of Government*, London: Macmillan.

Houlihan, B. (2005) 'Public sector sport policy: Developing a framework for analysis', *International Review for the Sociology of Sport*, 40(2): 163–185.

Houlihan, B. (2009) 'Mechanisms of international influence on domestic elite sport policy', *International Journal of Sport Policy and Politics*, 1(1): 51–69.

Houlihan, B., Bloyce, D. and Smith, A. (2009) 'Developing the research agenda in sport policy', *International Journal of Sport Policy and Politics*, 1(1): 1–12.

Houlihan, B. and White, A. (2002) *The Politics of Sport Development: Development of Sport or Development through Sport?* London: Routledge.

Hughson, J. (2004) 'Sport in the "city of culture" ', *International Journal of Cultural Policy*, 10(3): 319–330.

Hughson, J., Inglis, D. and Free, M. (2004) *The Uses of Sport: A Critical Study*, London: Routledge.

Isenberg, D. J. (2011) 'Introducing the entrepreneurship ecosystem: Four defining characteristics', *Forbes*. Available at <www.forbes.com/sites/danisenberg/2011/05/25/introducing-the-entrepreneurship-ecosystemfour- defining-characteristics/> (accessed 25 May 2015).

Jacobs, B. and Theeuwes, J. (2005) 'Innovation in the Netherlands: The market falters and the government fails', *De Economist*, 153(1): 107–124.

Katwala, S., (2000) *Democratising Global Sport,* London: The Foreign Policy Centre.

Kihl, L., Kikulis, L. and Thibault, L., (2007) 'A deliberative democratic approach to athlete-centred sport: The dynamics of administrative and communicative power', *European Sport Management Quarterly*, 7(1): 1–30.

Levermore, R. (2008) 'Sport: a new engine of development?', *Progress in Development Studies*, 8(2): 183–190.

Levie, J., Autio, E., Reeves, C., Chisholm, D., Harris, J., Grey, S., Ritchie, I. and Cleevely, M. (2014) *Assessing regional innovative entrepreneurship ecosystems with the global entrepreneurship and development index: The case of Scotland*, Global Entrepreneurship Research Conference, Barcelona.

Nooteboom, B. and Stam, E. (2008) *Microfoundations for Innovation Policy*, Amsterdam: Amsterdam University Press.

Nye, J., (2008) 'Public diplomacy and soft power', *Annals of the American Academy of Political and Social Science*, 616(1): 94–109.

Oakley, B. and Green, M., (2001) 'The production of Olympic champions: International perspectives on elite sport development systems', *European Journal of Sport Management*, 8 (Special Issue): 83–105.

Puig, M., Martinez, J. and Garcia, B. (2010) 'Sport policy in Spain', *International Journal of Sport Policy and Politics*, 2(3): 381–390.

Raco, M. and Imrie, R. (2000) 'Governmentality and rights and responsibilities in urban policy', *Environment and Planning A*, 32(12): 2187–2204.

Shane, S. and Venkataraman, S. (2000) 'The promise of entrepreneurship as a field of research', *Academy of Management Review*, 25(1): 217–226.

Silk, M. L., Andrews, D. L. and Cole, C.L. (eds.) (2005) *Sport and Corporate Nationalism*, Oxford: Berg.

Stam, E. (2015) 'Entrepreneurial ecosystems and regional policy: A sympathetic critique', *European Planning Studies*, 23(9): 1759–1769.

Stam, E., Bosma, N., Van Witteloostuijn, A., de Jong, J., Bogaert, S., Edwards, N. and Jaspers, F. (2012) *Ambitious Entrepreneurship. A Review of the Academic Literature and New Directions for Public Policy*, Den Haag: Adviesraad voor Wetenschap en Technologiebeleid (AWT).

Sternberg, R. (2007) 'Entrepreneurship, proximity and regional innovation systems', *Tijdschrift voor Economische en Sociale Geografie*, 98(5): 652–666.

Thibault, L., Kihl, L. and Babiak, K. (2010) 'Democratization and governance in international sport: addressing issues with athlete involvement in organizational policy'. *International Journal of Sport Policy*, 2(3): 275–302.

Thurik, R., Stam, E. and Audretsch, D. (2013) 'The rise of the entrepreneurial economy and the future of dynamic capitalism', *Technovation*, 33(8–9): 302–310.

Williams, R. (1958) *Culture and Society, 1780–1950*, London: Chatto & Windus.

Zhang, Y. and Li, H. (2010) 'Innovation search of new ventures in a technology cluster: The role of ties with service intermediaries', *Strategic Management Journal*, 31(1): 88–109.

12

"NOT OUT"? A SOCIOMATERIAL PERSPECTIVE ON DECISION REVIEW SYSTEMS IN PROFESSIONAL CRICKET

Ian McLoughlin and Patrick Dawson

Introduction

Management research on the relationship between sport and technology remains surprisingly limited given that the production and consumption of sporting events is increasingly interwoven with the use of new digital and network technologies (Kruse, 2010). For example, the increasing use of data analytics to track and evaluate on-field performance (Anderson and Sally, 2013), the use of mobile and other technologies to enhance the spectator experience (Kruse, 2010) and the globalisation of sporting markets and identities enabled by the network society (Hutchins and Rowe, 2013) are all transforming sport as a business and consumer experience. In this chapter we focus on the manner in which digital technologies are being deployed as aids to match officials – umpires, referees, etc. – in making on-field decisions during match play. The first and probably most well-known example of this type of innovation was the deployment of the "Hawk-eye" system in some "Grand Slam" tennis tournaments (Collins and Evans, 2008). This system used ball tracking technology to provide a means of determining the trajectory of the ball through computer generated images. In this way a ball could be deemed to be "in" or "out" or "over the line", etc. Our focus is on the "Decision Review System" (DRS) introduced into international test cricket over the past few years. As we will see, although intended to provide an on-field aid to umpires and eliminate human error in match adjudications, the deployment of this system has proved highly controversial.

Our aim is to explore the basis of this controversy but to do so through the "lens" provided by a sociomaterial perspective (Orlikowski, 2000; Scott and Orlikowski, 2014). We argue that, as in organisation studies more generally, this provides a rather different way in which we can view technological innovations in sport by re-casting our understanding of the relationship between technology and sporting social phenomenon. In particular, the approach challenges the view that technologies can be seen as separate entities with inherent properties that have impacts or determining effects. It also questions the view that technologies are themselves exclusively shaped by social phenomenon or that technical and social entities exist in some form of mutual relationship which shapes the other. Instead the ontological distinction between "technology" and the "social" as separate entities is rejected and viewed only as a relational phenomenon. We begin by outlining key aspects of the sociomaterial approach. The origins, technology and use of DRS in the sport of cricket are then reviewed and our research design and methods summarised. Findings from a study of the use of DRS during "critical incidents" in the back-to-back Ashes series held in England (2013) and Australia (2013–14) are then presented. Our conclusions highlight the ongoing uncertainty and ambiguity surrounding the use of DRS but suggest this be viewed as an ongoing feature of the materialisation of the phenomenon and not an aberrant outcome due to inherent technological and/or human failings.

A sociomaterial perspective on technological innovation

The sociomaterial perspective has recently gained ground in organisation studies and information systems research (for reviews see e.g. Leonardi, *et al.*, 2011; Nicolini, 2012; Cecez-Kecmanovic *et al.*, 2014). It owes its origins in part to the work of physicist Karen Barad (2003, 2007) and her argument for a "post humanist performative account of technoscientific and other naturalcultural practices" which more effectively represents the entanglement of matter and meaning in everyday practice (Barad, 2007, p. 32). The attraction of the approach is that it counters the tendency for dualism in much management theorising. Instead of seeking to explore the relationship between pre-defined entities or things which are assumed to have inherent properties or "essences" (Grint and Woolgar, 1997) such "things" are deemed to exist only when they are in relationship with each other in situated practices. As such "technologies" and "social phenomenon" do not have independent existences, capabilities and characteristics outside of situated actions and interactions. Materiality and meaning are thus an ongoing and emergent outcome of sociomaterial practices through which "things" are materialised and meanings associated with them established and institutionalised. As such: "Human action is not just dependent on materiality and material artefacts, but is constituted by them" (Doolin, 2012, p. 572).

The conventional view of technologies in much organisational research is that they are best regarded as more or less fixed structures (artefacts, products, systems) which embody human intentions (e.g. of designers, entrepreneurs, innovators). These structures are then appropriated (or not) through process of adoption by users in particular user domains and, where successful, diffused across similar settings. The sociomaterial lens, however, suggests that technologies are best viewed as an outcome (albeit contingent and transitory) not of appropriation but of their situated enactment in organisational practice. As such, rather than being fixed independent entities, technologies are continually enacted as "technologies-in-practice" through human actions and interactions with them whenever and wherever they are used (Orlikowski, 2000). Such a view invites us to move away from, "thinking about how technologies as discrete artifacts influence humans" to examine instead, "how actions and relations are materially constituted in practice" (Scott and Orlikowski, 2014, p. 874). In research terms, one key implication of this analytical stance is that, "rather than starting with the technology and [examining] how actors appropriate its embodied structures" it may be more realistic to adopt a position that, ". . . starts with human action and examines how it enacts emergent structures through recurrent interaction with the technology at hand" (Orlikowski, 2000, p. 407).

Key here is the notion that agency is not attributed to "either humans or their technical artefacts" but rather is conceptualised as a "capacity for action realised through the constitutive sociomaterial entanglement of the two" (Doolin, 2012, p. 573). The outcomes of such entanglements are both indeterminant and variable across different times, space and place. Important to understanding sociomateriality in a given context is the idea of "agential cuts" (Barad, 2003). These can be used to analyse how situated meaning is given locally to otherwise open, fluid and entangled material phenomenon. Agential cuts, ". . . are always enactments, producing and stablizing/destablizing particular distinctions, boundaries, and properties in practice" (Scott and Orlikowski, 2014, p. 879). Such cuts, for instance might (re-) define the authority, roles and responsibilities of decision-makers in specific contexts and/or act to de-stablise existing understandings of the same.

Many of these insights and concerns resonate with other sociologically informed attempts to understand the nature of the relationships between technical and social phenomenon (Cecez-Kecmanovic *et al.*, 2014). However, the sociomaterial lens provides a potentially more fruitful way of understanding how human agents and contemporary digital and network technologies interact. This is, in part at least, because of the inherent malleability and configurability of such systems in the situated organisational and other contexts in which they are deployed and used (Leonardi *et al.*, 2011). The use of such technologies in the practice of playing and experiencing professional sport provides a particularly compelling arena in which to explore such issues. This is because match play affords the opportunity to focus on highly situated "processes, changes and evolutions" where the action – for example on-field interactions between players and umpires and the interpretation and reflection on these events by media and other observers – requires description through "nuanced verbs" to capture "what people do" and "what happens to them" (Wolfe *et al.*, 2005, p. 205). Accordingly, we now review the background to the adoption of DRS, the nature of the "technology at hand" and how and why it has been taken up in international cricket.

The origins and the take-up of DRS

In cricket, and many other sports, the increased extent and sophistication of television coverage has been central to a new scrutiny of decision-making by on-field match officials (umpires, referees, etc.) who have been increasingly subject in many observers' eyes to "trial by television". Concerned by such developments, sports administrators have become interested in adopting technologies developed to enhance the viewing experience (e.g. action and slow-motion replays and the like) as decision-aids to assist match officials with the aim of overcoming the perception of their fallibility in circumstances where the human eye struggles to keep up with the action to determine "what really happened". In the case of cricket, this has resulted in the deployment of decision review systems (DRS) at the first-class international "test match" level of the game.

Although these initiatives have been backed by broadcasters and the sport's peak administrative bodies, the experience of their use has provided perhaps the most controversy of any sport (see Borooah, 2013). For example, prominent ex-players and former umpires have expressed concerns that the system is eroding the authority of the umpire and adding new pressures which have forced some officials to retire from the game (ESPN CricInfo, 2009). Others see DRS as really no more than a "gimmick" whilst some fear that it threatens the core values and character of the sport, turning it into "CSI Cricket" and a form of "computer game" (Smith, 2013). Among the first-class playing nations, India currently refuses to sanction use of the system in international test matches in which it is a participant because of concerns over its accuracy. The captain of the Indian national team famously remarked during the 2011 World Cup that the "adulteration of technology with human thinking was bad" (The Times of India, 2011). Finally, vendor claims that systems are inherently "accurate, reliable and practical" have been challenged by academic researchers – not always, it seems, to the amusement of the system suppliers – on the grounds that sources and margins of error exist in all scientific measurement (Collins and Evans, 2008, 2012; also Steen, 2011; Borooha, 2013).

The primary element of the DRS system used in cricket is based on Reconstructed Tracking Device (RTD) technologies (Collins and Evans, 2008). This is similar to the Hawk-Eye system used in professional tennis where computer-generated images of "what happened" are produced that also predict the trajectory of the ball and its relationship to aspects of play such as the court lines in tennis, or the batsman's position in relation to the stumps in cricket. The most well-known of these systems and the one used in professional cricket, tennis and more recently Association Football, is known as "Hawk-Eye". The origins of the RTD technology are said to be in research conducted by Gillette to try to identify the perfect means of assessing the closeness of the shave given by their products. Whether this is an authentic account or not, the first use of RTD was made by UK television broadcaster Channel 4 in its coverage of The Ashes cricket series in 2001. However, the coming of age of the technology occurred when it was adopted as a decision aid in the US Open Tennis Championship in 2006, followed by the Australian Open and then the Wimbledon Championship in 2007. It has been deployed to assist umpire decisions in professional cricket since November 2009, most notably in the Cricket World Cups held in India in 2011 and Australia in 2015, as well as in several test series, including the 2010–11,

196 Ian McLoughlin and Patrick Dawson

2013 and 2013–14 Ashes series between England and Australia (the latter two series providing the empirical focus for this paper). This represents a significant investment for the sport, one estimate suggests that US$60,000 on DRS-related infrastructure is required for each day of a test match (Borooah, 2013).

RTD tracking technology has particular application to the somewhat notorious "Leg Before Wicket" (LBW) law. The application of the game's "Law 36" governing LBW requires the human umpire to predict what the trajectory of the ball might have been en route to the stumps had it not been impeded by the batsman's body (rather than bat).[1] Such judgments call on immense experience and understanding of the game and from time to time the calls made in the heat of match play are not without controversy with different interpretations being revealed by TV slow-mo replays. Clearly a system that promises to accurately predict the tracking of a ball on the basis of its prior trajectory (i.e. in the context of cricket what would have happened if the ball's journey had not been disturbed by the batsman) would seem, if used as intended, to be a significant aid and means of eliminating, or at least significantly reducing, the margin of human error in such judgments.

Whilst RTD provides the core technology of the DRS system used in cricket, other technologies have also been incorporated into the system including of course replays and slow motion TV pictures. In addition to this thermal imaging, technology that can detect contact between the ball with the batsmen and their bat in the form of "heat spots" created by frictional engagement between the two (this system is known as "Hot Spot"), has also been adopted. There are also highly sensitive audio aids which use sound waves to detect similar contacts. However, whilst used by broadcasters for some time, this technology (known as "Snicko") has only very recently been incorporated into DRS due to time lags of several minutes in processing results. The first use of "real-time Snicko" was in the 2013–2014 Ashes series although it was not used in the 2015 World Cup (ESPN CricInfo, 2013a).

RTD and the other DRS technologies reveal different things, are subject to different degrees of accuracy, operate with different degrees of tolerance and, of course, rely on the availability of working equipment when required and can be affected by local environmental and other operational conditions. As we will see, the evidence they produce in practice (e.g. visuals, projections, heat, sound) does not speak for itself and sometimes appears to be ambiguous or even contradictory. How meaning is given to these material representations of "what really happened" by umpires, players and others provides the focus for our sociomaterial analysis and the manner in which DRS is constituted as a "technology in practice".

Research design

To align with our theoretical approach, the focus of our empirical attention is on the on-field actions and interactions of players and umpires during match-play and the observation and interpretation of these events, both live and after the

"Not Out"? Decision review systems in cricket **197**

match, by knowledgeable agents in the form of media commentators, journalists and pundits (many of whom are former players). We also examine the views and interventions of other key stakeholders such as game administrators and the technology suppliers. International cricket test matches between England and Australia are played for one of international sport's legendary prizes – "The Ashes". Each series consists of five "tests", each typically lasting up to five days, watched by large crowds. Matches are also covered in full and live through television and "ball-by-ball" radio broadcasts to sizeable global television and listening audiences. The Ashes also attracts extensive media coverage and comment before, during and after each series, especially in the two competing nations where the contest marks a strong rivalry born of common heritage. Online news media coverage of cricket is also increasingly important as both adjuncts to conventional broadcast (for example broadcasters and newspapers now provide online ball-by-ball live blogs of matches as they take place and post-match podcasts) and as a medium for comment, debate and discussion in their own right. In addition there are a plethora of cricket enthusiast and fan websites, blogs and other online arenas where the game is now routinely discussed and debated including the websites of system suppliers.

Our data is drawn from this array of sources and, in particular, the live broadcast of these events on television (which we recorded for subsequent analysis); ball-by-ball blogs provided by broadcasters and online versions of national newspapers, which can be analysed retrospectively, and key websites, which provide statistical records, comment and other information about on-field events and their aftermath. Using these sources we analysed the actions and interactions through which DRS was being constituted on-field as the events unfolded, and the practices of umpires, players and others as they enacted DRS during match play. We used this data to identify "critical incidents" during each test match where the DRS system was implicated either because it was called into play or, for some reason, was not. Background data was also collected by examining the history and deployment of DRS in the sport and from the observations of recorded TV pictures of its use in other selected international test matches. However, to make this task manageable in the context of resources available for the research, we decided to make our primary focus on the two test series played by England and Australia in the northern hemisphere summer of 2013 and during the return southern hemisphere summer of 2013–2014 (the series were held in back-to-back years on this one occasion due to the scheduling of the London Olympics in 2012). By this time, many of the issues which had emerged since the initial deployment of DRS in international cricket were coming to a head.

Through these methods a database was compiled documenting the key features of the critical incidents where DRS was used in each of the series and the ensuing discussions and debates that occurred. Our record of DRS incidents was corroborated by reference to websites such as ESPN CricInfo, which specialises in providing detailed ball-by-ball records. An example of a qualitative summary of critical incidents from the first test played in the 2013 series is given in Table 12.1

TABLE 12.1 Critical incidents identified concerning DRS in an Ashes Test Match

2013 Series	TYPE OF REFERRAL	OUTCOME	COMMENT
1st TEST: TRENT BRIDGE, Nottingham, UK			
England (ENG) 1st Innings (E1)	**Over:**	incorrect referral decision upheld	
	57.2 ENG refer out caught decision		
	57.6 AUS refer appeal for LBW not given	incorrect referral decision upheld	
Australia (AUS) 1st Innings (A1)			
	14.3 AUS refer out LBW decision	incorrect referral decision upheld	
	33.4 AUS refer out LBW decision	incorrect referral decision upheld	**Two incorrect referrals by AUS**
England 2nd Innings (E2)			
	1.3 AUS refer appeal for LBW not given	incorrect referral decision upheld	*Umpire judgement appears inconsistent with A1 14.3*
	7.4 AUS refer appeal for LBW not given	overturned umpire decision	*Controversial decision to overturn as hotspot evidence not available due to operator error*
	68.6 AUS refer appeal for LBW not given	incorrect referral decision upheld	
	78.6 ENG refer out LBW decision	overturned umpire decision	
Australia 2nd Innings (A2)			
	24.1 AUS refer out LBW decision	incorrect referral decision upheld	
	25.5 AUS refer out caught decision	overturned umpire decision	
	37.3 Umpire referral runout/stumping?	3rd Umpire advises not out	
	58.6 AUS refer out caught decision	incorrect referral decision upheld	**Two incorrect referrals by AUS** *prevents subsequent referral in "Broadgate incident"*
	61.5 ENG refer appeal for LBW not given	overturned umpire decision	*Marginal call in ENG favour*
	110.5 ENG refer appeal caught not given	overturned umpire decision	*DRS confirms "let's-take-a-gamble" referral'*

Source: ESPN CricInfo

"Not Out"? Decision review systems in cricket **199**

where we identified 14 incidents where the use or non-use of DRS was a matter of either record, comment or controversy amongst the participants and informed observers. Table 12.2 summarises the numbers of DRS reviews initiated by both teams in all the tests across the two series.

Our objective, as already noted, was to try to understand how DRS was constituted through the actions and interactions of participants in the sport, in particular umpires and players, in order to reveal the nature of the entanglements and agential cuts which lay at the heart of sociomaterial relations and practice. With this in mind, we were particularly interested in the ways that the deployment of DRS systems in professional cricket has made a difference in relation to the role of umpires and how this has been enacted through their actions and relations with players and others. We were concerned, therefore, with the manner in which existing boundaries, for example those which define where decision-making authority rests, might be being questioned and the roles of umpires destabilised. We were also interested in how agential cuts might include or exclude certain things (for example whether and when DRS evidence is admitted into the adjudication process or not).

TABLE 12.2 DRS reviews initiated by teams

Test	DRS reviews initiated by both teams	England (upheld/not upheld)	Australia (upheld/not upheld)
England Summer 2013			
1st	11	3 (1 not upheld/2 upheld)	8 (7 not upheld/1 upheld)
2nd	8	4 (3 not upheld/1 upheld)	4 (4 not upheld)
3rd	7	5 (2 not upheld)	2 (not upheld)
4th	12	6 (2 upheld/4 not upheld)	6 (3 not upheld/3 upheld)
5th	8	4 (4 not upheld)	4 (1 upheld/3 not upheld)
Series Total	46		
Average/Test	9.2		
Australia Summer 2013–2014			
1st	4	2 (2 not upheld)	2 (1 not upheld/1 upheld)
2nd	9	3(3 not upheld)	6 (4 not upheld/2 upheld)
3rd	2	1 (not upheld)	1 (not upheld)
4th	3	2(1 not upheld/1 upheld)	1 (not upheld)
5th	4	1 (not upheld)	3 (3 not upheld)
SERIES TOTAL	22		
Average/Test	4.4		
OVERALL TOTAL	68		

Source: ESPN CricInfo

DRS critical incidents from the test series

The introduction of DRS has arguably been the most radical on-field innovation in the history of the game, at least since overarm bowling was introduced. Significant institutional changes have of course also occurred in the organisation and governance of the sport, most notably the transition from an amateur pastime to a professionalised business during the last century (Wright and Zammutto, 2013). As part of this process the sport, as in many others, has become increasingly dependent for both its continued popularity and revenues on television and media coverage on an increasingly global scale. As noted, the technology underpinning DRS emerged through innovations of broadcasters intending to improve the game as a viewing experience. It is also perhaps representative of a new twenty-first century trend towards sport "as a global entertainment spectacle" where the representation of the game in a "virtual reality" of new digital and network media may itself be a further phase of institutional change where the only "reality" is a "virtual" one (McLoughlin and Dawson, 2013).

Significantly during the Ashes series it was the accuracy of DRS in providing a digital or virtual account of "what really happened" which was the major focus of discussion and debate. This prompted further concerns over the competence of umpires, the tactical nous of team captains and even the propriety of players who some alleged were seeking to find ways to "cheat" the system. As in other sports, cricket has developed within-game formal protocols which govern the use of the system during match play. These protocols also serve as indications of "agential cuts" since they frame the possibilities of interpretation of the meaning of the information provided by DRS systems in specific match incidents (e.g. an "LBW appeal"). These protocols provide the procedural and interpretative basis through which umpires and players call on the DRS system in the decision-making process during matches. As such the DRS protocol provides the frame through which interpretation of "what really happened" takes place.

The protocol covering the use of the DRS in cricket allows for each team – batting and bowling – to request reviews of umpire decisions (indicated by the team captain making a "T sign" with their hands) to a specified maximum of incorrect referrals per innings (in the first of the two Ashes series considered here the limit was two "incorrect referrals" per team, although this was subject to minor adjustment in the second series).[2] For example, the fielding team might call on DRS to dispute a "not out" decision by the umpire and likewise the batting side to contest an umpire's decision to give a batsman "out". At the same time umpires themselves may request a review of close decisions such as run-outs and stumpings where the action is normally rapid and sometimes obscured by events on the field of play. On accepting the challenge or initiating their own review the on-field umpires revert to a third off-field umpire who considers the DRS evidence. The third umpire then communicates the result of their deliberations to the on-field umpires using two-way radio. Their decision may be to uphold the on-field decision, over turn the decision or report an inconclusive result.

Significantly, there is recognition in the protocol of the limits of the accuracy of DRS ball-tracking technology and in certain circumstances the computer-generated evidence related to predicting the tracking of the ball is discarded because of this. Given all of this, as we will see, teams have also developed their own informal protocols with regard to how to exploit during match play the opportunities to challenge umpire decisions afforded by the formal protocol.

The critical incidents which occurred during the test series reveal the contingent nature of the boundaries and exclusions that the protocol enacts and the manner in which these were re-enacted in actual match play. First, the "accuracy" of DRS remained a matter of dispute throughout the series despite the protocol seeking to provide a boundary between when such evidence was accurate enough to be admissible to support decision-making. This concern was most evident during the series with respect to the infra-red detections system "Hot Spot". There were a number of incidents where seemingly ambiguous images were produced by the system leading at one point for the inventor of "Hot Spot" to suggest that it was not as reliable as assumed (Hoult, 2013) and at another for accusations to be made concerning players bat-tampering by applying tape to the edges to avoid DRS detection of contact by the ball (ABC News, 2013). In one incident in the first test at Trent Bridge, an English batsman was dismissed on the basis of what turned out to be misleading video evidence alone because the Hot Spot system was not available at that instant due to "operator error". The incident subsequently drew an apology from the International Cricket Council (ICC) and an admission that the umpires had made an error with their decision. After the 2013 series, one former England captain claimed that, "Hot Spot just creates confusion . . . Sometimes it shows up, sometimes it doesn't, so no-one really trusts it" (BBC Radio 5 Live, 2013).

Second, the adeptness of players and coaches in developing their own informal protocols with regard to DRS appeared to be becoming more decisive in determining the outcome of a match. Most commentators observed, for example, that England's on-field protocol for determining whether to initiate a DRS referral in the 2013 series was superior to that deployed by Australia and placed them at an advantage at key points during the series. For example, they did not waste referrals on erroneous cases and then, as a consequence, find themselves unable to challenge subsequent decisions which they regarded as incorrect (the extent of this "advantage" in the first series is indicated in Table 12.2). By the same token they were acutely aware of whether the opposing team had used its quota of referrals. This was clearly evident in one of the most controversial incidents, involving England player Stuart Broad, on day three of the first test at Trent Bridge in 2013. Here, having quite evidently to TV commentators and the viewing audience been dismissed, he stood his ground and awaited the umpire's decision (the accepted "sporting" behaviour, in some quarters at least, being for a batsman to walk before the umpire makes their decision in instances where they know they are out). In the event the umpire, to the evident dismay of the Australians and most neutral onlookers, declared Broad not out. Some sense of the fury over what was dubbed "Broadgate" is conveyed in the following from the BBC's on-line "as it happened" blog:

> Quite frankly, this is unbelievable. Broad, going back, edges Agar through to Michael Clarke at slip via a deflection off Brad Haddin's gloves. Appeal, must be gone, surely? No! Aleem Dar [the umpire] unmoved. The Aussies have no reviews, Broad, poker-faced, gives nothing away. Let's see the replay . . . it's a huge edge. How has Dar missed that? Michael Clarke angrier than a swarm of hornets. Darren Lehmann, expletives on the balcony, the coach looks like he might go into labour.
>
> *(Clarke, 2013)*

It was alleged Broad stood his ground in the knowledge that Australia had already made two incorrect referrals and were therefore not able to call for a DRS review under the protocol. Broad, it seemed, had judged that it was worth taking a chance on what the umpire would decide knowing that a DRS referral could not be called by the bowling team. In the subsequent series in Australia, such was the notoriety of this incident, Australian tabloids refused to mention Broad by name or to publish pictures of him!

Third, and following from the above, differences in the effectiveness of the deployment of DRS by each team highlighted for some commentators the emergence of a new skill requirement on the part of players over and above the ability to bat, bowl and field. As one informed observer put it, "in addition to the traditional skills", players now have to "learn a fourth skill – the ability to use DRS effectively" and that "a side can end up losing a match, not because it was deficient in terms of cricketing skills but because, compared to the opposition, it made poor use of DRS" (Borooah, 2013). For many observers lack of such skills was a major contributor to Australia's defeat in the 2013 series. In his diary of the tour published after the series, the Australian captain, Michael Clarke, sought to shift the blame to the system and its unreliability:

> The referral system – where captains have two unsuccessful referrals at their disposal – can distort the process . . . I don't like the tactics involved, where umpires and the teams know how many referrals are left, and change their decisions accordingly. It should be consistent for all players.
>
> *(Clarke, 2013)*

He went on to suggest that the game might be better off without DRS altogether and earned a reprimand from the cricket authorities when he ironically made a "T" sign in a non-international match not using DRS around the time of the diary's publication (*ESPN CricInfo*, 2013b). Ironically, perhaps, the use of DRS by the Australian team was a notable area of improvement in the following 2013–2014 series, although it was clear that the team's dominance in this series was more to do with an even greater improvement in the more conventional areas of batting, bowling and fielding. Australia defeated England by significant margins in each of the five test matches in this series.

Fourth, there was a growing realisation that, notwithstanding claims to technological accuracy, in practice human error could still occur in interpreting the evidence from DRS in the heat and excitement of a match. For example, in not only the opinion of the Australian Prime Minister, the umpire made a horrendous decision during the 2013 third test, seemingly ignoring all of the evidence presented to him by the DRS system. In this incident during the Australians' first innings, Swann had bowled to Khwaja and the ball had run through to the English wicket keeper. He immediately appealed "Howzat?" for a catch behind. The rest of the England fielders around the stumps with a good view of the incident joined the appeal in a similarly confident vein. The umpire agreed and raised his finger to give the batsman out. Khwaja, looking non-plussed, hesitated and did not leave the crease. Then after a few moments' delay he called for a review of the umpire's decision. A succession of replays of the DRS evidence ensued. The slow motion replay shown from a variety of angles was inconclusive. The "Hot Spot" replay seemed clearer showing no evidence of the ball making contact with the bat.

TV commentators looking at the DRS evidence, Shane Warne and Sir Ian Botham, both highly experienced, knowledgeable and respected former international players, declared that the decision would surely be overturned. This view seemed to be corroborated subsequently by the audio evidence from "Snicko" that there was no sound as the ball passed the bat (although, as noted above, this system was not part of the DRS review in this series and only available to the broadcasters). To the astonishment of both impartial observers and many others, on advice from the off-field umpire, the decision of "out" was confirmed. According to Warne, "the technology has shown clearly that there is enough evidence to overturn a mistake . . . that's a shocker, that's an absolutely shocking decision" (Fox Sports, 2013). The then Australian Prime Minister, Kevin Rudd, was sufficiently incensed by what he had witnessed to tweet: "I have just sat down to watch the test. That was one of the worst cricket umpiring decisions I have ever seen" (kevin.rudd@KRuddMP, 1st August 2013). Unsurprisingly the incident prompted a subsequent debate in the media expressing concerns over the level of competence of umpires. This was accompanied with a view articulated by at least one DRS vendor that cricket, compared to other sports, had not engaged in the same level of testing before implementing systems and had rushed into adoption without fully working out how the system would be deployed and how those charged with using it were best trained (Hawkins, 2013).

Fifth, the protocols around the use of DRS, rather than enable umpires and players to use the evidence generated to increase the accuracy adjudication and reduce the level of perceived "human error", seemed instead to confuse participants and therefore increase the possibility for errors (for a discussion see Date, 2013). This had been evident in earlier test series and the World Cup in India when a dismissal had been reversed on procedural grounds by the off-field umpire much to the bemusement of players and spectators. It also became apparent in the 2013 Ashes series that even the umpires were unsure as to how the protocol should work in practice, especially in relation to the role of the off-field umpire in being able to consult the DRS evidence and the implications of this for the on-field umpires.

One question that preoccupied commentary and debate throughout the series was whether the system was there to prevent obvious human errors on the part of umpires or instead to be deployed in an attempt to overturn umpire decisions on marginal calls. This issue is eloquently captured in the following observation made by Mike Jakeman of *The Guardian* newspaper in an assessment of the overall lessons from the two Ashes series. He suggests – in terms expressive of the kind of unavoidable entanglements between materiality and meaning at the core of the sociomaterial approach and the critical role of "agential cuts" – that "DRS is being asked to solve the wrong problem" (i.e. the agential cut is inappropriate):

> the authorities want to use technology to ensure that every umpiring decision is correct. However, human fallibility means that this will never happen, especially if umpires are given tools that create new ways for them to make an error. It would be better for cricket to reconcile itself with the idea that umpires get most things right, even with the use of DRS, and that their authority should be preserved.
>
> *(Jakeman, 2014)*

Sixth, one tradition cricket has preserved from its amateur origins and in the face of both professionalisation and transition into a business, perhaps more so than most other sports, is that the umpire's decision is accepted as final. In an interesting academic discussion of the implications of DRS for the umpire's authority, Collins (2010) makes the point that the investment in their "ontological authority" made in the rules and practice of the game is based on the umpire's "epistemological privilege". That is they have both a superior position on the field of play (i.e. they are closest to the action) and specialist skills and experience (e.g. as former players). In short they are believed to be in the best position to see and determine what happens. However, a belief in the infallibility of DRS implies that a "transparent" and unambiguous view of events is made available and that on-field injustices are now visible to all observers (Collins, 2010). In practice, the umpire's epistemological privilege is now more open to question if not even transferred to the spectator or viewer. As a result, "there is disharmony between the ontological authority and the epistemological privilege leading to loss of credibility of the match official and the sport" (Collins, 2010, p. 136). In short, the umpires' decision is no longer so final.

Significantly, the response of cricket authorities to public criticism of umpires in the context of this degradation of their epistemological privilege has been to seek to show how DRS has improved their decision-making. For example, such was the level of criticism of the standard of umpiring during the first series in England, the ICC felt obliged to publish data showing that the officiating umpires in the first series had typically got decisions right rather than wrong in by far the majority of instances a point reiterated by the General Manager of the ICC in a rare public defence of the system (see: www.icc-cricket.com/news/2013/media-releases/72599/icc-reveals-umpire-assessment-from-trent-bridge-test). According to the ICC, in the 2013 series in England the accuracy of umpire decisions was increased from 92.2 per cent to 97.3 per cent after DRS was deployed in adjudication (Waingankar, 2013).

Discussion: Re-constituting the sociomateriality of DRS

We have argued that the unfolding experience in the take-up and use of DRS in cricket, and indeed in other professional sports, might be usefully understood and interpreted through a sociomaterial lens. In particular, in this chapter we have revealed new ways in which the role of umpires, players and those who frame and interpret their actions might be better understood in terms of enacting DRS as a "technology in practice". This is because the sociomaterial lens questions the conventional assumption that technologies are "things" which interact with other equally independent social phenomenon. In the debates and discussion over DRS this is often reflected in the tension between claims that the technology inherently is or is not accurate and claims that the failings of DRS are more to do with the fallibility, cunning or other characteristics deemed to be inherent in the humans who play the game.

A sociomaterial approach seeks to avoid the attribution of cause and effect in this way and instead questions what are assumed to be separate and immutably defined boundaries and distinctions between "things" i.e. "technology", and "human agents". This alternative approach focuses upon the actions and relationships through which sociomaterial phenomena are constituted in practice – in other words, questions of "when, how and why they are used" (Leonardi, 2010, p. 10). This arguably allows an understanding to be developed of the evolving experience of using DRS systems as technologies in use where the principle at play is not the accuracy of technology versus humans but rather whether decisions can be seen to be just in the context of the core values of the sport (Collins, 2010).

DRS has been adopted within the sport of cricket in the belief that the technology is inherently more accurate than human agents and therefore capable of making better decisions than humans when left to their own devices. In Australia it has recently been suggested that the desire to use new media and related digital technologies to create more compelling viewing is having the consequence of re-shaping the nature of the sport, not just as a business, but as a global entertainment spectacle:

> The original philosophy in covering sport on television was to give the home viewer an experience of what it was like to be at the ground. But it's not like that anymore. If anything it's the opposite . . . We've become so

used to absorbing sport through television that if we are not confronted with television tropes we somehow think the experience is inauthentic. The risk for cricket is its hold on any kind of independent existence as a game rather than as a branch of the entertainment industry. It's become such a commodity now that it's almost losing touch with its reason for being.

(Haigh, 2013)

By adopting a protocol based on the belief that DRS is infallible the "umpire's decision" is no longer "final" and their competence and authority is inevitably made open to question by the greater transparency afforded to observers with regard to "what really happened".

However, other agential cuts which do not privilege the technology in this way would have different consequences. For example, as Collins suggests, technology should be used to "avoid errors which are obvious to all; human judgment should be used where there are no obvious errors" and technology "should not be used to make new kinds of judgment" (Collins, 2010, p. 143). This would require a protocol for executing decisions on the field of play which allows a more appropriate balance between human agency and technological aids and would be more congruent with the core values of the sport. To the extent that the protocols deployed to govern the use of DRS in cricket are still "a work in progress" (Selvey, 2010; Crowe, 2014), then there is an opportunity to enact a more appropriate form of technology in practice where the traditional authority of umpires is upheld and the limits and fallibility of the technology used to support them is as accepted as that of the sport's human participants.

Notes

1 "Law 36 Leg Before Wicket
   The striker can be out Leg Before Wicket if a ball, not being a no ball, strikes him on the person (not just the leg) and:

   The ball was not pitched outside leg stump
   The ball was not first touched by the bat of the striker
   The ball is definitely going on to hit the stumps.
   Only give a batsman out LBW if you are certain that the law is satisfied in full."
   Umpiring for Beginners, Cricket Victoria <www.cricketvictoria.com.au/files/umpires/2005-06/umpiring_for_beginners.pdf> (accessed November 18 2011).

2 The protocol is set out by the International Cricket Council (ICC) in an Appendix to the "Standard Test Match Playing Conditions" (ICC, 2012). For the 2013–2014 Ashes series the International Cricket Council adjusted the protocol in order that each team would be allowed a further two referrals once 80 overs have been bowled in the innings. The protocol was reviewed again in 2015 (Brettig, 2013).

References

ABC News (2013). 'Ashes 2013: Michael Clarke insists Australian players not tampering with bats to cheat DRS'. 8 August. <www.abc.net.au/news/2013-08-08/australia-players-are-not-cheating2c-says-clarke/4872652> (consulted, November 2013).

Anderson, C. & Sally, D. (2013). *The Numbers Game: Why Everything You Know About Football is Wrong.* London: Penguin.

Barad, K. (2003). 'Posthumanist performativity: towards an understanding of how matter comes to matter'. *Signs*, 28 (3), 801–831.

Barad, K. (2007). *Meeting the Universe Halfway: Quantum Physics and the Entanglement of Matter and Meaning.* Durham, NC: Duke University Press.

BBC Radio 5 Live (2013). 'Ashes 2013: No-one trusts Hot Spot, says Andrew Strauss'. 11 October. <www.bbc.com/sport/0/cricket/24493121> (consulted, November 2013).

BBC Sport (2013). 'Ashes 2013: England v Australia, First Test, day three as it happened'. <www.bbc.co.uk/sport/0/cricket/23277348> (consulted, November, 2013).

Brettig, D. (2013). 'Hawkeye, Realtime Snicko for World Cup'. *ESPN CricInfo.* 7 February. <www.espncricinfo.com/icc-cricket-world-cup-2015/content/story/827213.html> (consulted May, 2015).

Borooah, V. K. (2013). 'Upstairs and downstairs: The imperfections of cricket's decision review system'. *Journal of Sports Economics.* Published online 15 November.

Cecez-Kecmanovic, D., Galliers, R., Henfridsson, O., Newell, S. & Vidgen, R. (2014). 'The sociomateriality of information systems: Current status, future directions'. *MIS Quarterly*, (38) 3, 809–830.

Clarke, M. (2013). *The Ashes Diary.* Sydney: Pan Macmillan, Kindle Edition.

Collins, H. (2010). 'The philosophy of umpiring and the introduction of decision-aid technology'. *Journal of the Philosophy of Sport.* (37) 2, 135–146.

Collins, H. & Evans, R. (2008). 'You cannot be serious! Public understanding of technology with special reference to Hawk-Eye'. *Public Understanding of Science*, 17 (3), 283–308.

Collins, H. & Evans, R. (2012). 'Sport-decision aids and the CSI-effect: Why cricket uses Hawk-eye well and tennis uses it badly'. *Public Understanding of Science*, 21 (8), 904–921.

Crowe, M. (2014). 'Why the BCCI wont be swayed by Richardson's DRS'. *ESPN CricInfo*, March 24 <www.espncricinfo.com/magazine/content/story/730311.html> (consulted June, 2014).

Date, K. (2013). 'The DRS problem: It's not the humans'. *ESPN CricInfo*, 26 July. <www.espncricinfo.com/blogs/content/story/654847.html> (consulted November, 2013).

Doolin, B. (2012). 'Sociomateriality and boundary objects in information systems development'. *European Journal of Information Systems*, 21 (5), 570–586.

ESPN CricInfo (2009). 'Dickie Bird criticises review system'. 7 December. <www.espncricinfo.com/england/content/story/438444.html> (consulted November, 2013)

ESPN CricInfo (2013a). 'Real-time Snicko gets Ashes debut'. 19 November. <www.espncricinfo.com/the-ashes-2013-14/content/story/689909.html> (consulted December, 2013)

ESPN CricInfo (2013b). 'Clarke reprimanded for DRS signal'. 1 November. <www.espncricinfo.com/australia/content/story/684789.html> (consulted January, 2014).

Fox Sports (2013). 'Prime Minister Kevin Rudd joins chorus of outrage after dreadful DRS decision claims Usman Khawaja'. http://www.news.com.au/national/prime-minister-kevin-rudd-joins-chorus-of-outrage-after-dreadful-drs-decision-claims-usman-khawaja/story-e6frfkp9-1226689837138 (consulted September, 2016).

Grint, K. and Woolgar, S. (1997). *The Machine at Work: Technology, Work and Organisation.* Oxford: Polity Press.

Haigh, G. (2013). 'Interview from episode three of Sporting Nation written and presented by John Clarke'. *Australian Broadcasting Corporation*, DVD.

Hawkins, P. (2013). 'Cricket may have embraced technology too quickly, says Hawk-Eye founder'. *The Guardian*, 8 August. <www.theguardian.com/sport/2013/aug/08/cricket-embraced-technology-hawkeye-founder> (consulted January, 2014).

Hoult, N. (2013). 'Ashes 2013: Hot Spot can miss fine edges, admits inventor ahead of third England v Australia Test'. *The Telegraph*, 29 July. <www.telegraph.co.uk/sport/cricket/international/england/10209920/Ashes-2013-Hot-Spot-can-miss-fine-edges-admits-inventor-ahead-of-third-England-v-Australia-Test.html> (consulted November, 2013)

Hutchins, B. and Rowe, D. (2013). *Digital Media Sport: Technology, Power and Culture in the Network Society*. London: Routledge.

Jakeman, M. (2014). 'What the Ashes told us about the state of the Tests'. *Talking Sport, The Guardian*, 16 January. <www.theguardian.com/sport/blog/2014/jan/16/ashes-test-match-future> (consulted January, 2014).

Kruse, H. (2010). 'Multimedia use in a sport setting: Communication technologies at off-track betting facilities'. *Sociology of Sports Journal*, 27 (4), 413–427.

Leonardi, P. (2010). 'Digital materiality? How artifacts without matter, matter'. *First Monday*, 15 (8).

Leonardi, P., Nardi, B. A. & Kallinikoset, J. (2011). *Materiality and Organizing: Social Interaction in a Technological World*. Oxford: Oxford University Press.

McLoughlin, I. P. & Dawson, P. (2013). 'Ashes to Ashes: User Innovation and DRS in Professional Sport'. *6th International Society of Professional Innovation Managers (ISPIM)*, Symposium: Innovation in the Asian Century, Melbourne, Australia on 8–11 December 2013.

Nicolini, D. (2012). *Practice Theory, Work, and Organization: An Introduction*. Oxford: Oxford University Press.

Orlikowski, W. (2000). 'Using technology and constituting structures: A practice lens for studying technology in organisations'. *Organization Science*, 11 (4), 404–428.

Scott, S. and Orlikowski, W. (2014). 'Entanglements and practice: Performing anonymity through social media'. MISQ, 38(3) 873–893.

Selvey, M. (2010). 'Simple tweaks to stop bad judgement shocking the decision review system'. *Talking Sport, The Guardian*, 21 January. <www.theguardian.com/sport/blog/2010/jan/21/decision-review-system-icc> (consulted November, 2013).

Smith, M. (2013). 'Welcome to CSI Cricket'. *Yahoo7Sport*, 16 July. <www.au.sports.yahoo.com/cricket/blogs/b/-/18019256/welcome-to-csi-cricket> (consulted November, 2013).

Steen, R. (2011). 'Going upstairs: The decision review system – velvet revolution or thin edge of an ethical wedge?' *Sport in Society*, 14 (10), 1428–1440.

The Times of India (2011). 'Adulteration of technology with human thinking is bad: Dhoni'. February 28. <www.timesofindia.indiatimes.com/news/Adulteration-of-technology-with-human-thinking-is-bad-Dhoni/articleshow/7590694.cms> (consulted November, 2013).

Waingankar, M. (2013). 'ICC open to umpire review model for DRS: Allardice'. *The Times of India*, 5 September. <www.timesofindia.indiatimes.com/sports/cricket/interviews/ICC-open-to-umpire-review-model-for-DRS-Allardice/articleshow/22307762.cms> (consulted November, 2013).

Wolfe, R. A., Weick, K. E., Usher, J. M., Terborg, J. R., Poppo, L., Murrell, A. J., Dukerich, J. M., Crown-Core, D., Dickson, K. E. & Jourdan, J. S. (2005). 'Sport in organisational studies: exploring synergies'. *Journal of Management Inquiry*, 14 (2), 182–210.

Wright, A. & Zammuto, R. (2013). 'Wielding the willing: Processes of institutional change in English County Cricket'. *Academy of Management Review*, 56 (1) 308–330.

13

CONSUMER BEHAVIOR ANALYSIS

An innovation approach in non-profit sports organizations

Dina Miragaia and João J. Ferreira

Introduction

Nowadays, sport has been gaining an increasing role in society. Hallmann, Wicker, Breuer and Schönherr (2012) argue that sports not only help to meet individual needs, such as individual fitness, fun, and well-being, but also produce more global effects of social and economic relevance. Such social and economic importance prioritizes the improvement of sports services to make them more efficient, especially in terms of non-profit sports clubs, as they have a key role in the sports development of any country.

According to Nagel (2008), non-profit sports clubs aim to offer their members the opportunity to practice sports and provide recreational sport programs. They are organizations that are fundamentally financially supported by membership fees, government grants and donations or sponsorships (Wicker, Breuer and Hennigs, 2012). Thus, and given the financial difficulties such clubs usually experience, it is essential to innovate in their management strategies, optimizing their organizational capacity (Misener and Doherty, 2009; Wicker and Breuer, 2011), to provide a better sports offer to their partners and the community.

The inclusion of innovation in the services of non-profit sports clubs may allow the possibility of finding new sources of revenue, making the organization less dependent on government support. However, during this innovation process, the human resource structure that normally fits this type of organization should not be ignored. The non-profit nature of these organizations means that they are frequently managed by people who collaborate voluntarily and, given their uncertain technical skills, they may threaten the implementation of innovative management systems in a more conscious and structured manner.

Thus, sports organizations, including in the third sector, need to take a competitive posture to ensure their sustainability. It is therefore essential to maximize the available resources and a network of stakeholders towards the implementation of an organizational mission (Miragaia, Ferreira and Carreira, 2014). Given the competitiveness of markets, it is essential that organizations define their differentiation strategies. In this sense, the development of an innovative and quality service can be an option used by organizations to increase their competitiveness (Furman, Porter and Stern, 2002; Lovelock, 2000). For this reason, it is necessary to implement quality-control systems to allow managers to see if the service is operating within the desired parameters and in accordance with customer expectations (Kim and Kim, 1995).

To achieve this level of differentiation and innovation from the service point of view, it is necessary to define and collect indicators to ensure the quality of customer service (Howat, Absher, Crilley and Milne, 1996). According to Alexandris and Palialia (1999), to measure customer satisfaction is not a simple matter, because it is a multidimensional concept, as each customer has different needs and expectations, and the satisfaction of each is based on distinct dimensions of psychological, educational, social, physiological and aesthetic nature.

Given the above, regardless of new client acquisition strategies, managers of sports clubs should pay special attention to the process of loyalty of current customers, as customer retention is critical to the success of an organization (Ferrand and Vecchiatini, 2002; Oliver, 1980; Zeithaml, Berry and Parasuraman, 1996). For this reason, it is essential to create a competitive advantage by increasing quality and value to products and/or services provided, as the amount and diversity of sports offers is currently a great pressure on managers.

As a result of this context, the purpose of this study is to identify the consumer behavior of swimming according to the motivational approach through the perceptions of athletes and coaches.

Theoretical background

According to Herstein, Gilboa and Gamliel (2014), service organizations are increasingly developing strategies to produce and project their own brand. A client's connection with a brand makes the client feel fulfilled with the range of experience offered by an organization. This paradigm shift is nowadays visible in several sports organizations, namely, in the fitness industry. In this sector, it is usual to find the organizations previously presented to the market as "gyms" now currently identifying themselves as "health clubs", specifically showing that the organizational mission is more global. This change is not only in terms of nomenclature but also is associated with a more holistic range of services/products related to health and wellness. For this reason, it is possible to identify in the market several health clubs that, in addition to specific sports, also offer social events, beauty treatments and food and drinks.

Such attempts to improve services require an understanding of customer motivations to provide innovative service and quality (Albayrak and Caber, 2014;

McDonald, Milne and Hong, 2002), thus seeking to avoid an increase in drop-out rates (Gray and Wert-Gray, 2012; Guzmán and Kingston, 2011).

The studies developed to understand the motivations that lead athletes to engage in certain sports were mainly developed in psychology (Blanchard, Mask, Vallerand, Sablonnière and Provencher, 2007; Deci, Koestner and Ryan, 1999; Vallerand, 2004; Vallerand and Losier, 1999). However, this knowledge must be used as background information so sports managers can better understand the consumer profile of athletes and use this information to incorporate innovative elements within their clubs.

According to Ryan and Deci (2000), motivation is a key element in the involvement of take-up and abandonment of any activity and may even have performance implications (Bueno, Weinberg, Fernández-Castro and Capdevila, 2008; Duda, 1987; Gillet, Berjot and Gobancé, 2009; Mouratidis, Vansteenkiste, Lens and Sideridis, 2008). However, in addition to knowing the motivations of athletes, it is also essential to examine this issue from the point of view of a particular stakeholder, the coach. Several studies have shown that, in the delivery of service of sports clubs, coaches are the elements that most live and interact with and influence the athletes, and they can play a key role in performance, loyalty or, ultimately, a club's abandonment (Fraser-Thomas, Côté, & Deakin, 2008; Gould, Feltz, Horn, & Weiss, 1982; Smith, 2007). Consequently, it is essential that they have an adjusted perception of the reasons why athletes play sports to be able to interact in a more individualized and innovative way.

Therefore, the aim of this study is identify the consumer behavior of swimming according to the motivational approach through the perceptions of athletes and coaches.

Method

This study analyzes a swimming association in Portugal composed of 13 sports clubs, particularly two of its stakeholders: swimmers and coaches.

The Oregon Swimming Questionnaire proposed by Brodkin and Weiss (1990) was used to obtain information about the motivational reasons of swimmers and to analyze if the coaches have the same approach. The questionnaire was organized into two sections: 1) questions about the characteristics of the sample and 2) 35 items to assess the motivational reasons related to swimming practice. A five-point Likert scale (1 = not at all important to 5 = extremely important) was used to measure the degree of importance of each motivational reason.

To identify the motivational reasons of swimmers, an exploratory factor analysis was used to identify the reliability of the data. The oblimin rotation was applied to the 35 items that compose the questionnaire. Only factors with eigenvalues equal to or above 1.0 were retained, and the loading equal to or above 0.40 in each factor was used as reference to select the items of each factor. The Kaiser-Meyer-Olkin test and Bartlett's sphericity test assessed the data reliability.

To compare the approaches of coaches and swimmers regarding motivation reasons, a descriptive statistic of 35 items was carried out. Finally, the Mann-Whitney U test was used to analyze if significant differences exist between the two groups.

The SPSS program version 17.0 (SPSS, Inc., Chicago, IL, USA) was used to carry out the statistical analysis.

Results

The study included 156 swimmers (72 female and 84 male) and 13 coaches (one female and 12 male) belonging to the 13 clubs that constitute the swimming association. The swimmers were included in three competitive categories: juveniles (n=66), juniors (n=62) and seniors (n=28), and with an average age of 15.83 years (range, 13–30 years). The coaches had professional experience that ranged between 1 and 10 years and had a mean age of 34.4 years. All coaches already had experience with the three categories of swimmers (juveniles, juniors and seniors).

The application of the exploratory factor analysis has allowed the extraction of four factors that represent 50 per cent of total variance (see Table 13.1). The reliability was tested through the Kaiser-Meyer-Olkin test (0.85), and Bartlett's sphericity test (p<0.01) also confirmed the adequacy of the analysis.

The result of descriptive statistics concerning the 35 items that compare the ranking of coaches and swimmers can be seen in Table 13.2.

When the 35 items were analyzed comparing the approach of coaches to that of the swimmers, it was possible find significant differences in several motives (see Table 13.2). This analysis was done by comparing the approach of swimmers from each of the competitive categories to the perception of the coaches about the motivations associated with each of these levels (juveniles, juniors and seniors).

The results highlight an explicit divergence of approaches between coaches and swimmers, showing that coaches have a little in-depth knowledge of the motivations involved in each of the competitive categories.

It is important to highlight the significant difference identified in the item of belonging to a team (p= 0.001), which was considered by juveniles as the motive that most influenced their decision to participate (M= 4.65), unlike the perceptions shown by coaches (M= 3.69). The significant differences identified for the two items most highly valued by juniors (fun: M= 4.56, p= 0.001; liking physical exercise: M= 4.50, p= 0.001) also stand out with the disagreement with the coaches' perspective. Finally, also of note is the significant difference related to senior swimmers when choosing the "team spirit" as their first reason for participating (p= 0.021), contrary to coaches' perceptions.

Discussion

Innovations can be introduced to non-profit sports organizations through a better understanding of consumer profile. Therefore, understanding the consumer

Consumer behavior analysis 213

TABLE 13.1 Factor loadings of the reasons motivating swimmers

	Factor 1	Factor 2	Factor 3	Factor 4	Cronbach's α
HEALTH/FITNESS					
Having something to do	0.738				
I want to improve my health	0.693				
Be active	0.679				
I like using up energy	0.608				**0.85**
Improve physical appearance	0.591				
Get rid of my frustrations	0.507				
Get in shape or stronger	0.504				
I like physical exercise	0.473				
I like action	0.451				
I want to stay in shape	0.424				
SOCIAL STATUS/OTHERS' INFLUENCE					
I like to feel important		−0.818			
Be popular		−0.794			
I want others to notice me		−0.680			
My friends want me to participate		−0.605			**0.85**
To go to team dinners/lunches/ parties		−0.567			
Get out of the house		−0.519			
My family want me to participate		−0.499			
COMPETITION					
I like competing			−0.826		
I like going to meets			−0.800		
Competing at higher levels			−0.753		
I want to improve my skills			−0.592		**0.85**
I like winning			−0.573		
I like a challenge			−0.545		
Do something I am good at			−0.537		
Receive ribbons and trophies			−0.524		
AFFILIATION/FUN					
I like working as a team				0.806	
I like the team spirit				0.737	
I like being in a team				0.705	**0.80**
I want to be with friends				0.501	
I like swimming in the pool				0.484	
I like having fun				0.477	

TABLE 13.2 Ranking of swimmers' motivation and coaches' perception and significant differences

Items	Juveniles M ± SD	Coaches M ± SD	P	Juniors M ± SD	Coaches M ± SD	P	Seniors M ± SD	Coaches M ± SD	P
I like belonging to a team	4.65 ± 0.64	3.69 ± 0.75	< 0.001	4.27 ± 0.73	3.62 ± 0.65	0.003	4.29 ± 0.85	3.54 ± 1.88	0.017
I like to swim in the pool	4.58 ± 0.66	3.77 ± 1.09	0.004	4.35 ± 0.77	3.69 ± 1.11	0.034	4.11 ± 0.96	3.69 ± 1.11	
I like physical exercise	4.53 ± 0.81	3.23 ± 1.01	0.001	4.50 ± 0.76	3.31 ± 1.03	0.001	4.21 ± 1.13	3.31 ± 1.03	0.005
I like the team spirit	4.48 ± 0.64	3.77 ± 0.93	0.005	4.37 ± 0.71	3.85 ± 0.80	0.027	4.50 ± 0.64	3.77 ± 1.01	0.021
I like to have fun	4.45 ± 0.77	3.92 ± 0.95	0.036	4.56 ± 0.64	3.69 ± 1.03	0.001	4.32 ± 0.86	3.62 ± 1.04	0.033
I like to make new friends	4.42 ± 0.81	3.31 ± 0.75	< 0.001	4.02 ± 0.86	3.15 ± 1.21	0.002	3.82 ± 0.98	2.85 ± 0.38	0.002
I want to be with friends	4.41 ± 0.78	3.85 ± 0.99	0.038	4.18 ± 0.86	3.69 ± 0.86		4.43 ± 0.63	3.54 ± 0.97	0.004
I want to improve my skills	4.35 ± 0.79	3.92 ± 0.86		4.48 ± 0.70	4.08 ± 0.95		4.07 ± 0.94	3.92 ± 0.95	
I like teamwork	4.35 ± 0.73	3.54 ± 0.78	0.001	4.11 ± 0.77	3.38 ± 0.77	0.004	4.29 ± 0.90	3.46 ± 0.97	0.012
I like the challenge	4.29 ± 0.80	3.69 ± 0.95	0.026	4.03 ± 0.79	3.62 ± 0.96		4.04 ± 0.74	3.62 ± 0.96	
Get in shape or be stronger	4.24 ± 0.91	3.31 ± 0.75	0.001	3.94 ± 0.90	3.54 ± 0.66		4.14 ± 0.85	3.85 ± 0.99	
I want to stay in shape	4.21 ± 0.81	3.15 ± 1.07	0.001	3.90 ± 1.00	3.62 ± 0.87		4.18 ± 0.85	3.69 ± 0.86	
I like the coaches	4.18 ± 0.88	3.85 ± 0.80		4.37 ± 0.81	3.69 ± 0.75	0.004	4.46 ± 0.64	3.77 ± 0.73	0.006
I want to improve my health	4.15 ± 0.88	2.77 ± 0.93	0.001	4.03 ± 0.96	2.77 ± 0.93	0.001	4.04 ± 0.92	2.92 ± 1.04	0.003
Receive ribbons and trophies	4.15 ± 1.09	4.00 ± 0.82		3.58 ± 1.06	3.62 ± 1.12		3.21 ± 0.92	3.38 ± 1.12	
I want to learn new skills	4.12 ± 0.80	3.46 ± 0.88	0.013	3.92 ± 0.89	3.15 ± 0.80	0.013	3.64 ± 0.95	3.15 ± 0.99	
I like competing	4.11 ± 0.88	4.08 ± 0.64		4.03 ± 0.99	4.00 ± 0.58		4.07 ± 1.05	4.08 ± 0.95	
I like going to meets	4.11 ± 0.84	4.15 ± 0.69		4.06 ± 0.87	4.23 ± 0.73		4.04 ± 1.07	4.23 ± 0.93	
Competing at higher levels	4.09 ± 0.92	3.92 ± 0.76		3.95 ± 1.02	4.08 ± 0.86		3.64 ± 1.10	4.08 ± 1.04	
I like action	4.06 ± 0.82	3.38 ± 1.04	0.020	3.79 ± 0.87	3.15 ± 0.99	0.029	3.89 ± 0.88	2.85 ± 0.80	0.002
Do something I am good at	4.06 ± 1.01	3.62 ± 1.12		3.84 ± 0.87	3.46 ± 1.13		4.11 ± 0.96	3.46 ± 1.13	
Be active	4.00 ± 0.98	3.00 ± 1.23	0.005	3.90 ± 0.94	3.00 ± 1.08	0.005	4.11 ± 0.92	3.00 ± 0.91	0.001
I like excitement	3.92 ± 0.88	3.23 ± 0.83	0.011	3.73 ± 0.91	3.38 ± 0.87		4.18 ± 0.61	3.38 ± 0.96	0.006
I like winning	3.86 ± 1.12	3.85 ± 0.99		3.68 ± 1.00	3.77 ± 1.17		3.79 ± 0.10	3.77 ± 1.01	
Get rid of frustrations	3.83 ± 1.10	2.38 ± 1.12	< 0.001	3.69 ± 1.10	2.38 ± 1.04	0.001	3.43 ± 1.26	2.46 ± 1.13	0.025

(Continued)

TABLE 13.2 *(Continued)*

Items	Juveniles M ± SD	Coaches M ± SD	P	Juniors M ± SD	Coaches M ± SD	P	Seniors M ± SD	Coaches M ± SD	P
Improve my physical appearance	3.79 ± 1.17	3.00 ± 1.08	0.023	3.48 ± 1.23	3.23 ± 1.09		3.36 ± 0.91	3.08 ± 0.86	
Have something to do	3.58 ± 0.95	2.23 ± 1.17	< 0.001	3.29 ± 1.19	2.23 ± 1.01	0.005	3.00 ± 1.09	2.23 ± 0.93	0.030
To go to team dinners/lunches/ parties	3.50 ± 1.11	3.08 ± 1.19		2.98 ± 1.27	3.15 ± 0.99		3.46 ± 1.14	3.15 ± 1.14	
To get out of the house	3.48 ± 1.14	2.38 ± 1.19	0.005	2.65 ± 1.23	2.31 ± 1.11		2.50 ± 1.23	2.08 ± 0.95	
My family wants me to participate	3.47 ± 1.30	3.38 ± 0.87		2.68 ± 1.20	2.92 ± 0.64		3.68 ± 1.16	3.00 ± 1.08	
I like to use up energy	3.47 ± 1.04	3.00 ± 1.08		3.44 ± 1.03	2.92 ± 1.19		2.54 ± 1.23	2.62 ± 0.87	
My friends want me to participate	3.20 ± 1.22	2.85 ± 1.07		2.50 ± 1.24	2.54 ± 0.97		2.93 ± 1.46	2.46 ± 0.88	
I want others to notice me	2.68 ± 1.06	3.23 ± 0.93		2.10 ± 1.00	3.00 ± 1.00	0.004	2.32 ± 0.95	2.92 ± 0.95	
To be popular	2.41 ± 1.18	3.46 ± 1.33	0.008	1.95 ± 0.95	3.08 ± 1.12	0.001	2.07 ± 1.02	2.92 ± 1.04	0.017
I like to feel important	2.29 ± 1.15	3.62 ± 1.12	0.001	2.03 ± 1.04	3.15 ± 1.21	0.002	2.25 ± 1.01	3.00 ± 1.00	0.029

NOTA: 1 = not at all important; 5 = very important

motivations is an important tool to help understand the definitions of strategies that allow improving the sports service.

According to the results obtained, the athletes are motivated to practice swimming by a mix of intrinsic and extrinsic reasons (Deci *et al.*, 1999; Vallerand and Losier, 1999), as suggested by the factorial analyses through the four dimensions extracted: health/fitness, social status/others' influence, competition and affiliation/fun. When comparing these results to those obtained in the study developed by Brodkin and Weiss (1990), a similarity was found in several factors (characteristics of competitive swimming and health/fitness), despite the factors about social status, affiliation, others' influence and fun that constitute independent factors, whereas a fusion between them was found in the present study (social status/others' influence and affiliation/fun). Health/fitness is the only factor converging with the results obtained by Salguero, González-Boto, Tuero and Marquez (2003) in a study carried out on Spanish swimmers. Also, in a study performed on Brazilian swimmers by Andrade, Salguero and Marquez (2006), it was possible to identify an agreement on the competition factor. The same happened when comparing these results to another study applied to Portuguese swimmers (Salselas, González-Boto, Tuero and Marquez, 2007), finding convergence on the competition factor.

The differences identified between the studies mentioned might arise from cultural differences between the groups studied in each investigation and also from the difference in the sample number, which was the basis for each investigation. These results suggest that the consumer profile is influenced by the characteristics of the context, and for this reason, the sports managers should take this into consideration. The cultural experiences of each country may indicate different styles of sports consumption, and thereby, sports clubs should be prepared for this specificity.

However, so that all this information about the consumer can be useful for the process of innovation, it is also essential to consider the approach of one of the main stakeholders in this process – the coaches. Coach behavior can influence the intrinsic and extrinsic motivation of athletes (Mageau and Vallerand, 2003) and have a major impact on the loyalty or drop-out of sport. Thus, and according to the results found in this study, comparing the coaches' perceptions about the swimmers' motivations, a great discrepancy with the approach provided by the athletes was observed.

Through the ranking analysis of motives (see Table 13.2), it is possible to identify those that the coaches consider as the most important items ($M \geq 4$) for the juvenile involvement in swimming: the interest in going to meets, because they like to compete, and to receive ribbons and trophies. However, swimmers do not consider these reasons as priority. Regarding coaches' perceptions of items most highly valued by juniors, they indicated items predominantly associated with competitive reasons (going to meets, participating in important competitions, improving skills and because they like to compete). However, like in the juvenile category, juniors do not consider these items as the main reasons for their involvement on swimming. This group mentioned the "fun" motive as the main stimulus ($M = 4.56$).

This result reinforces the idea that youngsters need to strengthen relational components (Brodkin and Weiss, 1990). Finally, the results of the senior athletes' and coaches' perceptions of this category of swimmers once again highlight a different approach between the two groups. According to the coaches, this group valued primarily the competitive aspects (going to meets, participating in high-level competitions and because they like to compete), contrary to the approach of swimmers who value aspects associated with relational and social interactions (Andrade *et al.*, 2006).

Overall, coaches' perceptions were considerably different from the reasons pointed out by swimmers in the respective categories, and significant differences (see Table 13.2) were found in 22 items when comparing coaches to juveniles, 17 items between coaches and juniors, and 16 items in the case of coaches and senior swimmers. It is important to highlight the significant difference identified in the item of belonging to a team ($p= 0.001$), which was considered by juveniles as the motive that most influenced their decision to participate ($M= 4.65$), unlike the perceptions shown by coaches ($M= 3.69$). The significant differences identified for the two items most highly valued by juniors (fun: $M= 4.56$, $p= 0.001$; liking physical exercise: $M= 4.50$, $p= 0.001$) also stand out by the disagreement with the coaches' perspective. Finally, also of note is the significant difference related to senior swimmers when choosing the "team spirit" as their first reason for participating ($p= 0.021$), contrary to coaches' perceptions. It is also interesting to note that the item "improving health" was considered by coaches as one of the aspects that had least impact on the athletes' motives to participate in swimming, contrary to the indication given by the swimmers. In this sense, it is possible to identify some aspects that distinguish the three athlete groups, and this can be explained by the differences in the levels of their maturity.

Data revealed a gap in the coaches' approach. According to several studies, the understanding of sport motives should be taken into consideration, because the drop-out of swimming can result, in part, due to the coaches' behavior. Aspects, such as lack of fun and excitement, excessive pressure and hard training, are some of the main reasons given by athletes for dropping out of the sport (Fraser-Thomas *et al.*, 2008; Gould *et al.*, 1982; Molinero, Salguero, Álvarez and Márquez, 2009; Molinero, Salguero, Tuero, Alvarez and Márquez, 2006). Although this group of athletes is involved in this sport on a competitive level, there exist other motives to this engagement, namely, aspects focused on social relationships and health improvement. This information should be included on the strategic plan of the coaches', beyond the technical questions of team performance (Baker, Yardley and Côté, 2003; Keegan, Harwood, Spray and Lavallee, 2009).

Conclusion and some implications

The sustainability of non-profit sports organizations, like any other organizations, should increase the usage of management tools to enable the improvement of their efficiency. Their sustainability depends, among various elements, on their ability to address the needs of their stakeholders, including the athletes and members for those who develop sports services. The deeper understanding of consumer motives is a key component to define the intervention strategies to respond to the competitiveness that exists around the offer of sports services. Currently, the sports industry goes far beyond specific organizations in the sports context. Thus, sports managers should look to other sectors, such as tourism, health and education, as potential competitors or as potential partners. Thus, non-profit sports organizations, which are very important for the promotion of sports, must increasingly include services such as relational and social aspects, in order to improve the quality of life of their communities. Although some of these sports organizations provide a service associated with the competitive level, this does not invalidate the need for coaches to organize a more holistic intervention. This approach could improve sports performance and increase the loyalty of athletes in sports clubs. This process of knowing the consumer motives profile is not difficult to obtain and does not require large resources by a non-profit sports clubs.

It is suggested that, at the beginning of each season, clubs apply questionnaires to identify the participation motives of athletes, verifying periodically if there exists any change of interests, and to improve the sports services in accordance with these indicators. According to the data of this study, the reasons for the practice of swimming vary with different ages, as can happen according to gender or other targeting indicators. For this reason, it is important to explore the understanding of this profile as completely as possible to obtain data to innovate the several services that these clubs can offer to different types of consumers.

However, the low number of coaches (although corresponding to 100 per cent of the coaches involved in the clubs studied) could be appointed as a limitation of this study, because it was not possible to perform other robust statistical procedures. In future studies, it will be interesting to investigate this same model in a longitudinal perspective to understand what kind of motivational components changed. Furthermore, studying the reasons that lead the juvenile, junior and senior swimmers to give up sports participation could be another research study in the future. Finally, it is important to identify coaches' perceptions about this phenomenon and to know how this can help club managers make the right strategic decisions.

References

Albayrak, T. & Caber, M. (2014). 'Symmetric and asymmetric influences of service attributes: The case of fitness clubs'. *Managing Leisure*, 19(5), 307–320.

Alexandris, K. & Palialia, E. (1999). 'Measuring customer satisfaction in fitness centres in Greece: An exploratory study'. *Managing Leisure*, 4(4), 218–228.

Andrade, A., Salguero, A. & Márquez, S. (2006). 'Motives for sports participation in Brazilian swimmers'. *Fitness & Performance Journal*, 5(6), 69–83.

Baker, J., Yardley, J. & Côté, J. (2003). 'Coach behaviors and athlete satisfaction in team and individual sports'. *International Journal of Sport Psychology*, 34(3), 226–239.

Blanchard, C., Mask, L., Vallerand, R., Sablonnière, R. & Provencher, P. (2007). 'Reciprocal relationships between contextual and situational motivation in a sports setting'. *Psychology of Sport & Exercise*, 8(5), 854–873.

Brodkin, P. & Weiss, M. (1990). 'Developmental differences in motivation for participating in competitive swimming'. *Journal of Sport & Exercise Psychology*, 12(2), 248–263.

Bueno, J., Weinberg, R., Fernández-Castro, J. & Capdevila, L. (2008). 'Emotional and motivational mechanisms mediating the influence of goal setting on endurance athletes' performance'. *Psychology of Sport & Exercise*, 9(6), 786–799.

Deci, E., Koestner, R. & Ryan, R. (1999). 'A meta-analytic review of experiments examining the effects of extrinsic rewards on intrinsic motivation'. *Psychological Bulletin*, 125(6), 627–668.

Duda, J. (1987). 'Toward a developmental theory of children's motivation in sport'. *Journal of Sport Psychology*, 9(2), 130–145.

Ferrand, A. & Vecchiatini, D. (2002). 'The effect of service performance and ski resort image on skiers' satisfaction'. *European Journal of Sport Science*, 2(2), 1–17.

Fraser-Thomas, J., Côté, J. & Deakin, J. (2008). 'Understanding dropout and prolonged engagement in adolescent competitive sport'. *Psychology of Sport and Exercise*, 9(5), 645–662.

Furman, J. L., Porter, M. E. & Stern, S. (2002). 'The determinants of national innovative capacity'. *Research Policy*, 31(6), 899–933.

Gillet, N., Berjot, S. & Gobancé, L. (2009). 'A motivational model of performance in the sport domain'. *European Journal of Sport Science*, 9(3), 151–158.

Gould, D., Feltz, D., Horn, T. & Weiss, M. (1982). 'Reasons for attrition in competitive youth swimming'. *Journal of Sport Behavior*, 5(3), 155–165.

Gray, G. T. & Wert-Gray, S. (2012). 'Customer retention in sports organization marketing: Examining the impact of team identification and satisfaction with team performance'. *International Journal of Consumer Studies*, 36(3), 275–281.

Guzmán, J. F. & Kingston, K. (2011). 'Prospective study of sport dropout: A motivational analysis as a function of age and gender'. *European Journal of Sport Science*, 12(5), 43–442.

Hallmann, K., Wicker, P., Breuer, C. & Schönherr, L. (2012). 'Understanding the importance of sport infrastructure for participation in different sports – findings from multi-level modeling'. *European Sport Management Quarterly*, 12(5), 525–544.

Herstein, R., Gilboa, S. & Gamliel, E. (2014). 'The effect of private brands on leveraging service quality and satisfaction. *Services Marketing Quarterly*, 35(3), 222–235.

Howat, G., Absher, J., Crilley, G. & Milne, I. (1996). 'Measuring customer service quality in sports and leisure centres'. *Managing Leisure*, 1(2), 77–89.

Keegan, R., Harwood, C., Spray, C. & Lavallee, D. (2009). 'A qualitative investigation exploring the motivational climate in early career sports participants: Coach, parent and peer influences on sport motivation'. *Psychology of Sport & Exercise*, 10(3), 361–372.

Kim, D. & Kim, S. Y. (1995). 'QUESC: An instrument for assessing the service quality of sport centers in Korea'. *Journal of Sport Management*, 9(2), 208–220.

Lovelock, C. (2000). *Services Marketing – People, Technology, Strategy* (4th ed.). Upper Saddle River, NJ: Prentice Hall.

Mageau, G. A. & Vallerand, R. J. (2003). 'The coach–athlete relationship: a motivational model'. *Journal of Sports Sciences*, 21(11), 883–904.

McDonald, M. A., Milne, G. R. & Hong, J. (2002). 'Motivational factors for evaluating sport spectator and participant markets'. *Sport Marketing Quarterly*, 11(2), 100–113.

Miragaia, D. A. M., Ferreira, J. & Carreira, A. (2014). 'Do stakeholders matter in strategic decision making of a sports organization?' *Revista de Administração de Empresas*, 54(6), 647–658.

Misener, K. & Doherty, A. (2009). 'A case study of organizational capacity in nonprofit community sport'. *Journal of Sport Management*, 23(4), 457–482.

Molinero, O., Salguero, A., Álvarez, E. & Márquez, S. (2009). 'Reasons for dropout in youth soccer: A comparison with other team sport'. *Motricidad. European Journal of Human Movement*, 22, 21–30.

Molinero, O., Salguero, A., Tuero, C., Alvarez, E. & Márquez, S. (2006). 'Dropout reasons in young Spanish athletes: Relationship to gender, type of sport and level of competition'. *Journal of Sport Behavior*, 29(3), 255–259.

Mouratidis, A., Vansteenkiste, M., Lens, W. & Sideridis, G. (2008). 'The motivating role of positive feedback in sport and physical education: Evidence for a motivational model'. *Journal of Sport & Exercise Psychology*, 30(2), 240–268.

Nagel, S. (2008). 'Goals of sport clubs'. *European Journal for Sport & Society*, 5(2), 121–141.

Oliver, R. L. (1980). 'A cognitive model of the antecedents and consequences of satisfaction decisions'. *Journal of Marketing Research*, 17(4), 460–469.

Ryan, R. & Deci, E. (2000). 'Self-determination theory and the facilitation of intrinsic motivation, social development, and well-being'. *American Psychological Association*, 55(1), 68–78.

Salguero, A., González-Boto, R., Tuero, C. & Márquez, S. (2003). 'Development of a Spanish version of the Participation Motivation Inventory for young competitive swimmers'. *Perceptual and Motor skills*, 96(2), 637–646.

Salselas, V., González-Boto, R., Tuero, C. & Márquez, S. (2007). 'The relationship between sources of motivation and level of practice in young Portuguese swimmers'. *Journal of Sports Medicine and Physical Fitness*, 47(2), 228–233.

Smith, R. E. (2007). 'Toward a cognitive-affective model of athletic burnout'. *Essential Readings in Sport and Exercise Psychology*, 8(1), 36–50.

Vallerand, R. J. (2004). 'Intrinsic and extrinsic motivation in sport'. In C. Spielberger (ed.), *Encyclopedia of Applied Psychology* (Vol. 2, pp. 427–435). Florida: Elsevier.

Vallerand, R. J. & Losier, G. F. (1999). 'An integrative analysis of intrinsic and extrinsic motivation in sport'. *Journal of Applied Sport Psychology*, 11(1), 142–169.

Wicker, P. & Breuer, C. (2011). 'Scarcity of resources in German non-profit sport clubs'. *Sport Management Review*, 4(2), 188–201.

Wicker, P., Breuer, C. & Hennigs, B. (2012). 'Understanding the interactions among revenue categories using elasticity measures – Evidence from a longitudinal sample of non-profit sport clubs in Germany'. *Sport Management Review*, 15(3), 318–329.

Zeithaml, V. A., Berry, L. L. & Parasuraman, A. (1996). 'The behavioral consequences of service quality'. *Journal of Marketing*, 60(2), 31–46.

14

EXPLORING MOTIVATION OF MARATHON RUNNERS

Konstantinos Koronios, Marina Psiloutsikou and Athanasios Kriemadis

Introduction

The beneficial outcomes of regular exercise for physical and mental health are documented in detail and exercising has been promoted internationally via considerable provision of sport and recreation infrastructures. The enormous publicity of physical activity followed the acknowledgment of numerous benefits of sport participation, such as physiological, psychological and social benefits. Physiologically, sport participation is associated with a reduction in cardio-vascular risk, prevention/delay of diabetes and prevention of obesity. Psychologically, exercising is correlated with a decrease in anxiety and stress. Furthermore, sport participation heightens self-esteem and offers an apparatus for social interaction (World Health Organization, 2010). These benefits are correlated with a decline in medical care expenses, as well as with higher job efficiency (Alexandris and Carroll, 1997). A main stream of research has shown the majority of individuals in the developed world are knowledgeable about the necessity of being active and have an eagerness to be more active (Tsai, 2005). One of the prevalent types of systematic exercise since the 1970s is road running in general and more specifically half- and ultra-marathon running (Van der Nest, 2007). A main type of physical exercise with a significant increase over the last decade is marathon running. Although formerly thought of as purely a professional sport, marathon running has become commonplace worldwide among amateur individuals. The typical marathon range is 42.2 km and many athletes take part each year worldwide. Marathon running is a recreational activity which has experienced an exceptional development over the last years, as an increasing number of individuals consider it an appropriate alternative for recreationally based physical activity (Ridinger *et al.*, 2012).

Due to the fact that marathon participation is a highly demanding task, which necessitates months of devoted training and a high degree of commitment, there is an impressive development rate of half-marathons (21.1 km), in overall popularity and number. The development rate of half-marathons has far outbalanced the respective full-marathons, with half-marathons being one of the most rapid developing road races, with an annual increase of about 10 per cent (Hanson, *et al.*, 2015). On the contrary, less prevalent is the ultra-marathon, which encompasses any running distance that surpasses the classic marathon range of 42.195 km (American Ultrarunning Association, 2008). The most typical ultra-marathon courses include 50 kilometers, 80.5 kilometers and 161 kilometers, but they can also extend to 24/48 hours, multiday or even transnational. Even though the development rate of ultra-marathons is not as impressive as the simple marathons in absolute numbers, they are nevertheless rising in overall popularity and number (Hanson *et al.*, 2015).

Both ultra-marathons and half-marathons can be organized on or off-road and they are usually arranged to encompass a particular distance or cover a particular distance within a specific timetable. These types of marathons are largely segregated by harsh trail circumstances, such as rugged ground, altitude differences and nasty weather. Moreover, the amount of effort needed to participate in these types of marathons is certainly a long way off the training required to obtain elemental health benefits, which may cause tiredness and injury. Regardless of the great sacrifices correlated with training time and exertion, growing numbers of individuals are deliberately taking part in ultra-marathons and half-marathons systematically (Ogles and Masters, 2003). This contradiction makes one wonder about the factors influencing individuals' participation motives.

Several studies have investigated the motives of individuals for sport participation, but limited empirical support has been assigned to the motives of marathoners, individuals who train for very long periods and often in undesirable conditions. Many of the previous studies about marathoners have examined alterations of mood, stress and/or emotions, but have not straightforwardly assessed motivation to run. Furthermore, a contemporary review of the personality attributes of marathoners proved that there is a scarcity of knowledge concerning their motivation. A lot of individuals have the required capacity to perform adequately in running events, but lack the motivation for training and taking part. Motivation, therefore, is frequently the crucial factor in marathon running participation and performance (Hanson *et al.*, 2015).

Motivation can be defined as an internal force which evokes, devotes and organizes an individual's behavior (Funk, Toohey, and Bruun, 2007). Motivation performs a crucial role in recreational activities as it affects individuals' degrees of participation, the intensity of their commitment and eventually the result of their exertion (Kilpatrick *et al.*, 2005). In sport psychology, motivation is considered within the framework of participation, sport selection and degree of competition. Even though there are personal differences that regulate each individual's motivational behavior, a stream of research has focused on defining the motivational patterns that override personal characteristics. More specifically, individuals' intrinsic and extrinsic motivation for sport participation, has accumulated a high degree of attention from researchers in sport psychology (Vlachopoulos, Karageorghis and Terry, 2000).

This field of research is mainly based on the Self Determination Theory (Ryan and Deci, 2000) and it supports that whether the individual is intrinsically or extrinsically motivated will narrowly coincide with achievement objectives and conceptions of control and success. Intrinsically motivated behavior is character-ized by the pursuance of an activity for the contentment and fulfillment origin-ated from it. Therefore, the motive for taking part is basically situated in the participation itself instead of the need for an external award or evasion of negative after-effects correlated with non-participation (Vlachopoulos, Karageorghis and Terry, 2000). A person with intrinsic motives considers the participation in the specific activity as the reward. On the contrary, extrinsically motivated behavior derives from the need of the individual to acquire a reward or/and to avoid negative after-effects. In the context of sport, trophies, medals, monetary gain, outward appearance, etc., are among the main types of external awards. Both aspects of motivation are likely to exist within every individual who participates in sport, but in the majority of them, one aspect is more dominant than the other (Krouse, 2009). For the present study, motivation will presumably come from incentives already identified in the literature: sport attractiveness, recreation involvement, socializing opportunities, training habits, perception effect on physical and mental health, elements of sportscape and individual factors of gender (Alexandris et al., 2011; Funk et al., 2011; Koronios et al., 2015a; Koronios et al., 2015b).

The increasing popularity both of half-marathon and ultra-marathon running has led researchers to ascertain the multifarious factors that entice individuals to take part in sport. Various researches investigating the requirements, motives and behavioral attributes underlying half- and ultra-marathon runners have been recognized (Gillet and Kelly, 2006; Shipway and Jones, 2007), and have been found to be imbricating, with notions used correspondently, such as cognitive, emotional and physiological needs and motives. Due to inadequate studies on these specific types (half and ultra) of marathon running, information will also be extrapolated from researches on marathon running in general.

Half-marathon and ultra-marathon participation is the focus of this research due to their increasing popularity as leisure activities and due to the fact that they are correlated with a significant degree of constraints and loyalty. The participa-tion in these types of marathons impels a significant amount of time and exercise to prepare for and a higher degree of loyalty has been noticed in relation to running contests of different distances (Funk et al., 2011). The purpose of this study is two-fold. First, to single out the perceived significance level of factors associated with commitment to half- and ultra-marathon running, and more specifically to examine the relationships among attractiveness of the event, involvement with running, socializing opportunities, physical and mental health factors, training habits of individuals, elements of sportscape, as well as to explore the impact of gender on motivation in individuals who had taken part in such

224 Konstantinos, Psiloutsikou and Kriemadis

types of marathons. The second purpose of this study is to compare the motives to run between individuals who had taken part in a half-marathon and those who had participated in an ultra-marathon. The authors hypothesized that differences in motivation between these two distance groups, as well as among men and women, would be noticed.

Theoretical background

A lot of research has investigated motives of marathoners (Funk *et al.*, 2011), but inadequate consideration has been assigned to the notion of recreational involvement with running. Involvement can be described as an "imperceptible condition of motivation, insurrection or concernment about a recreational activity or correlated product" (Havitz and Dimanche, 1997). This circumscription mainly focuses on the social-psychological facet of involvement (Alexandris *et al.*, 2009). Sport activity involvement refers to the extent to which a person shows sympathy to a specific sport activity and in this research it is defined as a strong personal affiliation with running. More specifically, running involvement refers to an individual's inclination to marathon running, and has been described as one's assessment of his/her joining in a sport endeavor apropos of being an important part of her/his life, and one that gives both hedonic and symbolic value, affecting individuals' future participation and behavior (Ridinger, Funk, Jordan and Kaplanidou, 2012; Beaton *et al.*, 2011). Involvement with an activity is one of the variables recommended as a crucial determinant in comprehending recreation comportments, as previous researches have proved that individuals with a high degree of involvement with a specific activity are presumably more loyal customers (Kouthouris, 2009).

It is widely acknowledged nowadays that involvement is a multifaceted variable. A stream of research offered empirical evidence for the variable validity of the tri-dimensional model (Alexandris *et al.*, 2009; Kyle *et al.*, 2006; Kyle and Chick, 2004), with attraction, centrality and self-expression to be the three variables suggested. Attraction pertains to the anticipated significance that running holds for an individual, and the happiness, satisfaction and amusement that emanates from taking part in marathon running. Centrality pertains to the importance that running has in a person's way of life and embraces both social and individual factors (Walraven *et al.*, 2012). Individuals characterized by a high degree of centrality dimension are occupied with recreational activities which have a main role in their way of life (Iwasaki and Havitz, 2004). Lastly, self-expression pertains to "self-portrayal or the perception of the personality that people desire to reveal to others via taking part in the specific sport" (Kyle and Chick, 2004). This aspect is comparable to the variable of "extended-self" which is utilized in consumer behavior studies for interpreting individuals' buying behaviors (Alexandris *et al.*, 2009). In this respect, individuals have the intention to acquire goods/services the image of which harmonize with their self-image. In consonance with previous studies, involvement has been verified to be highly correlated with motivation (Funk, Ridinger and Moorman, 2004; Iwasaki and Havitz,

2004; Kyle *et al.*, 2006). More specifically, the attraction dimension was found to be affected by factors correlated to the sportscape of the sport activity, the centrality dimension found to be affected by socialization correlated factors, and the self-expression dimension to be affected by factors correlated to identification and role models (Funk *et al.*, 2004).

Various researches have investigated the motives of marathoners, but limited empirical support has been assigned to the notion of sport event attractiveness. An individual's experience from each marathon event will conduce to the evolvement of dispositions toward leisure time physical activities in general. Mass-participant sport events deputize a type of experiential consumption within the leisure framework via which sentimental reactions are received (Funk *et al.*, 2011). Leisure time physical activities can be innately delectable and the anticipated quality of services received may generate a higher degree of sentimentality. A high degree of sport event satisfaction can lead to an individual attributing more functional, emotional and symbolic meaning to this sport event. The higher the significance attributed to this meaning, the more pertinent the hedonic perspectives of the consumption experience. Therefore, contentment with the sport event has the capacity to strengthen the advancement of positive stances toward running commitment and future participation intentions (Funk *et al.*, 2011). The conception of the sport event experience will compose the basis of contentment. Synoptically, satisfaction depicts a mental evaluation of the grade to which a recreation efficiency enacts pertinent to an individual's substructure expectations (Petric, Morais and Norman, 2001). As for the perceived quality of services offered, the higher the anticipated quality of the event experience, the more positive stances of individuals toward running commitment and future participation intention (Tian-Cole *et al.*, 2002). Furthermore, as Wilson and Rodgers (2004) stated, satisfaction derived from participation in a sport event, is likely to affect future exercise intentions on a regular basis.

A main area of research has examined the influence of social motives on individuals' participation in sport activities. Sport can be regarded as one of the few social activities which can be acknowledged in practically every society and culture all over the world as a means of bringing individuals together (Allen *et al.*, 2010). Individuals generally enjoy being in a social environment and interacting with other people, and this is one of their main intentions when searching for a recreational activity. Social incentives operate in the sport and exercise setting (Gill and Overdorf, 1994), as for a large number of individuals one major motivating factor in sport participation is the wish to be a member of a tenacious group and internalize sensations of belonging (Hodge, Allen and Smellie, 2008), whereas for many of them sport participation is also inherently associated with their identity and self-concept (Weiss, 2001). Research has shown that people's initial intention when searching for a recreational activity is to find opportunities to interact with new people, and proposes that companionship and group acceptance affect individuals' willingness to participate in sport activities (Stuntz and Spearance, 2007).

The Social Motivation Theory is a contemporary field of research and according to its model "sport offers individuals the potentiality to indulge their needs for socializing and affiliation" (Hodge *et al.,* 2008). Social motivation orientation includes social status, social recognition and social affiliation, with recognition and affiliation being possible through active participation in marathons (Hill and Green, 2012). Affiliation can be defined as the individual's aspiration to be attached or consorted with other people. Previous studies in the context of sport have identified individuals' need for association with others, as a primary motive for sport participation. More specifically, affiliation and social influence were among the main factors which motivated individuals to take part in running activities (King and Burke, 2000), with affiliation motives to be age-dependent, as they increased with age (Lovett, 2011). Social recognition constitutes a main form of extrinsic award which can be a motivating factor for individuals in innumerable circumstances, and can be described as the personal need of individuals to be acknowledged and respected by other people. According to the literature, social recognition motives were found to be not only age-dependent, as they increased with age, but also gender-related. More specifically, older individuals were found to have more intense recognition motives, while women considered recognition to be a crucial factor for taking part in sport activities (Lovett, 2011).

Hence, socializing is an important aspect people scrutinize when choosing to take part in recreational activities. This kind of relationship among individuals with similar interests can occur through active participation in marathons (Hill and Green, 2012; Ogles and Masters, 2000).

Previous studies have investigated the motives of marathoners but limited empirical support has been assigned to the training habits of the individuals. Training habits of runners refer to the quality and the amount of effort invested by them in order to participate in major events and may include hours spent per week, distance covered per training, etc. Although in the past decades long-distance running was a sport mainly appropriate for professional athletes who exercised for intense competition with a severe training program, the arrival of "jogging" transformed long-distance running into a more common leisure activity, with many individuals considering it a proper form of recreation. Given this alteration in emphasis from a professional to a recreation basis, a lot of research has taken place in order to investigate the various types of recreational running and the training effort needed for each of them (Ogles and Masters, 2000). A specific group of long-distance runners, marathoners, are notably attractive to investigate owing to the immense effect training has on their way of life. More specifically, individuals who train in order to participate in a marathon intentionally compromise themselves to natural adversity while pursuing a meticulous time-consuming agenda in accordance with specific nutrition, which are a long way off the essential levels for general health and fitness (Ogles and Masters, 2000). Apart from the tiredness and soreness experienced during marathons, the training time needed for these events is overwhelming and is frequently more than twenty hours per week (Krouse, 2009).

The time spent by marathoners in training can be disheartening for other individuals, as marathoners have to adjust their personal life, family and business obligations along with training. Most of the time marathoners organize their holidays between cities hosting marathon events and prioritize their daily schedule based on the fact that training will be at the top of their to-do list. Furthermore, many individuals establish a marathoner identity which encompasses affiliation with running groups and frequent training. In some cases, so intense is the dedication demonstrated by individuals to running and training activities, many researchers have utilized the expressions of obligatory running or running addiction in order to depict the degree to which marathoners are devoted to training (Ogles and Masters, 2000). Despite the expressions used, individuals who participate in marathons assuredly compose a remarkable group of highly devoted runners involved in a unique leisure activity.

Hence, training habits are an important aspect affecting individuals' motivation for taking part in marathon events. Although to date a main stream of research has investigated the time spent by individuals in training and/or the average per training distance, the majority of these studies have investigated these variables as supplemental questionnaires outside the main research focus, and as a result they have not been thoroughly examined.

The research of sportscape factors in the framework of outdoor recreation is comparably newly equated to studies of the variable presented by geography and environmental psychology literatures (Moore and Graefe, 1994), with earlier studies being mainly focused on environment-behavior topics. A stream of geographical and environmental research supports that via the development of an attachment to a specific sportscape, individuals establish a bond that may grant emotional connotation to them (Kyle et al., 2004). Research about recreation activities was based on the above-mentioned theoretical premises and has applied the notion of sportscape attachment to recreation settings. Sportscape factors refer to the physical surroundings individuals face during their participation in a recreational activity, and consist of two aspects; functional dimension (pertaining to concrete activity requirements) and emotional – symbolic dimension. Put differently, a sportscape can be evaluated by an individual due to the fact that it is appropriate for undertaking the specific activity, or it may be important due to the fact that it is confronted as "special" for sentimental or symbolic reasons, or both (Kyle et al., 2004).

A crucial precondition of satisfying running experiences are participants' anticipated freedom and intrinsic motivation in selecting the conditions under which marathons will take place. In particular, among the most crucial decisions made either explicitly or implicitly by marathon participants is the physical surroundings of the marathon, which play a crucial role in the subsequent satisfaction and demand (Moore and Graefe, 1994). However, the significance of sportscape factors to the experience derived from participation in a running event enmeshes more than the physical surrounding. More specifically, the sentiments voiced by the marathon hosting area and its importance to individuals are also important.

This is acknowledged in the theoretical viewpoint of activity specialization, according to which, in some cases, increasing specialization in the recreation activity is associated with a higher degree on the physical surroundings of the activity and more intense inclinations for (and occasionally dependency on) specific sportscape (Moore and Graefe, 1994).

The framework of activity specialization aims to sidestep the apparent deficiencies of making plans and administrating for an "average" individual runner by recognizing significant subgroups of individuals within running. Similarly, differentiating between marathon runners on the basis of how they correlate to the specific sportscapes they participate in could be useful. A comprehension of how marathon runners appreciate, select and correlate to numerous sportscapes is crucial for researchers looking to comprehend recreation behavior and marathon officials looking to offer conveniences for maximizing recreation experiences. To this end, outdoor recreation researchers suggest that via the development of an attachment to a sportscape, individuals develop a bond which probably grants magnitude to them (Kyle *et al.*, 2004). More specifically, sportscape factors were found to influence individuals' affective experiences from the activity and also to have a direct link effect with their intention to participate (Hill and Green, 2012).

Various research has taken place in order to predict health-related motives of individuals' participation in sport activities, with two predominant aspects receiving the total amount of attention. In more detail, the first of the two notions is the preventive health and sickness avoidance aspect, while the second one is the cognitive behavioral aspect.

According to the preventive health and sickness avoidance aspect, the probability of taking up a preventive health comportment such as sport participation, rests on each individual's anticipation of a health danger and a confidence that the suggested activity will decrease that danger (Tsai, 2005). In more detail, the anticipated impact of the suggested precautionary activity relies on an individual's evaluation of the anticipated advantages of the recommended activity, in comparison with the actual or anticipated constraints for starting or carrying on the recommended activity. An exploration of the research about the application of health models in the forecast of exercise participation revealed contradictory results.

A stream of research displayed no linkages between the health-related constructs and exercise intention of individuals whilst other studies identified positive linkages (Tsai, 2005). At the other extreme, a few studies revealed negative correlations between anticipated health danger and the enactment of sport participation. In more detail, individuals who at first sensed themselves as healthy were more likely to continue their exercising than those who sensed themselves as less healthy (Tsai, 2005).

The endorsement of a preventive health and sickness avoidance aspect to anticipate and to advance commitment to regular sport participation is inadequate. This health aspect views sport participation as a kind of introjected regulation motivated by internal resources, needs, self-responsibility, or at most, a type of consolidated procedure of undertaking something that is personally significant (Tsai, 2005). Nevertheless, most research has shown that intrinsic reward is a crucial motivating factor which influences sport participation (Courneya and McAuley, 1994; Johnson and Heller, 1998). In accordance with this stream of research, sensations of amusement and well-being seemed to be more powerful motivations for prolonged sport participation. Hence, health-related advantages of sport participation did not seem to consistently provoke the enactment of a sport active lifestyle and seemed not to maintain individuals' interest in abiding participation. Instead, various non-health-correlated intrinsic rewards appeared to be important in preserving individuals' involvement in regular sport participation.

According to the second notion of the cognitive behavioral aspect, major social cognitive theories (i.e. theory of planned behavior, self-efficacy theory), adopt a more comprehensive perspective for the exploration of a sport active way of life, as they support the examination of both intrinsic and extrinsic rewards. A prevailing perspective in these cognitive theories is the expectancy-value formation of individuals' motivation (Tsai, 2005). In accordance with this perspective, the effectiveness of motivation to participate in sport activities relies on two tensions, with the first being the expectation that specific activities will generate the specific results and the second being the importance placed on these results. For instance, the higher the possibility of positive health-related outcomes from taking part in sport activities and the more valuable for individual's health these outcomes are, the more motivated the individual is to take part in sport activities. The contribution of the cognitive behavioral aspect in forecasting sport participation has been proved to be significant in various recreation studies (Tsai, 2005).

Based on the previous literature, sport participation offers a divergent assemblage of mental and physical benefits to individuals, such as reducing stress and anxiety, promoting well-being and avoiding health problems, and thus it could motivate individuals to participate in recreational activities such as marathon running (Funk et al., 2011).

One notable determinant, which also may differentiate the probability of participating in a marathon, is gender. Previous studies have, in general, limited evidence about gender differences in leisure time physical activities and have shown ambiguous results regarding the effect of gender on marathon participation motives. One of the most persistent results in the sport and exercise literature regards the deprived status of women (Guinn, Semper and Jorgensen, 2000). According to this stream of research, women's lower exercise levels, particularly in late youthfulness and pre-adulthood, distend beyond various sports and types of physical activities, with differences between the two genders being greater in arduous sport activities and types of exercise. More specifically, women were found to have lower overall leisure time physical activity in daily frequency as well as in weekly hours (Vilhjalmsson and Kristjansdottir, 2003). Furthermore, as Kilpatrick et al. (2005) stated, participation motives vary between the two genders, with men having more ego-oriented motives than women. On the contrary, no significant evidence were found about gender differences in levels of overall intense physical activities, such as marathon participation (Vilhjalmsson and Kristjansdottir, 2003). Additionally, as Koronios, Psiloutsikou, Kriemadis, Zervoulakos and Leivaditi (2015a) support, there is no significant evidence of linkage between gender and the intention to participate in marathon events. Hence, further research is required to identify the role of gender as a factor influencing participation in marathons.

However, research regarding marathoners' participation motives and the differences remains both tenuous and contentious, as the interactions between the proposed variables are complex and dynamic. Furthermore very little is known about the differentiation of motives between marathon and half-marathon runners. The challenges of competing in ultra-marathons are dissimilar to those of half-marathons.

The aim of this study is to single out the factors motivating individuals to take part in ultra-marathons and half-marathons. The factors examined were the degree to which individuals consider the event (half- or ultra-marathon) as attractive, the degree of attachment that individuals have with running, the socializing opportunities individuals have during their participation in the event, the physical and mental health factors which influence individuals' decision for taking part in exercise activities, as well as the sportscape factors individuals confront when taking part in a specific event. Furthermore, the training habits of half- and ultra-marathoners have not been examined previously and this research proposes to examine their impact as a motivational factor for future marathon participation. Additionally, the differentiation in motivation between men and women half- and ultra-marathoners is proposed to be significant.

Based on the literature, the suggested model (see Figure 14.1) proposes a number of factors affecting an individual's participation in half- and ultra-marathons.

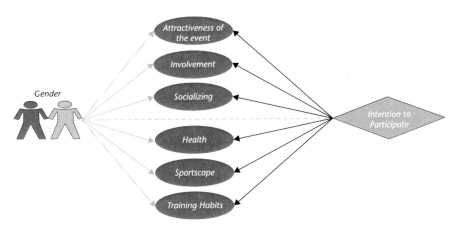

FIGURE 14.1 The proposed model about factors influencing participation in marathon events

All the hypothesized variables are displayed in the above-mentioned model, which critically investigates the following hypotheses:

H_1: Involvement with running increases the individuals' intention to participate in half- and ultra-marathons

H_2: Socializing opportunities increase the individuals' intention to participate in half- and ultra-marathons

H_3: Health factors increase the individuals' intention to participate in half- and ultra-marathons

H_4: Sportscape factors increase the individuals' intention to participate in half- and ultra-marathons

H_5: Individuals' training habits differentiate their intention to participate in half- and ultra-marathons

H_6: Events' (half- and ultra-marathon) attractiveness increases the individuals' intention to participate

H_7: The type of event moderates the effect of motivational factors and training habits to the intention to participate

H_8: The runners' gender moderates the effect of motivational factors and training habits to the intention to participate

Methodology

The present study investigates the factors influencing individuals' participation in marathons as measured from two different sport events. More specifically, elements were obtained from both a half-marathon (a mountain half-marathon of 22,400m) and an ultra-marathon event (246km/24h), following a similar procedure. Both events took place in southern Greece. A quantitative questionnaire was selected as the predominant means of collecting the data. The questionnaire developed for this study was based on previous research of similar subjects and populations (Hill and Green, 2012; Funk *et al.*, 2011). Items were assessed on interval scales and the time needed to complete the survey was 10–12 minutes.

To elaborate, a team of five researchers was responsible for distributing the questionnaires to the athletes and each one of them was randomly selected by the research team and politely asked to take part to the survey.

As far as the ultra-marathon event is concerned the questionnaires were distributed at the end of the award ceremony to each participant by the above-mentioned team of researchers and were completed in the presence of the surveyors, with 175 questionnaires successfully completed. In the case of half-marathon, the questionnaires were distributed, at the end of the race, to each athlete by the same team and the same procedure. The total number of questionnaires successfully completed from this event was 266. Particular circumstances on the field, such as the constant flow of athletes especially at the award ceremony of an ultra-marathon or the finish line of a half-marathon, favor the selected operation by the researchers. The

232 Konstantinos, Psiloutsikou and Kriemadis

total number of questionnaires successfully gathered from both events was 441 and they were analyzed by means of the SPSS.

Results – Discussion

Demographics

This research was based on 441 responses gathered from two distinct running events; a half-marathon race (HMR) and an ultra-marathon race (UMR). The responses gathered from the half-marathon race were 266 (60.3 per cent of the total sample) while those gathered from the ultra-marathon were 175 (39.7 per cent of the total sample). Approximately 2/3 of the respondents were men; 84 per cent in the HMR, 70.8 per cent in the UMR and 79.3 per cent in the total sample. Chi square analysis showed that the participation in the two events was not independent of gender ($X2=9.81$, $p<0.01$, Cramer's $V=0.149$). The comparison between observed and expected values showed that women were more likely to participate in the HMR than in the UMR. This is probably because an ultra-marathon event is more challenging in terms of strength and endurance.

The arithmetic mean of age was 39.19 years ($s=10.1$) for the total sample, 40 years for the HMR and 38.46 years ($s=11.85$) for the UMR. The majority of respondents in the total sample held a bachelor's degree (54 per cent) while 23.7 per cent had completed postgraduate studies. The respective percentages for the HMR were 47.6 per cent and 22.8 per cent and for the UMR were 40.5 per cent and 24.1 per cent. No significant differences were found in the age or the education of the participants between the two events.

Professionally, 56.4 per cent were employed in the private or public sector (also 56.4 per cent in the HMR sample and the UMR) while 27.5 per cent worked as freelancers (32.1 per cent in the HMR and 20.2 per cent in the UMR); 5.5 per cent were still studying (3 per cent in the HMR and 9.5 per cent in the UMR); 6.2 per cent were at the time unemployed (4.1 per cent in the HMR and 9.6 per cent in the UMR); 4.4 per cent were either retired or fully occupied with running their household (also 4.4 per cent in the HMR and 4.2 per cent in the UMR). Chi square analysis showed that the participation in the two events was not independent of the professional occupation ($X2=18.139$, $p<0.01$, Cramer's $V=0.204$). The comparison between observed and expected values showed that students and unemployed runners were more likely to participate in the UMR. Various occupations did not seem to have an effect on choosing either event.

In terms of marital status, 49.8 per cent were married or attached (50.4 per cent in the HMR and 49.2 per cent in the UMR), 44.1 per cent were single (45.9 per cent in the HMR and 42.1 per cent in the UMR) and 6.2 per cent were divorced or widowed (3.8 per cent in the HMR and 8.7 per cent in the UMR). Chi square analysis showed that the participation in the two events was not independent of marital status ($X2=6.61$, $p<0.05$, Cramer's $V=0.123$). The comparison between observed and expected values showed that divorced and widowed runners were slightly more likely to participate in the UMR.

The monthly income was under €1,000 for 47.5 per cent of the participants (45.5 per cent in the HMR and 50.8 per cent in the UMR), 39.7 per cent earned between €1,000 and €2,000 (42.5 per cent in the HMR and 34.9 per cent in the UMR), and 12.8 per cent earned more than that (12 per cent in the HMR and 14.3 per cent in the UMR). No significant differences were found in the income of the participants between the two events.

The participants practiced for their participation in running events on average 8.19 hours a week (s=7.5, mode=10); the respective values for the HMR's participants were m=7.71 hours, s=5.3 and for those of the UMR the values were m=8.56 hours, s=8.9. No significant differences were found in the training habits of the participants between the two events.

Key variables

The proposed model attempts to identify relationships between a number of motivational factors and the intention of the respondents to participate again in future running events. The description of the model's variables and their measurement in this survey are as follows.

Physical health refers to the degree to which benefits to physical health from running are perceived to provide motivation for participating in running events. It was measured with one variable on a 5-point Likert scale.

Mental health refers to the degree to which benefits to physical health from running are perceived to provide motivation for participating in running events. It was measured with five distinct variables on a 5-point Likert scale. Reliability analysis showed a good consistency (Cronbach's a=0.684).

Socializing refers to the degree to which opportunities to engage in social activities during running events are perceived as motivation for participating in them. It was measured with three distinct variables on a 5-point Likert scale. Reliability analysis showed a very good consistency (Cronbach's a=0.708).

Involvement with running refers to the general relationship that the participants have with the sport/habit of running in their everyday life. It was measured with four distinct variables on a 5-point Likert scale. Reliability analysis showed a strong consistency (Cronbach's a=0.894).

Attractiveness of event refers to the special features of a specific event and the attraction/motivation they alone provide to the participants. It was measured with five distinct variables on a 5-point Likert scale. Reliability analysis showed a good consistency (Cronbach's a=0.689).

Sportscape factors refer to the special features of the landscape where running events take place and the attraction/motivation they provide to the participants. It was measured with two distinct variables on a 5-point Likert scale. Reliability analysis showed an acceptable consistency (Cronbach's a=0.572).

Training habits refer to the time the participants spend on a daily basis for their training in order to be able to participate in running events. It was measured with a continuous variable.

234 Konstantinos, Psiloutsikou and Kriemadis

Intention to participate refers to the likelihood at which the participants estimate that they will continue to take part in running events. It was measured with one variable on a 5-point Likert scale.

Differentiation of motivation between events

The literature suggests that there are differences in the motivation of the runners when participating in various events. Furthermore, as already discussed this research has revealed a number of significant differences (although not very strong) between the profile of the participants in the HMR and the participants in the UMR. It is of interest to explore whether different factors motivate runners for different events or if they do so to a different degree.

A series of independent samples t-tests were performed and resulted in a number of interesting findings. Physical health, mental health and sportscape factors were perceived as more motivational for the participants in the HMR than for those in the UMR ($p<0.00$). Intention to participate in future running events was also higher for the participants in the HMR.

On the contrary, involvement with running was found to be more important for the ultra-marathon's runners. This is not surprising since UMRs are more challenging events that require a more consistent relationship between the participants and the sport of running. This particular relationship was the strongest of all; the difference of the two mean values was 0.7 on a 5-point scale. The others had a difference in the two mean values between 0.14 and 0.35. Moreover, the mean for the HMR was below three in the Likert scale, thus not important in terms of motivation, while the mean for the UMR was above three, thus important in terms of motivation. In all other factors, mean values were important for the participants in both HMR and UMR.

Socializing opportunities and the attractiveness of the event were not found to differ significantly between the participants of the two events.

All the above mentioned results are shown in detail in Table 14.1.

Differentiation of motivation between genders

The literature also suggests that there is a differentiation in the motivation between men and women to participate in running events. Independent samples t-test were used to explore such potential differences. Socializing opportunities ($MD = 0.26$, $p<0.01$), the involvement with running ($MD = 0.38$, $p<0.01$) and the attractiveness of the event ($MD = 0.18$, $p<0.05$) were found to provide higher motivation for women than for men.

The findings were similar when the half-marathon race was examined separately. Specifically, for the participants in the HMR, mental health ($MD = 0.27$, $p<0.01$), physical health ($MD = 0.2$, $p<0.05$), the involvement with running ($MD = 0.3$, $p<0.01$) and the attractiveness of the event ($MD = 0.31$, $p<0.01$)

Exploring motivation of marathon runners 235

TABLE 14.1 Independent samples t-test for the motivation of runners in different events

	Mean (HMR)	Levene's test for equality of variances F (sig)	t (sig, 2-tailed)+	Mean (UMR)	Mean difference (HMR-UMR)
Physical health	4.48★★	2.1 (0.148)	4.6 (0.00)	4.12	0.35
Mental health	4.05★	20.28 (0.155)	2.6 (0.01)	3.9	0.15
Involvement with running	2.59★★	1.052 (0.305)	−9.5 (0.00)	3.36	−0.77
Sportscape factors	4.39★★	46.19 (0.000)	10.6 (0.00)	3.69	0.70
Intention to participate	3.78★★	28.5 (0.00)	4.38 (0.00)	3.39	0.39
Socializing	*3.45*	*0.031 (0.86)*	*0.68 (0.49)*	*3.40*	*0.05*
Attractiveness of event	*3.26*	*1.911 (0.168)*	*−0.60 (0.54)*	*3.3*	*−0.04*

+Reported values were produced after taking into consideration the results of Levene's test
★p<0.05 ★★p<0.01

were differentiated by the gender. Again, they all provided higher motivation for women than for men.

However, when the ultra-marathon race was examined separately, only socializing (MD = 0.4, p<0.01) was found to provide motivation at different levels for men and women. Again, women found it to be of higher importance than men. This consistent finding is of great interest; it seems that the motivation factors proposed by the literature are more suitable for women participants than for men. Different areas should be considered in order to identify if there are other factors that provide a higher motivation for men to participate in running events.

Hypotheses testing

A series of linear bivariate correlation analyses were conducted to explore the relationship between the intention to participate in future running events and the motivation provided by each of the factors proposed by the model. All seven motivation factors were positively correlated with the intention to participate in future events; all seven relations were found to be statistically significant. Nevertheless, the correlations were weak or moderate; the respective correlation coefficient values varied from 0.132 to 0.363. The general involvement with the sport of running and the attractiveness of the event were the factors that had the strongest correlation with the intention of runners participating again in the future. On the other hand, the training habits and the physical health had the weakest correlation with the intention to participate again.

Next, a series of linear partial correlations was performed as control for the type of marathon event (HMR and UMR). All correlations were again positive and statistically significant. The effect on the values of the respective correlation coefficients was not notable, except for one; the correlation between the intention

236 Konstantinos, Psiloutsikou and Kriemadis

TABLE 14.2 Correlation coefficients between intention to participate in future running events and motivation factors

| | Intention to participate in future running events | |
	Linear bivariate correlation+	Linear partial correlation controlling for the type of running event+
Mental health	0.281** (0.000)	0.264** (0.000)
Physical health	0.206 **(0.000)	0.169** (0.000)
Socializing	0.230 **(0.000)	0.227** (0.000)
Involvement with running	0.363** (0.000)	0.503** (0.000)
Attractiveness of event	0.315** (0.000)	0.326** (0.000)
Sportscape factors	0.278** (0.000)	0.207** (0.000)
Training habits	0.132** (0.005)	0.144** (0.000)

+ Values are reported as Pearson's correlation coefficient (sig. 2-tailed).
**$p<0.01$

to participate in future events and the general involvement with running was increased from 0.363 to 0.503.

The results in detail are presented in Table 14.2.

A multiple regression analysis was run for the research model, which showed a statistically significant effect on the intention to participate again (IP) for four of the motivational factors proposed; notably, involvement with running (IR), mental health (MH), sportscape factors (SF) and training habits (TH). Physical health (PH), opportunities for socializing (S) and the attractiveness of the event (A) did not show a significant effect on the intention to participate in future events.

The fitness of the model was moderate, predicting 24.8 per cent of the total variance of the dependent variable ($R2 = 0.248$, $p<0.000$). The respective equation was:

$$IP = 0.318 + 0.382*IR + 0.363*SF + 0.156*MH + +0.010*TH$$

Regression coefficients of the involvement with running and the sportscape factors were significant at $p<0.05$ while the regression coefficients of the remaining variables were significant at $p<0.1$, with the estimated error value being marginally above $p= 0.05$.

The type of running event (TR) was used as a moderator variable to explore a potentially different relationship between the model's variables on different running events (Baron et al., 1986). It was found to have a significant and strong positive effect. The type of running event was entered as a dummy variable, with UMR coded as "0" and HMR coded as "1." Therefore, the positive effect means that there is a higher likelihood of participation in future events for the runners of the half-marathon event rather than those of the ultra-marathon. This is in

Exploring motivation of marathon runners **237**

consistency with the findings from the independent samples t-tests, which showed significant differences in the mean values of the model's variables between the HMR and the UMR runners.

The gender of the runners was also tried as a moderator variable, but no significant effect was found. This is in consistency with the results from the respective t-tests, which showed significant differences in socializing opportunities and the attractiveness of the event, factors that did not have a significant effect on intention to participate in future events. Involvement with running was the only factor that had a significant effect on the dependent variable and was found to have a mean value for women that was statistically different than the mean value for men. It is safe to assume that this effect was not strong enough for the gender to assume the role of a moderating factor.

After adding the type of marathon as a moderator variable, the fitness of the model was higher, predicting 32.8 per cent of the total variance of the dependent variable (R2= 0.328, p<0.000). The respective equation was:

$$IP = 0.314 + 0.512 \star IR + 0.648 \star TR + 0.176 \star MH + 0.158 \star SF + 0.011 \star TH$$

Regression coefficients of mental health and training habits were significant at p<0.05 while the regression coefficients of the rest were significant at p<0.00.

To account for the difference in the scales used for the various independent variables, the standardized coefficients were also calculated. The results of the full model are shown in Table 14.3.

The proposed model was not fully supported by the empirical evidence; three of the proposed relationships were not found to be statistically significant and neither was the effect of the runner's gender. The variance in the intention to participate was explained by four variables, measuring various kinds of motivation:

TABLE 14.3 Regression analysis for the proposed research model

	Unstandardized coefficient (B)	Standardized coefficient (Beta)	t	Sig. 2-tailed
Involvement with running	0.512★★	0.497	11.137	0.000
Type of running event	0.648★★	0.337	6.816	0.000
Mental health	0.176★	0.107	2.325	0.021
Sportscape factors	0.158★	0.120	2.342	0.020
Training habits	0.011★	0.086	2.207	0.028
Physical health		*0.024*	*0.490*	*0.625*
Socializing		*−0.004*	*−0.080*	*0.936*
Attractiveness of the event		*0.067*	*1.418*	*0.157*
Gender		*0.006*	*0.146*	*0.884*
	R= 0.328, p <0.000			
	Constant= 0.314			

★p<0.05, ★★p<0.01

involvement with running, mental health, sportscape factors and training habits. They all had a positive effect, which means that the more important a motivational factor is perceived to be, the higher the intention of the respective runner to participate in future events.

The general involvement with running had the highest effect. This means that intention – and consequently actual participation – is higher among runners or potential runners who develop a closer relationship with the sport rather than an occasional one. It is proposed, therefore, that organizers of running events focus their marketing efforts on targeting this specific group of people more, and investing in educating the broader population to view running as part of their lifestyle and make it part of their routine rather than considering it a distinct, occasional activity they may participate in.

The significant (even though not very strong) effect of the training habits on the intention of runners participating again supports the finding that the general involvement with running is the most important factor for repeated participation. The runners who spend more hours running and preparing for respective events on a weekly basis show a stronger intention to continue participating in them.

Furthermore, the benefits on mental health (less anxiety, relaxation, calmness, stress relief, etc.) were the second most important factor of motivation. Contrary to the intuitive thought that activities involving physical exercise would be more closely linked to physical health, this research showed that benefits to mental health are more important. This does not mean that people do not acknowledge the benefits of running to their physical health; it is rather an indication that promotion of mental health provides a higher incentive. Whether this is because people are currently more concerned with their mental health or because they associate their physical health more with other factors (e.g. nutrition, medical exams, etc.) rather than training for and participating in running events is something that needs to be explored further. In any case, promotion of mental health is more critical to enhancing future participation than are benefits for physical health or socializing opportunities.

Moreover, this research showed that the location where the running event takes place is of importance as far as the attractiveness of the landscape is concerned. This is more important than other elements of the venue, such as organization or the social program. This does not mean that the latter are not important; it means that they do not provide significant motivation for repeated participation. Whether or not this is the case because there are no perceived differences in the general attractiveness of the various events or because there is no direct effect on the intention to participate again, it is something that should be further explored. Further research is needed to better identify the kind of landscape that contributes to the motivation of runners.

The type of running event also contributed significantly as a moderator variable. The positive effect of the type of running event suggests a higher likelihood of future participation for the participants of the half-marathon event. This is an important finding that should be furthered explored in two ways. First, it is critical to identify the specific differences in the two types of events that cause the difference in the effect of motivation factors on intention to participate again. Second, more events should be compared in order to explore the extent of this moderation effect.

Physical health, socializing and attractiveness of the event were not found to have a significant impact. The runners' gender was also not found to have a moderator role in the relationship between motivation factors and the intention to participate in future events. This is despite the fact that certain factors (it varies between HMR and UMR) provide consistently higher motivation for women than for men. It seems that these differences are not enough to affect the intention to participate again. Nevertheless, it is an area that would benefit from further research on identifying more motivation factors for women and men.

References

Alexandris, K. and Carroll, B. (1997). 'An analysis of leisure constraints based on different recreational sport participation levels: Results from a study in Greece'. *Leisure Sciences*, 19: 1–15.

Alexandris, K., Funk, D. C. and Pritchard, M. (2011). 'The impact of constraints on motivation, activity attachment, and skier intentions to continue'. *Journal of Leisure Research*, 43: 56.

Alexandris, K., Kouthouris, C., Funk, D. C. and Giovani, C. (2009). 'Segmenting winter sport tourists by motivation: The case of recreational skiers'. *Journal of Hospitality Marketing and Management*, 18: 480–499.

Allen, J. T., Drane, D. D., Byon, K. K. and Mohn, R. S. (2010). 'Sport as a vehicle for socialization and maintenance of cultural identity: International students attending American universities'. *Sport Management Review*, 13: 421–434.

American Ultrarunning Association (AUA). Retrieved October 20, 2008, from the AUA official website: <www.americanultra.org>.

Baron, R. M. and Kenny, D. A. (1986). 'The moderator-mediator variable distinction in social psychological research: Conceptual, strategic, and statistical considerations'. *Journal of Personality and Social Psychology*, 51, 1173–1182.

Beaton, A. A., Funk, D. C., Ridinger, L. and Jordan, J. (2011). 'Sport involvement: A conceptual and empirical analysis'. *Sport Management Review*, 14: 126–140.

Courneya, K. S. and McAuley, E. (1994). 'Are there different determinants of the frequency, intensity, and duration of physical activity?' *Behavioral Medicine*, 20: 84–90.

Funk, D. C., Toohey, K. and Bruun, T. (2007). 'International sport event participation: Prior sport involvement; destination image and travel motives'. *European Sport Management Quarterly*, 7: 227–248.

Funk, D. C., Jordan, J., Ridinger, L. and Kaplanidou, K. (2011). 'Capacity of mass participant sport events for the development of activity commitment and future exercise intention'. *Leisure Sciences*, 33: 250–268.

Funk, D. C., Ridinger, L. and Moorman, A. M. (2004). 'Exploring origins of involvement: Understanding the relationship between consumer motives and involvement with professional sport teams'. *Leisure Sciences*, 26: 35–61.

Gill, K. and Overdorf, V. (1994). 'Incentives for exercise in younger and older women'. *Journal of Sport Behavior*, 17: 87.

Gillett, P. and Kelly, S. (2006). ' "Non-local" masters games participants: An investigation of competitive active sport tourist motives'. *Journal of Sport Tourism*, 11: 239–257.

Guinn, B., Vincent, V., Semper, T. and Jorgensen, L. (2000). 'Activity involvement, goal perspective, and self-esteem among Mexican American adolescents'. *Research Quarterly for Exercise and Sport*, 71: 308–311.

Havitz, M. E. and Dimanche, F. (1997). 'Leisure involvement revisited: Conceptual conundrums and measurement advances'. *Journal of Leisure Research*, 29: 245.

Hanson, N., Madaras, L., Dicke, J. and Buckworth, J. (2015). 'Motivational differences between half, full and ultramarathoners'. *Journal of Sport Behavior*, 38: 180.

Hill, B. and Christine Green, B. (2012). 'Repeat participation as a function of program attractiveness, socializing opportunities, loyalty and the sportscape across three sport facility contexts'. *Sport Management Review*, 15: 485–499.

Hodge, K., Allen, J. B. and Smellie, L. (2008). 'Motivation in masters sport: Achievement and social goals'. *Psychology of Sport and Exercise*, 9: 157–176.

Iwasaki, Y. and Havitz, M. E. (2004). 'Examining relationships between leisure involvement, psychological commitment and loyalty to a recreation agency'. *Journal of Leisure Research*, 36: 45.

Johnson, N. A. and Heller, R. F. (1998). 'Prediction of patient nonadherence with home-based exercise for cardiac rehabilitation: The role of perceived barriers and perceived benefits'. *Preventive Medicine*, 27: 56–64.

Kilpatrick, M., Hebert, E. and Bartholomew, J. (2005). 'College students' motivation for physical activity: Differentiating men's and women's motives for sport participation and exercise'. *Journal of American College Health*, 54: 87–94

King, J. and Burke, S. (2000). 'Motivations of marathon runners: Implications for sport and exercise'. *Sportpsyc Unpublished*. Retrieved July 10, 2004.

Koronios, K., Psiloutsikou, M., Kriemadis, A., Zervoulakos, P. and Leivaditi, E. (2015a). 'Factors influencing future marathon running participation'. Proceedings of the 8th Annual Euromed Academy of Business Conference: *Innovation, Entrepreneurship and Sustainable Value Chain in a Dynamic Environment*, Verona, Italy.

Koronios, K., Psiloutsikou, M., Kriemadis, A., Zervoulakos, P. and Leivaditi, E. (2015b). 'Factors influencing future marathon running participation'. Proceedings of the 23rd Conference of European Association for Sport Management, Dublin, Ireland.

Kouthouris, C. (2009). 'An examination of the relationships between motivation, involvement and intention to continuing participation among recreational skiers'. *International Journal of Sport Management Recreation and Sport*, 4: 1–19.

Krouse, R. Z. (2009). 'A descriptive study examining motivation, goal orientations, coaching, and training habits of women ultrarunners'. *Boise State University Theses and Dissertations*, 51.

Kyle, G. T., Absher, J. D., Hammitt, W. E. and Cavin, J. (2006). 'An examination of the motivation–involvement relationship'. *Leisure Sciences*, 28: 467–485.

Kyle, G., Graefe, A., Manning, R. and Bacon, J. (2004). 'Predictors of behavioral loyalty among hikers along the Appalachian Trail'. *Leisure Sciences*, 26: 99–118.

Kyle, G. and Chick, G. (2004). 'Enduring leisure involvement: The importance of personal relationships'. *Leisure Studies* 23: 243–266.

Lovett, D. (2011). 'An examination of the motives to participate in sprint distance triathlon'. *Dissertation Abstracts International*, DAI-B 72/10.

Moore, R. L. and Graefe, A. R. (1994). 'Attachments to recreation settings: The case of rail-trail users'. *Leisure Sciences*, 16: 17–31.

Ogles, B. M. and Masters, K. S. (2000). 'Older vs. younger adult male marathon runners: Participative motives and training habits'. *Journal of Sport Behavior*, 23: 130–143.

Ogles, B. M. and Masters, K. S. (2003). 'A typology of marathon runners based on cluster analysis of motivations'. *Journal of Sport Behavior*, 26: 69.

Petrick, J. F., Morais, D. D. and Norman, W. C. (2001). 'An examination of the determinants of entertainment vacationers' intentions to revisit'. *Journal of Travel Research*, 40: 41–48.

Ridinger, L. L., Funk, D. C., Jordan, J. S. and Kaplanidou, K. K. (2012). 'Marathons for the masses: Exploring the role of negotiation-efficacy and involvement on running commitment'. *Journal of Leisure Research*, 44: 155.

Ryan, R. M. and Deci, E. L. (2000). 'Self-determination theory and the facilitation of intrinsic motivation, social development, and well-being'. *American Psychologist*, 55: 68.

Shipway, R. and Jones, I. (2007). 'Running away from home: Understanding visitor experiences and behavior at sport tourism events'. *International Journal of Tourism Research*, 9: 373–383.

Stuntz, C. P. and Spearance, A. L. (2007). 'Coach-athlete and teammate holistic relationships: Measurement development and prediction of motivational factors'. *Journal of Sport and Exercise Psychology*, 29.

Tian-Cole, S., Crompton, J. L. and Willson, V. L. (2002). 'An empirical investigation of the relationships between service quality, satisfaction and behavioral intentions among visitors to a wildlife refuge'. *Journal of Leisure Research*, 34: 1.

Tsai, E. H. L. (2005). 'A cross-cultural study of the influence of perceived positive outcomes on participation in regular active recreation: Hong Kong and Australian university students'. *Leisure Sciences*, 27: 385–404.

Van der Nest, A. C. (2007). 'The motivation of ultramarathon runners: A comparison of different age, gender and race groups'. Dissertation, University of Johannesburg.

Vilhjalmsson, R. and Kristjansdottir, G. (2003). 'Gender differences in physical activity in older children and adolescents: The central role of organized sport'. *Social Science and Medicine*, 56: 363–374.

Vlachopoulos, S. P., Karageorghis, C. I. and Terry, P. C. (2000). 'Motivation profiles in sport: A self-determination theory perspective'. *Research Quarterly for Exercise and Sport*, 71: 387–397.

Walraven, M., Koning, R. H. and Van Bottenburg, M. (2012). 'The effects of sports sponsorship: A review and research agenda'. *The Marketing Review*, 12: 17–38.

Wilson, P. M. and Rodgers, W. M. (2004). 'The relationship between perceived autonomy support, exercise regulations and behavioral intentions in women'. *Psychology of Sport and Exercise*, 5: 229–242.

Weiss, O. (2001). 'Identity reinforcement in sport: Revisiting the Symbolic Interactionist Legacy'. *International Review for the Sociology of Sport*, 36: 393–405.

World Health Organization. (2010). 'Physical activity and women'. Retrieved October 2010 from: <www.who.int/dietphysicalactivity/factssheet_women/en/

15

SPORT ENTREPRENEURSHIP AND THE EMERGENCE OF OPPORTUNITIES

Towards a future research agenda

Vanessa Ratten and João J. Ferreira

Introduction

Sport has a big impact on society because of the various sport-related activities such as attendance, listening, participating and watching (Park *et al.*, 2015). Sport is one of the most popular recreational activities and is an important element of society. In the past decade, the sport industry has become more competitive due to the introduction of new sports but also competition from other leisure sectors. Due to this increase in global competitiveness, sport managers need to focus more on generating new ideas for sport in order to maintain competitiveness. This means that the development of new consumers is crucial for sport in the global competitive environment (Park *et al.*, 2015).

Sport has become more popular as a topic in business literature due to its role in society (Rundh and Gottfriedsson, 2015). Park *et al.* (2015, p.359) state "the size of the sport industry is estimated to become two times greater than the US automobile industry and seven times greater than the US movie industry." There are increasingly more entrepreneurs involved in sport due to the technological changes, which have created business opportunities. Despite this increase of sport entrepreneurs in the industry most of the current literature about sports is focused on marketing and management. This has meant there is abundant research about sports marketing in terms of promotions, advertising and communications. However, due to the innovative technologies and services being developed in the sport sector, it has become more apparent about the role of sports entrepreneurship. This has presented a challenge for sports marketers to incorporate more entrepreneurial thinking.

Many businesses use sport as a way to sell products and services due to sport's appeal with consumers and entrepreneurial capabilities. Sports products and services are developed often by consumers rather than businesses (Rundh and

Gottfridsson, 2015). There has been an increasing focus on entrepreneurship in sport with transformational applications to other industry contexts. This has meant dramatic new opportunities for sports entrepreneurship, the study of which is relevant. By understanding entrepreneurship in sport it can help identify sport as a distinct form of entrepreneurship and lead to our understanding of how sports entrepreneurship can develop.

The aim of this chapter is to bring together the latest research from the sports management and entrepreneurship disciplines to advance theoretical development about sports entrepreneurship. More attention needs to be given to the interplay between sport entrepreneurship as a theory and practice. This is due to sport entrepreneurship being an interesting topic due to the global appeal of sport in the marketplace. In addition, the contemporary relevance of sports entrepreneurship as a topic is important in creating a research community. Sport entrepreneurship as a theory is appealing due to its real-life application to sports companies. This has meant that the practice of sports entrepreneurship can utilize research to explain the development of business ventures in sport entrepreneurship. Sport entrepreneurship is a cutting-edge theoretically based discipline that can offer pioneering explanations for innovative behavior.

This increased presence of sport entrepreneurship signals the emergence of a new field in a growing exchange between sport and entrepreneurship scholars. This new field is contributing to our understanding of innovation, competitiveness and risk-taking in sport. The industry trends in sport reflect a growing need to be entrepreneurial in products, services, technologies and market development. Building on the entrepreneurship literature, this chapter indicates that sport studies are now utilizing more of an innovation approach.

This chapter makes two primary contributions about sport entrepreneurship. First, we offer an entrepreneurship perspective about sport, which helps to explain the multifaceted nature of the industry. This helps identify trends within the field, which can enable further research. Second, we provide a new perspective for including sport entrepreneurship as a theoretical framework for a more holistic view of the different types of entrepreneurship that occur in the sport context. As sport includes amateur, professional and non-profit entities, this will facilitate better positioning of sport entrepreneurship with management research. The identification of sport entrepreneurship as crucial to new studies will increase the impact of future research but also inform practitioners of new approaches.

Sport entrepreneurship theory

Sport entrepreneurship theory can inform the design of sport services and related ecosystems. This is due to sport entrepreneurship research having abundant opportunities for further study due to its practical relevance in informing the development of sport. Research in sport entrepreneurship is considered in its infancy due to the lack of theoretical development. The legitimacy of sports entrepreneurship as a research field is important for integrating the emotional value of sport with its business viability. Sports entrepreneurship has emerged as important for government policy because of the provision of funding and regulation to these initiatives. Sports entrepreneurship is defined as innovative, risk-taking and proactive behavior in the sports-related industry. This incorporates different types of sport from amateur, professional and educational that use innovations to solve problems. The lack of empirical research about sport entrepreneurship hinders exploration about the antecedents and factors influencing innovation in sport. This has led to a lack of theory-based advances on sport entrepreneurship since it is a promising global area deserving academic research and focused on contextual factors.

Contextual factors

Contextual factors can take a variety of different forms including institutional development, market trends and infrastructure availability (Hoskisson *et al.*, 2013). These contextual factors influence a firm's global competitiveness and ability to be entrepreneurial. An individual's social networks can mean that other contextual factors such as institutional and regulatory environments are overcome (Estrin *et al.*, 2012). Some entrepreneurs have contextual mobility from different environmental factors changing (Wright, 2011). This leads to contexts converging over time and space leading to changing entrepreneurial conditions (Zahra *et al.*, 2014). This evolution means that contexts are altering depending on the novelty of entrepreneurial activities (Zahra and Wright, 2011). Opportunities arise in a variety of ways including by chance or through deliberate assessment of future trends. The unplanned opportunities are referred to as serendipity and are influenced by contextual factors. The ability to choose the right opportunities can be difficult for individuals depending on the context (Zahra *et al.*, 2014). Some contexts make it easier to discover and exploit entrepreneurial opportunities (Saxenian, 1994). Contextualization refers to the natural setting of an action or behavior (Johns, 2001). This is helpful in assessing the cultural and historical elements to a setting (Zahra *et al.*, 2014).

Entrepreneurship research focuses on the premise that entrepreneurs have distinctive personality traits, which influence their behavior. The context in which entrepreneurial actions occur is an important consideration (Zahra *et al.*, 2014). Contextual influencers are inherent in both micro- and macro-processes that give rise to entrepreneurship (Foss *et al.*, 2013). This has meant that the study of contextualization within entrepreneurship helps to explain how the environment influences creative activity. The key contexts influencing entrepreneurial behavior are temporal, social, industry and market, spatial and ownership (Zahra *et al.*, 2014).

The temporal dimension concerns time and this is important for relevance in entrepreneurship (Zahra *et al.*, 2014). Timeliness of innovations is relevant for entrepreneurs in terms of their competitiveness (Bird and West, 1997). The role of time for sport entrepreneurship is important as there is a window of opportunity making new ventures possible. Some new sports need to be introduced into the marketplace by athletes or sports teams in order for there to be consumer acceptance. The value of opportunities is dependent on when they are introduced into the marketplace. Some sport entrepreneurial ventures face risk as they need to assess the willingness of consumers or businesses to adopt the innovation. This means that sport entrepreneurs need to exploit opportunities when they occur such as after winning an event or engaging in a novel activity on the sports field. Strategic action by entrepreneurs is influenced by the pace at which the industry is changing (Zaheer *et al.*, 1999). For some sport entrepreneurs, particularly professional athletes, there will be a need to build their brand reputation before starting a business venture.

The social dimension of context concerns the networks and relationships of an entrepreneur. Zahra *et al.* (2014, p. 12) state "networks refer to the constellation of relationships that develop among members of a social system." In sport, there are global networks developed from being involved in the sport, which help individuals share information. The social nature of sport gives rise to potentially close network relationships to exist between sport organizations and external business providers. This helps sport entrepreneurs connect with relevant sources of business knowledge. There tends to be more mutual trust in sport due to its collaborative nature. This leads to sport entrepreneurs having easier access to innovations and greater ability to use their social network. Social networks enable individuals to access information, marketing and resources (Stuart and Sorenson, 2007). Over time networks develop making it easier for firms to make strategic choices based on help from network sources that affect their performance. Often the radical technological change disrupts existing network relationships causing new entrants to enter the market (Zahra *et al.*, 2014).

Industry and markets are contextual factors influencing sport entrepreneurship. The industry a firm operates in provides the context for the type and frequency of innovations (Porter, 1980). Some industries are more competitive than others due to the nature of their products and services (Zahra *et al.*, 2014). The sport industry provides opportunities in a number of different ways including complementary building on existing business relationships. This helps sport entrepreneurs to utilize complementary assets that may exist from sports activities. Market factors involve assessing demographic and social trends, which affect demand for sports services. The timing of entering a market is important to the success of a business (Grant, 2012). Competition between firms means that markets and industries will change based on entrepreneurial activity. Established companies can enter markets quickly by buying new businesses or refocusing their existing assets. Zahra *et al.* (2014, p. 8) state that "some markets cannot support the profitability and growth goals of a large number of new ventures." Industries can be in decline, growth or maturity, which affects how firms compete (Grant, 2012). Some industries, whilst in the decline stage, may still be highly profitable because of the limited number of firms. An industry's landscape will shift based on regulatory, technical and social change.

Cultural expectations also trigger markets to develop in different ways depending on business circumstances. In addition, the entry and existence of firms particularly by international companies influences the context of competition (Bradley *et al.*, 2011). Industry and markets change based on shifts in new venture strategies from dynamic competition (Bradley *et al.*, 2011). New ventures can often use innovative technologies, making it easier for them to position themselves as market pioneers (Zahra *et al.*, 2011). Markets are also influenced by the mode of internationalization new ventures use to learn about technology (Zahra *et al.*, 2000).

The spatial dimension of context incorporates geography and location, which are important for entrepreneurship (Zahra *et al.*, 2014). Geography is often discussed in terms of clusters of firms locating in a specific region because of resource endowments. The place where businesses are located is linked to their ability to access stakeholders and other relevant knowledge networks. Geography has been seen as important for entrepreneurs as it links to locational advantages (Clark *et al.*, 2000). Economic geography is considered as influencing international markets by explaining the type and growth of new ventures (Clark *et al.*, 2006). For these reasons, space in terms of location can explain the intensity of entrepreneurial ventures (Zahra *et al.*, 2004). Other factors apart from geography are also important for entrepreneurship as seen in countries with location disadvantages who are still achieving high economic growth rates (Bruton *et al.*, 2013). This has become more evident with technological advances in communication and transportation making it easier for businesses in developing and less urban country locations (Zahra *et al.*, 2011). The importance of physical distance for entrepreneurship has lessened with the rise of the digital economy (Zahra *et al.*, 2014). Despite the assertion that the internet has changed the way entrepreneurship is conducted, some still see the physical location as being important to creating an entrepreneurial ecosystem (Nachum and Zaheer, 2005). Knowledge spillovers from entrepreneurs locating in close geographic areas make it possible for unintended innovations to develop. This helps entrepreneurs use their social capital to focus on the discovery of potential opportunities. For sport, this is important as stadiums and event facilities impact tourism, health and education industries.

The organizational dimension of context includes aspects about ownership and governance (Zahra *et al.*, 2014). Maitland *et al.* (2015, p. 501) state "sport organizations are commonly associated with specific values and a great variety of symbols, stories, myths and rituals." Entrepreneurship often occurs in self-managed organizational structures where the entrepreneur also acts as the leader. Start-ups are considered entrepreneurial due to their ability to focus on innovation. Other organizational forms include small businesses, corporations and government entities. Small businesses may facilitate entrepreneurship due to their ability to act quickly and respond to market demand. Often small businesses in sport facilitate the early introduction and testing of innovations. Corporations take a different, more bureaucratic style of ownership and structure, which can restrict creativity and the development of innovation. Despite the more bureaucratic formal structure of corporations, some suggest that the resource endowments of large sport businesses facilitate innovation.

Organizations have different exploitation and objectives depending on their ability to access markets. For some, the opportunity recognition process is the most important part of their organization and they devote resources to incubators to achieve this objective. Spin-offs from universities are often utilized as an organizational structure to achieve entrepreneurship goals (Zahra *et al.*, 2007). Commercialization of ideas originating from government organizations is important and sometimes the spin-offs offer the appropriate organizational structure (Wennberg *et al.*, 2011). Other important types of organizational contexts for entrepreneurship, especially for sport, are non-profit or social entities. These allow sport organizations to have both a business and social objective.

New venture development

Within sport the contextual dimensions influence new venture development. New ventures are started by teams of people rather than by individuals (Wright and Vanaelst, 2009). The prevalence of teams in new start-ups means it is important to have the right social networks (Zahra *et al.*, 2014). For individuals who play team sports, they have experience and aptitude for working with a number of others, which can help them form new ventures. Teams have certain dynamics that need to be harnessed in order for them to work well. Some entrepreneurs retain the same team members whilst others have new teams for each venture (Zahra *et al.*, 2014). There have been innovations with new sports emerging that link lifestyle aspects with sport pursuits. This includes lifestyle sports, which in the past were at the periphery of professional sport but have become more mainstream activities. One of the most famous proponents of lifestyle games is the X Games, who pioneered the way sports are viewed and seen by large global audiences. The television network ESPN started the X Games as an innovative way to capture new audiences but also highlight new adventure and lifestyle sports as part of the entrepreneurial development process.

The entrepreneurial process usually begins with the discovery of opportunities (Shane and Venkataraman, 2000). Individuals scan the environment for opportunities that combine different kinds of knowledge (Kuada, 2015). This challenging of existing practices incorporates accessing relevant knowledge that seems unrelated (Kirzner, 1997). A relevant type of entrepreneurship for sport is growth-orientated. Entrepreneurship that is concerned with a desire for growth is important for economic development (Kuada, 2015). During business venture growth, there are less resources used by creative entrepreneurs. Growth-orientated entrepreneurs disregard the resources they possess but are more concerned with opportunities. In the sport context, growth-orientated entrepreneurs are more prevalent in adventure sport as there is more emphasis on creativity and innovation. There is also an emphasis by growth-orientated entrepreneurs on developing professional sports because of the opportunity to add media and technology services.

Some sport entrepreneurs are considered lifestyle entrepreneurs because they are using the social networks they have built during their sports careers. Lifestyle entrepreneurs convert social capital from their personal, political and social networks into business opportunities (Kuada, 2015). This enables them to continue their relationship with a sport whist building a financial revenue stream. Some of these lifestyle entrepreneurs may be interested in social and sustainability elements to sport that mean they are likely to maintain a personal connection with the sport business. Normally, entrepreneurs who have a greater resource platform are able to achieve more long-term growth (Gilbert *et al.*, 2006).

Corte (2013, p. 25) states lifestyle sport has "its ethos of anti-competitiveness, anti-regulations, high risk, personal freedom and artistic expression." This means that lifestyle sports have developed in association with popular culture and media. Lifestyle sports are different to traditional mainstream sport as they emphasize art, as well as physical activity (Corte, 2013). There is more emphasis in lifestyle sports on creativity, invention and personal expression (Wheaton, 2004). The artistry associated with lifestyle sports has given rise to more linkage with the creative industries such as music. The emphasis in lifestyle sports is on individuality rather than conforming to stereotypical behavior. This has led to lifestyle sports growing in popularity due to their innovativeness. The individuality associated with lifestyle sports has further differentiated the way sport is measured. Wheaton (2004) argues that compared to traditional sports, lifestyle sports have given rise to stylistic nuances that cannot be taught as they are inherent in an individual's personality. Despite the rebel nature of lifestyle sports they have been commercialized to enable greater international access (Corte, 2013). This has meant lifestyle sports have professionalized but also achieved global recognition by being included in the Olympics.

Sport and creativity

Context is significant for the occurrence of creative outcomes (Shalley *et al.*, 2009). Creativity is enhanced when combined with a supportive context that enables synergy to occur (Zhang and Zhou, 2014). Support can be in the form of personal factors such as social relationships, which encourage team projects to occur (Zhou and Hoewes, 2014). The social context means that creators and entrepreneurship for sport is embedded in social relationships. In sport, there is social contact that enables individuals to interact with others to implement innovative ideas. The social contacts obtained from sport enables people to discuss and refine innovations that can lead to the creation of business ventures. Entrepreneurs' social networks are an important part of their ability to start new ventures (Stuart and Sorenson, 2007). Opportunities arise from social networks that make the obtainment of funds easier (Baer, 2010). In the sport context, individuals often belong to multiple social networks, which increases access to information that can facilitate entrepreneurial ventures.

Team creativity is important to encourage the diversity of viewpoints and to increase knowledge transfer (Taggar, 2002). Groups that have diverse members enhance their capabilities and knowledge required to facilitate creativity (Perry-Smith and Shalley, 2014). Entrepreneurial team members can apply diverse ideas to increase creative output. The thought processes of team members make it useful in the ideation and invention phase of entrepreneurship. Facilitating entrepreneurial ideas is part of a team's strategy when formatting ideas. The process of creativity involves behaviors such as challenging assumptions, tolerating ambiguity and making novel connections (Shalley *et al.*, 2004). In the sports context, developing creative ideas can include assessing the environment for problems that need solutions. For sport entrepreneurs, creativity helps in identifying opportunities by also finding ways to exploit them. The sports entrepreneurs who succeed in getting their ideas into the marketplace are creative in pitching and developing their ideas. The fundamental part of entrepreneurship involves the ability of individuals to put their ideas into the marketplace.

Innovation involves using new, revised or combined knowledge to come up with ideas that can change existing business practices (Anderson *et al.*, 2014). Creativity is linked to innovation due to the role it has as part of the process of selecting and varying existing patterns (Feist, 1998). The selection of ideas which are most promising involves entrepreneurs who allocate resources to making ideas become a reality. The personal factors associated with creativity include being open to new ways of doing things, thinking in a different way and being futuristic in thinking (Jabri, 1991). These personality traits associated with being creative are linked to being non-traditional and solving problems in different ways (Costa and McCrae, 1992). Entrepreneurship involves people with creative personalities coming up with ideas that have business applications (Barron and Harrington, 1981). Sometimes entrepreneurial passion is used to describe the personality of entrepreneurs who go into previously unknown business ventures. This means that entrepreneurs have a passion for creating new businesses because of their intrinsic motivation to be innovative (Hitt *et al.*, 2011). In sport, this entrepreneurial passion can be seen in individuals wanting to find new ways of increasing performance.

Sport, entrepreneurship and innovation

The aim of this book is to integrate the research on sport, innovation and entrepreneurship. There is a large body of research on each of these areas but there is a lack of integration despite the overlaps. In order to understand how these areas are becoming intertwined this book has taken an interdisciplinary perspective. This helps to understand how innovation and entrepreneurship are related to sport. This enables the benefits of combing the knowledge from each research stream to integrate theory with practice. This book will move the sport entrepreneurship and innovation field forward to incorporate a more dynamic global perspective. This book comprised a number of chapters written by prominent international scholars that are integrating sport, innovation and entrepreneurship research.

This book has examined how entrepreneurship and innovations can enhance research about sport management. There has been little overlap between scholars from entrepreneurship and innovation backgrounds with sport researchers. This has meant lost opportunities, which is the reason for this book focusing on sport entrepreneurship and innovation. There are benefits from using an entrepreneurial and innovation lens to study sport in a variety of different contexts. This can help enhance sport research by placing emphasis on entrepreneurship and innovation. This book provides an approach to the study of sport that recognizes the role of entrepreneurship and innovation.

More sport scholars are using different disciplines for their research (Knoppers, 2014). Most of the current literature on sport management has focused on practical issues and less on theoretical frameworks. The lack of entrepreneurship studies in sport is surprising given the large number of sport companies that are innovative. There is entrepreneurship and innovation in sport due to the way it shapes participation amongst sport enthusiasts but also surrounding industries.

There are limited authors who publish both in sport, entrepreneurship and innovation management. Entrepreneurship theory is rarely used in sport management despite its appeal and ability to link sport to business. Sport scholars should pay more attention to work that goes on in entrepreneurship as it provides useful information about innovation, risk-taking and competitiveness which are ingrained in sport. Entrepreneurship scholars can also use a sports-thinking lens to be critical about the competitiveness of business, which can be similar to a sport setting. Sports managers are an important part of the entrepreneurial process as they are involved in the resourcing and organization of their team, organizations and individuals. Sports managers hire, motivate and train employees by constructing an organizational strategy (Knoppers, 2015). The role of leaders includes a number of functions from implementing regulations to shaping a productive organizational culture (Collinson, 2014).

There has been little empirical work on entrepreneurial leadership of sports entities. Most sport management research takes an organizational theory approach that focuses on behaviors consistent with previous work (Frisby, 2005). The reliance on sport as having a managerialist nature in the literature has meant there is limited research about entrepreneurship. Due to the historical development of sport management most studies come from the health sciences rather than the business domain. This has been changing with the growth of sport as a business and increasing interest about the commercialization of sport. Sociology of sport originated from the physical education discipline (Knoppers, 2015). The use of an entrepreneurship approach to sport enables scholars to explore innovative practices and to pay attention to changing dynamics within sport. The current practices of sport can be transformed by questioning existing practices that produce entrepreneurial outcomes.

The combination of sport and entrepreneurship can provide value to organizations when used together. The use of entrepreneurship and innovation perspectives requires sport researchers to address new areas of context. This includes questioning how innovations developed by sports fans are then commercialized. A sport enterprise may be involved in sport they are actively engaged in and this leads to innovative approaches being developed. More questions about sport entrepreneurship leaders and how they build businesses is needed. Some sport entrepreneurs share the responsibility of advancing their sport by coming up with innovative products and services. Little attention has been given to how entrepreneurship is embedded in sport leaders. Those who study sport management are urged to use entrepreneurship and innovation theory to explore creativity in sport dynamics. Few sport management researchers have taken up the task of using a contextual approach to entrepreneurship. More research is needed that explores how innovation in sport informs business growth. The practice of sport is based on challenging the opponent by taking an innovative approach to competition. Yet little is known about how innovative structures of sport shape the development of sport practices. Research is needed to examine the benefits of sport entrepreneurship from both profit and non-profit perspectives. The impact of negative sport innovations would absorb the source of information about how user knowledge affects customer value of sport services.

The role of gender-based sport entrepreneurship is needed to see how professionalization of sport has led to better ability of females to bring ideas to fruition. This could include looking at how gendering of leadership is practiced in sport organizations (Knoppers, 2015). Knoppers (2015, p. 499) states "critical research on managerial fashions needs to be conducted not only in sport organizations but also in educational institutions that prepare individuals to become sport managers." Entrepreneurship theories should be used to understand more about how innovations in sport are produced and the results of these changes. This book has proposed an intersectional approach to sport, innovation and entrepreneurship that places creativity at the centre of the research. There is little known about how creativity works in sport organizations and if this process is specific to sport. Sport organizations shape society by acting as a cultural and business centre of activity. Entrepreneurship in sport is a topic that could benefit from more critical analysis. The aim of this book is to stimulate more entrepreneurship and innovation research about sport.

Future research opportunities

Our discussion indicates that more opportunities to research sport entrepreneurship are becoming apparent. Some attention has been given to revealing fruitful avenues for future research about sport entrepreneurship. There are a range of sport-related disciplines including injury prevention, physical training, rehabilitation, sports psychology and sports tourism (Maitland *et al.*, 2015). There are three main streams for sport entrepreneurship research to follow, which are athletes and teams, marketing and processes, and competitive environments. The first stream about athletes and teams has interesting possibilities due to sport-related entrepreneurship becoming more evident in the industry. It is meaningful to better understand why athletes during and after their sports career are drawn to business ventures. There has been some speculation that sports people are better at business due to their competitive natures. An interesting opportunity for future research is to look at sports psychology of athletes to see how their behavioral traits are linked to entrepreneurial orientation. Another useful way to uncover why athletes are often drawn to new business ventures would be to examine whether risk-taking propensity and athleticism are linked for team sports and entrepreneurship. There is a need to look into previously unconnected linkages between collaborative activity and success of business ventures. This means investigating how team skills learnt as a member of a sport team are linked to entrepreneurship. This would help understand the skills and expertise of sports teams and athletes that may make them more entrepreneurial than others.

Second, the entrepreneurial nature of sports marketing and processes needs to be explored. Many advertising campaigns for sport products and services are innovative, due to the ability to link sport with entertainment. Entrepreneurial sports markets have used athletes in a new way in campaigns in order to encourage fans who have emotional attachments with sport to buy certain products and services. Sport processes in terms of buying tickets online and game-day events are also entrepreneurial and need more research attention. This may help build sports entrepreneurship as a research discipline linked to marketing and advertising. The nature of sports marketing has led to increased efforts to do creative things in order to increase viewership and buyer behavior.

Third, competitive environments in sport influence entrepreneurship. This is due to new sports being introduced into the marketplace that compete with traditional sport. Time is a strategic resource as it enables firms' advantages of newness and first-mover advantage (Autio *et al.*, 2000). Global environmental changes in technology and social attitudes towards sport affect entrepreneurial new ventures. Examples of this have included the Ultimate Fighting Championship's use of the Octagon, which is an innovative development of mixed-martial arts. Social changes in women in sport have been reflected in women fighters in the Ultimate Fighting Championships such as Ronda Rousey and racing car driver Danica Patrick. In addition, regulatory adjustments in sport have been entrepreneurial such as night-time cricket and the priority rule in surfing enabling fairer access to waves during events. The emergence of these changes to sport has also been influenced by technology changes such as real-time access to sports events made possible by mobile communication. Future research needs to probe into global environmental influencers on the development of entrepreneurship in sport. Thinking about change in sport as a form of entrepreneurship will have research potential for scholars interested in sport entrepreneurship.

Conclusion

There are a number of ways to advance the field of sport entrepreneurship. Sport entrepreneurship is a new field with limited studies specifically focusing on this area. Despite the big role entrepreneurship plays in the sport, fitness and health industry there are few research studies about sport entrepreneurship. A promising area of study for sport entrepreneurship is sport organizations and associated athletes, coaches and members (Maitland *et al.*, 2015). There has been an increase in interest in recent years linking sport entrepreneurship to other fields such as social and community development but also technological innovation. This increase signals the growing significance of sport entrepreneurship as a field of research. This is helping researchers in the sport management and entrepreneurship disciplines strengthen our understanding of the relevance of sport entrepreneurship. The increased interest in sport as an entrepreneurial industry has enabled new direction for future research to be forged. This helps indicate that sport entrepreneurship is a contribution to entrepreneurship scholarship, but also the innovation management community. As more policy and industry are focusing on sport entrepreneurship there will be increased interest from scholars. More interest from management areas of leisure and tourism studies has resulted in more integration of entrepreneurship in sport research. This means that the study of entrepreneurship within sport is gaining momentum as scholars understand its relevance. The emergence of entrepreneurship within sport research represents a pivotal point in the influence of sport research as a field of research. This has led to implications for the conversations around sport entrepreneurship development and the theoretical premises of this field. Sport entrepreneurship will continue to evolve as more research is focused at an interdisciplinary level but also on the practical role that sport has in society and the global economy.

We hope this book will serve as a catalyst for more research to focus on sport entrepreneurship. There is potential for research from the sport, innovation and entrepreneurship area to be integrated in order to understand how sport can be entrepreneurial. Each of the chapters in this book has a number of suggestions for future research about sports entrepreneurship. The main areas for future research we will highlight here in order to provide a succinct agenda for sports entrepreneurship. We suggest that more research should focus on how sports managers, organizations and entrepreneurs can encourage more innovations that have business potential. Much of the innovation that occurs in sport happens by chance rather than through direct intervention. It is critical to cultivate a supportive environment for sport-related innovations to be developed. This can include more research about the contextual factors that help sport innovations become entrepreneurial business ventures. One of the most promising areas for sport entrepreneurship is local and amateur sport clubs or associations that have the potential to influence market trends. Our understanding about how creativity is used in this context needs more attention to spur further research. There is a need to understand how entrepreneurial passion is utilized in sport to understand social and economic activity of local sports clubs. The integration of creativity into local, amateur and non-profit sports clubs is encouraged.

In conclusion, we believe the chapters in this book provide an important addition to research on sport, innovation and entrepreneurship. Each of the chapters in this book provides an integration of sports and entrepreneurship in order to facilitate more interest in this interdisciplinary research area. This book represents a way to better understand how sport utilizes innovation and entrepreneurship.

References

Anderson, N., Potocnik, K. and Zhou, J. (2014) 'Innovation and creativity in organizations: A state-of-the-science review, prospective commentary and guiding framework', *Journal of Management*, 40(5): 1297–1333.

Autio, E., Sapienza, H. J. and Almeida, J. G. (2000) 'Effects of age at entry, knowledge intensity and imitability on international growth', *Academy of Management Journal*, 43(5): 909–924.

Baer, M. (2010) 'The strength-of-weak-ties perspective on creativity: A comprehensive examination and extension', *Journal of Applied Psychology*, 95(3): 592–601.

Barron, F. and Harrington, D. M. (1981) 'Creativity, intelligence, and personality', *Annual Review of Psychology*, 32(1): 439–476.

Bird, B. and West, G. P. (1997) 'Time and entrepreneurship', *Entrepreneurship Theory and Practice*, 22(2): 5–9.

Bradley, S.W., Shepherd, D.A. and Wiklund, J. (2011) 'The importance of slack for new organizations facing "tough" environments', Journal of Management Studies, 48(5): 1071–1097.

Bruton, G., Filatotchev, I. and Si, S. (2013) 'Entrepreneurship and strategy in emerging economies', *Strategic Entrepreneurship Journal*, 7(3): 169–180.

Clark, G., Feldman, M. P. and Gerder, M. (Eds.) (2000) *The Oxford Handbook of Economic Geography*, Oxford, Oxford University Press.

Clark, G., Feldman, M. P. and Gerder, M. (Eds) (2006) *The Oxford Handbook of Economic Geography*, Oxford, Oxford University Press.

Collinson, D. (2014) 'Dichotomous, dialectics and dilemmas: New directions for critical leadership studies?', *Leadership*, 10(1): 36–55.

Corte, U. (2013) 'A refinement of collaborative circles theory: Resource mobilization and innovation in an emerging sport', *Social Psychology Quarterly*, 76(1): 25–51.

Costa, P. T. and McCrae, R. R. (1992) 'Four ways five factors are basic', *Personality and Individual Differences*, 13(6): 653–665.

Estrin, S., Korosteleva, J. and Mickiewicz, T. (2012) 'Which institutions encourage entrepreneurial growth aspirations?', *Journal of Business Venturing*, 24(4): 564–580.

Feist, G.J. (1998) 'A meta-analysis of personality in scientific and artistic creativity', *Personality and Social Psychology Review*, 2(4): 290–309.

Foss, N. J., Lyngsie, J. and Zahra, S. A. (2013) 'The role of external knowledge sources and organizational design in the process of opportunity exploitation', *Strategic Management Journal*, 34(12): 1453–1471.

Frisby, W. (2005) 'The good, the bad, and the ugly: Critical sport management research', *Journal of Sport Management*, 19(1): 1–12.

Gilbert, B. A., McDougall, P. P. and Audretsch, D. B. (2006) 'New venture growth: a review and extension', *Journal of Management*, 32(6): 926–950.

Grant, R. (2012) *Contemporary Strategy Analysis* (8th Ed.), Hoboken, New Jersey, John Wiley.

Hitt, M. A., Ireland, R. D., Sirmon, D.G. and Trahms, C. (2011) 'Strategic entrepreneurship: Creating value for individuals, organizations and society', *Academy of Management Perspectives*, 25(2): 57–75.

Hoskisson, R., Wright, M. and Filatotchev, I. (2013) 'Emerging multinationals from mid-range economies: The influence of institutions and factor markets', *Journal of Management Studies*, 50(7): 1295–1321.

Jabri, M. M. (1991) 'The development of conceptually independent subscales in the measurement of modes of problem solving', *Educational and Psychological Measurement*, 51(4): 975–983.

Johns, G. (2001) 'In praise of context', *Journal of Organizational Behavior*, 22(1): 31–42.

Kirzner, I. M. (1997) 'Entrepreneurial discovery and the competitive market process: An Austrian approach', *Journal of Economic Literature*, 35(1): 60–85.

Knoppers, A. (2015) 'Assessing the sociology of sport: On critical sport sociology and sport management', *International Review for the Sociology of Sport*, 50(4–5): 496–501.

Kuada, J. (2015) 'Entrepreneurship in Africa – A classificatory framework and a research agenda', *African Journal of Economic and Management Studies*, 6(2): 148–163.

Maitland, A., Hills, L. A. and Rhind, D. J. (2015) 'Organisational culture in sport – A systematic review', *Sport Management Review*, 18: 501–516.

Nachum, L. and Zaheer, S. (2005) 'The persistence of distance? The impact of technology on MNE motivations for foreign investments', *Strategic Management Journal*, 26(8): 747–767.

Park, S., Mahony, D. F., Kim, Y. and Kim, Y. (2015) 'Curiosity generating advertisements and their impact on sport consumer behavior', *Sport Management Review*, 18(3): 359–369.

Perry-Smith, J. E. and Shalley, C. E. (2014) 'A social composition view of team creativity: The role of member nationality heterogenous ties outside the team', *Organization Science*, 25(5): 1434–1452.

Porter, M. (1980) *Competitive Strategy*, New York, Free Press.

Rundh, B. and Gottfriedsson, P. (2015) 'Delivering sports events: The arena concept in sports from a network perspective', *Journal of Business and Industrial Marketing*, 30(7): 785–794.

Saxenian, A. (1994) *Regional Advantage: Culture and Competition in Silicon Valley and Route 128*, Cambridge, MA, Harvard University Press.

Shalley, C. E., Gilson, L. L. and Blum, T. C. (2009) 'Interactive effects of growth need strength, work context, and job complexity on self-reported creative performance', *Academy of Management Journal*, 52(3): 489–505.

Shalley, C. E., Zhou, J. and Oldham, G. R. (2004) 'The effects of personal and contextual characteristics on creativity: Where should we go from here?', *Journal of Management*, 30(6): 933–958.

Shane, S. and Venkataraman, S. (2000) 'The promise of entrepreneurship as a field of research', *Academy of Management Review*, 25(1): 217–226.

Stuart, T. E. and Sorenson, O. (2007) 'Strategic networks and entrepreneurial ventures', *Strategic Entrepreneurship Journal*, 1(3–4): 211–227.

Taggar, S. (2002) 'Individual creativity and group ability to utilize individual creative resources: A multilevel model', *Academy of Management Journal*, 45(2): 315–330.

Wennberg, K., Wiklund, J. and Wright, M. (2011) 'The effectiveness of university knowledge spillovers: Performance differences between university spinoffs and corporate spinoffs', *Research Policy*, 40(8): 1128–1143.

Wheaton, B. (2004) *Understanding Lifestyle Sports: Consumption, Identity and Difference*, London, Routledge.

Wright, M. (2011) 'Entrepreneurial mobility', in Bergh, D. and Ketchen, D. (Eds.) *Research Methodology in Strategy and Management*, Bingley, Emerald Publishing, pp. 137–159.

Wright, M. and Vanaelst, I. (2009) *Entrepreneurial Teams*, Cheltenham, Edward Elgar.

Zaheer, S., Albert, S. and Zaheer, A. (1999) 'Time scales and organizational theory', *Academy of Management Review*, 24(4): 725–740.

Zahra, S. A. and Wright, M. (2011) 'Entrepreneurship's next act', *Academy of Management Perspectives*, 25(4): 67–83.

Zahra, S. A., Ireland, R. D. and Hitt, M. A. (2000) 'International expansion by new venture firms: International diversity, mode of market entry, technological learning and performance', *Academy of Management Journal*, 43(5): 925–950.

Zahra, S. A., Neck, H. and Kelley, D. (2004) 'International corporate entrepreneurship and the evolution of organizational competence', in Shepherd, D. and Katz, J. (Eds.) *Advances in Entrepreneurship Research*, New York, JAI Press, pp. 145–171.

Zahra, S. A., Van de Velde, E. and Larraneta, B. (2007) 'Knowledge conversion capability and the growth of corporate and university spin-offs', *Industrial and Corporate Change*, 16(4): 569–608.

Zahra, S. A., Abdelgawad, S. G. and Tsang, E. (2011) 'Emerging multinationals venturing into developed economies: Implications for learning and entrepreneurial capability', *Journal of Management Inquiry*, 20(3): 323–330.

Zahra, S. A., Wright, M. and Abdelgawad, S. G. (2014) 'Contextualization and the advancement of entrepreneurship research', *International Small Business Journal*, 1: 1–22.

Zhang, X. and Zhou, J. (2014) 'Empowering leadership, uncertainty avoidance, trust and employee creativity: Interaction effects and mediating processes', *Organizational Behavior and Human Decision Processes*, 124(2): 150–164.

Zhou, J. and Hoewes, I. J. (2014) 'Research on workplace creativity: A review and redirection', *Annual Review of Organizational Psychology and Organizational Behavior*, 1: 333–359.

INDEX

Note: Information in figures and tables is indicated by page numbers in italics.

activation control strategies 78
activity specialization 228
administrative innovation 16
adrenaline sports: risk and 7
adventure sports: risk and 7
advertising *see* sport marketing
aesthetics 77
affiliation 226
agency 194
ambition *109*
America's Cup 120
Asturias 63
Athens Olympic Games 118–19
atmospherics, environmental 77
autocratic leadership 80–1
awareness-building *99*

Barad, Karen 193
Barcelona Olympic Games 118
barriers: to innovation 45–6; to sport
    innovation *46*, 52–3, *54*
beach volley 24
behavior: in sporting events 33; sport
    leadership 81–3, *82; see also* consumer
    behavior analysis
blue ocean: awareness-building and *99*;
    change assimilation phase and *104*;
    characteristics *90*; clients *vs.*
    non-clients in *97*; competition factors
    and *98*; competitive advantage and *93*,
    94; complementary products and

services and 111; core tools in *91*;
customer-specific solution orientation
and *99*; economic policy and *102*;
emotional stimulus and 111–13;
employee participation and *109*;
enforcement-orientation and *99*; in
fitness and health clubs 110–13, *112*;
future lines of research with 113–14;
impact of *91*; and innovation with
value *93*; "islandhopping" in *92*;
leadership in, *vs.* conventional
leadership *93*; literature review 89–110,
90–109; new markets and *93*; overview
of 84; purchaser chain and 111; as
strategic concept 89–110, *90–109*;
structuralist view and *91, 92*; value and
89, *90–4, 98–100, 102–4, 108,* 110–11;
value-cost tradeoff and *90*; "value to
the client" categories and *100*
Botham, Sir Ian 203
bottom-up innovation 45, 50
boxing 47
Brazil 119–20
bricolage 45
business: leadership in, vs, sport 79, *80*;
    links between sport and 75–6; sport
    psychology and 77–9
business performance: leadership and 84
butterfly effect 158–9

Càceres International Open 37

258 Index

capabilities system 167–8
capacity, innovative 62, 70
champion, innovation 21
change assimilation phase *104*
clarity, of vision *109*
Clark, Michael 202
coaches *see* leadership; sport leadership
cognitive behavioral aspect, in motivation 229
coherence 168–71, *170, 172–3, 174*
coherency diagnostic *170*
collaboration: as innovation driver 53
commentary 77
commercialization 25; sport innovation and 1–2
Commonwealth Games 120
communication, open 75
community sport organization 144–6, *145*
comparative advantage 171
competition: among non-profit sports organizations 13; entrepreneurship and 245, 252; factors *98*; as sport segment 153
competitive advantage *93, 94,* 168–71, *170, 172, 174*
complementary products and services 111
construal level theory 126
consumer behavior analysis 209–18, *213–15*
consumers: behavior of 33; as developers 242–3; emotional stimulus provided to 111–13; financial risk and 7; marketing for interest of 76; motivation of 77; psychological factors in 7–8; service innovation and 4; sport innovation and 1; suspicion of innovation on part of 6; in user dimension 20
contingency model, of leadership 81
continuous improvement 68, *68, 71*
creativity 248–9
cricket 192–206, *198, 199*
cultural significance 184–5
culture: embeddedness of sport in 179; entrepreneurship and 246; organizational 68, *68, 71,* 159–60; sport 23–4; sport policy and 181–2
customer orientation 68, *68, 71*
customer-specific solution orientation *99*
customer target identification 160–2
customer value proposition 161–3

daily physical activity 42–3
data analytics 192
"Decision Review System" (DRS) 192–206, *198, 199*

democratic innovation 45, 50
differential advantage 171
diffusion: of innovation 5
digital economy 246
drivers: of innovation 45; of sport innovation *46,* 52–3, *54*
DRS *see* "Decision Review System" (DRS)

economic barriers, to innovation 45–6
economic motivation 77
economic policy *102*
economy: digital 246; mixed 24–5
education: innovation in 47; sport policy and 182–3
elite athletes 182
elite sport systems 82
emotional stimulus 111–13
employee-driven innovation 45
employee participation, blue ocean and *109*
employee recognition 75–6
enforcement-orientation *99*
entertainment 77
entrepreneurial ecosystem approach 187–8, *188*
entrepreneurship *see* sport entrepreneurship
environment, psychological, leadership and 79
environmental atmospherics 77
equipment, as segment 153
equity 48
E-RecS-QUAL scale 111
escape 77
E-S-QUAL scale 111
ethical leadership 80
eustress 77
events *see* sporting events
evolutionary innovation 17
excellence models 61
exclusion 42, 43, 48–9
expansionary innovation 17
expectancy-value model 126
expressionism, human: sport as 76

family 77
fan interest: marketing for 76
fans *see* consumers
financial barriers, to innovation 45–6
financial dimension: in non-profit sport organizations 20–1
financial risk 7
financing *see* public financing
fitness market 88–9, 110–13, *112*

flexibility: of non-profit organizations 14–15
Football World Cup 119–20, 132
'Fosbury flop' 47
fun 78–9

gender: in marathon runner motivation 229–30, 234–5; sport entrepreneurship and 251; *see also* women
gender bias, in sport leadership 82–3
geography, entrepreneurship and 246
girls *see* women
governance, sport leadership and 80–1
Greece 118–19

"Hawk-eye" system 192, 195
health: inactivity and 42–3
health clubs 88–9, 110–13, *112*
high jumping 47
human expressionism: sport as 76
human resources: dimension 21; leadership and 78; management 63, *68, 71*

image incentives 8–9
imagery, mental 77–8
inactivity, in Norway 42–3
inclusion *see* social inclusion
industry, size of 242
inequality 42
inflation 129
initial conditions, dependence on 158–9
innovation: administrative 16; as amorphous concept 43; barriers 45–6, 52–3, *54*; bottom-up 45, 50; collaboration and 53; competition and 13; as context-specific 44; creativity and 249; definitions of 43, 44; democratic 45, 50; diffusion of 5; drivers 45, 52–3, *54*; economic barriers to 45–6; in education 47; employee-drive 45; entrepreneurship and 249–51; evolutionary 17; expansionary 17; financial barriers to 45–6; invention *vs.* 5; knowledge barriers to 46; management-driven 45; non-beneficial 25; in non-profit organizations 14–15; organizational 54; process 5, 15; product 16; in public organizations 59–60; regulation barriers to 46; resistance to 7–8; social 44–5; for social inclusion 49–50; social inclusion and 43–6; sport policy and 179, 180, 186–9, *188*; in sports medicine 47; structural barriers to 46; suspicion of 6;

technology and 62; timeliness of 244–5; top-down 45, 50, 53; Total Quality Management and 62–4, 72; value 6; with value *93; see also* service innovation; sport innovation; technology innovation
innovation capability: in non-profit sports organizations *19,* 19–23
innovation champion 21
innovation management 4
innovation systems approach 187–8
innovative capacity 62, 70
instant replay 47
integrative outcomes 183
internal voice 78
invention: innovation *vs.* 5
investment: as barrier 20–1
involvement 224–5, 233, *235, 236, 237,* 238
Ireland 63
"islandhopping" *92*
Italy 63

Jakeman, Mike 204
Japan 141–51, *143–5, 147–50*
jogging 226

knowledge barriers, to innovation 46
knowledge creation: service innovation and 4–5
knowledge development 5
knowledge transfer: performance risk and 7

LBW *see* "Leg Before Wicket" (LBW) law
leadership: autocratic 80–1; blue ocean *vs.* conventional *93*; business performance and 84; characteristics 79; commitment 21; fun and 78–9; human resources and 78; listening and 79; literature review 77; management 63; management capabilities and 76; psychological environment and 79; in sport *vs.* business 79, *80*; transactional 81; transformational 67, *68, 71,* 81; value and 79; *see also* sport leadership
"leapfrogging" *92*
"Leg Before Wicket" (LBW) law 196, 206n1
lifestyle sport 248
life-work balance 78
listening 79
location, of stadium 77

260 Index

management-driven innovation 45
managerial implications 9
marathon running 221–39, *230, 235–7*
market: access, entrepreneurship and 247; factors in entrepreneurship 245; fitness 88–9
market choice orientation 14
market freedom: non-profit sports organizations and 20
marketing *see* sport marketing
markets: innovation and 3; new *93*
masculinity 82
media commentary 77
medicine *see* sports medicine
mental imagery 77–8
mixed economy 24–5
monopolies 21
motivation 77; affiliation and 226; cognitive behavioral aspect in 229; in consumer behavior analysis 210–11, *213, 214–15*; defined 222; involvement and 224–5, 233, *235, 236, 237,* 238; of marathon runners 221–39, *230, 235–7*; preventive health in 228–9, 233, *235, 236, 237*; role of 222; in Self Determination Theory 223; sickness avoidance in 228–9, 233, *235, 236, 237*; social 225–6, 233, *235, 236, 237*; in Social Motivation Theory 226; sportscape in 223, 227–8, 230, 233, *235, 236, 237,* 238; theoretical background of 224–31, *230*

networks 8, 245
new markets *93*
noise pollution 130
non-linear system 158–9
non-profit organizations (NPOs): change in 17–18; flexibility in 14–15; innovation in 14–15; market freedom and 20; process innovation in 15; risk in 15
non-profit sport organizations (NPSOs): competition among 13; financial dimension in 20–1; innovation capability in *19,* 19–23; innovation in 14–15, 18–19; mixed economy of 24–5; regulated 23–4; strategic dimension in 19–20; user dimension in 20
Norway 42–3, 50–3
NPSOs *see* non-profit sport organizations (NPSOs)

Olympic Committee 117, 120
Olympic Games 117, 118–19, 132, 133

open communication 75
open organization 63
Oregon Swimming Questionnaire 211
organizational culture 68, *68, 71,* 159–60
organizational innovation 54
organizations *see* non-profit sport organizations (NPSOs)

participants: in sporting events 34–5
P.E. *see* physical education (P.E.)
performance risk 7
physical activity, in Norway 42–3
physical education (P.E.): innovation in 47
policy *see* sport policy
Portugal 60, 65, 159, 211–12
power recognition 75–6
preventive health aspect, in motivation 228–9, 233
price inflation 129
processes management 63
process innovation 5, 15
product innovation 16
professionalization 25, 82
psychological environment, leadership and 79
psychological factors 7–8
psychology *see* sport psychology
public financing: of America's Cup 120; of Commonwealth Games 120; and host country citizens 121; of Olympic Games 118–19; requirement for 117; of sports events 118–22; of Super Bowl 121; support for 121–2; of World Cup 119–20
public organizations 59–60

quality: evolution of concept 61; service innovation and 4; *see also* Total Quality Management (TQM)
quality control and measuring *68,* 71, *71*
Queensberry rules, in boxing 47

rafting 146–7, *147, 148*
reasoned action theory 126–7
Reconstructed Tracking Device (RTD) 195–6
red ocean 84, *90, 94, 96; see also* blue ocean
regulation 23–4
regulation barriers, to innovation 46
religion, sport as 184–5
resource allocation 3
resource dependence theory 21
resources: entrepreneurship and 163–8, *166–7*; imitability of *166*; intangible

163–4; ordinary 165; organization and *167*; rareness of *166*; strategic 165; tangible 163; value of *166*; VRIO framework for 164, *166–7*
right to win 154–5
Rio de Janeiro Olympic Games 120
risk: financial 7; in non-profit organizations 15; performance 7; social 8; in theoretical framework 7
RTD *see* Reconstructed Tracking Device (RTD)
'Run For You' 17
running 221–39, *230, 235–7*

self-assessment 61–2
Self Determination Theory 223
self-talk 78
service innovation 4–5, 16–17; types of 17
SIA *see* social impact assessment (SIA)
sickness avoidance, in motivation 228–9, 233, *235, 236, 237*
skateboarding 50–3, *54*
social development, community sport organization and 144–6, *145*
social exchange theory 124–6
social exclusion 42, 43, 48–9
social impact(s): administrative *128*, 133–4; classification of *127–8*, 127–34; commercial *127*, 129; conceptualization of 122; conflict as 131–2; construal level theory and 126; cultural *128*, 130–1; defining 122; economic *127*; environmental *128*, 130; evaluation of 122–4; expectancy-value model and 126; explanatory theories 124–7, *125*; lack of study on 117; legacy and 123–4; negative 129, 130, 131–2, 133–4; physical *128*; political *128*, 133–4; psychological *128*, 132–3; rationality and 126; reasoned action theory and 126–7; resident perceptions and 126; social exchange theory and 124–6; sport-related 131; standard of living and 123, 131; taxes and 121, *127*, 129; theoretical frameworks for *125*; tourism as *127*; urban regeneration as 129
social impact assessment (SIA) 122–4
social impacts, tourism as *127*, 129
social inclusion: innovation and 43–6; innovation for 49–50; new sports and 54–5; physical activity and 42–3; in skateboarding 50–3, *54*; in sport 48–9; sport innovation and *46*, 46–8; of women 50–3, *54*

social innovation 44–5
socialization 226, 233, *235, 236, 237*
Social Motivation Theory 226
social networks 8, 245
social risk 8
socioeconomic impact: of sporting events 32–3, *34*, 38–9
South Africa 119
Spain 63; Barcelona Olympic Games in 118; tourism in 31–2
specialization, activity 228
sport culture 23–4
sport entrepreneurship: butterfly effect and 158–9; capabilities and 163–8, *166–7*; coherence and 168–71, *170, 172–3, 174*; competition and 245, 252; competitive advantage and 168–71, *170, 172, 174*; consumers in 242–3; contextual factors in 244–7; creativity and 248–9; cultural expectations and 246; customer target identification in 160–2, *161*; customer value proposition in 161–3; design 154–5; digital economy and 246; environmental factors in 156–7; future research in 251–2; gender-based 251; geography and 246; increased presence of 243; industry factors in 245; influential elements of options in 156–60, *158*; innovation and 249–51; in Japan 141–51, *143–5, 147–50*; as lifestyle entrepreneurship 248; market access and 247; market factors in 245; marketing and 252; networks and 245; non-linear system and 158–9; as open system 157; opportunity discovery in 247–8; organizational culture and 159–60; organizational dimension in 246–7; personality traits in 244; resources and 163–8, *166–7*; right to win and 154–5; social dimension of 245; spatial dimension in 246; technology and 252; temporal dimension in 244–5; theory 243–4; value and 156, 157, 160, 161–7, *166, 170, 172–3*; venture development and 247–8
sport industry, size of 242
sporting events: behavior of individuals in 33; competitors in *36*; interest level at 77; participants in 34–5; physical legacy of 130; public financing of 118–22; residents in *36*; socioeconomic impact of 32–3, *34*, 38–9; travelers in 35, *36*; users of *36*; wealth creation by 32; *see also* social impacts

262 Index

sport innovation: barriers to *46, 54*; commercialization and 1–2; consumers and 1; drivers to *46, 54*; exploitative 2; explorative 2; focus of 1; image incentives in 8–9; importance of 1; innovation *vs.* 1; managerial implications in 9; psychological factors in 7–8; risk reasons in 7; social inclusion and *46,* 46–8; theoretical framework for 5–9; usage reasons in 5–6; value incentives in 6; *see also* innovation
sport leadership: attitudes *82*; behavior 81–3, *82; vs.* business 79, *80*; contingency model of 81; ethics in 80; evaluation in 80–1; future research in 83–4; governance and 80–1; key behaviors in 81; marketing and 83; masculinity and *82*; scale 81; skills 81–2; transactional 81; transformational 81; women in 82–3; *see also* leadership
sport marketing: audience and 77; entrepreneurship and 252; leadership and 83; *vs.* other types of marketing 77; types of 76
sport organizations *see* non-profit sport organizations (NPSOs)
sport policy: constituent 183; contextual factors in 181; cultural significance and 184–5; culture and 181–2; education and 182–3; elite athletes and 182; entrepreneurial ecosystem approach and 187–8, *188*; future research in 189; government and 180, 181, 186–7; impact of 180; independent variables in 181–2; innovation and 179, 180, 186–9, *188*; innovation systems approach and 187–8; integrative outcomes and 183; interest in 180; international 185–6; literature review 181–3; policy analysis and 183–4; processual factors in 181–2; social relations and 184; specific factors in 182; sustainability and 182
sport psychology: business and 77–9; mental imagery in 77–8
sportscape, in motivation 223, 227–8, 230, 233, *235, 236, 237,* 238
sports equity 48
sports medicine: innovation in 47
stadium location 77
standard of living 123, 131
status quo 6
strategic management 63
strategy, innovation 3
streams, innovation 3

structural barriers, to innovation 46
structuralism *91, 92*
Super Bowl 121
suspicion: of innovation 6
sustainability 182
swimming 211–12, *213, 214–15*
Sydney Olympic Games 132

taxes: and entrepreneurship *188*; and social impact of sporting events 121, *127, 129*
team creativity 249
team unity 75
"technologies-in-practice" 194
technology 192; agency and 194; capabilities and 163, 165; entrepreneurship and 252; as fixed structure 193; innovation and 47, 62; internationalization and 182, 246; performance risk factors and 7; sociomaterial perspective on 193–4; *see also* "Decision Review System" (DRS)
technology innovation: performance risk and 7; process innovation and 16
tennis 192
theoretical framework 5–9
timeliness, of innovations 244–5
top-down innovation 45, 50, 53
top-down leadership 81
Total Quality Management (TQM): defining 61; history of 61; innovation and 62–4, 67–9, *68, 69,* 71, *71*; literature review 60–2; methodology in investigation of *64,* 64–6, *66*; pillars of 61–2
tourism: analysis model in 36–7, *37*; methodology used with 37; promotion of 142–3; segmentation 35; as social impact *127,* 129; in Spain 31–2; sport as complementary to 31
Tourism Nation Promotion Basic Law (Japan) 142–3
Tourism Satellite Accounts (TSA) 31
tourists, visitors *vs.* 35
traffic 130
training habits 226, 233
transactional leadership 81
transformational leadership 67, *68,* 71, 81
TSA *see* Tourism Satellite Accounts (TSA)

umbrella organizations 21
umpires 195
unity, team 75
urban regeneration 129

usage reasons 5–6
user dimension 20

Valencia America's Cup 120
value: blue ocean and 89, *90–4, 98–100, 102–4, 108,* 110–11; coherence and 169; entrepreneurship and 156, 157, 160, 161–7, *166, 170,* 172–3; generation 2–3; incentives 6; innovation 6; innovation and 2–3; leadership and 79; of opportunities 245; quality management and 68; of resources 154; social 77
"value shop" 175n10
"value to the client" *100*
venture development 247–8; *see also* sport entrepreneurship
video refereeing 47
vision, clarity of *109*
visitors: tourists *vs.* 35
voice, internal 78

volleyball 24
volunteers 21
VRIO framework 164, *166–7*

Warne, Shane 203
wellness with users 153
women: in leadership 82–3; marathon running and 229–30, 234–5; social inclusion of, in skateboarding 50–3, *54; see also* gender
work-life balance 78
World Conference on Sport and Tourism 31
World Cup 119–20, 132
World Fighting Championship 8
World Tourism Organization (WTO) 35
WTO *see* World Tourism Organization (WTO)

'Zorbing' 17
Zumba 17

Taylor & Francis eBooks

Helping you to choose the right eBooks for your Library

Add Routledge titles to your library's digital collection today. Taylor and Francis ebooks contains over 50,000 titles in the Humanities, Social Sciences, Behavioural Sciences, Built Environment and Law.

Choose from a range of subject packages or create your own!

Benefits for you
- Free MARC records
- COUNTER-compliant usage statistics
- Flexible purchase and pricing options
- All titles DRM-free.

Benefits for your user
- Off-site, anytime access via Athens or referring URL
- Print or copy pages or chapters
- Full content search
- Bookmark, highlight and annotate text
- Access to thousands of pages of quality research at the click of a button.

 REQUEST YOUR FREE INSTITUTIONAL TRIAL TODAY — Free Trials Available. We offer free trials to qualifying academic, corporate and government customers.

eCollections – Choose from over 30 subject eCollections, including:

Archaeology	Language Learning
Architecture	Law
Asian Studies	Literature
Business & Management	Media & Communication
Classical Studies	Middle East Studies
Construction	Music
Creative & Media Arts	Philosophy
Criminology & Criminal Justice	Planning
Economics	Politics
Education	Psychology & Mental Health
Energy	Religion
Engineering	Security
English Language & Linguistics	Social Work
Environment & Sustainability	Sociology
Geography	Sport
Health Studies	Theatre & Performance
History	Tourism, Hospitality & Events

For more information, pricing enquiries or to order a free trial, please contact your local sales team:
www.tandfebooks.com/page/sales

 Routledge Taylor & Francis Group | The home of Routledge books

www.tandfebooks.com